Reframing Human Capital for Organizational Excellence

Reframing Human Capital for Organizational Excellence

Editors

G.D. SARDANA
TOJO THATCHENKERY

BLOOMSBURY

LONDON • NEW DELHI • NEW YORK • SYDNEY

BLOOMSBURY PUBLISHING INDIA PVT. LTD.
London New Delhi New York Sydney

ISBN: 978-93-82563-40-2

Published by Bloomsbury Publishing India Pvt. Ltd.
VISHRUT Building, DDA Complex, Building No. 3, Pocket C-6 & 7
Vasant Kunj, New Delhi 110 070

Typeset by FORTUNE GRAPHICS
WZ-911/2, Shankarlal Street, Ring Road, Naraina, New Delhi

Printed at ANVI COMPOSERS
1 DDA Market, Block A-1B, Pachim Vihar, New Delhi 110 063

Contents

Acknowledgements   ix

Introduction   xi
  G.D. Sardana and Tojo Thatchenkery

PART I: Cases Using Appreciative Intelligence-based Interventions

1. Appreciative Intelligence for Change Management:
    A Case Study of a Community College   3
    R. Mikel Lemons and Tojo Thatchenkery

2. An Appreciative Inquiry Study: Sustaining Fundraising Enablers   21
    Kristine Brands and Debora Elam

3. Discovering Possibilities: An Applied Appreciative Inquiry
    Analysis of Core Organizational Values   34
    Rod Hagedorn

4. Homeowners: The Other Side of Management Through Ontological
    Storytelling   52
    Krisha M. Coppedge and David M. Boje

5. Student Opportunity for Achieving Results (S.O.A.R.)   65
    Barbara Carter, Joan Marie Johns and Kenneth Wall

6. Using Appreciative Intelligence and Positive Approaches for Change
    Management   74
    Beverley E. Powell III and Tojo Thatchenkery

7. Nonprofit Board Service: A Qualitative Investigation using
    Appreciative Inquiry   90
    Tonya Henderson Wakefield, Alfonso Robertson and Kenneth Wall

8. Appreciative Sharing of Knowledge (ASK) Research Case:
    Undergraduate College (USA)   103
    James T. Colvin, Jr. and James M. Thorpe

9. Simplified Cost-Effective Strategic Artificial and Business Intelligence
    at Gulf Shores Company   115
    Asma Qureshi and Jeff Stevens

10. Virtual Appreciative Sharing of Knowledge for Global Teaming   126
     Ken Long and Parag Dighe

11. Perceptions of the United States' New Healthcare Reform Law,
     the PPACA, as Exemplified by the NFIB, a Lobbyist Organization
     for Small Businesses   141
     Divya Srinivasan, Tojo Thatchenkery and Anne L. Washington

12. Data Conversion for Electronic Medical Records: A Case Study of SGN   163
     Yaw M, Parag Dighe, Monty Miller and Kenneth Wall

PART II: Cases in Knowledge Management, Talent Management, and Education

13. Enhancing the Edge: Innovative Management of Knowledge at
     Sapient Corporation   181
     Mohammed Arshad Khan and Santanu Roy

14. Talent Management Practices and its Effectiveness at Grasim Industries   192
     Jaya Gupta and Megha Singh Tomar

15. Retaining Talent in Bharat Heavy Electricals Limited: An Indian PSU   210
     Geeta Rana and Alok Goel

16. Understanding the Essential Principles for Integrating Theory and
     Research Knowledge to the Realm of Practice: Lessons from the
     Scholar-Practitioner   224
     Ramkrishnan (Ram) V. Tenkasi and George W. Hay

17. Open Innovation Space   242
     Tero Montonen and Päivi Eriksson

18. Case Studies and Research in Management science   251
     Lamy Erwan and Lapoule Paul

PART III: Cases in Human Capital Development

19. Employee Retention at Jindal Steel and Power Limited   269
     Shuchi Agarwal and Manosi Chaudhuri

20. Branding the Training at Finfare Limited   278
     Parameswar Nayak and Sanjana Tyagi

21. Impact of Compensation on Motivation, Job Satisfaction and Turnover
     Intentions in the Retail Industry: A Study of NCR   293
     Pooja Misra, Shreya Jain and Abhay Sood

22. Competency Assessment of the Retail Staff and Preparing to
Launch Retail HR Processes in Top Stores of Adidas India   311
Sakshi Puri and Manosi Chaudhuri

PART IV: Cases in Leadership, Organization Development

23. How Do Leadership Styles Affect Followership Styles in a
Large Christian Church?   325
Arnold R. Anderson Anderson and Cheryl R. Anderson

24. Perspectives of Charismatic Leadership   334
Ronald Newton

25. Forging the ABCS in Graduate International Programs:
Team Performance and Leadership Development   344
Daphne D. DePorres, and Monty G. Miller

26. Harmonizing Western OD Methods and Thai Hospitality Culture:
A Case Study of a Hotel   354
Vilas Wongtrakul and Bruce Hanson

27. Guided Professionalization in the Cleaning Industry with
CIMS and CIMS GB: A Case Study   368
Nathan Walla

PART V: Cases in Global Culture and Organizational Change

28. The Social Construction of Entrepreneurs, Success, and Wealth:
A Case Study of Management Students' Perceptions from
Three Different Cultural Contexts   379
Beata Glinka and Tojo Thatchenkery

29. The 'Sense of Community' in Geographically Dispersed Organizations:
A Case Study of the Organization of Burners   397
Karla R. Peters-Van Havel

30. Community Engagement Practice of a Joint Venture Petroleum
Company Operating in Sudan   412
*Eiman H. Ibrahim, Siti Nabiha Abdul Khalid, Dayana Jalaludin
and Yousif Abdelbagi*

31. Growth Concerns of a Social Enterprise: The Case of
'Sammaan Foundation'   421
Bhawna Anjaly and Arun Sahay

32. The Impact of Cultural Values in Shaping Economic Growth and
     Development: A Case of Ubuntu Economy   433
     Ruchi K. Tyagi and Symphorien Ntibagirirwa

Author Index   443
The Editors   445

Acknowledgements

The papers included in this volume represent selected manuscripts received from across the globe for presentation at the International Conference on Management Cases, ICMC 2012, organised by Birla Institute of Management Technology, Greater Noida, and the School of Public Policy, George Mason University, Arlington, VA, USA, at the BIMTECH Campus on November 29-30, 2012.

Every paper has undergone a double blind review. We are grateful to reviewers who took great pains to go through the manuscripts and provide critical comments in many cases to improve the papers. In some of the cases, the papers underwent revisions necessitating re-reviews by the same reviewer. It is a time consuming job, needs patience and a passion to carry out the responsibilities. We wish to acknowledge the very valuable help we received from our peers, former colleagues, research scholars, our past -students who came forward to extend their support. The reviewers include: Tojo Thatchenkery, Kenneth Wall, Harjit Singh, Nikunj Aggarwal, Archana Shrivastav, Ruchi Tyagi, Raveesh Agarwal, Alok Goel, Smriti Pande, Sriparna Basu, John Walsh, Abha Rishi, Mayur Dande, Pratigya Kwatra, Krishna Akalamkam, Ken Long, Bob Palk, Angela Parish, Wallace Edson, Jackie Bsharah, Kevin LeGrand, Keith Hosea, Julie Huffaker, Keli Yen, Kerry Mitchel, Bob Lucius, Aaron Finney, Andrea McCormick, Eric Matheny, Warren Vaughan and G.D. Sardana.

Prior to the blind review, all the papers were subjected for Originality report and Similarity index, using Turnitin Soft ware installed at BIMTECH Library. We wish to thank Subhash Sharma, Priyanshi Rastogi and Naqi Murtaza all office bearers at the library for taking up the task often at short and urgent notice.

Proof reading and language corrections of such a large volume of papers in a such a short time of four weeks is literally a neck-breaking job. This became possible because of full understanding and support from our respective family members, who often shared the load of proof reading.

We also express our thanks to Mr. Suresh Gopal, Publisher-Special Projects and Ms. Jyoti Mehrotra, Development Editor, Bloomsbury Publishing India Pvt. Ltd. for their support, cooperation and attention to details for timely publication of this book.

G.D. Sardana
Tojo Thatchenkery

Introduction

GD Sardana and Tojo Thatchenkery

All fields of management are meant to strive towards organizational improvement. Making organizations a better place to work is a goal shared by all stakeholders. While there may not always be agreement on how to do this, considerable consensus exists about the notion that the human capital in an organization is one of the most "leveragable" assets to accomplish organizational excellence. People make the difference. The focus on human capital is thus not new. Human capital has always been important. What is different is the reframing that has been applied to it. Significant changes in human capital have become necessary thanks to unprecedented technological innovation. According to Manoj Saxena (2012), General Manager of IBM's cutting edge Watson Solutions, "Ninety percent of the world's information was created in the last two years, but 80% of that 90% is unstructured or semi-structured information, like doctor's notes or product reviews on Amazon" (p. 129) One of the implications of this Big Data onslaught in our lives is that we have to learn to make decisions with information that might feel excessive or overwhelming. The human capital requirement has thus changed in dramatic ways. Organizations today are looking for human talent that is highly resilient and adaptable. One of the most valued competencies in this context is the ability to think outside the box or the capacity to reframe. It has become a necessity, not just a desirable ability.

The capacity to reframe is a component of Appreciative Intelligence (Thatchenkery & Metzker, 2006). Appreciative Intelligence® is the ability to perceive the positive potential in a given situation and to act purposively to transform the potential to outcomes. In other words, it is the ability to reframe a given situation to recognize the positive possibilities embedded in it but is not apparent to the untrained eye, and to engage in the necessary actions so that the desired outcomes may unfold from the generative aspects of the current situation (Thatchenkery & Metzker, 2006). Appreciative Intelligence holds significant promise in leveraging human capital for organizational excellence because it is directly linked to innovation in organizations and industry (Thatchenkery, 2011). The case studies in this edited volume show that by internalizing the various components and qualities of Appreciative Intelligence, it is possible to generate productive innovations in organizations.

Appreciative intelligence has its origins in leveraging human capital. Thatchenkery coined the term Appreciative Intelligence in 1996 after studying the phenomenal growth of entrepreneurship in the Silicon Valley in California, U.S.A. As articulated by Saxenian (1996; 1999) through her pioneering study of immigrants in the Silicon

Valley, talents of all sorts congregated around a small region in Northern California during the 1980s and 1990s. Entrepreneurs, venture capitalists, academics, researchers, and immigrants (primarily from Asia) worked together to make the best use of human talent and created some of the most ubiquitous innovations we see today (from companies such as Apple, HP, Ebay, Oracle, and Cisco). Appreciative Intelligence is the individual ability that partly contributed to the creation of the exceptional human capital and success of the Silicon Valley (Thatchenkery, 2011).

Appreciative Intelligence® has three components: *reframing, appreciating the positive,* and *seeing how the future unfolds from the present.* Framing is the basic psychological process in perception where a person constructs or interprets a context, issue, or scenario in a certain way. Reframing is about changing the immediately available framing to a different one intentionally. Appreciating the positive is the second component of Appreciative Intelligence whereby the reframing leads to seeing something good in a situation even though what might be apparent is something negative. The third component of Appreciative Intelligence, seeing how the future unfolds from the present, is the critical last step for generating successful results. It is not enough to reframe or recognize positive possibilities. One must know what to do in the present moment. The future possibility must be realized in the current reality through purposive action. Leveraging human capital with Appreciative Intelligence entails breaking down one's actions into a series of workable, time-sensitive small steps (Thatchenkery, 2011). Many of the case studies in this volume point to the leveraging of human capital with Appreciative Intelligence. There are many examples where the leaders or stakeholders reframed and saw positive possibilities in many of the challenges that they had faced, and acted with conviction to make the new possibilities come true.

The leveraging of human capital for organizational excellence is exemplified at the macro level in Appreciative Inquiry (Cooperrider & Srivastva, 1987). Widely regarded as one of the most influential Organization Development (OD) interventions during the last two decades, Appreciative inquiry is a form of organizational analysis that focuses on what works in a system. The methodology has been widely used in hundreds of OD interventions (Whitney & Trosten-Bloom, 2010; Cooperrider & Whitney, 2005). It has also been applied to knowledge management (Thatchenkery & Chowdhry, 2007) and knowledge sharing (Thatchenkery, 2005). Overall, the appreciative inquiry and Appreciative Intelligence models are embedded in the positive approaches to organizational transformation, as was showcased by Sardana and Thatchenkery (2011). Several leading universities such as University of Pennsylvania, University of Michigan, and Case Western Reserve University have established centers for positive psychology or organizational behavior. The number of books, conferences, and publications exploring the positive approaches has skyrocketed during the last five years. Following in that tradition, the first section of this edited volume features case studies using appreciative inquiry and Appreciative Intelligence to various functions and arenas of management such as OD, knowledge utilization, knowledge sharing, product development, innovation, and customer service.

The first offering in this section "Appreciative Intelligence for change management: a case study of a community college" by Lemons and Thatchenkery explores the intricacies of the leadership challenges faced by a community college and its efforts to deal with the various aspects of the resistance to change that unfolded. The authors identified the core values of the community college using Appreciative Intelligence-based interviews and created various scenarios for transformation that were participatory and were based on empowering all stakeholders for a collective future. In the next chapter "an appreciative inquiry study: sustaining fundraising enablers-" Kristine Brands and Debora Elam use a customized approach of the Appreciative Inquiry (AI) organizational analysis model to examine a non-profit organization's fund raising enablers. They were able to discover possibilities for increasing fundraising levels to meet the growing needs of the Pike region community in Colorado, USA. "Discovering possibilities: an applied appreciative inquiry analysis of core organizational values", authored by Hagedorn is yet another use of the positive approaches to create positive change, this time at a for-profit educational entity. Hagedorn describes the AI methodology and results in detail which includes a valencing survey that compared core organizational values captured in a large-group session with individual employee perceptions of values expressed in the form of possibility propositions. Results of the study were used to generate four pragmatic action items which were later presented to the top administrators of the organization for implementing OD and change initiatives.

"Homeowners: the other side of management through ontological storytelling" is a narrative about the dark side of the mortgage crisis that has plagued the United States for the last four years. Coppedge and Boje go behind the scenes and let us know – through the lenses of empathic understanding, the experience of the betrayal and hardships faced by six homeowners who suffered mortgage foreclosure. Using the increasingly popular story telling methodology the authors provide an engaging narrative of the challenges faced by the homeowners and their resilience against adversity. The authors conclude that coercion, mistaken evidence, and duress impacted participants' mortgage foreclosures and suggest ways to prevent such social injustice in the future. Against the backdrop of the present housing crisis in the United Sates, their findings are poignant. In the following chapter Carter, Johns, and Wall discuss an initiative titled Student Opportunity for Achieving Results (SOAR) that focuses on barriers to student success. By reframing barriers and obstacles as opportunities- an instance of Appreciative Intelligence, SOAR entails the introduction of appreciative inquiry with targeted results and specific outcomes. Powell and Thatchenkery next describe a process intervention that took place at a military accounting facility to improve employee retention. An OD intervention known as Appreciative Sharing of Knowledge (ASK), which is based on Appreciative Inquiry (AI) and Appreciative Intelligence, uncovered several core values held by the staff but not being fully supported by the leadership. The case study shows how participants worked through conflicting information with an eye towards the positive.

Wakefield, Robertson, and Wall in the chapter that follows "Nonprofit board service: a qualitative investigation using appreciative inquiry", present an appreciative-inquiry inspired study conducted in support of efforts to improve opportunities for young people seeking nonprofit board service. The case study identifies critical board member skills specific to this community and explores related topics including training and fundraising. Colvin and Thorpe present results of a study on a Human Resource Management (HRM) intervention. They used Appreciative Sharing of Knowledge (ASK) methodology to explore core competencies and uncovered several areas of improvements including accountability, student focus, retention and proactive communications. "Simplified cost effective strategic artificial and business intelligence at Gulf Shores Company" is the next case study featured where Qureshi and Stevens discuss how artificial intelligence supports an organization's business intelligence processes by simplifying them and making them more cost effective. Theirs is an analysis that is both conceptual and practical. Long and Dighe present a case on application of Virtual Appreciative Sharing of Knowledge (VASK) to develop a mutually supportive learning organization. This unique application of ASK (Thatchenkery, 2005) to the virtual domain is very pragmatic and provides a rich set of qualitative and quantitative data for analysts.

Perceptions of the United States' new healthcare reform law, the PPACA, as exemplified by the NFIB, a lobbyist organization for small businesses" is the next case study by Srinivasan, Thatchenkery, and Washington. They analyze how perceptions toward the Unites States' new healthcare reform law, popularly called ObamaCare, or more technically the Patient Protection and Affordable Care Act (PPACA), are shaped by influence tactics of the National Federation of Independent Business (NFIB) and other lobbyist organizations. In this time of intense presidential election political campaign, the language used to attack or defend ObamaCare acquires new significance. The power of language and our capacity to reframe to bring out what we want to both see and ignore are amply evident in this case study, making us wonder how socially constructed are our views about such important public policy issues. The last chapter in this section by Yaw, Dighe, Miller, and Wall explores data conversion for electronic medical records. As healthcare cost spirals out of control, Health Maintenance Organizations (HMO) have recognized the economic benefits of maintaining electronic medical records for patients. However, the transition from paper to digital or more recently to cloud computing has not been easy. Using appreciative inquiry, the author show how these challenges can be managed as they did so in Shri Ganapati Netralaya (SGN), a well-known Eye Hospital in India. All in all, the dozen case studies in this section show the power of Appreciative Intelligence® and AI and how the two can be synchronized to create total system changes that are sustainable and positive.

Another aspect of leveraging human capital centers on knowledge and talent management along with educational reform. This is the focus of section two of this edited volume. Thanks to the high state of globalization and advances in technology, organizations will have to make the best use of their tacit knowledge and human talent for value creation. Useful knowledge represents the accumulation of experience in the organization which is the result of experimentation and enduring transformation processes, most of which exist in the tacit form. The modern organization faces challenges to capture and retain the tacit knowledge so gathered (Thatchenkery & Chaudhry, 2007). The cases covered in this section highlight the strategies, methods, and practices followed in some of the most successful organizations in managing tacit knowledge and talent. More than half the cases pertain to the Indian context and validate the propositions and observations made by Thatchenkery and Stough (2006) and Thatchenkery, Kash, Stough (2004) regarding the way India transitioned from an agrarian to a knowledge intensive society, despite rampant bureaucracy and regulations.

Khan and Roy in the first chapter of this section explicate the innovative steps by the IT major Sapient Corporation ("Enhancing the edge: innovative management of knowledge at Sapient corporation"). The analysis is geared towards understanding the impact of such initiatives on organizational performance. Gupta and Tomar analyze the effectiveness of talent management practices at Grasim Industries of the Birla Group in India. The authors refer to creation of talent pool and the intricacies of managing it. According to their research, many of the non-talent pool members feel that the transparency in the talent management process is low. In the next chapter, Rana and Goel examine the talent retention practices in Bharat Heavy Electricals Limited (BHEL), a massive knowledge intensive public sector organization in India. Their findings are of significant value not just to BHEL but to the hundreds of similarly large public sector entities in India and South Asia. Tenkasi and Hay next elucidate the basic principles and key competencies underlying integration of theory and research knowledge to the realm of practice in the context of a study of scholar-practitioners. Their case study suggests employment of six strategies for interrelating theory and practice and two meta-strategies. Montonen and Eriksson next analyse how innovation and entrepreneurship have been taught at a Finnish higher education institution. The case study demonstrates success story of a new model of teaching to initiate and enhance a transparent and practice oriented innovation process as part of the business degree curriculum. As a nation, Finland has been lauded very positively for their innovative educational system and the case study explains some of the success factors behind it.

Noted case writers Erwan and Paul in the final chapter in this section highlight the complexity of management situations when it comes to using case studies as a teaching tool. The reality is always more complicated than the classroom and yet the case writer should strive to maintain a deep embeddedness to the real world. The authors share various fine tuning of the pedagogy of case studies in management education based on their long years of practice in this area and present a survey of current trends to choose a topic for a case. All in all, the half a dozen cases in this section portray the dynamic world of tacit knowledge sharing and talent management and the role of reframing human capital.

The third section of this edited volume focuses on human capital development. As pointed out by Mabey (2003) Human Resource Development (HRD) practice can be understood from multiple perspectives and one of them is based on human capital management. This is so because in the final diagnosis it is the human capital which is called upon to discover new solutions in the highly competitive global market place. Human resource is also the carrier of intellectual capital. The management of human capital thus emerges as the biggest challenge and opportunity. For example, Bolman and Deal (2009) through their well-known reframing approach has shown the importance of leveraging human capital. The four cases in this section explicate some of these issues facing the management of human capital. The cases cover the success stories and lessons learned from failures, both in an engaging and narrative format. The reader benefits from seeing how reframing works in the real word when it comes to leveraging human capital.

The first such exploration is by Agarwal and Chaudhuri who present a case study conducted at Jindal Steel and Power Limited (JSPL), one of the largest materials and energy companies in India. The study recognizes factors such as work climate, growth opportunities, non-monetary incentives, and flexibility and clarity in work as contributing to employee retention and productivity. Nayak and Tyagi next discuss a financial services company's learning and development programs to address the issue of absenteeism. The case brings out both strengths of learning curriculum and weaknesses of classroom training. Misra, Jain, and Sood present an exploratory study in Indian retail industry. They analyze the impact of compensation components (both financial and non-financial rewards) and organizational justice on motivation, job satisfaction, and turnover intentions. In the final case study in this section, Puri and Chaudhuri examine initiatives of competency assessment at ADIDAS India to change the way its franchisee stores managed their human resources. The analysis uses in-depth interviewing and observations and brings out insightful findings. Overall, the four chapters in this section present a convincing case for human capital development in organizations of all sorts.

The fourth section lists several cases on reframing in the domain of leadership and organizational development. One of the most researched concepts in organizational science is leadership. It has been looked at from multiple angles, and one of the newest such approaches is the notion of quiet or invisible leadership (Thatchenkery & Sugiyama, 2011). Most of leadership training today is focused on charismatic or visible leadership. Leadership is also intimately tied to entrepreneurship. Against this backdrop of the history of focusing on developing only one type of leadership, Thatchenkery and Sugiyama (2011) call for valuing quiet leadership, one that is focused on collaboration, mindfulness, and bringing out the best from everyone. The five chapters in this section discuss several cases from new perspectives on leadership and organization development. They were chosen from diverse fields to highlight application of these approaches to differing circumstances – cultural, political, and economic. The first chapter by Anderson and Anderson explores leadership issues in administration of a large church facing a vocal minority group in blocking an effort to relocate and expand the church. Their narrative brings out the dependencies between followership and leadership and reveals the fine balance between faith and autonomy. Newton in the next chapter explores the theory and characteristics of charismatic leadership behavior in order to illuminate various perspectives of transformational leaders through their understanding of existing charismatic leadership behavior. Such a topic is of significance as corporations today try to balance the need for valuing multiple styles of leadership, not just charismatic (Thatchenkery & Sugiyama, 2011).

Based on their long years of experience and research, DePorres and Miller explore the inner working of international student programs. Their study provides ten steps that faculty teaching in "study abroad" programs may use to build and reinforce the attitudes, behaviors, and commitments (ABCs) of students participating in such programs. Their advice is pragmatic and is supported by data. The next research case from Thailand-based Wongtrakuland and US-based Hanson discusses the impact of an Organizational Development Intervention (ODI) on the improvement of employee motivation, commitment, and customer satisfaction in a Thai subsidiary of a multinational hotel chain. The lessons learned are highly valuable for anyone looking for insights about managing staff in multinational corporations. The last case study in this section is from Walla who examines the processes needed to guide professionalization of organizations in the cleaning industry from both environmental and social sustainability standards. All together these cases bring to surface the nuances and subtleties of organizational development and leadership.

A good way to conclude this edited volume is to bring it to full circle by examining cases in global culture and organizational change. Similar to leadership, scholars in organizational sciences have examined culture from every conceivable angle. In this volume we have cases focusing on both organizational culture and global culture. Management scholars and practitioners have for long recognized that ignoring the cultural differences across geographies can lead to significant problems for organizations operating in global markets (Thatchenkery & Gopakumar, 2005; Adler,

2001; Bartlett & Ghoshal, 2004; Boyacigiller and Adler, 1991; Hofstede, 2003). The descriptions of two such mishaps by Mann (1989) and Brannen and Wilson, (1996) are worth noting. Mann shows how US executives miscalculated the organizational culture of Chinese businesses and made poor decisions while investing in China. In the end, according to Mann, the Chinese acquired valuable new technology at virtually no cost by outgunning the U.S. executives by deception and manipulation. Brannen and Wilson analyze the efforts of Walt Disney to replicate its entire organizational policies and practices in France after successfully completing a similar exercise in Tokyo. However, this ended up as a failure and the company had to suffer negative perception for urging French employees to enact behaviors alien to their culture.

Managers who target growth in global markets believe that while dealing with heterogeneity across cultures and markets, going to the other extreme of paying too much attention to cultural uniqueness can lead to equally severe tragedies (Thatchenkery & Gopakumar, 2005). For example, Percy Barnevik, the first Chief Executive Officer (CEO) of ABB, a global leader in power and automation technologies notes that while global managers respect and appreciative of cultural differences, "they are also incisive; they push the limits of the culture. Global managers don't passively accept it when someone says, 'You can't do that in Italy or Spain because of the unions 'or 'You can't do that in Japan because of the Ministry of Finance.' They sort through the debris of cultural excuses and find opportunities to innovate" (Quoted in Taylor, 1991, p. 93).

Despite this growing realization among management practitioners that culture can no longer be considered as a static and discrete entity which characterizes national identities, the major approaches in cross cultural OD have continued to emphasize that when OD practitioners are in various countries, they should stay away from a "U.S.-Euro centric" view of OD and instead customize their offerings to suit the local culture (Thatchenkery, 2006). Others have suggested that the applicability of OD in the international context may depend on the congruence of national cultural values and OD values (Fagenson-Eland, Ensher, & Burke, 2004). For example, Hofstede (1993) described overseas Chinese firms as extremely cost-conscious, applying Confucian virtues of thrift and persistence, thereby less likely to make use of OD practitioners. Lau, McMahan, and Woodman (1996) compared the organization development practices in the U.S. and Hong Kong and pointed out differences such as that the Hong Kong firms spent one quarter of their time on strategic planning in lieu of the 16.3 percent for the U.S. firms.

Singh and Krishnan (2004) studied the transformational aspect of organization development in India by conceptually separating its leadership dimension into universal and culture-specific leadership. Their results implied a 56% weight for various culture-specific factors in the corporate sector such as nurturing, personal touch, expertise, simple living, loyalty, and sacrifice. Another study was by Fagenson-

Eland, Ensher, and Burke (2004) who compared differences in OD intervention in seven countries, namely Finland, Ireland, the Netherlands, New Zealand, South Africa, and U.K. If the above studies are any indication, most OD researchers and practitioners are of the view that OD as practiced in the West or the U.S. should only be used for organizations in other countries with appropriate customization to accommodate the local cultures (Thatchenkery & Gopakumar, 2005).

Arguments for culture specific OD interventions are based on the analytical distinctions of 'Global versus Local' and its attendant dichotomy of 'Homogeneity versus Heterogeneity' both of which no longer holds the same relevance that they once had (Thatchenkery & Gopakumar, 2005). Evolution of these arguments need to be understood in the context of how assumptions of modernity and later, post modernity has influenced the field and how global modernity is taking over the current discourse about organizational development practices. In the context of globalization and its related experiences of global modernity, the notion of culture will have to illustrate the commonality of experiences generated at the global level. Although it is important to recognize differences across cultures, it is equally necessary to recognize that these differences derive meaning from a common experience of globalization (Thatchenkery & Gopakumar, 2005).

Case studies in this section show that understanding the phenomenology of global cultural identity requires a nuanced and dialectical approach. A recognition of the simultaneous existence of two realities is desired. First, the increasing global interconnectedness makes people across the world subject to the same determining forces and processes. Second, the movement of culture between geographical areas always involves adaptation as the 'receiving culture' brings its own imprint upon 'cultural imports'. This recognition in turn implies that the assumptions of neither modernity nor late modernity would be sufficient to deal with the complexities of contemporary global context (Thatchenkery & Gopakumar, 2005; Burke, 2004; Bradford & Burke, 2004). Thus organizations today understandably face new realities in multiple domains, culture being one of the most intricate among them all. The organizations owe their existence to society and pay back to it in various forms as social responsibility and community development. There are new concepts such as conscious capitalism (Mackey & Sisodia, 2013), corporate social responsibility (CSR), and social consciousness related to generation of capital. In the other extreme, as organizations move out to outsourcing or search for cheaper resources beyond the national frontiers they face cultural diversity among employees and customers. Cultural context has its own impact for the smooth functioning of systems, procedures, and human relations. This has been evident in several labor conflicts seen recently in several countries. This section examines some of these sensitive issues through case studies.

Glinka and Thatchenkery present a case study to seek answers to the vexed question of how culture might influence management students from three radically different large world metropolises. This study covered management students in Warsaw (Poland), Delhi (India), and the Washington, D.C. (U.SA). The authors collected data through a carefully designed questionnaire and their findings reveal the role of bureaucracy in Poland and India and free markets in the U.S. They show how globalization has made the world more homogenous and yet how deep rooted cultural values persist. In the next chapter, Peters-Van Havel focuses on a case study to develop an understanding of the psychological sense of community within a geographically dispersed organization. She articulates a workable definition of community as applicable in a non-traditional environment and her analysis shows the ambiguities, challenges, and opportunities afforded by such an attempt.

Ibrahim, Khalid, Jalaludin, and Abdelbagi discuss a case about community engagement practice of JOC Petroleum (JOC), a petroleum company operating in the south of Sudan. They examine corporate community engagement practice for a balanced and equitable development. In the next chapter Anjaly and Sahay illustrate a success story of a social entrepreneur who decided to improve the life of thousands of poor rickshaw pullers in India. The last case study in this section as well as the volume is from Tyagi and Ntibagirirwa. They explore the economic success of South East Asia and compare it with failure of economic development in sub-Saharan Africa. The authors conclude that economic growth and development of a nation need to be a substantiation of the beliefs and values of its citizens.

All in all, the 33 case studies in this volume covered a diverse range of topics, controversies, and new developments using the approach of reframing for leveraging human capital. We believe that we have touched on the surface of a highly promising area of new research from a global perspective and look forward to seeing additional research in reframing for leveraging human capital.

REFERENCES

Adler, N. (2001). *International dimensions of organizational behavior.* Cincinnati, OH: Southern-Western.

Barlett, C.A., and Ghoshal, S.(2004). *Managing across borders.* Boston, MA: HBS Press.

Bauman, Z. Is there a postmodern sociology? Theory, Culture, and Society, 2-3, 1988, 217-39.

Boyacigiller, N.A. & Adler, N.J. (1991). The parochial dinosaur: Organizational science in a global context. *Academy of Management Review.* 16 (2), 262-90.

Bradford, D., & Burke, W. (2004) Introduction: Is OD in Crisis? *The Journal of Applied Behavioral Science, 40*: 369-373.

Brannen, M.Y., & Wilson, J.M. (1996). Recontextualization and internationalization: Lessons in transcultural materialism from the Walt Disney Company. *Community of European Management Schools Business Review.* 1(1), 97-110.

Burke, W. (2004). Internal Organization Development Practitioners: Where Do They Belong?

The Journal of Applied Behavioral Science, 40: 423-431.

Cooperrider, David., & Whitney, Diana. (2005). *Appreciative inquiry: A positive revolution in change*. San Francisco: Berrett-Koehler.

Cooperrider, D.L., & Srivastva, S. (1987). Appreciative inquiry in organizational life. *Research in Organizational Change and Development* 1, 129-169.

Fagenson-Eland, E., Ensher, E.A., & Burke, W.W. (2004). Organization development and change interventions: A seven nation comparison. *Journal of Applied Behavioral Science, 40* (4), 432-464.

Hofstede, G. (1993). Cultural constraints in management theories. *Academy of Management Executive. 7* (1), 81-94.

Hofstede, G. (2003). *Culture's consequences: Comparing values, behaviors, institutions and organizations across nations*. Beverly Hills, CA: Sage.

Lee, B. Deal, T. (2009). Reframing Organizations: Artistry, Choice and Leadership Jossey-Bass.

Lau, C.M., McMahan, G.C., & Woodman, R. (1996). An international comparison of organization development practices: The U.S.A. and Hong Kong. *Journal of Organizational Change Management, 9* (2), 4-14.

Mann, J. (1989). *Beijing Jeep: The short, unhappy romance of American business in China*. New York: Simon and Schuster.

Mabey, C. (2003). Reframing Human Resource Development. Human Resource Development Review, 2. 4, 430-452.

Mackey, John., & Sisodia, Raj. (2013). Conscious Capitalism: Liberating the Heroic Spirit of Business. Boston, MA: Harvard Business Review Press.

Saxena, Manoj (2012) quoted by Gertner, John. (2012). Calling Dr Watson. Fast Company, November 12, 129.

Saxenian, Annalee. *Regional Advantage: Culture and Competition in Silicon Valley and Route 128*. Cambridge, MA: Harvard University Press, 1996.

Saxenian, Annalee. *Silicon Valley's New Immigrant Entrepreneurs*. San Francisco: Public Policy Institute of California, 1999.

Sardana, G.D., Thatchenkery, Tojo. (Eds.). (2011). *Positive Initiatives for Organizational Change and Transformation*. New Delhi. Macmillan.

Singh, N., & Krishnan, V. (2004). *Towards understanding transformational leadership in India: Grounded theory approach*. Jamshedpur, India: Xavier Labor Relations Institute.

Taylor, W. E. (1991). The logic of global business: An interview with ABB's Percy Barnevik. *Harvard Business Review. 69*(1): 93–105.

Thatchenkery, Tojo. (2011). Appreciative Intelligence for Transformative Conversations. In

Sardana, G.D., Thatchenkery, Tojo. (Eds.). *Positive Initiatives for Organizational Change and Transformation* (pp. 63-77). New Delhi. Macmillan.

Thatchenkery, Tojo., & Sugiyama, Keimei. (2011). Making the Invisible Visible: Understanding Leadership Contributions of Asian Minorities in the Workplace. New York: Palgrave Macmillan.

Thatchenkery, T., and Chaudhry, D. (2007). Appreciative inquiry and knowledge management: A social constructionist perspective. Cheltenham, U.K. Edward Elgar.

Thatchenkery, Tojo., & Metzker, Carol (2006). *Appreciative Intelligence: Seeing the Mighty Oak in the Acorn.* San Francisco: Berrett-Koehler.

Thatchenkery, Tojo., & Stough, Roger (2006). Information Communication Technology and Economic Development: Learning from the Indian Experience. Cheltenham, U.K. Edward Elgar.

Thatchenkery, T (2006). Organization Development in Asia. In Michael Brazzel & Brenda Jones (Eds). *The NTL Handbook of Organization Development and Change*: San Francisco:

Thatchenkery, Tojo (2005). Appreciative Sharing of Knowledge: Leveraging Knowledge Management for Strategic Change. Chagrin Falls, Ohio: Taos Institute Publishing.

Thatchenkery, Tojo., & Gopakumar, G. (2005). Organization development in the global context: A critique. Paper presented for the *Academy of Management Annual Meetings*, August 6-10, Hawaii.

Thatchenkery, T., Kash, D., & Stough, R., (Eds.). (2004). Information technology and development: The Indian experience. *Technological Forecasting and Social Change, 71*(8), 771-879.

Tsing, A. (2000). The global situation. *Cultural Anthropology*, 15 (3), 327-360.

Whitney, Diana ., & Trosten-Bloom, Amanda. (2010). The Power of Appreciative Inquiry: A Practical Guide to Positive Change . San Francisco: Berrett-Koehler.

PART I: Cases Using Appreciative Intelligence-based Interventions

As mentioned in the introduction, Appreciative Intelligence® is a key component in leveraging human capital for organizational excellence. Human resource and organization development professionals during the last decade have been able to make the best use of many aspects of human capital such as emotional intelligence, social intelligence, and analytical intelligence. Appreciative Intelligence is the latest entrant those efforts. The capacity to reframe and see the positive potential in otherwise gloomy situations is a critical skill needed for stakeholders and leaders in all types of organizations. Developing Appreciative Intelligence goes one more step- the capacity to take action by bringing the future desired state into an awareness of the present. It is possible to think of this third component of Appreciative Intelligence as a type of applied mindfulness, as revealed by many chapters in this section.

This section also makes a strong link between Appreciative Intelligence and Appreciative Inquiry. The former is an individual level ability while the latter is an organizational analysis tool and approach. The two build on each other as vividly demonstrated in several case studies in this section. For example, engaging in a system-wide appreciative inquiry project may lead to enhancing the Appreciative Intelligence of participants by allowing them to discover the positive potential in the challenging situations that they had faced and acting to transform the opportunities to purposeful outcomes using the future-present scenarios (FPS) or possibility propositions models inherent in the appreciative inquiry model. The case studies show that AI takes various approaches to recognize the potential embedded in a multitude of organizational realities but not initially visible to an untrained eye. The case studies presented and methodologies described will help an interested reader not familiar with AI to understand the logic and rationality of this emerging and popular management tool. The one full dozen cases covered in this part are from diverse organizational and cultural situations and have direct bearings for applied actions. Such a strong link only goes to stress the usefulness of AI and its application to a wide spectrum of management situations.

The first chapter in this section is a case study by Mikel Lemons and Tojo Thatchenkery who explore the intricacies of the leadership challenges faced by a community college and its efforts to deal with the various aspects of the resistance to change that unfolded. The authors identified the core values of the community college using Appreciative Intelligence-based interviews and created various scenarios for transformation that were participatory and were based on empowering all stakeholders for a collective future which in turn was built on principles of ecological and social sustainability for education. In the next chapter, Kristine Brands and Debora Elam use a customized approach of the Appreciative Inquiry (AI) organizational analysis model to examine a non-profit organization's fundraising enablers. The research was used to discover possibilities for increasing fundraising levels to meet the growing needs of the Pike region community in Colorado, USA. Lessons learned were also shared in a usable manner. In the chapter that follows Rod Hagedorn discusses yet another case of appreciative inquiry to identify positively-oriented action items at a for-profit technical college. The survey method was used to validate ideal state versus present state possibility propositions posited via a qualitative analysis.

The next chapter by Krisha Coppedge and David Boje explores the experiences of six homeowners who suffered mortgage foreclosure in the United States. Using the increasingly popular story telling methodology the authors provide an engaging narrative of the hardships and challenges faced by the homeowners and their resilience against adversity. The authors conclude that coercion, mistaken evidence, and duress impacted participants' mortgage foreclosures and suggest ways to prevent such social injustice in the future. Against the backdrop of the present housing economic data, their findings are extremely valuable and poignant. In the following chapter, Barbara Carter, Joan Marie Johns, and Ken Wall discuss an initiative titled Student Opportunity for Achieving Results(SOAR) that focuses on barriers to student success. By reframing barriers and obstacles as opportunities- an instance of Appreciative Intelligence, SOAR entails the introduction of appreciative inquiry with targeted results and specific outcomes. Beverley Powell and Tojo Thatchenkery next describe a process intervention that took place at a military accounting facility to improve employee retention. An OD intervention known as Appreciative Sharing of Knowledge (ASK), which is based on Appreciative Inquiry (AI) and Appreciative Intelligence, uncovered several core values held by the staff but not being fully supported by the leadership. The case study shows how participants worked through conflicting information with an eye towards the positive and a generative future.

Tonya Wakefield, Alfonso Robertson, and Ken Wall in the chapter that follows present an appreciative-inquiry inspired study conducted in support of efforts to improve opportunities for young people seeking nonprofit board service. The case study identifies critical board member skills specific to this community and explores related topics including training and fundraising. James Colvin and James Thorpe present results of a study on a Human Resource Management (HRM) intervention. Appreciative Sharing of Knowledge (ASK) methodology is used to explore core competencies in this instance.Their case study uncovered several areas of improvements including accountability, student focus, retention and proactive communications.Asma Qureshi and Jeff Stevens in the next chapter discuss how artificial intelligence supports an organization's business intelligence processes by simplifying them and making them more cost effective. Theirs is an analysis that is both conceptual and practical. Ken Long and Parag Dighe present a case on application of Virtual Appreciative Sharing of Knowledge (VASK) to develop a mutually supportive learning organization. This unique application of ASK to the virtual domain is very pragmatic and provides a rich set of qualitative and quantitative data for analysts.Divya Srinivasan, Tojo Thatchenkery, and Anne Washington next analyse how perceptions toward the Unites States'new healthcare reform law, popularly called ObamaCare, or more technically the Patient Protection and Affordable Care Act (PPACA), are shaped by the National Federation of Independent Business (NFIB) and other lobbyist organizations. The power of language and our capacity to reframe to bring out what we want to see and ignore are amply evident in this case study, making us wonder how socially constructed are our views about such important public policy issues.

The last chapter in this section by Yaw M, Parag Dighe, Monty Miller, and Ken Wall explores data conversion for Electronic Medical Records. As healthcare cost spiral out of control, Health Maintenance Organizations (HMO) have recognized the economic benefits of maintaining electronic medical records for patients. The transition from paper to digital or more recently to cloud computing has not been easy. Using appreciative inquiry, the authors show how these challenges can be managed as they did in Shri Ganapati Netralaya (SGN), a well-known Eye Hospital in India. All in call, the dozen case studies show the power of Appreciative Intelligence® and AI and how the two can be synchronized to create total system changes that are sustainable and positive.

Appreciative Intelligence for Change Management: A Case Study of a Community College

R. Mikel Lemons* and Tojo Thatchenkery**

ABSTRACT

This case study explored the intricacies of the leadership challenges faced by a community college in the United States in dealing with the resistance to change and how they could be reframed into opportunities using Appreciative Intelligence-based approaches. Results showed that creating and maintaining a significant amount of personal communication and knowledge sharing among all participants was critical during leadership transition. To reframe the notion of resistance to change as a constructive quality, various core values of the organization were identified using Appreciative Intelligence-based interviews. An elaborate Appreciative Inquiry-based organizational analysis was conducted building on the core values and several "future-present scenarios" were generated for implementation. The power of the unconditional positive questions in communication meetings to create a positive organizational climate was demonstrated in this case study. As a pre-test had revealed a resistance to change among internal stakeholders, Appreciative Intelligence-based communication programs were designed and implemented to address it. Post-tests indicated that the effort was successful in helping others "see the mighty oak in the acorn". The key learning from this study was that higher education leaders should proactively create a readiness for change in the faculty, staff, and administration prior to making radical changes by leveraging the goodwill and positive energy that exist in the institution. This was best accomplished by reframing resistance to change as an opportunity and redefining personal communication meetings as a tool for knowledge sharing and for creating a positive organizational climate.

Keywords: Resistance to change, appreciative intelligence, community colleges, organizational climate.

INTRODUCTION

This case study was conducted on a medium sized community college campus in the southwestern United States which had approximately 6,000 students, 118 faculty

* Lemons is with Odessa College, USA.

**Prof. Tojo is with George Mason University, Arlington, Virginia, USA.

E-mail: thatchen@gmu.edu, mlemons@odessa.edu

members, 108 administrative and professional staff, and 115 non-professional staff. Most educational institutions have mechanistic and hierarchal bureaucracies because of the rigid rules and policies and procedures developed to be a guide for the educational processes (Jones, 2007). They are often characterized by autocratic rule because public institutions are evaluated by boards of trustees, governing boards, coordinating boards and taxing authorities from county, state and national government agencies on their effectiveness in meeting public needs (Heller, 2003). All of these agencies expect a level of productivity, efficiency and predictable outcomes. At the same time, because of the rapidly changing economic conditions, educational institutions are facing new challenges to create more flexible processes and procedures in order to respond effectively to the regional demands.

This research examines the attitude of the faculty and staff in the face of a restructuring of the upper level management in the community college. The faculty and staff were concerned that the new President did not proactively communicate the changes reshaping the administration. For example, though the previous President's Council was made up of the Vice Presidents and the Divisional Deans, the new President's Council comprised the Vice Presidents, the Director of Research and Institutional Effectiveness, and the Director of State and Federal Grants but not the deans. The four deans were the critical communicative link to the faculty and staff. As a result of this, the department chairs who reported directly to the dean were also left out of the communication structure.

Participants were interviewed to understand their ambivalences towards these changes, and the lack of communication to and from the administration. This case study research used the 4D method of Appreciative Inquiry (Cooperrider & Srivastva, 1987; Cooperrider & Whitney, 2005; Ludema, Cooperrider, & Barrett, 2001). The pretest interview data taken from sixteen stratified random interviews was entered into three Appreciative Intelligence-based matrices (Thatchenkery & Metzger, 2006) to obtain information to apply the 4D method and for the design of the intervention programs. These programs were implemented for one year. A post-test survey gathered quantitative and a limited amount of qualitative data to measure the effectiveness of the programs.

The initial interview questions revealed information about the attitudes of the administration, faculty and staff toward the changes in the administrative structure. The information also gave clues to the nature of the programs that might increase communication and feedback. The case study also explored the power of the unconditional positive question (Ludema, et al., 2001; Heelan & Transure, 2005) used in communication meetings in dealing with resistance to change and the role of electronic communications relating to psychological ownership and change management. The unconditional positive question (Ludema, et al, 2001) entails asking a positive question without attaching conditions about the type of responses expected.

The case study explored whether communication meetings (in person and electronic) using the power of the unconditional positive questions would have an impact in dealing with the resistance to changes in policies and procedures.

APPRECIATIVE INQUIRY AND APPRECIATIVE INTELLIGENCE

Cooperrider and Srivastva (1987) and several others such as Ludema et al. (2001), Thatchenkery & Chaudhary (2007), have advocated the use of Appreciative Inquiry in the research process for change in organizations. "Appreciative Inquiry involves in a central way, the art and practice of asking questions that strengthen a systems capacity to apprehend, anticipate, and heighten positive potential, it centrally involves the mobilization of inquiry through the crafting of the unconditional positive question" (Heelan & Transure, 2005 p. 8). Using the power of the unconditional positive question in focus groups and meetings can aid in generating knowledge about the changes that need to be implemented (Greenwood & Levin, 2007). The focus groups were made up of the faculty, administration and staff and generated an atmosphere of unbiased observation about the current issues facing the community and the college. The positive questions were used as a tool to bridge the personal communications gap from administration to faculty and staff, help in the positive communication between departments and for knowledge generation about the changes that needed to be implemented.

To better understand Appreciative Inquiry in research, Appreciative Intelligence-based principles (Thatchenkery & Metzger, 2006) can be used as a method of coding data to arrive at the Life Giving Forces (LGF's). Identifying the LGF's of an organization is a way to see the "mighty oak in the acorn" (Thatchenkery & Metzger, 2006) or to see the future opportunities available to the organization. These LGF's along with the five organizational factors used as guidelines with the data applied to different matrices can help a researcher better understand the concepts of "the best of what is", "envisioning what could be", "co-constructing what should be" and then "sustaining what will be".

This research used a pre-test interview to collect information on the attitudes, feelings and opinions of the members of four divisions of the institution. The qualitative data were incorporated into several Appreciative Intelligence (Thatchenkery & Metzger, 2006) matrices, and these in turn were used to identify needs and design programs to aid the institution in an intervention. The research team conducted sixteen interviews among a stratified random sample of faculty, staff and administrators to collect valuable qualitative data of the feelings and opinions of the subjects (Gall, Borg, & Gall, 1996). A post-test survey was designed and used to collect qualitative and quantitative data about the effects of the interventions. The post-test survey instrument was administered approximately one year after the four intervention programs were instituted.

This case study used a modified version of the 4D model of Appreciative Inquiry (Ludema et al. 2001). The study team used five phases: (1) topic of choice, (2) discovery (identifying he needs), (3) dream (envisioning what could be), (4) design (co-constructing what should be) and (5) destiny (sustaining what will be) (Ludema et al. 2001, p. 192). The modifications were the change of positive topic of choice (1) and additions to (5) Destiny. To measure the success or failure of destiny, a survey with qualitative and quantitative questions was designed and administered. The data from the survey instrument yielded information for sustainability of the programs and or methods used in the intervention and possible alterations, improvements and new programs. The 4D model of Appreciative Inquiry is Fig. 1 below.

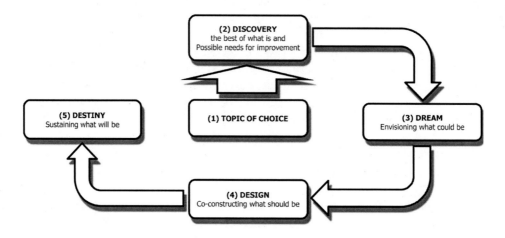

Fig. 1: 4D Model

Topic of Choice

The first phase was to identify the topic of choice.   Interview data revealed that there was resistance to the changes in organizational structure that created fear of the unknown among faculty and staff. There seemed to be a lack of communication between the administration and faculty and staff. The research department of the institution conducted surveys from time to time, but faculty were known "to give them what they want to hear". The faculty could give all positive comments in upward communication, while passing rumors and "hear say" in horizontal communication. The 4D model of Appreciative Inquiry was modified to fit the intervention process. The division between labor and administration was evident. Conversations between faculty members were more often negative in reference to the administration. Interview questions were designed in accordance with the Appreciative Interview Protocol (Ludema et al. 2001). This would aid in gathering the information to code and apply to the three Appreciative Intelligence-based (Thatchenkery & Metzger, 2006) matrices. Sixteen pretest interviews were conducted in a stratified random sampling to better understand and design the intervention programs.

Pre-test Analysis

The answers from the interviews were divided into one hundred to obtain a percent value for each answer. The pretest interview data revealed resistance to the changes in the reshaping of the administration and changes in policies and procedures. This was caused by a lack of communication to create a readiness for change prior to the restructuring. The main core values of the institution's culture were identified as student success, teamwork, pride in the organization and professionalism. Eleven of the participants (68%) mentioned student success as the main core value of the institution. Five of the participants (31.25%) identified teamwork and pride in the organization as one of the life-giving forces, while four respondents (25%) identified professionalism as a core value. Other core values were academic freedom and being community minded (one participant each). A table identifying the four main core values or LGF's of the institution and the rank of each from the interview process is detailed in Table 1.

Table 1: Core Values

Rank	Main Core Value	# Interviewees who Mentioned	% of interviewees who Mentioned
1	Student Success	11	68%
2	Teamwork	6	37.5%
3	Pride in Organization	5	31.25%
4	Professional	4	25

Rank of Main Core Values or Life Giving Forces (LGF's)

The negative comments were identified as resistance to the changes in policies and procedures caused by the lack of communication from the administration to the professional staff, faculty and staff. One comment to the question pertaining to the institutions best practices was that "we are disorganized and there is a lack of communication from the top down". A comment heard more often in the interviews was "the left hand does not know what the right hand is doing". This pointed to the lack of communication, which could be improved by the use of appreciative inquiry meetings. The common suggestion was to have face to face meetings with the administration and receive feedback from the other participants.

Six interviewees (37.5% of the interviewees) mentioned face to face communication meetings as a hope for the future. Eight of the participants (50%) identified better communication from administration to the faculty in that category. Six participants (37.5%) identified better teamwork as a hope for the future and five (31.25%) chose more effective leadership.

Better communication was rated as high as the most important hope for the institution, because it was identified in 50% of the interviews. Face to face or personal communication as one of their hopes for the future was rated at moderately important being identified in 37.5% of the interviews. Better teamwork was rated as a moderate hope with 31.25% of the respondents listing this as an important hope for the future of the organization. Better marketing was rated as moderate with 37.5% value of the answer. More effective leadership was rated as moderate in the hopes for the institution, because of a 31.25% answer value. Two interviewees answered that their hope for the future of the institution would be that the administration work better with faculty which garnered a score of 12.5% and was rated as low. Only one participant listed a hope for a more progressive institution which was rated as low with a score value of 6.25%. The value of the interview answers is shown in Table 2.

Table 2: Value of Interviews

Rank	Hope for the Future	# of Interviewees who Mentioned	% of Interviewees who Mentioned
High	Better communication	8	50%
Moderate	Face to face or personal communication	6	37.5%
Moderate	Better teamwork	6	37.5%
Moderate	More effective leadership	5	31.25%
Moderate	Better marketing	6	37.5%
Low	Administration work with faculty	2	12.5%
Low	More progressive institution	1	6.25%

Value of Interview Answers of hopes for the future

The final question of the pretest interview asked the participants to rate their attitude towards the changes in administrative structure, and changes in policies and procedures. The rating of one was listed as resistance and five was labeled as acceptance. Four (25%) rated the resistance as one, while six (37.50%) scored it as a two and five (31.25%) rated it as a three. Ten of the sixteen participants rated their attitude as resistance while only one rated the attitude as acceptance to the changes. Five respondents rated the resistance as a three which could mean they were indecisive on the issue. This was the only statistical question of the interview process.

Discovery

The second phase was discovery. Data from answers to interview questions 4-7 helped the researcher define the four LGF's of the organization. These LGF's offered most often were student success, teamwork, pride in the institution, and professionalism. The five organizational factors used in the matrices were the organizational structure, decision making, leadership, communication, and organizational practices. These were applied to three separate matrices to gain a clear perspective of what was good and what was lacking in the organization. Thatchenkery & Metzger (2006) argued that "thematic analysis is one of the most widely used qualitative research methods in the social sciences" (p. 138). Furthermore, a theme is a statement or a meaning that runs through the data like a thread and carries a factual impact (Thatchenkery & Metzger, 2006).

Answers to the interview questions revealed that communication was lacking and some form of communication between the faculty, staff and administration was needed. The researcher scheduled a meeting with the President to explain the problem and offer the information gleaned from the Appreciative Intelligence Matrix (Refer Table 3)

Table 3: Matrix 1 ("The best of what is")

Org. factors	Main Core Values			
	Student Success	Teamwork	Pride in Organization	Professionalism
Organizational Structure	Strive for student success***	Need for teamwork*	Pride in what we do*****	Willing to do anything* Academic freedom*
Decision Making	Student success**	Need better coordination*	Helping Students*	Whatever it takes*
Leadership	Faculty works hard for students*	Team oriented** Dedicated*	Helping students*	Community minded*
Communication	Teachers get students excited**	Lacking**	Departments communicate*	Whatever it takes*
Organizational Practices	We make people successful***	Can do attitude**	Innovative* Work hard*	Forward thinking*

(Asterisks= number of times the answer was mentioned)

For example, if the answer to the question was that the leadership was dedicated or team oriented, that would be applied to the cross section of the Teamwork column (Main Core Values) and the Leadership column (organizational Factors) of Matrix #1. If the same answer was repeated in other interviews, an asterisk would be placed by the answer that was already in the matrix to denote rank of the answer.

The President suggested a meeting with the President's Administrative Council to introduce the research and obtain permission for further research from the entire group. Questions from the panel ranged from how the research would be conducted to the amount of involvement would be expected from the institution. After answering question, the President's Council voted to allow the research to take place.

Dream

The third phase was to dream or "envisioning what could be". This process builds on the life-giving-forces to discover the possibilities. Questions 8-10 asked participants to give their three highest hopes and dreams and most pressing problems of the institution. Other questions of the interview asked for the participants to offer suggestions of what they would like to contribute to help the institution reach its highest hopes and dreams. This information along with the thematic analysis of the main core values of the organization allowed the President's Administrative Council to dream up ideas of "envisioning what could be". A second matrix designed with the four core values across the top and the six organizational factors down the left hand column with responses to the questions of the possibilities for the future put in their appropriate areas to determine the needs for a program or programs. (Refer Tables 4)

Table 4: Matrix 2 ("Envisioning what could be")

Org. factors	Main Core Values			
	Student Success	Teamwork	Pride in Organization	Professionalism
Organizational Structure	More student success	More progressive institution	Pride in what we do	Pride in this organization
Decision Making	Better marketing*****	Form a winning team***	Better training*	Respect of faculty**
Leadership	Value students*	Admin work with faculty*	We can do better*	More effective leadership*
Communication	Open door to all students*	Personal communication	Better communication****	Improve communication****
Incentives	Lack of monetary funds*	Team oriented**	Better communication*	Lack of monetary funds*
Organizational Practices	Helping students* Pride in traditions*	Pull together to become a team*	More positive* Pride in traditions*	Better communication***

(Asterisks= number of times the answer was mentioned)

For example, if an interview answer was "pride in traditions of the school", it would fit in the cross section of Main Core Values column of Pride in Organization and the Organizational line of Organizational Practices. Each answer was categorized and placed in the best fit area of the matrix.

Design

The fourth phase of design allowed for the design of several programs because of the "envisioning of what could be" into "co-constructing what should be" (Thatchenkery & Chaudary, 2007). The situation was discussed and the possibilities were examined. Many of the President's Administrative Council offered ideas of an organization working with a total team effort to complete the mission of the institution. Others offered ideas of passing a bond issue to strengthen the organization financially to better educate the public and possibly change the attitude of the faculty by offering higher salaries. The evidence of the problem was also discussed and all agreed that programs should be developed to reduce the level of resistance to changes and create a culture of better communication amongst all divisions. The use of Appreciative Inquiry and the power of the unconditional positive question were explained to the group. The dream phase allowed the administration to "see the mighty oak in the acorn" (Thatchenkery & Metzger, 2006, p. 5). All of the ideas and propositions would take cooperation and communication between faculty and administration.

Information from the coded data was used to offer information for propositions to be used to develop intervention programs that would possibly improve the areas lacking. The different propositions were labeled as Novelty if it was a totally new program or Continuance if it was a program that could be redesigned to fit the Appreciative Inquiry guidelines. The Appreciative Inquiry team developed the following Propositions:

PROPOSITION #1; (NOVELTY); "Lunch with the President": This meeting is designed for a more intimate conversation between the president and the employees. Twenty employees will be invited to have lunch with the president on a given day of the month. Employees will be formally invited by letter with RSVP. Lunch will be served in a separate room from the dining hall to allow for personal conversation and questions. This communication meeting will enable each employee to have a conversation with the president to address issues that pertain to their position. These communication meetings will aid in knowledge generation for the president to learn more about each employee and each department. Seventeen lunch meetings will be held each year during the fall and spring semester to accommodate all 341 employees. All employees will be urged to attend when invited.

PROPOSITION #2 (NOVELTY); "Coffee and Conversation": This meeting is free for all employees to attend when time is allowed and to discuss any issue with all of the administration attending. Meetings will be held once per month on the second Tuesday morning at 6:45am. This would permit all employees an opportunity to attend and be at their post by 8:00am. These meetings will be very informal with the first thirty minutes for coffee and conversation with other employees and then a time for questions and answer with the administrative officials.

PROPOSITION #3 (CONTINUANCE); "Supervisor training": This is a lunch meeting held to help with communication between the administration and the department chairs.

A topic is chosen for each meeting that helps to inform the chairs and deans of important happenings at the institution. The speaker introduces of a topic that needs to be discussed and taught. The group is then provided lunch with time for personal communication between faculty, staff, professional staff and administrative officials. The speaker completes the topic and then the president has the "Final Fifteen" minutes to update the deans and department chairs of anything or changes that might be happening. This meeting is limited to the department chairs, deans and administration. These positions have the greatest power to change the culture and attitudes of the rest of the employees.

PROPOSITION #4 (NOVELTY); "Wrangler Chat" This E-Communication meeting was designed to allow all employees the opportunity to ask questions and receive answers from any department or official through the use of computer technology. This Web-log (BLOG) will be a non-treatment group with non-personal communication available to all employees.

PROPOSITION #5 (NOVELTY); "Appreciative Input Meeting" (AIM): This meeting is a large scaled meeting of all employees held in the auditorium. Everyone sits with their respective departments. Each department has two minutes or less to tell something good that their department is doing. There is no applause until every department has had time to speak. This happens in a "rapid fire" fashion and it is up to the moderator to hold each department to two minutes or less and quickly go from department to department. This happens in 40 minutes or less. There is a three minute break to stand up, applaud and visit with other departments.

The next session permits a different speaker from each department the same allotted time to tell something good that another department is doing. The statements cannot be duplicated and applause is held until each speaker has completed the "good news". Time for applause is three minutes and then the President gets to speak to the entire congregation for the "final fifteen" minutes.

These meetings could be held the first Thursday of each month at 4:00 pm. The departmental speakers for each meeting rotate so that each employee has a chance to speak for the department. This meeting will develop a pride in the organization, help develop leadership in individuals, teamwork, quick decision making skills, and better communication between departments. It is recommended that this (AIM) also be held in inner departmental meetings to develop pride in the department and other skills listed.

(This proposition was canceled because of time limitations, but was later suggested as an addition to the "Supervisor Training" to improve the meeting).

A third matrix was developed with the four main core values across the top and the organizational factors down the left hand column. The coded data were used to assure that the programs designed would accommodate the needs assessed in the second matrix. The number of the proposition was applied to the cross section of the appropriate main core value and the line of organizational factor for the "best fit" for the intervention programs. Many propositions fit well in several areas of the matrix. The Appreciative Intelligence Matrix #3 is as depicted in Table 5:

Table 5: Matrix 3 (Propositions)

Org. Vactors	Main Core Values			
	Student Success	Teamwork	Pride in Organization	Professionalism
Organizational Structure	1,2,3	1,2,3,4	1,2,3,4	1,2,3,4
Decision Making	1,2,3	1,2,3,4	1,2,4	1,2,3,4
Leadership	1,2	1,2,3,4	1,2,3,4	1,2,3,4
Communication	1	1,2,3,4	1,2,3,4	1,2,3,4
Incentives	1	1,2,4	1,2,4	1,2,4
Organizational Practices	1,2,3	1,2,3,4	1,2,3,4	1,2,3,4

Numbers represent the different Propositions that could be used to strengthen each Organizational factor as it applied to the Main Core Values.

Three personal communication programs were designed and implemented along with the creation of a web log for e-communication to discover what programs would be the most effective. "Coffee and Conversation" (Proposition #2) was developed to allow all employees to have personal communication with the administration. "Lunch with the President" (Proposition #1) was developed to give the President the opportunity to interact with each and every employee on a more intimate level over a meal. "Supervisor Training" (Proposition #3) was developed to be a personal communication venue and educational meeting for the midline (Deans and Department Chairs) and administration (strategic apex). "Wrangler Chat" (Proposition #4) was designed as an E-communication meeting for all employees. This would be the quasi-control group for the study with no Appreciative Inquiry concepts applied.

"Wrangler Chat" would be for questions asked by participants with the appropriate official answering the question. "Appreciative Input Meeting" (AIM) (Proposition #5) was proposed to continue the positive dialogue amongst departments, but it met with disapproval because of the time element. The meetings would be time consuming, but could possibly be used in smaller formats. The intervention programs were designed and implemented for one year. To gauge the results, a thirteen question paper survey was sent out to all participants in a campus mail.

Post-Test Qualitative Analysis

The qualitative data of the post-test survey was designed to obtain information about the change in attitudes of the participants after one year of the intervention programs. Questions were designed to mine information about what each participant enjoyed most about their work, the best practices of the organization and their most important hopes for the future of the institution. A paper copy of the survey instrument was mailed to all employees in the campus mail. The information from the returned surveys was coded and applied to a fourth Appreciative Intelligence matrix to aid in "sustaining what will be". The answers to the questions revealed information about the change in the organizations cultural attitude and its effects on positive organizational behavior along with the added organizational factor of the participants "hope for the future". The Appreciative Intelligence Matrix #4 is as in Tables 6.

Table 6: Matrix 4 ("Sustaining What Will Be")

Org. factors	Main Core Values			
	Student Success	Teamwork	Pride in Organization	Professionalism
Organizational Structure	Student success/ student oriented (29)	Teamwork/ Professionalism (25)	Pride in what we do (3)	Professionalism/ communication (15)
Decision Making				
Leadership				
Communication				
Organizational Practices	Student oriented (27)	Teamwork (3)	Better Leadership (6)	Professionalism (46)
Hopes for the Future			Better Leadership (11) Better communication/ Community support (57)	

(XX) Number of comments

Seventy-seven surveys were returned. This was divided into one hundred to get the percent value of each answer, thus each answer would have a value of 1.29%. The responses were coded. The answers were applied to an Appreciative Intelligence matrix with the four main core values listed across the top and the organizational factors listed down the right hand column with an added factor of hope for the future to establish a picture of "sustaining what will be". Student success or a student oriented culture was listed as the aspect most liked about the employees work. This was evident in 37.41% of the responses. Professionalism/Teamwork was listed twenty five times for a value of 32.25%. These two were ranked as high while good communication was ranked moderate in regard to the culture of the organization. Good communication was identified in 15 responses for a value of 19.35%. These three have a total of 89.01% of the responses and was evidence of a more positive organizational behavior and improved culture. Three survey respondents listed pride in the organization as a value of the culture for a value of 3.87%. There were only eight surveys with this question left blank for a total of 10.32% having no comment. (Refer Table 7.)

Table 7: Survey Responses

Rank	Organizational Structure	# of survey Respondents who Mentioned	% of Survey Respondents who Mentioned
High	Student success/student oriented	29	37.41%
High	Teamwork	25	32.25%
Moderate	Professionalism/communication	15	19.35%
Low	Pride in the organization	3	3.87%

Forty-six respondents listed good communication as the best practice of the organization for a value of 59.34%. Helping students was a second choice for the best practice with twenty seven listing it as a best practice for a value of 34.83%. This was labeled Student Oriented on the matrix. Three respondents listed teamwork as the best practice of the organization for a value of 3.87%, although there was a high rank of the similar answer to the organizational culture. These values represent a more positive attitude. Three respondents left this question blank and one response was that there were no best practices of the organization. This was the only negative response to this question. Other respondents indicated they were required to attend too many meetings (Refer Table 8).

From these totals, the number one Life Giving Force was "good communication/ teamwork (from the top down in the column) with a score of 61 responses. The second highest LGF was "student success/student oriented with 56 responses, while the third LGF was "professionalism/teamwork" with 25 responses (Refer Table 9).

Table 8: Value of Survey Answers to Best Organizational Practices or Life Giving Forces

Rank	Best Practices	# of Survey Respondents who Mentioned	% of Survey Respondents Who Mentioned
Very High	Professionalism	46	59.34%
High	Student oriented	27	34.83%
Low	Teamwork	3	3.87%

Table 9: Value of Life Giving Forces

Life Giving Force	# of Survey Respondents who Mentioned	% of Survey Respondents Who Mentioned
Communication/ Teamwork	61	78.69%
Student Success	56	72.24%
Professionalism/Teamwork	25	32.25%
Pride in the Organization	3	3.87%

A question of the most important hopes for the institutions future showed a change in attitude from internal lack of communication to one with a more external thought of better communication with the community and more community support. This question along with question and answers in the personal communication meetings allowed for the inclusion and understanding of the "shadow" or "darkside" (see Fitzgerald & Oliver 2006) for greater success of the intervention programs. Fifty of the seventy seven responses listed this as one of the most important hopes for the institution for a value of 64.5%. Eleven responses listed a need for better facilities for a value of 14.19%. Six respondents listed a need better leadership as the most important hope for a value of 7.74%. Ten survey respondents left this area blank. The blank responses were attributed to the lack of interest in the questions while the negative responses were low. (Refer Table 10)

Table 10: Survey Results

Hope for the Future	# of survey Respondents who Mentioned	% of Survey Respondents Who Mentioned
Better Communication/ community support	57	73.53%
Better facilities	11	14.19%
Better leadership	6	7.74%

Hopes for the Future of the Organization

Post-Test Quantitative Results

This research used paired t-test on questions 4 and 5 of the post test survey which ask respondents to rate their opinion of learning of changes through e-mail and to rate their opinion of learning of these changes through personal communication meetings to determine their preference for either the e-communications or personal communications. Using a 5-point Likert-type scale ranging from 1 (high resistance) to 5 (high acceptance), the mean response needed to be above 3 (neutral) to show less resistance to change from the group. Based on the paired t-test, there was sufficient evidence indicating that the mean opinion ratings differed on learning the information through e-sources versus personal communication. (t= -6.493, df =76, p value was smaller than .001). The mean response for e-communications was 3.17 while the mean response for personal communication meetings was 4.27.

Personal Communication vs. e-communication

Question 8 of the survey ask respondents to rate their opinion of the intervention programs "Wrangler Chat, "Lunch with the President", "Supervisor Training" and "Coffee and Conversation". "Wrangler Chat" was the e-communication and was not tested for a positive response. This research used a t-test to determine if the sample mean response to 8b, 8c, or 8d was greater than 3. Using a scale of 1 being low, 2 being low medium, and three being neutral with 4 being moderate and 5 being high, the mean response needed to be above 3.

Of the 77 who responded to the survey, forty-six had attended "Lunch with the President". All employees were invited throughout the year, but not all attended. The opinion of the respondents for 8b "Lunch with the President", had a p-value of (p=.0015) (df =45) (t=3.199). Thus, those who attended "Lunch with the President" had a mean response greater than 3 on their opinion of "Lunch with the President".

"Supervisor Training" was limited to the administration, divisional deans and department chairs. Twenty six participants out of 77 respondents attended the "Supervisor Training", thus n=26 (t= -1.041) (df =25) (p=0.846). The opinion was rated in question 8c. There is not sufficient evidence indicating that those who attended "Supervisor Training" have a mean opinion score of greater than three. This could be due to the educational component of the meeting being less than adequate for the extra time spent on Friday afternoon for the sessions and thus the ratings were low.

The response to 8d had a total of 49 of the 77 respondents in attendance for "Coffee and Conversation" for n=49. (t=6.387) (df =48) (p value of less than .001). There is sufficient evidence indicating that those who attended "Coffee and Conversation" have a mean value score greater than 3. The mean score for "Coffee and Conversation" of 6.387 indicates that the participants were more informed and this particular type of personal communication meeting was more successful than other personal communication meetings.

Effectiveness of intervention programs

Hypotheses

The null hypothesis for question 1 was: Communication meetings using the power of the unconditional positive question will have no significant effect on the attitude of resistance to changes in policies and procedures.

The null hypothesis for question 2 was: There will be no significant difference between e-communication and personal communication meetings as it relates to psychological ownership and a "team embrace" in change management.

Considering the information mined from the research instruments, the null hypothesis H1 (communication meetings using the power of the unconditional positive question will have no significant effect on the attitude of resistance to changes in policies and procedures) was not accepted. Although there was evidence that "Supervisor Training" meetings did have a negative impact. This was possibly due to the content of the program. Qualitative answers from the survey indicated that the value of the program was good, but the content was not accepted or approved by the participants. The alternative hypothesis H2 (communication meetings using the power of the unconditional positive question will have a positive effect on the attitude of resistance to changes in policies and procedures) was accepted.

The qualitative and quantitative data support the alternative hypothesis H2. The null hypothesis H3 of there will be no significant difference between e-communication meetings as it relates to psychological ownership and a "team embrace" in change management was not accepted. However, the alternative hypothesis of personal communication meetings will have more positive impact than e-communications as it relates to psychological ownership and a "team embrace" in change management was accepted because of the supporting qualitative and quantitative data.

Conclusion and Implications

The findings of this study indicated that there is a need for positive personal communication meetings to aid in creating a culture of positive organizational behavior. Meetings need to be informative and have an element of a feedback loop for knowledge generation. This feedback and knowledge generation was an aid in inclusion of the shadow (Fitzgerald and Oliver, 2006). To discover and better understand how communication affects the attitude and culture of the institution, the research team interviewed members of each division. Appreciative Intelligence Matrices (Thatchenkery & Metzger, 2006) were developed to aid in understanding the interview data. The interviews identified a need for positive personal communication meetings designed to aid in creating a culture of readiness for change and positive organizational behavior. These data identified "the best of what is", and "envisioning what could be" (Ludema et al., 2001) was the second and third phase of the 4D model of Appreciative Inquiry. The committee and the researcher designed three personal communication meetings to aid in communication and knowledge generation and one E-communication meeting. The design of the intervention programs of co-constructing "what should be" (Ludema et al., 2001) was the fourth phase of the 4D model of Appreciative Inquiry. The intervention programs were implemented and continued for one year. The post-intervention survey indicated the positive communication programs had a positive influence on the culture of the organization.

A post-test survey was administered after one year of the intervention programs to gather qualitative information and measure the impact. A fourth matrix (Thatchenkery & Metzger, 2006) was developed to help the researcher better understand the value of the intervention programs in "sustaining what will be" (Ludema et al., 2001). The respondents were more positive about the personal communication meetings than the e-communications. Some personal communication meetings had a greater impact on the positive outcome of the research than others. The "Supervisor Training" meeting garnered a negative rating of $t= -1.041$. "Lunch with the President" had a positive impact of $t=3.199$. This was due to the small number of participants in the meeting and the personal conversation with the president. "Coffee and Conversation" achieved the highest rating of $t=6.387$. This meeting could be attended by any employee and with a large group, there is some anonymity. Therefore, "Coffee and Conversation" and "Lunch with the President" were successful in knowledge generation and feedback. These two meetings were recommended to the President and the Administration as programs to help in creating a sustainability of the readiness for change in the organization.

ACKNOWLEDGEMENT

The authors would like to thank Tanya Hughes, Executive Director, Chief of Staff, Odissa College for the support provided in carrying out this research.

REFERENCES

Cooperrider, D. & Whitney, D (2005). Appreciative Inquiry: A Positive Revolution in Change. San Francisco: Berrett-Koehler.

Cooperrider, D.L. and Srivastva, S. (1987). Appreciative Inquiry in Organizational Life. *Research in Organizational Change and Development*, 1, 129-169.

Cooperrider, D.L. and Whitney, D. (1999). *Collaborating for Change: Appreciative Inquiry,* San Francisco: Barrett-Koehler.

Cummings, T.G., & Huse, E.F. (1989). *Organizational Development*. Mason, OH: South-Western.

Fitzgerald, S.P. & Oliver, C. (2006). *Walking the dark side of positive organizational behavior: Appreciating the role of the shadow.* Proceedings CD-ROM, Southern Management

Association Meeting. Clearwater Beach FL.

Gall,M.D., Borg, W.R., & Gall, J.P. (1996). *Educatio*nal Research: An Introduction. White Plains, NY: Longman.

Greenwood, D.J. and Levin, M. (2007). *Introduction to Action Research.* Thousand Oaks, CA: Sage.

Heelan, C. and Transure, P. (2005). *College-Wide Planning That Works.* Community College Review. **75**(6): 8-10.

Heller, D.E. (2003). Not all institutions are alike. *Chronicle of Higher Education,* **50** (12), B7-B9.

Jones, G.R. (2007). *Organizational Theory, Design and Change.* New York: Pearson.

Judge, W.Q. (1999). *The leaders shadow: Exploring and developing the executive character.* Thousand Oaks, CA: Sage.

Lipnack, J. & Stamps, J. (1987). *A network model.* The Futurist, **21**(4), 23-25.

Ludema, J.D., Cooperrider, D.L. and Barrett, F.J. (2001). Appreciative Inquiry: the Power of the Unconditional Positive Question. In Peter Reason and Hillary Bradbury (eds.) *Handbook of Action Research.* London: Sage.

Thatchenkery, T. and Chaudary, D. (2007). *Appreciative inquiry and knowledge management: A social constructivist perspective.* Cheltenham, U.K.: Edward Elgar

Thatchenkery, T. and Metzger, C. (2006). *Appreciative Intelligence: Seeing the mighty oak in the acorn.* San Francisco: Barrett-Koehler.

An Appreciative Inquiry Study: Sustaining Fundraising Enablers

Kristine Brands* and Debora Elam**

ABSTRACT

The demands on non-profit organizations to support the increasing needs of communities during economic hardships require these organizations to look for alternative and creative fundraising options. This study used a customized approach of the Appreciative Inquiry (AI) organizational analysis model to examine a non-profit organization's fundraising enablers and to identify how the organization could sustain its fundraising levels during the economic challenges of 2009. This process-consulting model was used to focus on the organization's strengths to allow the organization to build on them. A three-member doctorate student research team not affiliated with the organization conducted this research project using a multiple phased process to collect and analyse data. The research was used to ultimately identify possibilities for increasing fundraising levels to meet the growing needs of the Pikes Peak Region community in Colorado.

Keywords: Appreciative inquiry, organizational analysis, fundraising.

INTRODUCTION

The Organization

The Pikes Peak Region Non-Profit Organization (PPRNPO)is an independent community-based non-profit organization located in Colorado Springs, Colorado, United States. It has approximately 20 staff members, 10-15 board of trustee members, over 50 trained corporate and civic volunteers serving on a committee that allocates funds to various community organizations, approximately 100 community leaders participating on a visionary planning council, and over 500 volunteers helping

* Assistant Professor, Regis University, Colorado Springs, CO, USA.

**Team Leader, Software Engineering Process, New York Air Brake, Colorado Springs, CO, USA.

E-mail: kbrands@regis.edu, deboraelam@comcast.net

throughout the community.PPRNPO serves the El Paso and Teller counties on Colorado's Front Range. It is also part of a national network of over 1,300 other non-profit organizations.The PPRNPO's three major focus areas include partner support, community programs, and local assistance resource information and referral services.

The PPRNPO serves the local community's most needy residents through an annual community fundraising campaign with an annual goal of approximately $6 million; its annual budget is approximately $5.9 million. The funds are allocated annually to over 40 partner agencies.In addition to focusing on the community's needy residents, PPRNPO works to identify the local community's most serious problems in order to create long lasting change.

In addition to supporting its partner agencies, PPRNPO runs a community assistance resource information and referral hotline that can be reached by phone or accessed online.It provides the community with information about resources to pay for living necessities such as rent or mortgages,and referrals to community health and human services agencies.In the first half of 2008 alone, the organization serviced approximately 22,000 calls.The PPRNPO also supports community programs to identify critical community issues, administers dedicated funds to provide emergency monetary grants to local area non-profit organizations, and manages a shelter to address the area's homeless issues.

According to its Chief Operating Officer (COO) (personal communication, February 27, 2009), fundraising levels for 2009 were expected to be flat due to the economic downturn in late 2008.Despite having many established fundraising programs, the organization faced fundraising challenges and needed to identify possibilities for increasing fund levels to meet the growing needs of the community. The organization was interested in working with the research team to explore ways to sustain its fundraising goals.

OBJECTIVE

The purpose of this project was to use a customized approach of the Appreciative Inquiry (AI) organizational analysis model to examine PPRNPO's fundraising enablers and to identify how it can sustain fundraising levels during the economic challenges of 2009 that are expected to continue through 2010. The PPRNPO executive leadership recognized the knowledge and value that an AI process would provide to their organization because it would give them a different perspective and viewpoint of the organization and would also help them recognize what programs are regarded as important to employees in the organization.

RESEARCH METHODOLOGY

Description of the Model

The research model used for this project was the AI process-consulting model that combined "action research and theory of how organizational realities evolve" (Thatchenkery, 2009, p. 2).This organization analysis model represents a methodology that focuses on identifying an organization's core values or life-giving-forces in order to fully develop the organization's potential (Thatchenkery, 2005).In contrast to a problem-solving consulting model, AI focuses on what is working in an organization (Thatchenkery, 2009) to leverage its future potential through a collaborative process of inquiry and examination.

AI focuses on a key view that"every living system has a core of strengths that is often hidden and/or under utilized - what is known as its positive core" (Stetson, 2007, p.2). The AI process-consulting modeloriginally developed by Cooperrider and Srivastva (1987) looks for "the best in people, their organizations, and the relevant world around them" (Cooperrider & Whitney, 2009, p.1).The organization's life-giving forces or core values represent an organization's unique structural and organizational footprint that allows its existence (Cooperrider and Srivastva, 1987).AI goes beyond the organization's structure by representing a more holistic view of the organization including the organization's value system, beliefs, and culture (Thatchenkery, 2009). These core values represent the DNA of the organization, which give it a unique character.It is this unique character that lets the AI model leverage the organization to develop its potential to be the best it can be in "economic, ecological, and human terms" (Cooperrider & Whitney, 2009, p.1).While AI refers to a quest for knowledge to develop the organization's potential, it also focuses on "a theory of intentional collective action which is designed to help the normative vision and will of a group, organization, or society as a whole"(Cooperrider & Srivastva, 1987, p.159).When"the positive core is revealed and tapped into, it provides a sustainable source of positive energy that nourishes both personal and organizational change" (Stetson, 2007, p. 2).

The research team customized the traditional AI model to focus on a specific characteristic of PPRNPO: its fundraising enablers. Except for this scope modification, the research protocol follows the AI model. The objective of using this model is to create a collective image of the future state through analysing the best of what is and has been(Cooperrider & Srivastva, 1987) in the PPRNPO fundraising and to draw on the collective strength of the organization's past and current fundraising efforts.

AI contrasts with traditional consulting because the latter focuses on problem solving in an organization. Problem-based consulting does not focus on positive aspects of an organization, but rather with what is wrong with the organization. Thus, the organization's key strengths and processes upon which positive changes could be based might be overlooked. Leveraging changes based on what works in an organization might improve the organization's ability to sustain the change (Thatchenkery, 2009).AI focuses on unlocking the potential in an organization rather than on viewing an organization as a problem to be solved (Cooperrider & Srivastva, 1987).

The AI process-consulting model focuses on an inquiry of the organization through asking the organization's members questions to "strengthen a system's capacity to apprehend, anticipate, and heighten positive potential" (Cooperrider & Whitney, 2009, p. 1).This process, outlined in the methodology section, focuses on exploring fundraising enablers from an "appreciative, applicable, provocative, and collaborative perspective" (Thatchenkery, 2009, p. 6) by guiding the organization through a systematic discovery and unconditional positive examination (Cooperrider & Whitney, 2009) of its future potential. Weick reinforces this positive approach by noting that if individuals work with negative or weak images of an organization, then they are more likely to identify weak theories or outcomes (Weick, 1982).

The final phase of the model addresses the intervention or the recommendation phase, which is intended to promote change. Cooperrider says that "the arduous task of intervention gives way to the speed of imagination and innovation; instead of negation, criticism, and spiralling diagnosis, there is discovery, dream, and design" (Cooperrider & Whitney, 2009, p. 1).The entire model is framed in positive terms harnessing the positive energy of the organization. This phase also breaks away from the traditional problem-solving model that often frames the intervention or recommendations in critical terms.

Finally, the research team modified the steps of Thatchenkery's (2005) model to fit the customized approach in the following way: identify fund-raising enablers, use appreciative interviews to explore the fundraising enablers, perform thematic analysis of the step two interviews organized in a matrix,identify possibility propositions constructed with the PPRNPO staff, and validate the possibility propositions.

Data Collection Devices/Instruments

Using the AI process-consulting model developed by Thatchenkery (2005), a multiple phased approach to collect data was used. The research team members developed questions for each phase based on the guide for leveraging knowledge management and AI (Thatchenkery, 2005).Once the research team developed the questions for each phase, they submitted the questions to Thatchenkery for review prior to moving to the next phase.

First phase questions were taken directly from Thatchenkery's (2005) guide for conducting paired mutual interviews. The research team developed interview questions for phase two based on the knowledge enablers the PPRNPO staff members identified during the first phase and the guide for leveraging knowledge management and AI

(Thatchenkery, 2005).Two approaches were used for the one-on-one interviews. One was a matrix approach using the fund-raiser enablers and organization factors, and the other used a series of questions focusing on each of the fundraising enablers. This dual approach was selected to provide alternative options to obtain the information in case participants struggled with one approach.

For the final phase, using the data collected from the previous future-present scenario (possibility propositions) development phase, the research team members created a survey to validate and rank each of the possibility propositions. The research team members, on the advice of Thatchenkery, decided to use the online survey tool Survey Monkey(www.SurveyMonkey.com) to facilitate the data collection process.The research team used Thatchenkery's (2005) guide for reaching consensual validation to structure the survey questions. One modification was made because of the survey's limitation. It was necessary to deviate from the format of the third question for each possibility proposition to conform to the format of the first two questions.One research team member created the surveyand one other research team member reviewed and tested it. The online link was then emailed to each of the PPRNPO participants.

Participant Selection

Purposeful sampling by PPRNPO was used to select participants for the project (Maxwell, 2005).Although the organization is very large with the inclusion of volunteers, partners, and donors, the research team only had access to the PPRNPO staff members. Selected staff members (12 total) were invited to participate during the two phases by email by the research team's PPRNPO sponsor, the COO.The twelve staff members were selected from the marketing, media, and campaign departments; executive staff members were also invited to participate. Nine members (75%) participated during the first phase and ten members (83%) were interviewed during phase two; eight of the ten participated in the first phase.For the third phase, three of the four invited members participated (75%); the participants were all from the annual campaign department.For the final phase, the research team distributed the survey to all ten members who participated in the earlier phases; five anonymous survey responses were received (50%).

Data Collection

The data for this research project was collected through a series of in-person interviews conducted at the client organization's headquarters and using surveys.To kick-off the research project, two members of the research team met in person with the PPRNPO project sponsor to discuss the project.The project plan was presented and a tentative schedule was agreed upon.Subsequent meetings were arranged via email and telephone conversations between PPRNPO members and the research team.During the first data collection phase,the full research team met with staff members to identify the knowledge enablers for the organization's fundraising efforts.The staff members broke into pairs and interviewed each other and then presented the results to the entire group.Members of the research team took notes as each staff member presented their results.Then, as a group, PPRNPO staff members identified various themes, which the research team recorded on post-it notes.Finally, the staff members categorized the themes into knowledge enablers that the research team recorded.

During the second phase, the research team conducted individual interviews with PPRNPO staff members. Interviews were assigned to research team members based on availability to ensure each research team member had equal opportunity to conduct interviews.Interviews were conducted at PPRNPO'sheadquarters. Research team members transcribed notes from his or her interviews and saved them electronically.

During the third phase, the research team facilitated a brainstorming session with PPRNPO staff members to develop possibility propositions.The participants wrote their ideas on post-it notes, which the research team collected. Then, the research team transcribed the notes and saved them electronically.The research team consolidated the input from the PPRNPO members and possibility propositions identified by the research team members from Internet searches of similar organizations. The research team then created a list of possibility propositions to be validated and ranked.From this list, the research team conducted a survey for the PPRNPO staff members to validate and rank the possibility propositions.Upon completion of the survey, the research team downloaded the results recorded by the online survey tool.

The research team was impressed with the staff members' enthusiasm and willingness to participate.Participants were open and comfortable during the interviews,expressed their excitement about the process, and seemed genuinely interested in the outcome.

DIAGNOSIS AND ANALYSIS

This section presents an analysis of the results of the AI interviews by focusing on a quantitative summary of the interview data by classifying the results by organization factor (organization structure, decision making, leadership, communication, incentives, and organization practices) and by fundraising enabler (education, action, collaboration, and commitment).The data was analysed by reviewing the responses from the AI interview transcripts.The research team coded the transcripts by using the thematic analysis of the organization factor/fundraising enabler matrix. An Excel worksheet was prepared for each fundraising enabler. Figure 1 summarizes the responses by showing the number of response occurrences for fundraising enablers by organization factors. Figure 2 summarizes the results.

Fig. 1: Interview Results Summarized by Organization Factor and Total Fundraising Enabler Response Occurrence

Organization Factor	Fundraising Enablers				Total	%
	Education	Action	Collaboration	Commitment		
Organization Structure	1	0	0	3	4	4%
Decision Making	0	0	1	3	4	4%
Leadership	0	1	6	3	10	11%
Communication	14	1	2	1	18	19%
Incentives	3	2	1	6	12	13%
Organization Practices	5	17	13	12	47	49%
Total	23	21	23	28	95	100%
%	24%	22%	24%	29%	100%	

Fig. 2: Fundraising Enabler Responses by Organization Factor

Organization Factor	Fundraising Enablers			
	Education	Action	Collaboration	Commitment
Organization Structure	4%	0%	0%	11%
Decision Making	0%	0%	4%	11%
Leadership	0%	5%	26%	11%
Communication	61%	5%	9%	4%
Incentives	13%	10%	4%	21%
Organization Practices	22%	81%	57%	42%
Total	100%	100%	100%	100%

Analysis Limitation

Quantitative analysis was limited because coding was based on qualitative interview responses preventing statistical analysis and correlation of the responses.Coding was judgmental and could result in researchers' bias.The nature of the AI methodology and its focus on qualitative data collection means the major focus of the analysis is on interpreting and analysing the interview results and placing them in a conceptual and theoretical context.

AI Interview Results

The 'organization practices' factor dominated the results at 49%, representing almost the combined total of the other factors at 51%.According to Thatchenkery (2005) 'organization practices' represent the organization's infrastructure characteristics that are the norm for the organization's operational habits.This includes teamwork, hiring, performance, and promotion practices, cross-functional teams, and organizationalvalues. The organization factors ranged from four to 49%.However, the fundraising enabler results were very close with responses ranging between 21 and 28%.The standard deviation of the organization factors is 16.15 and 2.99 for the fundraising enablers.

The 'organization practices' factor showed strong responses for all fundraising enablers. The PPRNPO shows many characteristics of a high involvement organization and an organization structure that "supports high levels of employee involvement"(Cummings & Worley, 2009, p. 367). While the other organizational factors contribute to PPRNPO's effectiveness, high involvement organization characteristics play a significant role in the organization's success.PPRNPO is a flat, lean organization; the job design emphasizes employee autonomy and independence, and the culture promotes from within and fosters employee commitment to the organization.

Another reason for the strong responses for this factor is that organizational practices facilitate PPRNPO's goals. Thatchenkery (2005) notes that after establishing organizational routines, they "free up valuable organizational energy for more proactive strategies and action" (p. 63).One interviewee said he likes working for PPRNPO because corporate politics are practically non-existent, allowing him to focus on organizational goals.

The AI interviews provided a rich collection of positive examples of how the elements of organization structure support fundraising enablers.Significantly, the process was conducted by building on PPRNO's unique qualities. It also followed the AI process because each of the interviews was "appreciative, applicable, provocative, and collaborative" (Thatchenkery, 2009, p. 6).The results provided a strong basis for what the organization does well today. They also served as a platform for PPRNPOto bridge the gap between "what is" and "what might be" (Thatchenkery, 2009, p. 14).

While organization factors were analysed individually against the fundraising enabler, they needed to be viewed as an interrelated system.All six of the organization factors need to exist in the organization to support fundraising enablers.They provide the framework and the infrastructure to the organization to support fundraising.The factors need to co-exist because they are interdependent and cannot exist without each other (Thatchenkery, 2005).

PPRNPO has established several sound fundraising practices.The question is how can PPRNPO sustain and build on these fundraising efforts to ensure the needs of the community are met?Based on the results of using the AI process, PPRNPO staff members and the research team identified 19 possibility propositions. Of these 19, 18 were evaluated and prioritized; one was inadvertently omitted from the survey. Fifty percent (five out of the ten surveyed) responded to the consensual validation of propositions survey. The individual results were totalled and average; results are summarized in Figure 3.

Questions	Q1	Q2	Q3	Q4	Q5	Q6	Q7	Q8	Q9	Q10	Q11	Q12	Q13	Q14	Q15	Q16	Q17	Q18
How much of an ideal is it?	4.8	4.6	4.2	3.8	4.4	3.8	3.8	3.2	2.2	4.0	3.6	2.2	4.6	3.8	3.8	4.2	3.4	4.4
How much of it may already be present now?	3.0	3.8	3.2	1.2	1.4	1.4	1.4	1.8	1.0	1.4	1.2	1.2	3.0	1.4	2.2	1.4	1.2	2.6
Realistically, do you want this to happen quickly?	4.2	4.0	3.6	2.6	3.4	3.6	3.2	3.4	1.6	3.2	2.8	1.8	3.8	2.6	3.6	3.8	2.8	3.8

Fig. 3: Consensual Validation of Propositions Survey Results Summary

Each question needed to follow the same format and scale. To meet these criteria, the research team adjusted the results by reversing the scale. This was necessary because of limitations of the survey tool and the need to adequately analyse the data. This is summarized in Figure 4.

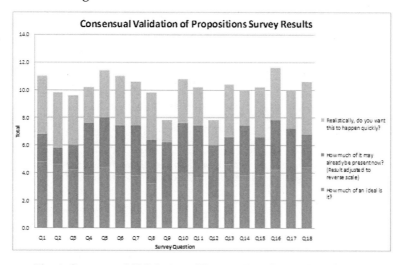

Fig. 4: Consensual Validation of Propositions Survey Results

The research team created a prioritized list of possibility propositions from the results based on ranking. Weighting its ideal rating and how fast it could be implemented broke ties. The prioritized list of possibility propositions (ranked from highest to lowest) is shown in Figure 5.

Prioritized List of Possibility Propositions (Ranked from Highest to Lowest)			
Priority	Possibility Proposition	Question	Ranking
1	PPRNPO has a mobile giving initiative to allow donors to text their donation.	16	11.8
2	We sponsor the Young Professionals Leadership Council to engage them in leading a fundraising effort.	5	11.4
3	PPRNPO promotes its efforts in leadership on solving the root causes of community problems in addition to the safety net of services provided. We use our website, our newsletter, and the local media to communicate this message.	1	11
4	We partner with colleges and universities to run PPRNPO fundraising campaigns at the schools.	6	11

5	Every two years, we host a fundraising practices summit with all Colorado United Way organizations to share best practices.	10	10.8
6	PPRNPO staff educates and engages El Paso and Teller county policymakers on the goals and priorities of PPRNPO and its partner organizations, quality of life indicators for the Pikes Peak region, and other community needs.	18	10.6
7	We partner with local sports events (e.g., Sky Sox baseball, CC Tiger hockey, bike or running event, etc.) to raise funds for PPRNPO.	7	10.6
8	Our redesigned web site has become the central community hub of information to learn about key community issues, commit to long-term projects, donate, volunteer, and how to run or participate in a PPRNPO fundraising activity.In addition, our website is linked to all of our partnership agencies. Our website also explains how PPRNPO can help companies setup CSR programs and PPRNPO fundraising activities.	13	10.4
9	Annually, we ask the community to vote on a quality of life indicator for the Pikes Peak region to focus on.The selected issue is then highlighted.Also, donors can contribute funds directly towards the solving the root cause of this issue.	15	10.2
10	We sponsor volunteer fundraising projects run by high school students and young professionals.	4	10.2
11	We engage neighbourhoods and communities to get involved with PPRNPO through block parties, small community events, and community projects to raise money.	11	10.2
12	We send fund raising staff members to regional and national fund raising conferences using donated airline miles and hotel points.	14	10
13	During Make a Difference Month we have donation collection boxes throughout local businesses in El Paso and Teller counties.	17	10
14	We collect personal stories about the positive impact of PPRNPO programs on individuals and organizations at all PPRNPO meetings. We share these stories on our website and our newsletter, and through the local media.	2	9.8
15	We are using new fundraising events to reach new donors.Each year, we pick a new event.	8	9.8
16	We have an internship program for college and university students to develop their professional knowledge and skills in non-profit management. As part of their internship, the students manage fundraising activities for PPRNPO.	3	9.6
17	We have a Care and Share Food Bank collection box in the PPRNPO headquarters lobby.	12	7.8
18	We host an annual PPRNPO charity art auction. Local artists donate all items and all the proceeds go directly to PPRNPO Charity Fund.	9	7.8
*	We have a loyal contributor recognition program, recognizing committed donors (e.g., 5+ year donors, 10+, etc.).We honour these loyal contributors through printed materials, public "thank you," employee meetings, etc. -Inadvertently omitted from the survey, so it was not included in the validation and prioritization process. (Inadvertently omitted from survey).		

Fig. 5: Prioritized List of Possibility Propositions

The AI interviews provided a rich collection of positive examples of how the organization structure elements support fundraising enablers.The process was conducted by building upon the unique qualities of PPRNPO (Thatchenkery, 2009). It also followed the AI process because it applied specifically to PPRNPO in a collaborative and appreciative setting during each one of the interview phases, by fully engaging PPRNPO in the process (Thatchenkery, 2009).The results showed what the organization does well today and served as the platform for developing the possibility propositions to bridge the best of PPRNPO today with what its image of the future might be (Thatchenkery, 2009).Based on the analysis results, the research team members made recommendations to assist PPRNPO's staff in implementing an action plan using possibility propositions that PPRNPO's staff members identified as important and desirable.

RECOMMENDATIONS

The recommendations included creating and executing an implementation plan; collectively, the research team and staff members identified the possibility propositions and action items, and formed implementation teams for action items (Thatchenkery, 2005).The research team recommended the organization develop an intervention to enable PPRNPO to sustain their fundraising programs. An interventionis "a set of sequenced planned actions or events intended to help an organization increase its effectiveness" (Cummings & Worley, 2009, p. 151).Cummings and Worley (2009) identify three criteria for an effective intervention. The first is how much the intervention meets the needs of an organization.Effective interventions are based on valid information, which is needed to accurately diagnose an organization.The second is based on the knowledge of specific outcomes and how they can be achieved.Finally, effective interventions are ones that result in an organization's increased ability to manage itsown change.

The research team identified two possible types of interventions to recommend to PPRNPO.The first intervention involves changing the PPRNPO organization into a learning organization.Organizational learning enhances an organization's capability to acquire and develop new knowledge (Cummings & Worley, 2009, p. 538).It is important for PPRNPO to become a learning organization because new knowledge will be generated with this change.A learning organization is one that is skilled at creating, acquiring, interpreting, transferring, and retaining knowledge, and at purposefully modifying its behaviour to reflect new knowledge and insights (Cummings & Worley, 2009, p. 542).The PPRNPO can become a learning organization by using four interrelated activities:discovery, invention, production, and generalization, as it relates to its information systems.Discovery involves analysing processes in the organization with gaps.Invention is aimed at devising solutions to close the gap between desired and current conditions.This involves gathering information and figuring out how to implement a new process.The production process involves implementing solutions, and generalization includes drawing conclusions about the effects of the solutions and extending that knowledge to other relevant situations (Cummings & Worley, 2009, p. 543).The research team recommended the organizationuse double-loop learning to change the existing assumptions and conditions at PPRNPO.By using double-loop learning,PPRNPO might create new programs and funding opportunities.

The second type of intervention is a transorganizational change intervention, which will allow PPRNPO to forge new partnerships in the community.A transorganizational change helps organizations transcend the perspective of a single organization and address the needs and concerns of all involved organizations (Cummings & Worley, 2009, p. 560).The research team recommended PPRNPO establish strategic alliances with organizations in the community outside their current partners.The first step in establishing a beneficial partnership involves understanding why it is important for an alliance in the first place.The second step involves selecting an appropriate partner that has the same mission as PPRNPO's mission.The third step involves structuring the partnership, and building and leveraging trust in the relationship.Once the strategic alliance is created, the final step can be carried out, analysing the state of the partnership and making appropriate adjustments to the partnership when needed. Looking for new organizational partnerships will benefit PPRNPO because these new partners will bring it much needed resources.

Each of the interventions discussed will benefit PPRNPO. However, the researchers believe the transorganizational change intervention is the best.By fundamentally changing how new partnerships are brought into PPRNPO, valuable resources will be added and is consistent with one of the fundraising enablers, collaboration.In contrast, changing the organization into a learning organization might come with a high price tag because PPRNPO will have to fundamentally change its entire organizational structure.

The possibility proposition list (Figure 5)represents the culmination of the AI process, representing the PPRNPO assessment of their organization and their willingness to make these possibility propositions a reality (Thatchenkery, 2005).The researchers recommended PPRNPO create an action plan using this list as a guide and then implement these action items through the formation of an implementation team comprised of members that participated in the research project as they might be the best advocates for the initiatives (Thatchenkery, 2005).

CONCLUSION

It was clear to the research team that staff members were dedicated and enthusiastic about what they did. The environment of nonprofit organizations such as PPRNPO is changing, adding pressure to ensure its survival and to address growing needs within the community (Siebart, 2005). This project endeavored to identify and build on the positive aspects of PPRNPO to meet these increasing demands.

Because PPRNPO runs successful fundraising campaigns and has a solid fundraising history, changes to the established organization and its practices might cause resistance, making it difficult to implement improvements (Cummings & Worley, 2009).Cummings and Worley (2009) identify three strategies in managing resistance to change:empathy and support, communication, and participation and involvement. The AI process focuses on the organization's member involvement throughout the process.Participation of organizational members is considered one of the most effective strategies for overcoming resistance to change (Worley & Cummings, 2009). PPRNPO has already taken the essential steps to managing resistance to change and is positioned well to implement the research team's recommendations.

Using the AI process to analyze PPRNPO as an organization was a positive experience providing a valuable learning opportunity for the research team.Based on the feedback received from PPRNPO staff members who participated, this process was very rewarding, allowing them to participate throughout the entire process. This research project ended with identifying possibility propositions that will further support the fundraising enablers and allow PPRNPO to continue providing essential support to the community in these difficult economic times. The next step belongs to PPRNPO to create the action plan and to implement it.

REFERENCES

Cooperrider, D. L., & Srivastva, S. (1987). Appreciative inquiry in organizational life. In Pasmore, W., Woodman, R. (Eds.), Research in organization change and development (Vol. 1). Greenwich, CT: JAI Press.

Cooperrider, D. and Whitney, D. (2009)."A positive revolution in change: Appreciative inquiry." Retrieved June 3, 2009, from http://appreciativeinquiry.case.edu/intro/whatisai.cfm

Cummings, T., & Worley, C. (2009). *Organization Development & Change*. Mason, OH: South-Western Cengage Learning.

Maxwell, J. (2005). Qualitative research design: An interactive approach (2nd ed.). Thousand Oaks, CA: Sage Publications, Inc.

Siebart, P. (2005). Corporate governance of non-profit organizations: cooperation and control. *International Journal of Public Administration*, 28(9/10), 857-867.

Stetson, N. (2007). "Aligning strengths through appreciative inquiry." *Consulting Today*. Retrieved June 3, 2009, from http://appreciativeinquiry.case.edu/uploads/Aligning%20Strengths%20through%20Appreciative%20Inquiry.pdf

Thatchenkery, T., and Metzker, C. (2006).*Appreciative Intelligence: Seeing the mighty oak in the acorn*. San Francisco, CA: Berrett-Koehler

Thatchenkery, T. (2005). *Appreciative Sharing of Knowledge: Leveraging Knowledge Management for Strategic Change*. Chagrin Falls, OH: Taos Institute Publications.

Thatchenkery, T. (2009). *A guide to appreciative organizational analysis*. School of Public Policy. George Mason University, Arlington, VA.

Weick, K. (1982). Affirmation as inquiry. *Small Group Behaviour*, 13, 441-442.

Discovering Possibilities: An Applied Appreciative Inquiry Analysis of Core Organizational Values

Rod Hagedorn*

ABSTRACT

This study uses an applied appreciative inquiry methodology to identify positively-oriented action items at a for-profit technical college located in the north central United States, hereby ficticiously referred to as XYZ Technical College. The methodology is described in detail, along with results of an organization wide employee survey used to validate ideal state versus present state possibility propositions posited via a qualitative analysis of 12 one-on-one appreciative interviews. Results of the study are used to generate four pragmatic and positively-oriented action items intended to narrow the most significant gaps between ideal state and present state possibilities.

Keywords: Applied appreciative inquiry, thematic analysis, positive organizational behavior, organization development, appreciative interviewing, action research

INTRODUCTION

Recent years have seen the movement away from deficit-based psychology toward an increasing emphasis on positive psychology, reflected in the management literature in the form of positive organizational behavior. Luthans (2002) notes that, historically, most psychologists focused on "being concerned with what is wrong with people, human frailties and weaknesses" (p. 696). This contrasts with positive psychology, which aims to "shift the emphasis away from what is wrong with people to what is right with people—to focus on strengths (as opposed to weaknesses)" (Luthans, 2002, p. 697).

Applying positive psychology to the field of organizational behavior is defined by, Luthans (2002) as positive organizational behavior—"the study and application

* Colorado Technical University, Colorado Springs, Colorado CO, USA.
E-mail: rodhagedorn@quest.net

of positively oriented human resource strengths and psychological capacities that can be measured, developed, and effectively managed for performance improvement in today's workplace" (p. 698). In a related article, Luthans & Church (2002) argue that positive organizational behavior, unlike concepts such as positive thinking or various popular business books, can be applied to the workplace as a scientific discipline. They assert that the field of positive organizational behavior can serve to "begin to build bridges between the academic OB field and the popular business bestsellers" (Luthans & Church, 2002, p. 58). Later, Wright (2003) echoes the call for and notes the growing interest in a more positively-oriented approach toward the study and practice of managing organizational behavior.

Several scholars have argued in favor of continued research in methods and practices related to positive organizational behavior. For example, Roberts (2006) argues in favor of more studies that are grounded in positive organizational behavior to better understand factors that result in improved quality of work-life by stating:

The idea is to identify and understand the generative mechanisms that create positive deviance in people, groups, and organizations. In so doing, positive scholarship represents a quest or desire to understand the processes that produce certain collective and individual states that are less commonly addressed by current organizational studies, such as processes that build integrity, resilience, and compassion. (Roberts, 2006, p. 294)

Likewise, Luthans & Youssef (2007) propose that research emphasizing positive organizational behavior should complement, rather than replace, the existing body of knowledge related to either positively or negatively-oriented organizational behavior research. Caza & Caza (2008) echo this sentiment by suggesting that studies focusing on positive organizational behavior should be viewed as an alternative to traditional deficit-based research.

Appreciative inquiry is a pragmatic tool to support positive organizational behavior in the workplace. Formalized as a research method by Dr. David Cooperrider in his 1986 doctoral dissertation, appreciative inquiry is an approach which is strengths-based rather than deficits-based (Reed, 2007, pp. 22-24). It emphasizes the positive potential in both organizations and in people, appreciating what is and what can be—what the organization does especially well and how it can capitalize even further on those strengths. Cooperrider & Whitney (2005) stress the importance of focusing on an organization's "positive core" and how doing so "enhances its collective wisdom, builds energy and resiliency to change, and extends its capacity to achieve extraordinary results" (p. 10). Reed (2007) states that in using appreciative inquiry, "the emphasis is firmly on appreciating the activities and responses of people, rather than concentrating on their problems" (p. 2). Reed (2007) also notes the ability of appreciative inquiry to be used for action research by stating that action research is an "obvious link between AI, research, and [organizational] change" (p. 63). By emphasizing that the "aim of action research is to *change practice*", Reed (2007, p. 193) argues that one of the most effective tools for doing so can be appreciative inquiry.

This study did not attempt to confirm or disconfirm the efficacy of appreciative inquiry as research method. Nor did it seek to create new empirical knowledge related to the field of positive organizational behavior. Rather, the purpose of this study was to test and illustrate how an appreciative inquiry-based methodology could be used in the field to identify untapped potential expressed in the form of pragmatic and positively-oriented recommendations for action within a complex organizational system.

METHODOLOGY

The methodology and data collection process used for this study was based on *A Guide to Appreciative Organizational Analysis*, a supplemental guide by Thatchenkery (2010) for the doctoral Process Consulting and Intervention course at Colorado Technical University in Colorado Springs, Colorado, USA. Specifically, the process consisted of the following five steps:

1. Identification of life-giving forces (LGFs) or core values

2. Expansion of LGFs or core values using appreciative interviews

3. Thematic analysis of appreciative interview data as the basis for the development of possibility propositions

4. Constructing possibility propositions

5. Consensual validation of the possibility propositions

These five steps can be associated with the 4-D appreciative inquiry model described by Ludema & Fry (2008, pp. 282-284) and illustrated in Figure 1 next page.

In appreciative inquiry, the Discovery stage seeks to "search for, highlight, and illuminate those factors that give life to the organization, the 'best of what is' in any given situation" (Ludema & Fry, 2008, p. 283). As it related to this study, the primary objective in this stage was to identify core organizational values, or those values that give meaning to the organization. This was accomplished in a large group session with the organization's faculty and administration (step 1). The Dream stage of appreciative inquiry is described by Ludema & Fry (2008, p. 283) as "what could be"; whereas, the Design stage is described as "what should be" (Ludema & Fry, 2008, p. 283). In this study, the Dream stage was enabled via feedback from one-on-one appreciative interviews (step 2). Design was enabled via a thematic analysis of appreciative interview data, forming the basis for 22 possibility propositions which were later validated via the use of a valencing survey distributed to all employees (steps 3-5). Results of the valencing survey were subsequently used to form the basis for pragmatic and positively-oriented recommendations by comparing ideal state to present state variances. These recommendations were presented and discussed with top administrators of XYZ Technical College, serving to fulfill the final stage of appreciative inquiry; Destiny, described by Ludema & Fry (2008) as "an invitation to construct the future through innovation in action" (p. 283).

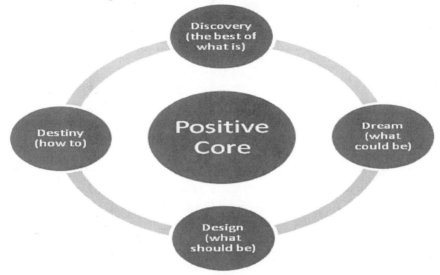

Fig. 1: Appreciative Inquiry 4-D Model. Ludema & Fry (2008)

Each of these steps is outlined in detail in the paragraphs that follow.

Step 1: Identification of LGFs or Core Values

The study began by leveraging another research project, which was completed at the same organization in the late summer and early fall of 2009. Its purpose was to determine if participatory action research could affect attitudinal change among faculty members. Because that study also required the identification of core organizational values, its findings were used for step 1 (Discovery).

To facilitate Discovery in the 2009 study, a large group meeting with approximately 25 members of the faculty and administration was held to identify the key themes summarized in Table 1. Modeled after a case study at Roadway Express in Ludema & Fry (2008) and adopted from the guide developed by Appreciative Inquiry Commons (2001), participants were placed in pairs and interviewed each other by sharing stories and mental images of key themes focusing on what XYZ Technical College does best. Following the completion of these interviews, participants were then placed in groups of four to six and asked to share their interview responses. These groups then identified the top three or four key themes that emerged from the interviews. The final themes were then shared with the entire group and captured on a whiteboard.

Table 1: Discovery: The Best of What is at XYZ Technical College—Key Themes

Student-Customer Satisfaction	Faculty Real World Experience
Ongoing Professional Development	Student Flow/Enlightenment
Faculty Support/Commitment	Faculty Mentoring
Student Success/Capstone	Knowledge Transfer
Faculty Motivation	Personalized Curriculum
Challenge Faculty to Be Their Best	Helping Students Graduate

For this study, detailed notes taken from the 2009 Discovery meeting were carefully evaluated and it was determined that a consistent pattern emerged in which the key themes identified in Table 1 could be consolidated into the following four core values:

1. Faculty Commitment   2. Professional Growth
3. Student Satisfaction   4. Student Success

These four core values were then later applied to the remaining steps in this study.

Step 2: Expansion of LGFs or Core Values Using Appreciative Interviews

A deeper analysis of core values was conducted via appreciative interviews on an individual basis. Twelve individual interviews were conducted, all of which were conducted on-site and in-person. Given that there were 94 employees in the organization, this resulted in interviewing 13 percent of the total. A random sample of employees was selected, primarily on the basis of participant availability and included a cross-section of both faculty and administrative staff. There was, however, more access to and availability with the administrative staff. Therefore, interviews were somewhat skewed toward the administrative side of the organization. Despite this potential concern, the author's contention is that study results are still valid due to the heavier participation of faculty in the discovery of core values (step 1), and given that the interview questions were designed to gauge behaviors of faculty members as well as administrative support staff. Finally, the dynamics of this particular organization fostered a very cohesive work group in which perceptions and attitudes appeared to be relatively uniform across functions. A count of the roles for those who participated in appreciative interviews is listed in Table 2.

Table 2: Appreciative Interview Participant Roles—Number of Participants

Faculty and faculty administration	3
Admissions reps	6
Administrative support	3

Interview questions were focused on asking participants to provide positively-oriented examples that they had observed or experienced at XYZ Technical College for each of the four core values. For each core value, participants were asked to provide their own description and one or two incidents where they recalled seeing each core value at its best. They were also asked to describe what factors or conditions facilitate the existence of each core value. Finally, to further elaborate, participants were asked to provide an example where a colleague may have observed each core value and how that colleague might describe the factors or conditions that lead to their existence.

Interviews were recorded via the means of a digital audio recorder and later transcribed in detail. To ensure accuracy, a research assistant employed by the author's management consulting practice carefully reviewed and edited all transcriptions. All interviews were conducted over a period of approximately two months from December 7, 2010 to January 27, 2011.

Step 3: Thematic Analysis of Appreciative Interview Data

Thematic analysis of appreciative interview data was completed via the use of HyperResearch qualitative research software. All interview transcriptions were downloaded into HyperResearch, carefully reviewed line-by-line, and coded based on recurring themes related to the four core values previously identified. Codes were also assigned for six different organizational factors, as recommended by Thatchenkery (2010), and included the following:

1. Communication
2. Decision Making
3. Incentives
4. Leadership
5. Organizational Practices
6. Organizational Structure

As transcriptions were reviewed, codes were assigned which associated the four core values with each of the above six organizational factors. This was done by carefully analyzing the statements made by each of the interview participants and categorizing significant and/or recurring statements of a similar nature into each one of the core value-organizational factor combinations. Interview participant statements related to these core value-organizational factor combinations, were placed in cells within a six-by-four matrix, with the six organizational factors listed in rows and the four core values listed in columns. Table 3 lists the most often mentioned core value-organizational factors.

Recurring themes were also captured in the same manner by carefully reviewing interview transcripts and coding using HyperResearch. These themes, along with detailed data related to the core value-organizational factor combinations, are captured in Appendices 1-2. Themes were reviewed for consistency with the core value-organizational factor combinations and for the identification of patterns to support subsequent recommendations.

Table 3: Counts of Most-Often Mentioned Core Value-Organizational Factors

Student Success – Organizational Practices	22
Student Success – Organizational Structure	17
Faculty Commitment – Organizational Practices	13
Professional Growth – Leadership	13
Student Satisfaction – Organizational Structure	11
Faculty Commitment – Communication	10
Professional Growth – Organizational Practices	10

Step 4: Constructing Possibility Propositions

Upon completion of the thematic analysis, the next step was to review the results for the development of possibility propositions. The objective was to identify consistent patterns that would form the basis for possibility propositions to be used in a valencing survey. Working with data directly pulled from the codes stored in HyperResearch, each of 169 interview participant statements that were translated into core value-organizational factor combinations were carefully evaluated. This data was used to develop possibility propositions, which were also incorporated into a six-by-four core value-organizational factor matrix, based on the guidelines outlined by Thatchenkery (2010). The final possibility propositions matrix is included in Appendix 3.

Step 5: Consensual Validation of the Possibility Propositions

The possibility propositions identified in step four, above, were then used as the basis for questions included in a valencing survey distributed online to all 94 employees. This distribution included the entire population of faculty and administrative support staff, and thus provided a final means of cross-validation for study findings. Design of the survey was also based on the guidelines outlined by Thatchenkery (2010), with the primary intent being to identify gaps between current and ideal state possibilities. Twenty-six individuals completed the survey in its entirety for a 28 percent response rate over a period of five business days. Valencing survey ratings are included in Appendix 4, and all questions followed the same structure as shown in Figure 2, with each possibility proposition serving as a question.

How much of an ideal is it?							
	5 Very Much		4		3 Neutral	2	1 Not Much

How much of it may already be present now?

	5 Very Much		4		3 Neutral	2	1 Not Much

Realistically, how soon do you want this to happen?			
	Immediately	Short Term—within 6 months	Long Term—within 2 years

Fig. 2: Faculty Commitment – Communication

There is a high level of camaraderie among faculty, in addition to an open and informal communication process that is very effective

RESULTS AND OBSERVATIONS

There are several observations that can be made based on both the appreciative interviews and the valencing survey. These observations were made using the data analysis capabilities embedded within HyperResearch and the results of the valencing survey via the use of the analytical tools embedded within Microsoft Excel. Once data has been coded, HyperResearch has the capability to run frequency reports and descriptive statistics including distribution, minimum and maximum counts of various codes, as well as the mean and standard deviation of various codes. It is important to note that, given the appreciative nature of this study, only comments of a positive nature were coded.

Table 4 lists some of the descriptive statistics that were pulled from HyperResearch for all core value-organizational factor combinations and themes that were coded with more than ten appreciative comments across all interview participants. The data can be interpreted as follows:

Total Count: Total number of times an appreciative comment related to this core value-organizational factor combination or theme was coded across all participants.

Minimum: The smallest number of times an appreciative comment related to this core value-organizational factor combination or theme was coded for any participant.

Maximum: The largest number of times an appreciative comment related to this core value-organizational factor combination or theme was coded for any participant.

Mean: The average number of times an appreciative comment related to this core value-organizational factor combination or theme was coded across all participants.

Standard Deviation: The distribution of the number of times an appreciative comment related to this core value-organizational factor combination or theme was coded across all participants (larger values indicate more variability).

Table 4: Aggregate and Individual Interview Counts of Core Value-Organizational Factors and Themes Coded Ten Times or More

	Total Count (All Interviews)	Min	Max	Mean	Std Dev
Student Success – Organizational Practices	22	0	6	1.833	1.85
Student Success – Organization Structure	17	0	4	1.417	1.24
Faculty Commitment – Dedicated	13	0	3	1.083	.9
Faculty Commitment – Organizational Practices	13	0	2	1.083	.669
Student Success – Helping People	13	0	3	1.083	1.165
Professional Growth – Leadership	13	0	5	1.083	1.505
Student Satisfaction – Organizational Structure	11	0	3	.917	.996
Faculty Commitment – Communication	10	0	3	.833	1.115
Professional Growth – Organizational Practices	10	0	2	.833	.718

Per Thatchenkery (2010), the objective was to identify the largest gaps between ideal state possibilities and present state possibilities. This resulted in identifying nine possibility propositions that had a variance of 0.6 or greater. The most significant gaps are listed in Table 5.

Table 5: Significant Possibility Proposition Gaps between Ideal State and Present State

	Difference Between Ideal and Present State
Professional Growth – Communication: "Information is usually available on advancement opportunities, and we always try to help each other succeed in our jobs."	1.1
Student Success – Organization Practices: "At XYZ Technical College, we do everything we can to remove barriers to student success, including hiring faculty and staff that care, convenient class times for non-traditional students, and ensuring that the various support services work together in a coordinated fashion."	.88
Student Satisfaction – Incentives: "Students feel like they have an incentive to attend class on a regular basis."	.82
Student Satisfaction – Organization Practices: "Our programs at XYZ Technical College are consistently high in quality and we are able to be flexible and adaptable to student needs."	.77
Professional Growth – Leadership: "Our leaders here at XYZ Technical College, including the deans and faculty chairs, routinely provide performance feedback and mentoring in a positive and supportive manner."	.73

Student Satisfaction – Organization Structure: "At XYZ Technical College, we have created a flexible environment which is conducive to learning including, good facilities and equipment, and integrated support systems."	.65
Professional Growth – Organization Structure: "Our organization is growing and our student body is diverse; as a result, there are always opportunities for growth and advancement."	.64
Professional Growth – Organization Practices: "We have plenty of opportunities to grow professionally across the organization, including tools for ongoing training, advancement, and mentoring."	.61
Faculty Commitment – Leadership: "Our administration is directly involved with student issues and has created a caring, open environment which includes regular feedback to instructors."	.6

RECOMMENDATIONS

Following the compilation of all HyperResearch and valencing survey data, study results were carefully evaluated for the development of actionable recommendations. This consisted of identifying recurring patterns in both the HyperResearch and valencing survey data which resulted in the following four recommendations. All possibility propositions with a gap between the ideal and present state of .7 or greater were used as the primary basis for these recommendations. Further, it was determined that all possibility proposition gaps between .6 and .69 were at least indirectly related to those with gaps of .7 or more; making it possible to consolidate recommendations.

Recommendation One—Focus on Developing Faculty and Staff Strengths

A recurring theme in the individual appreciative interviews and in the group discovery session was that XYZ Technical College tended to place a developmental emphasis on weaknesses rather than strengths. This had been manifested in the form of classroom observations and quarterly performance reviews which were often perceived as somewhat negative by faculty and staff. Both the discovery group participants and the appreciative interview participants frequently noted a need to develop faculty and staff in a more positive and supportive manner. These perceptions were also reflected in the valencing survey results.

Given this finding, a recommendation was made to incorporate some of the tools and concepts discussed by Buckingham & Clifton (2001) in their popular business book, *Now, Discover Your Strengths*. It was suggested that this book could form the basis for training and awareness programs at the organization's ongoing quarterly faculty and staff development meetings. This also included leveraging access to an online "strengthsfinder" profile (included with new copies of Buckingham & Clifton's book) which could be incorporated into quarterly performance reviews. By focusing on strengths instead of weaknesses, the way could be paved for improved performance, as well as improved attitudes and perceptions on the part of faculty and staff. Simply moving toward creating a strengths-based culture may serve to lift morale.

Recommendation Two—Customized Faculty Training and Development Programs

Discovery group session and appreciative interview participants, particularly faculty and faculty administration, expressed some frustration over "boilerplate" training and development programs. For example, it was noted by participants that even highly experienced senior faculty sourced from other institutions are required to take online "teaching 101" training modules. Participants noted that this serves to de-motivate individuals by creating the perception that their talents and strengths are not recognized or appreciated, and that elementary-level training for other than novice employees is a waste of time. Recommendation two, therefore, was related to recommendation one in the sense that the recognition of individual strengths and talents should form the basis for employee development. Whenever possible, it was recommended that faculty training and development should be customized to the needs, existing talents, and strengths of the individual.

Recommendation Three—Consistent Internal Communication of Career Opportunities

While not observed in the group discovery session, many appreciative interview participants indicated that there was a lack of awareness of internal career development and promotion opportunities. Although it was somewhat infrequently mentioned in the interviews, it came out in the valencing survey as having the largest possibility proposition gap. More research would need to be done in order to develop specific recommendations in this area. However, it was recommended that the organization should make note of this finding and review processes and procedures for communicating promotional opportunities internally.

Recommendation Four—Establishment of a Student Forum

A surprising finding in this study was the apparent disconnect between individual and group perceptions of student support services. While the core value-organizational factors Student Success-Organizational Practices and Student Success-Organizational Structure were, by far, the leading appreciative comments captured by interview participants, the results of the valencing survey did not reflect this view. In fact, Student Success-Organizational Practices had the second largest gap of all possibility propositions. Immediately following were large possibility proposition gaps in Student Satisfaction-Incentives and Student Satisfaction-Organizational Practices. This led to the conclusion that there may have been a disconnect between the internal perceptions of student support services and the perceptions that students themselves may have, based on student comments recalled by interview participants. Therefore, the final recommendation was to establish a student forum in which the organization's student-customers could offer suggestions and voice concerns. It was suggested that this might be executed in the form of an online discussion board or social networking web site. Alternatively, it might also take the form of a physical group which meets on a regular basis with student representatives.

CONCLUSION

The methodology used in this study illustrates how appreciative inquiry can be used as a pragmatic tool for the development of actionable recommendations, supported by the notion of positive organizational behavior. Appreciative inquiry combined with action research's emphasis on pragmatism is noted as a strength by Reed (2007, pp. 194-195). Yet, while appreciative inquiry has been shown to be effective in organizational change efforts, Zandee & Cooperrider (2008) note that its unconditional emphasis on strengths and positive outcomes has sometimes been a source for concern. For example, Collinson (2012) argues that leaders who are too positively-oriented risk perceptual distortion in the sense that they may not adequately consider negative viewpoints. Cameron (2008) notes that "human inclinations toward the positive as well as learned human tendencies to react strongly to the negative create a positive change paradox—both conditions can be important enablers for positive change, but negative is emphasized far more than positive" (p. 8). Researchers should, therefore, carefully consider the objectives and overall context of each research application before using appreciative inquiry as a methodological basis.

Despite these concerns, numerous studies have demonstrated the efficacy of approaches grounded in positive organizational behavior, including appreciative inquiry, such as those by Giardini & Frese (2008), Luthans, Norman, Avolio, & Avey (2008), Peelle (2006), Sekerka, Zolin, & Smith (2009), and Muse, Harris, Giles, & Field (2008). Further, Donaldson & Ko (2010) reviewed 172 peer-reviewed articles related to positive organizational behavior published between 2001 and 2009, including 16 that focused on positive organizational change and development. They concluded that the "findings suggest that efforts to improve organizations can become more effective and less stressful when interventionists use positive ODC approaches and processes" (Donaldson & Ko, 2010, p. 182).

Regardless of the direction of future scholarship, appreciative inquiry has demonstrated consistent usefulness as a practitioner's tool for organizational development. Cooperrider, Whitney, & Stavros (2008, pp. 27-30) note that appreciative inquiry's effectiveness stems from the way it "liberates power and unleashes human potential" by giving organization members more freedom to be known, heard, dream, contribute, act, and be positive. Moreover, as this study illustrates, it can be effectively used as a framework for conducting organizational analysis and for developing specific recommendations which are practical, actionable, and positively-oriented. This may be particularly true for organizations which are accustomed to a more deficit-based approach. The act of simply moving from an emphasis on weaknesses to an emphasis on strengths may be something which alone enables empowerment, hope, and visions of future potential among organization members, resulting in enhanced levels of engagement and organization performance.

ACKNOWLEDGEMENT

The author wishes to thonk Richard R. Aman Dean, Academic Affairs ITT Technical Institute Eden Prairie MN, USA for the support provided, including conducting individual interviews to carry out the research study.

REFERENCES

Appreciative Inquiry Commons. (2001). AI summit worksheets—Roadway. In *Positive questions and interview guides detail*. Retrieved August 24, 2009 from http://appreciativeinquiry.case.edu/practice/toolsQuestionsDetail.cfm?coid=1166

Buckingham, M., & Clifton, D.O. (2001). *Now, discover your strengths*. New York, NY: The Free Press.

Cameron, K.S. (2008). Paradox in positive organizational change. *The Journal of Applied Behavioral Science, 44*(1), 7-24.

Caza, A., & Caza, B.B. (2008). Positive organizational scholarship: A critical theory perspective. *Journal of Management Inquiry, 17*(1), 21-33.

Collinson, D. (2012). Prozac leadership and the limits of positive thinking. *Leadership, 8*(2), 87-107.

Cooperrider, D.L., & Whitney, D. (2005). *Appreciative inquiry: A positive revolution in change*. Williston, VT: Berrett-Koehler Publishers.

Cooperrider, D.L., Whitney, D., & Stavros, J.M. (2008). *Appreciative inquiry handbook: For leaders of change*. Williston, VT: Berrett-Koehler Publishers.

Donaldson, S.I., & Ko, I. (2010). Positive organizational psychology, behavior, and scholarship: A review of the emerging literature and evidence base. *The Journal of Positive Psychology, 5*(3), 177-191.

Giardini, A., & Frese, M. (2008). Linking service employees' emotional competence to customer satisfaction: A multilevel approach. *Journal of Organizational Behavior, 29*(2), 155-170.

Ludema, J.D., & Fry, R.E. (2008). The practice of appreciative inquiry. In P. Reason & H. Bradbury (Eds.), *The Sage handbook of action research: Participative inquiry and practice* (2nd ed., pp. 280-296). Thousand Oaks, CA: Sage Publications.

Luthans, F. (2002). The need for and meaning of positive organizational behavior. *Journal of Organizational Behavior, 23*(6), 695-706.

Luthans, F., & Church, A.H. (2002). Positive organizational behavior: Developing and managing psychological strengths. *Academy of Management Executive, 16*(1), 57-72.

Luthans, F., & Youssef, C.M. (2007). Emerging positive organizational behavior. *Journal of Management, 33*(3), 321-349.

Luthans, F., Norman, S.M., Avolio, B.J., & Avey, J.B. (2008). The mediating role of psychological capital in the supportive organizational climate—employee performance relationship. *Journal of Organizational Behavior, 29*(2), 219-238.

Muse, L., Harris, S.G., Giles, W.F., & Field, H.S. (2008). Work-life benefits and positive organizational behavior: Is there a connection? *Journal of Organizational Behavior, 29*(2), 171-192.

Peelle, H.E. (2006). Appreciative inquiry and creative problem solving in cross-functional teams. *The Journal of Applied Behavioral Science, 42*(4), 447-467.

Reed, J. (2007). *Appreciative inquiry: Research for change.* Thousand Oaks, CA: Sage Publications.

Roberts, L. (2006). Shifting the lens on organizational life: The added value of positive scholarship. *Academy of Management Review, 31*(2), 292-305.

Sekerka, L.E., Zolin, R., & Smith, J.G. (2009). Be careful what you ask for: How inquiry strategy influences readiness mode. *Organization Management Journal, 6*(2), 106-122.

Thatchenkery, T. (2010). *A guide to appreciative organizational analysis. School of Public Policy, George Mason University. Arlington, VA.*

Wright, T.A. (2003). Positive organizational behavior: An idea whose time has truly come. *Journal of Organizational Behavior, 24*(4), 437-442.

Zandee, D.P., & Cooperrider, D.L. (2008). Appreciable worlds, inspired inquiry. In P. Reason & H. Bradbury (Eds.), *The Sage handbook of action research: Participative inquiry and practice* (2nd ed., pp. 190-198). Thousand Oaks, CA: Sage Publications.

APPENDICES 1-2: HYPERRESEARCH DATA

Core Value - Organizational Factor Codes

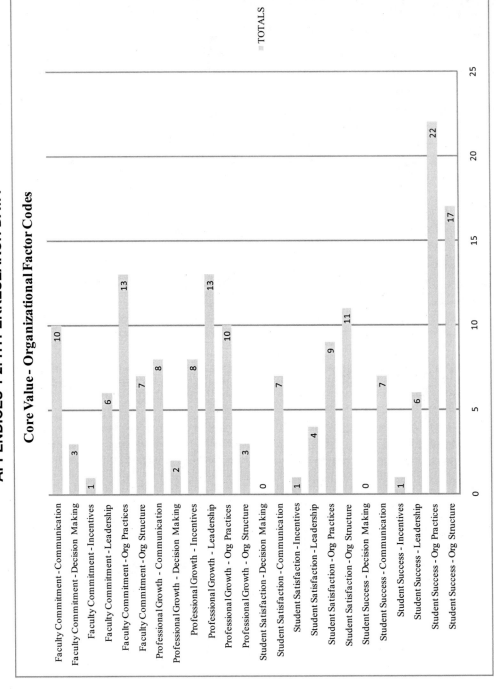

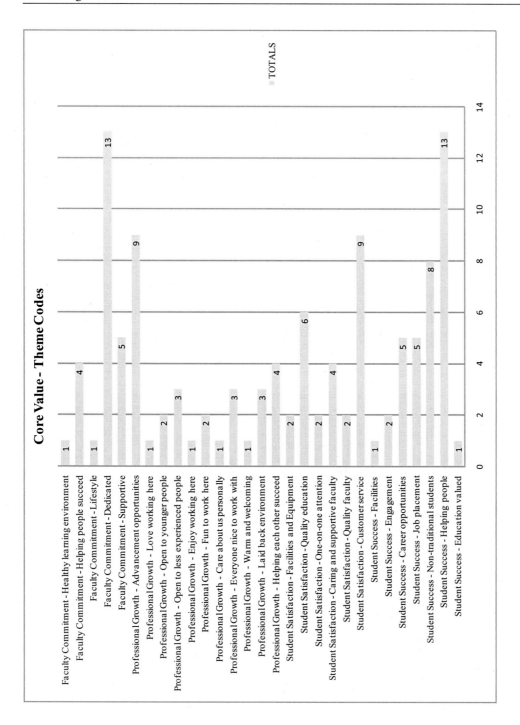

APPENDIX 3: POSSIBILITY PROPOSITIONS MATRIX

	Faculty Commitment	Professional Growth	Student Satisfaction	Student Success
Communication	There is a high level of camaraderie among faculty, in addition to an open and informal communication process that is very effective.	Information is usually available on advancement opportunities, and we always try to help each other succeed in our jobs.	Here at XYZ Technical College, instructors and administration always have an "open door" for students and provide them with highly personalized attention.	Our students enjoy an intimate campus setting which enables open and coordinated communication.
Decision Making	XYZ Technical College hires faculty that genuinely care about students and like to help people succeed.	Here at XYZ Technical College, careful decisions are made when hiring faculty and staff.	N/A (no interview statements made)	N/A (no interview statements made)
Incentives	It is very reasonable for someone to be able to work at a full-time job and still teach here at XYZ Technical College part-time.	At XYZ Technical College, we have strong incentives and opportunities to grow professionally, including such things as advancement, promotion, and tuition reimbursement.	Students feel like they have an incentive to attend class on a regular basis.	Our students feel successful when they graduate.
Leadership	Our administration is directly involved with student issues and has created a caring, open environment which includes regular feedback to instructors.	Our leaders here at XYZ Technical College, including the deans and faculty chairs, routinely provide performance feedback and mentoring in a positive and supportive manner.	The XYZ Technical College leadership team is actively involved with students' needs and concerns, including encouraging an open channel of communication as needed.	XYZ Technical College leaders, including the deans and faculty chairs, genuinely care about our students and will go above and beyond to help them succeed.
Organizational Practices	The faculty here at XYZ Technical College are extremely dedicated, they will do almost anything to help their students succeed.	We have plenty of opportunities to grow professionally across the organization, including tools for ongoing training, advancement, and mentoring.	Our programs at XYZ Technical College are consistently high in quality and we are able to be flexible and adaptable to student needs.	At XYZ Technical College, we do everything we can to remove barriers to student success, including hiring faculty and staff that care, convenient class times for non-traditional students, and ensuring that the various support services work together in a coordinated fashion.
Organizational Structure	At XYZ Technical College, we are careful to hire talented faculty who are genuinely interested in our students' success.	Our organization is growing and our student body is diverse; as a result, there are always opportunities for growth and advancement.	At XYZ Technical College, we have created a flexible environment which is conducive to learning including, good facilities and equipment, and integrated support systems.	XYZ Technical College caters to the needs of our students by offering convenient, consistent support to help them succeed.

APPENDIX 4: VALENCING SURVEY RATINGS

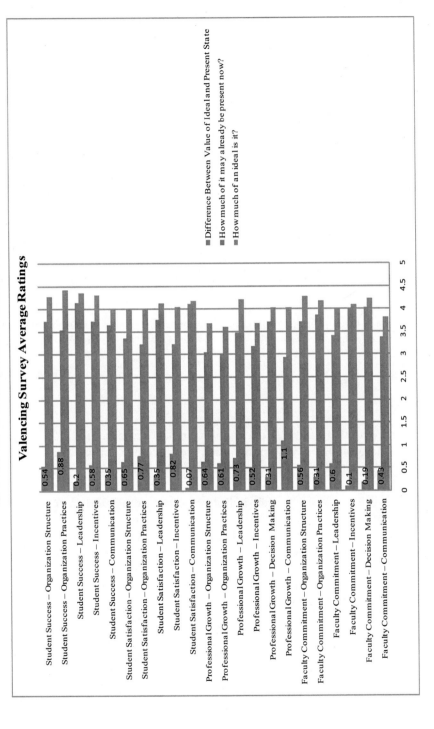

Valencing Survey Average Ratings

■ Difference Between Value of Ideal and Present State

■ How much of it may already be present now?

■ How much of an ideal is it?

Homeowners: The Other Side of Management Through Ontological Storytelling

Krisha M. Coppedge* and David M. Boje**

ABSTRACT

Through this qualitative research study, we explored the experiences of six homeowners who suffered mortgage foreclosure in the United States. The purpose of the study was to share homeowners' ontological stories that detail each homeowner's unique journey through the experience of mortgage foreclosure and evaluate which themes related to consentology affected their experiences. Our method involved reviewing different types of homeowner experiences from the perspective of the homeowners' unmanaged disciplines through a series of consents made between multiple parties. The findings revealed the differences between each homeowner's journeys through an investigation of their consentology. We analyzed particular scenes from the results and identified journey themes as well as differences between each homeowner's significant experiences. Many homeowners have lost their homes because they lack homeownership experience, experience in managing their personal finances, and effective decision-making skills. Factors that led to the participants' mortgage foreclosures included coercion, mistaken evidence, and duress.

Keywords*: Consentology, homeowner, mortgage foreclosure, ontology, storytelling.*

INTRODUCTION

Many individuals who were initially excited to purchase their homes faced mortgage foreclosure due to lack of effective homeownership experience, management, decision-making skills, understanding, and knowledge. Some homeowners' struggles with mortgage foreclosure began when they encountered opposition to their hesitance to buy and decided to go against their better judgment, the internal voice that told them, "Don't do it!" From a theoretical viewpoint, mortgage foreclosure is defined as the repossession of homes by banks, utilizing a third party (attorneys), due to homeowners' failure to pay their mortgage. NeighborWorks America (2011) reported

---

* Krisha M. Coppedge is with Colorado Technical University; Colorado, CO, USA.
**David M. Boje is with New Mexico State University, Las Cruces, NM, USA.
E-mail: Krishaj2@verizon.net

that 250,000 homes have been foreclosed as of 2012 in the United States. This indicates that many homeowners continue to experience mortgage foreclosure, yet their sides of the story remain unheard.

Bakhtin (1973) distinguished between narrative and story by explaining that "narrative genres are always enclosed in a solid and unshakable monological framework" (1973, p. 12). Bakhtin noted that story, by contrast, is more of a plurality: "The plurality of independent and unmerged voices and consciousness and the genuine polyphony of full-valued voices ... plurality of equal consciousness and their world" (Bakhtin, 1973, p. 4). The *microstoria-antenarrative*, however, is a third sort of voice, what Boje called an *antenarrative* (Boje, 2001, 2008a, 2008b, 2011a). The antennarative is defined as a bridge between living story (embodied lived story) and narrative (disembodied abstract thematics). In writing historical narratives, oftentimes the "little people's" microstoria, both its antenarrative and its living-story qualities, becomes diluted or edited. Antennarative methods retrace ways living stories get emptied out in narratives' quests for abstract thematics (Boje, 2008a). This may be a way to explore the root causes of important problems such as how mortgage-banking narratives marginalize those microstorial voices. Homeowners' stories may contain underlying themes regarding ethical and moral practices of homeowners, financiers, mortgage lenders, and bankers; hence, recording and investigating these themes may assist in creating a plan of action that may deter mortgage foreclosures in the future. Therefore, the need for this case study is crucial. Evaluating the "little people's" stories may encourage future homeowners to assess their personal management styles and decision-making prior to entering a mortgage loan. Additionally, recording these stories may motivate individuals who have been misguided homeowners in the past to consider (Boje, 2012a) and develop an alternate plan of action that would teach other homeowners the importance of remaining responsible for the continuity of their mortgage payment (Boje, 2012a).

OBJECTIVES

The main objectives of the current study were the following:

1. To provide a greater awareness of homeowners who have lost their homes to mortgage foreclosure and motivate others to share their stories of mortgage foreclosure worldwide.
2. To determine which themes related to *consentology* affected the experiences of those who have lost their homes to mortgage foreclosure.

We aimed to determine the ways in which *consentology* journey findings may have influenced the homeowners' decision-making processes regarding their mortgages. Consentology is a state of mind in which one decides to accept an ethical and moral responsibility to act. Here, the expression of consentology occurs through the exchanging of vows or promises to one another. The obstacles involved in these consentology journeys may arise if outside influences challenge homeowners' free wills. In the current study, we conducted interviews with six homeowners who lost their homes to mortgage foreclosure in the state of Pennsylvania. We addressed the in-depth structure of homeowner's accountability, responsibility, and consentology methods through default patterns of their interactions with others. These methods emerged from the opacity of each homeowner's self-account through interrupted ontological-storytelling narratives (Butler, 2005). Therefore, continuing to avoid remittance and sustainability; as well as accommodating homeowners' misunderstanding of homeownership, which is due to lack of knowledge, education, and learning; can impede practices of ethical accountability and responsibility through consentology (Butler, 2005). Through the interviews, we found that none of the participants realized the dire outlook of their homeownership (Coppedge, 2012). The homeowners did not understand that they signed for a mortgage loan they could not afford, which later led to the painful outcome of mortgage foreclosure.

This oversight affected not only the homeowners, but also their spouses, children, grandchildren, foster children, friends, parents, and communities. The stronger, overpowering opinions of others persuaded each homeowner to move into the direction of "homeownership havoc." These external opinions ultimately violated the homeowner's sense of better judgment regarding what is "truth" and what is a "lie." This exemplifies what Heidegger (1962) called the "they-self," how one is influenced to follow others (i.e., the they-self) instead of growing into one's own potentiality-for-Being-a-whole-Self (Boje, 2012b, 2012d, 2012f, 2012g,). The mortgage foreclosure crisis, which occurred because of the homeowners' lack of responsibility, answerability, virtue ethics, and deficiencies of consentology, further demonstrates this.

RESEARCH METHODOLOGY

The hypotheses for the current research study were as follows:

H_1: Homeowners' insufficient planning and lack of foresight were the primary reasons for their home foreclosures.

H_2: Homeowners' insufficient planning and lack of foresight were consequences of their consentology.

This methodology involved gathering comprehensive, living examples of homeowners' experiences in a non biased setting. We designed this case study to focus on questions posed to the homeowners about the decision-making processes they used in their unique experiences and to eliminate any potential bias associated with those who have lost their home to mortgage foreclosure. However, my challenge as the interviewer was to determine a favorable atmosphere. In addition, we encouraged interviewees to recapture the meaning of their mortgage foreclosure by storytelling those experiences in their own way, particularly depicting how they felt about the loss of their homes. The design further depended upon the participants' willingness to re-live, discuss, and share emotional experiences in a private, one-on-one setting with a mutual feeling of confidentially, trust, honesty, loyalty, and openness between the researcher and the participants.

PARTICIPANTS

Participants' ages ranged from 35 to 60 years, and each participant who chose to engage in the interviews had purchased a home. Four homeowners interviewed for this study were males, and two were females (Coppedge, 2012). Two of the participants referred to those homes as their "Dream Home." With this study, we sought to explore the ethics of answerability. The assumption was that when homeowners first applied for mortgage loans, they each met the necessary criteria for attaining the loan, which included the following: (a) the individual had a stable job, (b) the individual held that job for an acceptable amount of time, (c) the individual's bank accounts and amounts available were sufficient, (d) the individual's monthly and annual earnings were satisfactory, and (e) the individual's credit history was adequate. However, these homeowners were naive in their knowledge of subprime mortgage loans and the fact that lenders were authorized in many cases to waive documentation for homeowners to acquire a home loan.

PROCEDURE

Three rounds of interviews provided us with the opportunity to explore their stories about their situations.

First round of interviews. We designed the following questions to help the interviewees feel comfortable in sharing their journeys by telling their own stories in their own way:

1. Tell me the story of your mortgage loan.
2. Did it work out as you expected?
3. What was unexpected about it?
4. What could have been different?
5. What were the turning points?
6. How was the loan process conducted?
7. What sort of care did the mortgage loan officer take with regard to how the loan would play out?

Second round of interviews. We developed the second round of interview questions to contrast four ethical approaches: answerability, categorical, virtue ethics, and instrumental-ethics. The purpose of the second set of interview questions pertained to the ontological, heartfelt, ethical journey involving the body, mind, and spirit. Some answers to these questions revealed intentions, or unfounded presumptions, by comparing and contrasting the responses. The questions were as follows:

1. Who would you say is responsible for homeowners' foreclosures? Why?

2. Could you explain any reasons you think the bank should bear some responsibility in your foreclosure?

3. How might advice from family or friends be helpful in making the decision to purchase a home?

4. Do you believe that there may have been some unforeseen circumstances that, if you had been aware of them prior to investing in a home, might have affected your decision to buy your home?

5. What strategic plan of action do you suggest be put in place to divert such devastations in the future?

Third and final round of interviews. This became an increasingly collaborative endeavor by further investigating participants' responses to the following questions:

1. I have presented the types of journeys that I interpreted. What would you like to add?

2. I have presented the types of ethical encounters in those journeys, and what would you like to add or comment upon?

3. What would you like to see this research accomplish in the future in preventing homeowners from losing their homes, or saving their home from mortgage foreclosure?

4. What do you think could be done to return homeowners back to their homes after they have lost them to mortgage foreclosure?

5. How do you feel now about your experience of foreclosure after talking with me about it?

After the interviews, we isolated specific instances of various ethical approaches for the content and theme analysis of the interviews. We examined each participant's story for instances of categorical, answerability, action or emotion, and instrumentalist legalizations in what may be considered "malpractice" in mortgage banking.

These stories may offer some implicit or explicit ethical stances to assist researchers in understanding what happened in these homeowners' stories of mortgage foreclosure. The so-called "little people's microstorias" of homeownership was an essential component in evaluating the results of this study.

In summary, this study's designed methodology incorporated qualitative methods used to identify ethical and moral practices of homeowners, financiers, mortgage lenders, and bankers to prevent mortgage foreclosures in the future. This case study's design required an innovative qualitative research style that ultimately captured the essence of the mortgage foreclosure problems.

DIAGNOSIS AND ANALYSIS

Henry Mintzberg (2009) deliberated that the way in which individuals manages the various aspects of their lives, which include external, organizational, job-related or professional, chronological, and personal management, intertwine. While these managing concepts may be realized, the fact that "consistency is found only where you look for it" remains true (Mintzberg, 2009, p. 13). Based on homeowners' stories, we observed an ironically consistent lack of consistency in both the decision to buy against their better judgment and the way in which they managed their homeownership affairs. Therefore, we deduced that these homeowners, who signed for their mortgage loans without deep consideration and consistency, demonstrated an "unbalancing act" in consciousness.

Pastor John Hagee (2012) stated, "There are two sides to every conflict: the truth and the lie, light and darkness, and good and evil" (p. 21). In the context of this case study, the homeowners' extensive interviews included examples of *truthfulness* verses *untruthfulness*. Correctly identifying who is accountable for the mortgage loan and responsible for paying the mortgage on a monthly basis was the "truth," or fell into the category of truthfulness. In this case study, the decision to pass blame on another was the "lie," or fell into the category of untruthfulness. With that said, depending on how individuals choose to manage their lives and the decisions they make as homeowners, "'you are either going to disrupt' that which is already working well for you, or you are 'going to disrupt'" (p. 20) the quality of not only your life, but the quality and life of your family, which includes your spouse, children, and communities in which you live. This stems from one's own lack of personal management capabilities and ethical consentology.

During the interview sessions, the homeowners' discovered that facing mortgage foreclosure and the fear of eviction, possibly by the County Sheriff, were the final factors that led to their devastation (Hagee, 2012). Over time, these homeowners, who experienced suffering, persecution, and humiliation, no longer held a victimized attitude; rather, they gratefully developed an attitude of ethical enlightenment. These homeowners finally accepted the fact that, regardless of the reasons why they chose to enter into a mortgage agreement, they were solely accountable for the outcome. The homeowner's signature is that individual's consent to proceed.

Wherefore, from their responses, we found that each individual homeowner consciously granted consent to the mortgage lenders, banks, and realtors through their signature, which relates to a new concept known as consentology.

The homeowners' storytelling revealed emotional, personal struggles and conflicts of interest. Participants shared the ontological impact that had affected their sense of self and free will in their decision-making abilities as *free moral agents* for choices they made. A free moral agent in this context is one who makes choices and is able to evaluate, from an honest perspective, their personal decisions in regards to their personal life journey. Understanding the elements of consentology can assist in creating awareness of those dynamics described herein. I, therefore, analyzed the intrinsic decision-making processes the homeowners were willing to explain.

Coercion is the first theory of consentology which influenced participants Bailey, Jonathan, Doneeta, and Marie. Coercion is the journey in which these participants were persuaded by stronger influences other than their own. For example, Bailey was coerced to believe that his friend Florence, who is also a relative, makes better decisions than he does and that he should "just follow her lead." Jonathan's coercion stemmed not only from his secretive gambling problem but also from his desire to purchase a home he could not afford. Doneeta's coercion resulted from blind trust and misguided information; she did "not know what [she] was doing." In her case, Doneeta allowed others to lead her into a complex situation that she did not fully understand which eventually cost her her home. Similarly, Marie's coercion situation stemmed from her lack of self-dependability to decide for herself. A second theory of consentology, mistaken evidence led to Sammy's foreclosure situation. In this context, mistaken evidence is willful neglect. Sammy's mistaken evidence was a direct result of a mental conditioning that caused him to follow the directions of others unnecessarily. His independent, critical-thinking process was arrested by a mental condition, which affected his decision to pay his mortgage. Duress, a third theory of consentology, affected Smitty's consentology journey. In this context, duress is an influential and negative force. Smitty was under duress because of his wife's unfavorable influences and forces when she demanded for her needs to be met.

In theory, through this investigation into the events of these six homeowners, we objectively identified the error in their consentology thinking. With this study, we hope to provide research that may prevent mortgage foreclosure, due to similar occurrences in the future. By utilizing the methodology to ensure "Ontological-Storytelling Inquiries," We identified themes from each interviewee's speech intonations, hesitations or moments of expressions, and body language interruptions based on their emotional behaviors due to the stressors of their self-reflections and emotional stories as they unfolded (Boje, 1991).

LIFE-PATH CHOICES OF OTHERS: NOT YOUR OWN CHOICE

Metaphorically, all of the participants have walked on what Boje classified as "deeply rutted" paths. These homeowners chose to allow a another individual to convince them to make decisions that later caused them hardship and loss of stability (Boje, 2012a, 2012b, 2012c, 2012d, 2012e, 2012f, 2012g). Some individuals who acted as leaders possibly thought that they provided the homeowners with good advice. However, through coercion, mistaken evidence, and duress, the homeowners later learned that their advised "paths" led them to mortgage foreclosure.

Boje explained (2012a) how "occupants of each particular historical world can sense something beyond, a sort of free space opening and closing beyond the work-world…. (p. 14)." Homeowners should have had the ability to sense that the unethical guidance of others impacted their personal, ethical way of thinking about purchasing a home that they could not afford. Did these homeowners see the opportunity to purchase a home in a partial aspect, perhaps without noticing the space-time dynamic or *spiraling* (the upward pull into the spiral of liberation, and the downward pull into the spiraling abyss of mortgage failure and its aftermath)? In Coppedge's (2012) dissertation research study, analyses revealed how each homeowner was deterred from their typical *life-path choices* by moving away from their existing path and detouring off to the left or to the right. This change, from their ordinary life-path choices and *keeping-straight ahead* (Boje, 2012a, 2012b) as opposed to following the curve, created unforeseen, negative outcomes in each of their lives. After several years, the homeowners' recovery process started. Following the life-path of another's decision for one's life without any *self-reflexivity* and no *self-efficacy space* has proven to be quite dangerous for "people in organization" (Boje, 2011b, 2011c; 2012d, 2012f, 2012g). The same may be true for homeowners and the way in which they manage their personal affairs and make decisions.

Participants were able to identify their own dysfunctions during the process. They also revealed examples of their "hidden costs," which included loss of job, lack of income, divorce, depression, illness, alcoholism, and others. For participants who discovered their dysfunctions, findings from this study reveal the truths as to why those "hidden costs" were hidden. Were participants unaware of the potential dangers of owning a home because of lack of understanding, education, or training? Previous researchers have found that a foundation in financial resource stability is necessary in owning and keeping one's home during the housing crisis (Bonnet & Cristallini, 2002). The "little peoples" stories are often overshadowed by "grand narratives" in the media and large social institutions such as banking.

Allowing these participants to tell their own stories enabled them to adopt a willingness to explore some core values about ethics, morality, responsibility, answerability, and virtue ethical (Thatchenkery & Metzker, 2006). By further investigating these core values, some homeowners improved their ability to reflect on their own decision-making processes that might have contributed to the consequences of the loss of their homes (Merriam, 2009). Perhaps these participants' experiences may provide the opportunity for them to buy another home in the future. The differences in the way participants might approach purchasing a home now, as opposed to their previous experience, raises the question of how might a potential homebuyer prevent a future mortgage foreclosure? By applying this methodology, we hoped to create an understanding of the directionality of homeowners' experiences with mortgage foreclosure devastations during the housing crisis in the United States, as well as to foresee the existential, ontological consentology in-Being of ante-narrative storytelling continuously unfold.

HOMEOWNERS ETHICAL REALIZATION DIALOGUES

This section includes ethical realizations that were recognized after two out of the six homeowners, Marie and Jonathan, had experienced foreclosure. During the research interviews, these homeowners admitted that the true reasons for their mortgage foreclosure stemmed from both their lack of understanding and consentology as homeowners.

First, Marie's indecisive dependability path contributed to her mortgage foreclosure experiences. The paths towards Marie's foreclosure experience resulted from her indecisiveness and consent to a loan for which she was unprepared. Marie signed for a mortgage loan that she could not afford to pay back. However, through coercion, another individual influenced her to purchase the home. She admits this repeatedly, as evidenced by her statement, "I believe I was rushed into a situation I really was never prepared for" (Coppedge, 2012).

Marie expressed how she regretted the fact that that losing her job and losing her home were turning points she could not easily accept. She realized that not being in control of her own personal affairs and being unable to make her own final decisions were not beneficial in the end. Marie had lost everything, including control of her personal affairs and thoughts. She later understood that she would have been in a better position had she decided to temporarily rent a home until she had found secure employment.

In Jonathan's case, his secretive paths and behaviors towards his spouse impacted their mortgage foreclosure. Jonathan explained, "We reached the decision to go ahead and buy a home, and we went forward with it" (Coppedge, 2012), however, Jonathan had a secret gambling habit that his family did not know about that affected his financial situation after first establishing consent. Jonathan's withholding of this secret was one of the primary causes of his family's mortgage foreclosure and permanent separation from his family. Jonathan stated, "I had a gambling problem that I never really talked to anybody about because I was too ashamed." By admitting that this was the driving force behind his misfortunes, he soon realized the need for his reform.

The theme of greed is an element of gambling. The sense of failure in gambling also contributed to Jonathan's lack of control over his family's security and financial stability. Jonathan had "detoured" himself from the path of truth and reality and followed a road of risk and the "impoverishment of Being" (Bakhtin, 1993, pg. 16). He ceased in his sense of personal uniqueness by failing to remember that marriage is about oneness. As a consequence of that decision, he failed to share his gambling secret with his wife, which ultimately led to foreclosure and the destruction of his marriage. Gambling, therefore, related to self-greed, which results in "losing oneself" (Bakhtin, 1993). Because Jonathan's premise was false, in that he assumed that gambling was an appropriate activity, nothing that followed was successful. Jonathan since has learned that gambling is not a wise choice in life-planning and decision-making when one's family is at risk.

Consequently, U.S. Army Major General Marcia Andersen has stated, "If you are not stable then you are on the menu" (2012), which is a general principle for homeowners to consider. By comparing her statement to these homeowners' statements, homeowners should better prepare themselves to handle the challenges of homeownership. Additionally, every homeowner must become stable financially, emotionally, and intellectually in order to withstand the pressures and influential practices of those around them. If individuals choose to become homeowners, they must be prepared to protect themselves against those with the intent of earning money who are not necessarily thinking of the homeowners' best interest.

RECOMMENDATIONS

When confronting critical issues about a homeowner's accountability, answerability, and responsibility ethics, future researchers must acknowledge personal consentology, which explores the difficulties of confronting "democracy and emancipation" (originally freedom of slavery; Boje, 2008a, p. 136). Homeowners in the United States live as part of a democratic society, not a "Republic of," as indicated in the United States Constitution. The conflict between moral philosophy in the corporate structure and ethical practice of the individuals in charge remains objective when dealing with public policy administration. Boje explained "being set free" under the idea of emancipation of "the people" (2008a, p. 137).

It is suggested that future researchers remain objective in order to avoid the possibility of creating a bias. In dealing with homeowners' responsibility, accountability, and answerability from an outside and ethical standpoint of view, some researchers may fault the corporations' business operations rather than the individuals within the corporations when determining accountability for the decisions made. Based on the interviews, the issues occurred stemming from homeowners' personal choices. Those individuals remain hidden under corporation names, and the public cannot identify those individuals for accountability and answerability for their personal decisions.

According to Boje, the researcher must understand that the foregoing will involve human rights regarding differences in moral relativism in controversy with social justice in relationship to homeowners' problems in foreclosure (2008a,). Therefore, future researchers may discover the value of seeing the big picture of the homeowner in the economy. This involves corporations understanding basic business principles in society.

CONCLUSIONS

In reviewing past literature, homeowners have not received the opportunity to share their side of the story with a research interviewer regarding why they lost their homes to a mortgage foreclosure. Homeowners have attempted to tell their side of their story to a loan modification counselor, to a mortgage company or representative who called to collect overdue payments, to a bank, and finally, to the judge, but "Who Listens?" (Coppedge, 2012). None of those mentioned were able to assist the homeowner; as a result, the homeowners were foreclosed upon, evicted from their homes, and left devastated, in many cases with nowhere to go.

We hope that these findings will provide a greater awareness of homeowners who have lost their homes to mortgage foreclosure and motivate others to share their stories of mortgage foreclosure worldwide. Our goal is to enable homeowners in the United States of all cultures to share their stories of mortgage foreclosure. Sharing stories stems from a "♥-of-Care" (Boje, 2012a) and can encourage homeowners to make better decisions regarding the wellbeing of their lives and those for whom they are responsible.

We believe that homeowners telling their stories may help to deter further foreclosures around the country because of education and knowledge. The participants' stories may prevent others from making the same mistakes and encourage future homeowners to assess their personal management styles and decision-making prior to entering a mortgage loan. Additionally, through this study, we hope that individuals who have not listened to homeowners in the past may learn and understand the impact of their decisions and consider adapting to a ♥-of-Care (Boje, 2012a). In other words, judges, attorneys, and the mortgage companies may adopt a change of heart for these individuals by implementing an effective plan of action that, before eviction, would first teach homeowners the importance of remaining responsible for the continuity of their mortgage payment or negotiate an arrangement to return the home to the bank without drastic force. Every story contains two sides, and we believe that homeowners should receive the opportunity to tell theirs as well.

Through exposing these ontological living stories, we hope to reveal conjectural boundaries approaching futuristic enlightenment about homeownership and mortgage foreclosures globally. Our main objective for pursuing this critical problem relating to homeowners is to expose the necessity of empowering homeowners with sufficient knowledge and understanding to manage their finances so that they can make better decisions for the stability of their lives. Homeowners can benefit from a firm understanding of consentology, knowledge, insight, accountability, and responsibility in long-term homeownership. The findings from this case study may inspire further research in a universal modus (Bansal & Corley, 2012).

Finally, the overarching goal of this research is to start a foundation which will help homeowners "under water" in their mortgages to recover from this devastating journey. A goal of this emerging foundation is to assist those who have lost their homes to mortgage foreclosure by finding them a home and removing them from unsafe living situations such as parks, tents, shelters, and automobiles. This plan of action through the foundation will be centered on homeowners' willingness to undergo a homeownership educational and training program for approximately year.

REFERENCES

Anderson, M. (2012, July 22). *Washington watch: What career opportunities are available for women in the military?* [Video]. Retrieved from http://www.bcnn3.tv/2012/07/washington-watch-what-career-opportunities-are-available-for-women-in-the-military.html#more

Bansal, P. T., & Corley, K. (2012). What's different about qualitative research? *Academy of Management Journal, 55*(3), 509-513.

Bakhtin, M. M. (1973). *Problems of Doestoevsky's poetics.* (R. W. Rostel, Trans.).

Ann Arbor, MI: Ardis.

Bakhtin, M. M. (1993). *Toward a philosophy of the act.* (V. Liapunov, Trans., M. Holquist & V. Liapunov, Eds.). Austin, TX: University of Texas Press.

Boje, D. M. (1991). The storytelling organization: A study of story performance in an office-supply firm. *Administrative Science Quarterly, 36*(1), 106-126.

Boje, D. M. (2001). *Narrative methods for organizational and communications research.* Thousand Oaks, CA: Sage.

Boje, D. M. (2008a). *Critical theory ethics for business and public administration.*

Charlotte, NC: Information Age Press.

Boje, D. M. (2008b). *Storytelling organization.* London, England: Sage.

Boje, D. M. (2012a, January). *The ♥-of-care of the life-path of organizations through landscapes of quantum fields.* Retrieved from http://peaceaware.com/Boje/index.htm

Boje, D. M. (2012b) *Quantum spirals for organization consulting.* Retrieved from http://business.nmsu.edu/~dboje/448/QUANTUM%20SPIRALS%20for%20Business%20Consulting%20a%20book%20by%20David%20M%20Boje%20July%209%202012.pdf

Boje, D. M. (2012c, March). *Quantum storytelling.* Presented at seminar, Lille, France.

Boje, D. M. (2012d, May 25). *Quantum storytelling: Blacksmithing art in the quantum age* [Video]. Retrieved from http://www.youtube.com/watch?v=a7pm_mRwL-0

Boje, D. M. (2012e, June). *Quantum storytelling.* Retrieved from http://business.nmsu.edu/~dboje/448/The%20Quantum%20Physics%20of%20Storytelling%20in%20book%20format%20Jan%202011%20Boje.pdf

Boje, D. M. (2012f). Reflections: What does quantum physics of storytelling mean for change management? *Journal of Change Management.* Advance online publication. http://peaceaware.com/vita/paper_pdfs/JCM_BojeReflections_July%2021%202011.pdf

Boje, D. M. (2012g). *What is living story?* Retrieved from http://peaceaware.com/Boje/What%20is%20Living%20Story.htm

Bonnet, M. & Cristallini, V. (2002). Enhancing the efficiency of networks in an urban area through socio-economic interventions. *Journal of Organizational Change Management, 16*(1), 72-81. doi:10.1108/09534810310459783

Butler, J. (2005). *Giving an account of oneself.* New York, NY: Fordham University Press.

Coppedge, K. M. (2012). *An ontological-storytelling inquiry into homeowners' socioeconomic-ethics in mortgage foreclosure* (Unpublished doctoral dissertation). Colorado Technical University, Colorado Springs, CO.

Hagee, J. (2012). The outcome of conflict: We are more than conquerors through him who loved us. *All the Gospel to All the World and To All Generations, 24*(4), 20-21.

Heidegger, M. (1962). *Being and time.* (J. Macquarrie & E. Robinson, Trans.). New York, NY: Harper Row.

Merriam, S. A. (2009). *Qualitative research: A guide to design and implementation.* San Francisco, CA: Jossey-Bass.

Mintzberg, H. (2009). *Managing.* San Francisco: Berret-Koehler.

NeighborWorks America. (2011). *Foreclosure statistics: Homeowners facing foreclosure.* Retrieved from http://www.fdic.gov/about/comein/files/foreclosure_statistics.pdf

Thatchenkery, T., & Metzker, C. (2006). *Appreciative intelligence: Seeing the mighty oak in the acorn.* San Francisco, CA: Berrett-Koehler.

Student Opportunity for Achieving Results (S.O.A.R.)

Barbara Carter*, Joan Marie Johns* and Kenneth Wall*

ABSTRACT

Positive impacts on neighborhoods of collaborative re-entry initiatives assist post incarcerated populations in successful community transition. Collaborative efforts of agencies working in tandem increase quality of human lives, rebuild families, promote community safety, and conserve agency budgets by collectively interrupting cycles of criminality and substance abuse. The Marion County Sheriff's Office, in Salem, Oregon sponsors one such initiative. The Student Opportunity for Achieving Results (S.O.A.R.) focuses on barriers to student success. This initiative invites an opportunity for the simultaneous introduction of appreciative inquiry within a mutual and equal environment; while having the potential to increase the appreciative intelligence of a team. An increased level of appreciative intelligence assists team members in uncovering their own leadership strengths as they work in cost effective ways to strengthen families. The introduction of appreciative intelligence using a blended model of trauma sensitivity and appreciative inquiry has the potential to enhance effectiveness of collaborative teams.

Keywords: Appreciative intelligence, appreciative inquiry, coordinated community response.

INTRODUCTION

Jack, known to his friends as "Brutus', and after less than 24 hours out of prison, finds himself in jail again after having had unauthorized contact with his wife against a legally mandated no contact order. After meeting her in a hotel room, beating her to unconsciousness, leaving her there to die, and then leaving the scene to use drugs, the police found him intoxicated and fighting in a bar. More charges and probably an even longer prison sentence await "Brutus." In his mind, Brutus is likely thinking

---

* Research scholars, Colorado Technical University, Colorado Springs, Colorado, CO, USA.

E-mail: barbc99@comcost.net, pebbyjohns844@msn.com, kwall@coloradotech.edu

that he just had a bad day. Perspectives of intervention and treatment providers probably involve conversations focusing on how the system could have responded more quickly to increase Brutus' chances for success and subsequently meet the needs of the community by promoting victim safety. Corrections department reality is that Brutus has not yet been adjudicated of a new felony, so statistically and technically he cannot be classified as a recidivating offender. Community attitude is more likely than not that this is just one more example of a high risk felon who should never again see the light of day. Finally, tax payer opinion is probably that attempts at rehabilitation is a waste of dollars and community resources; and at the same time wondering just how many more felons like Brutus are about to be released; providing offenders opportunities to contaminate communities, and waste time, money, and resources that are better served elsewhere.

An estimated 600 corrections supervised clients are discharged into Marion County, Oregon communities yearly (Marion County Re-entry Initiative (MCRI, 2010). Almost half of those discharged are back on the streets without housing; almost 70% struggle with substance abuse problems, and a majority of those released also have no means of transportation (MCRI, 2010). Almost two thirds are parents, (MCRI, 2010). Addressing this serious social issue requires significant levels of collaboration.

Travis (2005) discusses record breaking numbers of men reintegrating to communities after incarceration. Elevated numbers of those incarcerated are creating financial and community resource stress. The Student Opportunity for Achieving Results (S.O.A.R.) team discusses the potential impact of successful reintegration on decreasing recidivism in this nascent area of study. Pilot studies similar to the S.O.A.R. project are surfacing to address familial and community aspects of successful reintegration and the impact on recidivism (Travis, 2005). Collaboration between partners is crucial to the success of these pilots.

S.O.A.R. objectives include: reducing recidivism, saving tax payer dollars, improving community safety, and positively impacting lives and families. This program affords assistance to those reentering the community from incarceration providing access to opportunities for assistance with shelter options, employment skills training, job skills development, mentoring, transportation options, treatment for mental health, and substance use and dependence issues (MCRI, 2010). These services are collectively provided through collaboration with a variety of partners including: The Corrections Education Department at Chemeketa Community College, Marion County Sheriff's Office Parole and Probation Department, The Marion County Health Department, The Mid Valley Mentors (MVM), The Mid-Willamette Valley Community Action Agency, The Center for Family Success, and The Quest for Change, (a 12 bed, ninety day transition housing option).

With all of these organizations, and financial and human resources addressing the problems of criminality, addiction, and person-to-person violence: How can the introduction of appreciative intelligence using a blended model of trauma sensitivity and appreciative inquiry enhance effectiveness of collaborative teams? The S.O.A.R. project addresses this question through their collective participation and from each of their perspectives, with a goal of effectively performing their duties. The introduction of appreciative intelligence by promoting appreciative inquiry in a violence free environment process was essential to the team's ability to acknowledge everyone's reality and give everyone a voice that is heard (Cooperrider & Whitney, 2005; Thatchenkery & Metzker, 2006). This process in itself moved the team a step closer to improved collaboration and a sanctuary model.

Bloom, (1997) in her discussion of sanctuary discusses the significance of an organization's ability to provide services in a way that is trauma-informed. A trauma-informed team, system, or organization is an environment where services are strength based, survivor centered, recovery focused, culturally sensitive, gender-specific, empowering, engaging, collaborative, unconditionally respectful, and are provided in a violence-free and civil atmosphere (Bloom, 1997). Team members provide services in a way that appreciates the developmental influence of violence, abuse, and trauma at all levels including physical impact, psychological effects, cognitive behavioral experiences, as well as the social, educational, work related and spiritual spheres. Team members demonstrate an ability to provide student services in a way that deliberately and purposefully minimizes and avoids relational and environmental re-traumatization either by words, behaviors, or intervention approaches (Bloom, 1997).

Organizationally, the provision of a safe and civil, violence-free environment, from the top down, lays the foundation for trauma sensitive services for students and staff (Bloom, 1997). The S.O.A.R. team's ability to create a sanctuary model in which to provide an appreciative inquiry (AI) approach is a way to reduce the numbers of incident reports, enhance team sustainability, reduce staff turnover, assist staff in identifying and employing their own leadership qualities, increase trust between staff and students, and as a result create and maintain a strong team that makes effective use of resources as families and communities are rebuilt. Creating and maintaining a sanctuary model is a perfect setting for providing a variety of collaborative services to offenders who are re-entering the community using an appreciative inquiry approach.

ISSUES/NEEDS FOR STUDY

Despite prior successes of the S.O.A.R. project, stakeholders continue to seek out training and new ways to improve teamwork, self-identify, employ leadership characteristics, and provide student services in a collaborative and trauma-sensitive way to create student success. In addition to student success, stakeholder's interest is in program sustainability and ongoing continued improvement. The aim is to enable team members in the self identification and development of individual and team skills in a way that most benefits the high risk clients they serve. They are open to evidence-based and creative approaches that help them to identify and enhance what works well (Cooperrider & Whitney, 2005) continue to do what works well, and at the same time create a civil, trauma-sensitive and violence-free environment of ongoing improvement in the context of sustainability (Ref. Fig. 1.).

In the context of an organizational change process, assessment of sustainability requires a variety of perspectives and ongoing analysis in a way that moves progress forward resulting in ongoing improvement (Sardana & Thatchenkery, 2011) aligning with team and program objectives. What better way to promote progress and sustainability in a way that supports objectives of student success and community safety than to to blend this idea with the motive of providing required services in a violence-free setting that promotes sanctuary?

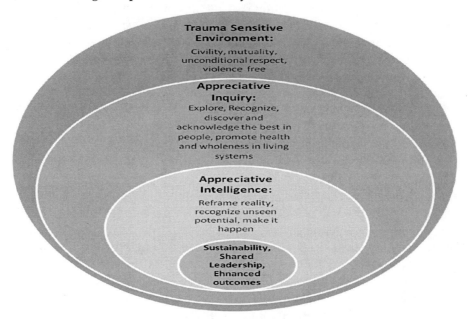

Fig. 1: Creation of Trauma Sensitive Environment

OBJECTIVES

Team objectives are to introduce appreciative intelligence to a team using a combination of a sanctuary model and appreciative inquiry through a series of experiential workshops that assist team members in identifying their individual leadership strengths. The team must apply this new knowledge to increase their collective performance resulting in organizational improvement, program sustainability, increased creativity, and team work. An idea is to clearly identify what works well, repeat those behaviors, and obtain ongoing training and information that contributes to these objectives in a civil and trauma sensitive setting. Opportunities created are the development of a blended model integrating appreciative inquiry in a trauma-sensitive environment as a way to increase a team's appreciative intelligence resulting in improved program sustainability, supports community safety, and makes the best use of financial and community resources. Challenges are in maintaining high levels of collaboration of multiple-involved agencies at all levels, and providing services to a difficult high-risk population while working to rebuild families and maintain community safety, which helps answer the question of: How does the introduction of appreciative intelligence using a blended model of trauma sensitivity and appreciative inquiry enhance effectiveness of the S.O.A.R. team when employing the appropriate research methodology?

RESEARCH METHODOLOGY

This S.O.A.R. team demonstrates collaborative community partner involvement while simultaneously addressing the social issues of: seamless prisoner reentry; re-building families; interrupting criminality; treating substance abuse; and reinforcing community safety. They seek ways to improve teamwork through trauma sensitivity, self-identification of their own leadership skills. Using those traits to promote collaboration and maximize quality client services is a perfect methodological fit for introducing appreciative intelligence by blending appreciative inquiry with a sanctuary setting (Bloom, 1997; Miller & Rollnick, 2002; Thatchenkery & Metzker, 2006). Qualitative inquiry and motivational interviewing are employed as a foundation to support the identified framework with objectives of uncovering what works best for S.O.A.R., which enables the team members in voicing and delivering those results in their own language and terminology.

An effective framework for this study centers on a conversation with team members using four successive steps: Objective, Reflective, Interpretative, and Decisional (ORID). This ORID process lays the foundation of a logical course of thinking about the specific issue of improving S.O.A.R. services. Designing a series of probing questions enabling team members to reflect on specific issues using their own perspectives and experiences is a way to move forward with this study (Stanfield, 1997). This process is consistent with Thatchenkery, (2005).

The appreciative inquiry (AI) process (Thatchenkery, 2005; Thatchenkery & Metzker, 2006) was used by the S.O.A.R. team to seek out the root causes of successes and build upon what the team identified as successful improvement ideas (Carter, Johns, Sampayo, Boyd, Keyser, Laverty, Trevedi, & Wall, 2011). AI is also promoted as an innovative and widely accepted change management tool used to focus on what is working well and then planning to make improvements to identified elements. The process builds on the team's existing strengths. Tangible outcomes of a series of inquiry results were a description of where the team wants to be by reliving what has worked well through storytelling as a tool. Periods of ongoing reflection enables team members to identify, and assess new data (Carter, et al, 2011). The S.O.A.R. team consists of a variety of agency representatives who, through a series of training activities, are able to appreciate not just their own perspectives, but the realities of other stakeholders. This is significant to effective diagnostic and analytic processes.

DIAGNOSIS AND ANALYSIS

There are approximately 19 individual S.O.A.R. team stakeholders from a variety of community agencies. Five are managers and/or supervisors, which is a perfect combination for the facilitation of an iterative process designed to increase service effectiveness from the top down.

A first step in this iterative and thematic process is an action learning conversation with S.O.A.R. when deliberately hearing, writing, and thinking together as a team assists them in uncovering innovative ideas (Stanfield, 1997). Uncovering the best answers involved a series of ORID questions including: Objective: How does the S.O.A.R. team currently function in order to perform duties? Observable data was uncovered by reviewing historical and current experiences that helped to identify what is currently known about how the team performs.

Reflective: From your own perspectives how do S.O.A.R. team members currently function in order to perform their duties? Each team member took the opportunity to make written reflections and then share them in a safe setting from their own perspectives. This form of storytelling using their own language and terminology assisted in uncovering their realities and then compare them to those of other team members, which was a natural next step in making sense of current circumstances.

Interpretative: What does the current reality mean in the context of S.O.A.R. team performance? This conversation uncovered individual and team assumptions, values, and beliefs about how the S.O.A.R. team performs their duties. Identifying implications on community safety and student success lead to a discussion of decision related inquiry.

Decisional: The S.O.A.R. team was able to effectively identify commitments to inform future action involving continued use of appreciative inquiry processes in the S.O.A.R. pilot project duties at all levels by all partners. They began with an agreement to continue a series of trainings and workshops designed to enhance service delivery by developing a trauma-informed environment in which to deliver those services (Stanfield, 1997).

Recently, a series of experiential trainings and team meetings proved useful in the collection of qualitative data. A deliberate and purposeful blending of methodologies enhanced initial project outcomes. The AI process with S.O.A.R. uncovered an appreciation for team members' differences in individual realities in the context of enhanced team work. That was the beginning of facilitating their pursuit in identifying individual leadership strengths and the best of leadership skills in individual partners as they related to one another and to their own organizations (Thatchenkery, 2005). The next step in this process is measuring individual and team buy-in in order to uncover initial outcomes.

INITIAL OUTCOMES

Results of written team surveys suggest a 100% buy-in from the top down to employ an AI model in a trauma sensitive environment. All participants identified a positive experience through this process. All were able to identify their individual leadership characteristics that contribute positively to S.O.A.R. objectives. All participants identified that an AI process in a trauma informed setting is a combination that promotes collective learning and positive experiences in a safe environment. All the participants voted to continue moving forward with an AI process in a sanctuary setting with a goal of increasing levels of appreciative intelligence individually, as a team, and as an organization from their own perspectives. In periodic surveys team members revealed how the use of a blend of trauma sensitivity and appreciative inquiry has enhanced the effectiveness of the S.O.A.R. team. Using a manual word count, language describing team improvement is identified. A goal was to uncover attitudes and behaviors consistent with Bloom, (1997) and her description of trauma sensitivity as well as language consistent with the benefits of appreciative inquiry (Thatchenkery, 2005). It should be noted that for the purposes of this study, language is only listed that was identified by all of the team members from the top down.

When asked to describe positive experiences from their own perspective of the initiation of the blended model in this study; all team members used the following language: willingness to remain on the S.O.A.R. team (without transferring to another program); experienced a peaceful, violence- free/profanity free setting; allowed to exercise personal leadership traits; affirmed, empowered, and experienced mutuality and equality; experienced civility from the top down; looked forward to team meetings and left happy. When asked to use language describing areas of increased effectiveness of S.O.A.R. services from their own perspectives resulting from this process; the following terminology was used: improved collaboration, total elimination of a group think dynamic, less time writing and addressing incident reports, less numbers of student-related security incidents, more frequent student breaks, classes run on time, students and staff more engaged and more frequent conversations are recovery focused, less tardiness and absences, students, staff, and supervisors are expected to take responsibility for a trauma-sensitive environment from the top down. Qualitative data form these initial findings imply increased appreciative intelligence and have the potential to contribute to short and long term recommendations.

RECOMMENDATIONS

Recommendations are for continued coaching, training, and consultation of the S.O.A.R. team as they continue to develop individual and organizational appreciative intelligence. Action steps moving the team forward include the following and are supported by the team. First, continue weekly team meeting using an appreciative inquiry 4-D format to drive the team discussions (discover, dream, design, and deliver) (Cooperrider, & Whitney, 2005). Members of all levels of the S.O.A.R. team agree to attend weekly meetings. Second, schedule a series of workshops for S.O.A.R. team members who will receive additional education in appreciative inquiry processes within trauma informed environments. Third, the S.O.A.R. team agrees to work together to identify acceptable behaviors that promote civility and create a safe environment from the outside in; in which to perform S.O.A.R. duties. Fourth, continue to provide education and training to students in the context of their responsibility to contribute to a trauma free environment as a way to promote health and wholeness from the inside out. Fifth, progress checks at 6 months and a year later will likely uncover evidence of the effectiveness of an AI process in prison re-entry teams blended with a sanctuary model. Opportunities are for identified benefits to the S.O.A.R. team, capability to contribute to team and program sustainability, and student success. This combination of opportunities has community, political, and family implications as well as the potential to drive systemic improvements through policy change. Challenges that can easily be managed are: time, money, and staff scheduling.

CONCLUSIONS

The S.O.A.R. team is well defined, and individuals and team members from the top down are invested in creating and maintaining a trauma-sensitive environment while at the same time facilitating an appreciative inquiry process with the potential to increase depths of appreciative intelligence in a way that promotes ongoing positive change at individual, team, student, community and program levels. All of the team members from the top down express interest in creating healthy internal relationships and stakeholder collaboration. All of the team members express a desire to be open-minded and willing to try creative and innovative trauma-sensitive techniques blended with an AI approach that are in the best interest of the students, the team, and the community. Their willingness to devote time and energy to a process of ongoing reflection and pose well-thought-out questions that keep the process moving forward is crucial to outcome benefits. They express confidence at the process and consistently attend meetings and trainings. Outcome results imply a 100% buy-in, enthusiasm, and excitement, as potentials for ongoing improvement. The S.O.A.R. team motivation level maximizes the possibility of success in meeting team and organizational goals of enhancing the appreciative intelligence of the S.O.A.R. team (Thatchenkery & Metzker, 2005). The process improves reflection on the question of the benefits of continued research.

Areas of additional research as the result of this study might include an investigation in measurement of levels of appreciative intelligence and improved service delivery when appreciative inquiry is promoted in a trauma-informed setting. Qualitative follow up with this particular S.O.A.R. team in the near future can uncover more specific improvements contributing to program sustainability including staff turnover, uses of financial and human resources, and a collective experience of program stability. These qualitative inquiries have the potential to assist in more deeply answering the question of: How can the introduction of appreciative intelligence using a blended model of trauma-sensitivity and appreciative inquiry enhance effectiveness of collaborative teams?

ACKNOWLEDGEMENT

The authors would like to thank Marion County Sheriffs Office per their permission to use data, information and records in development of this case.

REFERENCES

Bloom, S. L. (1997). Creating sanctuary: Toward the evolution of sane societies. New York: Routledge.

Carter, B., Johns, J., Sampayo, J., Boyd, M., Keyser, R., Laverty, P., Trevedi, M., & Wall, K. (2011). Leadership Pikes Peak, a community development organization: Creating a robust training program. As cited In: Sardana, G.D., Thatchenkery, T. (Eds.). (2011). Positive initiatives for organizational change and transformation. New Delhi. Macmillan. Original paper presented at the International Conference on Management Cases, Greater Noida, India, December 1-2, 2010.

Cooperrider, D., & Whitney, D. (2005). Appreciative inquiry: A positive revolution in change. San Francisco: Berrett-Koehler.

Marion County Re-Entry Initiative, (MCRI). (2010). MCRI partner agencies. Retrieved from: http://marioncountyreentry.com/about-2/about/#MCSOi

Miller, W. R., & Rollnick, A., (2002). Motivational interviewing: Preparing people for Change. New York: Guilford.

Sardana, G.D., & Thatchenkery, T. (2011). Building competencies for sustainability and organizational excellence. New Delhi. Macmillan.

Stanfield, B. (1997). The art of focused conversation: 100 ways to access group wisdom in the workplace. New Society Publishers. Canadian Institute for Cultural Affairs. Gabriola Island, BC. Canada.

Thatchenkery, T. (2005). Appreciative sharing of knowledge: Leveraging knowledge management for strategic change. Chagrin Falls, Ohio: Taos Institute Publishing.

Thatchenkery, T., & Metzker, C. (2006). Appreciative intelligence: Seeing the mighty oak in the acorn. San Francisco: Barrett-Koehler.

Travis, J. (2005). But they all come back: Facing the challenges of prisoner reentry. The Urban Institute Press. Washington, D.C., 20037.

Using Appreciative Intelligence and Positive Approaches for Change Management

Beverley E. Powell III* and Tojo Thatchenkery**

ABSTRACT

This paper describes a process intervention that took place at a defense accounting facility to improve employee retention. Senior leadership was faced with various challenges emanating from miscommunication, high turnover, and a deterioration of employee trust in leadership. In recent months, this particular facility had a significant decrease in employee retention. In addition, the majority of the remaining staff were beginning to show a reduction in performance. An intervention called Appreciative Sharing of Knowledge (ASK) was used to bring about long lasting change and to address underlying collective problems that were suspected. The ASK approach, based on Appreciative Inquiry (AI) and Appreciative Intelligence, uncovered several core values held by the staff that were not being fully supported by the leadership. The ASK protocol was conducted using both personal interviews and group sessions. Twenty-six of the fifty-two staff members participated. Many of the values derived from the ASK validators—known as Knowledge Enablers (KE)—were combined with the Knowledge Infrastructure Factors (KIF) to create Future Present Scenarios (FPS). The emphasis between the top four KEs and KIFs was examined through a prioritizing ("valencing") survey that produced an average KE ranking. This survey determined two factors: the KE/KIF combination needed to be implemented sooner as well as the standard deviation of the participant's desires. The results allowed leadership to reduce employee turnover by increasing communication and employee trust in leadership.

Keywords: Appreciative intelligence, appreciative sharing of knowledge, knowledge management, culture change.

INTRODUCTION

During the last decade, positive approaches for creating organizational changes have become the preferred method (Seligman, 2011; Thatchenkery & Chowdhry, 2007;

---

* Colorado Technical University, Colorado Springs, Colorado, CO, USA.
** George Mason University, Arlington, Virginia, USA.
Email: evans.powell@gmail.com, thatchen@gmu.edu

Cameron & Spreitzer, 2011; Golden-Biddle & Dutton, 2012; Roberts & Dutton, 2009). All of them accentuate original ideas that derive from the social construction of reality (Burgan and Luckman, 1966) and demonstrate the role of language in creating positive outcomes. This case study situates itself in a positive organizational behavior discourse and shows how an intervention based in that manner was able to help the director. It does so by fleshing out the underlying values and core enhancers specific to the personnel within the organization. The organization was faced with the challenge of explaining a high turnover rate while also under the strain of being undermanned." A typical, mainstream approach would have focused on problem identification and problem-solving paradigm. Consultants using such an approach assume that organizations are full of problems that need to be solved and thus, good consulting equates positive and effective problem solving (Thatchenkery, 2005). In contrast, Appreciative Inquiry (Copperrider & Srivastva, 1987), focuses on what is currently working in an organization versus what is not. By exploring events when employees are at their best as far as productivity, mood, behavior, etc, appreciative inquiry identifies employees' core values that they cherish and explores ways to nurture them into the everyday work environment. The inquiry begins with a process of affirming the basic "goodness" that exists in a group or organization and tries to create a climate of collaboration and true inquiry within the unit. In essence Appreciative Inquiry is an attempt to co-create a shared and new future of an organization by exploring its core competencies and values.

Related to Appreciative Inquiry is the construct of Appreciative Intelligence (Thatchenkery & Metzker, 2006), which is defined as the ability to perceive the positive potential in a situation and to act purposively to transform the potential into outcomes. AI is the process of acting immediately so that the desired outcomes may unfold from the generative aspects of the current situation. While Appreciative Inquiry is an organizational analysis methodology, Appreciative Intelligence focuses on individual ability. The two are related, as they operate at the macro and micro level respectively.

APPRECIATIVE SHARING OF KNOWLEDGE (ASK)

The Appreciative Sharing of Knowledge, or 'ASK,' is an approach to knowledge management based on the tenets of Appreciative Inquiry (Thatchenkery, 2005; Thatchenkery & Chowdhry, 2007). According to Thatchenkery (2005), in the "last five years, most Chief Information Officers of large corporations have realized that knowledge management is not about managing but about sharing" (p. 20). In order for an organization to nurture a culture that shares knowledge, it is important for leadership to avoid managing or controlling knowledge. This shift in the traditional knowledge management practices requires top management to first discover what enables the knowledge sharing and then incorporate what is found back into the organization's infrastructure.

The first objective in the ASK process is the identification of Knowledge Enablers (KE). This is accomplished by identifying, exploring and enhancing the values, competencies, and organizational factors that enable people to share knowledge. After the ASK process identifies, explores, and enhances various knowledge sharing competencies those competencies are incorporated into the organizational structure and culture. These KEs are integrated and strengthened using five Knowledge Infrastructure Factors (KIFs): decision-making, organizational practices and routines, incentives for knowledge sharing, leadership, and communication (Thatchenkery, 2005). Both the KEs and the KIFs are essential for a successful ASK process.

According to Thatchenkery (2005), there are seven steps for conducting ASK.

Step 1:   Set the stage. Present the appreciative knowledge sharing paradigm and negotiate top management commitment and support.

Step 2:   Through paired interviews, elicit positive stories from organizational members of successful knowledge sharing behaviors already occurring in the work area.

Step 3:   Identify Knowledge Enablers (KE).

Step 4:   Analyze the data using Knowledge Infrastructure Factors (KIF).

Step 5:   Construct possibility propositions known as Future Present Scenarios (FPS).

Step 6:   Consensually validate and rank possibility propositions

Step 7:   Formulate and implement ways to incorporate findings into the work environment

This case study used the above sequence to determine the underlying issues behind the declining performance and low employee job satisfaction. However, instead of asking what created low morale and satisfaction, the ASK process focused on occasions when employees experienced high morale and job satisfaction. This was instance of reframing, one of the components of Appreciative Intelligence.

THE CASE STUDY: THE ASK INTERVENTION IN AN ACCOUNTING ORGANIZATION

The office that participated in the ASK is a geographically detached division of a government funded finance company. The main organization oversees and processes payroll and accounting for over 500 million military and civilian employees while the facility that participated in this case study processes payroll for approximately 50 thousand military and civilian personnel. There are many satellite offices throughout the world, such as this, that act on behalf of the main organization. Each separate facility functions as the local subject matter expert for government service members and civil service employees. Each facility is typically divided into several sections that address and process specific payee inquiries regarding travel expenses, pay, allowances, specific entitlements, cash advances, etc. Each facility sends a monthly 'scorecard' to the main headquarters that shows the overall payments, account reconciliations, and customer inquiries processed. This facility was staffed with about 50 employees, which included two supervisors, five team leads, and one director. There were 17 sections, each covering a specific aspect of payroll and accounting. The director monitors the two supervisors who monitor the team leaders; in turn, these team leaders monitor 5-10 employees each. All departments communicate with the other internal departments as needed. Through frequent conversations with the director, it was learned that the director had concerns that there was a degradation of employee motivation combined with a decaying level of communication within and between different departments. The director believed that this was stemming from a perceived loss of employee trust in the leadership. Since this division often set the standard for the other facilities of the main organization, the director was interested in regaining the trust of his employees. He was interested in exploring how an ASK intervention would help uncover the contributing factors behind trust within the organization and learning about and possibly implementing the recommendations that might come from the intervention.

METHODOLOGY

The ASK process applied in this study can be categorized as a post-positivist qualitative approach. This mixed study quantifies qualitative findings using matrices and surveys. ASK challenges traditional foundations of positivism and is based on the philosophical premises of social construction of reality (Berger and Luckman, 1966; Gergen, 1999; Gergen & Thatchenkery, 2004). In ASK, participants in the project co-create the desired reality. Hughes (1994) argues that reality does not exist within a vacuum; it is the result of what we do and who influences them. Proctor (1998) posits that the creation of reality is heavily influenced by culture, gender, and cultural beliefs. These and other variables affect the relationship between individual behaviors, attitudes, and social interactive situations. Language thus has a *real* effect on individual perceptions of reality and subsequently, on organizational outcomes, such as how people perceive and appreciate sharing of knowledge.

Sample Size and Demographics

The ASK process involves gathering relevant data from organizational members by deconstructing positive stories told by the employees and fleshing out common core themes such as trust and respect. Doing so requires data gathering sessions where participants can share personal stories using interviews. A full scale participation of the staff was supported by the division director. However, initially there was a problem obtaining participants since nearly half the employees were contract workers. The contract existing at that time was ending soon and they were nervous whether their jobs would be renewed. The launch of ASK may have generated additional stress and decreased the researchers' ability to secure full participation and positive input. The director could not control the outcomes one way or the other and updates regarding the status of contract negotiations were sparse and inconclusive.

The total participant sample obtained for the intervention was 26 out of a staff of 52. Below is the detailed breakdown:

- Initial discovery session (KEs)/including story telling—1 supervisor, 20 pay clerks
- Individual interviews—1 supervisor, 1 team lead, 4 military pay clerks (each met separately)
- Future-Present Scenario (FPS) session—1 supervisor, 1 team lead, 16 military pay clerks
- Prioritizing survey—1 supervisor, 1 team lead, 13 military pay clerks

Data Collection

The primary method used to gain the data was the solicitation of positive storytelling. This was accomplished through both group and individual interviews. Participants were asked to describe real life examples of when they felt most satisfied and motivated to be working in the organization. The objective was to record positive stories and look for common themes that underpinned what motivated them. For example, an employee tells a story about her enjoyment with her department when others voluntarily pulled together and worked as a team, the resonating theme would be recorded as teamwork. Deficient or negative storytelling was not encouraged. If and when participants began to engage in a negative scenario, they were guided back to recalling and describing positive situations. However, they were not criticized for having negative stories since doing so would have been an unappreciative act on the part of the researchers.

Session Scheduling

When the director initially approved the project, there were no reasonable time slots available that would allow large group sessions due to various time constraints on an already strained and understaffed organization. This facility was understaffed by 10 personnel though the facility performance benchmarks were not reduced. Additionally, there was a week's worth of corporate mandated training needing to be scheduled, which would take precedence over participation in the project if and when any free time became available.

A mass email was sent out by the director supporting the ASK project and encouraging volunteers to participate in the personal interviews requested. Only six staff had volunteered in five days. On the sixth day, it was proposed to the supervisors that if their employees would attend a group session during their lunch break, a meal would be provided in exchange for their participation. The next day, 21 employees volunteered and two one-hour group sessions were scheduled. The first session was for discovering the KEs and the second was for developing Future-Present Scenarios (FPS) using the KEs and KIFs developed during the first session. The group sessions were set to be held at the employee conference room with a long meeting table and plenty of chairs so participants could face and interact with each other. The supervisors gave verbal approval to their staff that if the sessions went over an hour, they were permitted to stay until finished. The participants were not taped or filmed. All notes and recording of core values were made on large lecture paper in full view of the participants. After the first session, the resulting KE list was recorded in Microsoft Word and placed in an Excel spreadsheet matrix with the KIFs. The subsequent empty matrix boxes that intersected each KIF with each KE became the focus of the second group session.

Personal Interviews

Interviews lasted between 45 and 75 minutes and were conducted in the participant's office or work station. Each participant was asked a standardized set of questions. None of the interviews were video recorded or taped. All notes were taken by hand and transferred to Word documents immediately afterwards. After establishing underpinning themes within the stories told, the participants were asked to confirm their accuracy. Once confirmed, the themes were added to a master list that would be included during the group sessions.

Discovery Session

In this first group session, participants were given the same questionnaire used in the personal interviews. As each person shared their stories with the other participants, those listening were asked to identify resonating themes. One master list of themes from both individual and group sessions was compiled for all the stories. If a particular theme such as teamwork came up more than once, it was once again recorded and counted. Once the storytelling was finished, the top four most popular themes mentioned were labeled as the four primary KEs.

Future-present Scenario (FPS) Session

This second and last session began with all participants being divided into groups of three. Each group was provided with one blank KE/KIF matrix using the top four KEs discovered in the previous sessions. Each group was asked to provide a FPS for each cell that intersected with a particular KE and KIF. FPSs are positive scenarios that describe an example of a situation that is within the context of the intersecting KE and KIF. In order to create specific FPSs, participants were asked to imagine and describe a scenario describing a situation where the KIF and KE were part of a situation taking place regularly in the work environment; hence the term, future-present scenarios. For example, if the matrix showed an intersection of teamwork (KE) and communication (KIF), a participant might state: "when our department falls behind, both supervisors regularly pitch in to help us meet the goals." It should be noted that this example is not a desire to see something in the future and is stated in the present-tense as if this has already happened.

Once completed, each group shared their FPSs with the entire group. The most popular FPSs were chosen by majority vote and placed into a master KE/KIF matrix at the head of the conference table for all to see. The final matrix was completed during this session and a majority agreement was reached (See Appendix A).

Validation Survey

The survey used a 1-5 Likert scale format with a multiple choice selection regarding the rated importance of each KE as well as a preferred timeline for enactment (See Appendix B). At the conclusion of the FPS session, participants completed a survey that rated the importance of each KE/KIF on a scale of 1-5, 1 being the least and 5 being the most important. This survey also asked participants to choose a preferred time-frame (such as immediately, short term, or long term) that they would like to see each FPS incorporated into their everyday work environment.

Findings and Analysis

Trust, relationships, recognition, and teamwork were found to be the most common knowledge enablers emerging out of the positive storytelling exercise. As shown next, several common related themes were extracted from the storytelling sessions that helped create the final themes. 1). Trust—reliability, faith, confidence, belief. 2). Relationships—contacts, connections, commonalities, ties, friendships, acquaintances. 3). Recognition—rewards, acknowledgement, credit, appreciation. 4). Teamwork—reliance, sharing, responsibility, positivity. It was notable in all sessions and interviews that these themes carried both a social and emotional effect.

The matrices were compiled by the employees. The FPSs were created using the KE/KIF matrix developed by the participants attending the second group session. Individual interviews and group sessions with 26 employees revealed 103 possible FPS scenarios which were discussed and consolidated into what is listed in the FPS matrix.

The focus of the data analysis centered on the following:
- Most emphasized KE/KIF coupling

- How soon each employee wanted to see the FPSs incorporated
- Ranking of KIFs against the KEs

The discovery and FPS session, along with the prioritizing ("valencing") survey, yielded a rich amount of data that were organized in an Excel spreadsheet that was formulated to calculate preference averages and Standard Deviation (stdev). The FPS matrix blocks were numbered in sequence with the rating survey. This made it simple to track the data, input results into a spreadsheet, and mathematically rank each KE/KIF according to importance of the participants as well as calculate their standard deviation. The preference averages and stdev were then compared to determine the overall rankings. Only 15 individuals completed the prioritizing survey. Their results reflect 26 percent of the facility staff. However, the matrix this survey valenced was compiled collectively by 26 employees (50 percent of the facility's staff).

OVERALL THEME RANKINGS

Employee preference for ranking the importance of the four KEs was ranked on a decimal scale of 0.0 to 5.0; 0.0 being no importance and 5.0 being most important. The overall preference rankings for the four KEs were:

Trust	5.00
Teamwork	4.90
Relationships	4.85
Recognition	4.50

Each KE was also "valenced" with each KIF, which gave deeper insight to where individual preferences fell among the different infrastructure factors.

Theme—Recognition

Recognition, although receiving the lowest ranking, still showed to be a priority to the staff. The largest stdev was between recognition and incentives at 1.34. The smallest was between recognition and practices at 0.74.

Theme—Relationships

This KE also showed a wide range of variance in employee preference. The highest stdev showed to be between relationships and decision making. The smallest stdev was 0.6 for relationships and leadership.

Theme—Teamwork

Teamwork had the narrowest set of stdev. The lowest was 0.36, held by teamwork and both leadership and communication. The highest stdev was 0.85 for teamwork and decision making.

Theme—Trust

Trust yielded the most collective measure importance overall. Interestingly it also showed the widest range of stdev between KEs and KIFs. The highest stdev was between trust and practices at 1.31. The lowest stdev, which also ranked the most important KE and KIF relationship, was trust and communication.

DISCUSSION OF KE/KIF RESULTS

Recognition

Although there are occasional meetings when recognition is given out to employees, the practice was inconsistent. This was mentioned several times prior to reframing stories. The recognition KE was broken into two categories: formal and informal. Formal recognition came in the form of official notice by the management and usually took place in full view of management and coworkers. This occurred during the occasional monthly meetings and less publically in the team settings with the supervisors and director. Informal recognition was provided in the form of encouragement and praise of the team during informal meetings and in the regular work environment throughout the work day.

Although the leadership had held reward and recognition meetings in the past, the staff stated clearly that they wanted more such meetings in the form of consistently scheduled events. Several participants also wanted to see more open and public acknowledgement of their teammates when standards were met or exceeded. Many participants recalled occasions where individuals were recognized outside scheduled meetings and in front of their colleagues for meeting or exceeding the job requirements. The majority of participants, however, were in agreement that they all looked for incentives set forth by the management as a matter of practice. It was equally important for management to regularly schedule and follow through (and not cancel) the monthly awards and recognition meetings. They spoke of setting their own personal goals based on the possibility of recognition. Recognition served as a measure for their individual success as well. Recognition was not cited for incentives alone. Many stories talked about simpler and more subtle forms of recognition such as acknowledging when another coworker or leader did something nice for another member of the organization. Several people mentioned that acknowledging these little things with a 'thank you' or some kind of compliment went a long way in making a person feel appreciated. This has also been supported by other research that examined employee interpretations regarding fair treatment by leadership (Scott & Colquitt, 2007).

Teamwork

This KE got the most emphasis while all the other three factors showed lowest KE and KIF stdev. Even though there were 17 departments and only 52 employees, teams were often developed across different departments. In two separate storytelling sessions, examples were given about how the deficiency of another value such as trust or recognition greatly determined one's contribution to the team effort. This was based on the amount of social capital (also referred to as trust) that individual members of the teams held for management and each other. In both the discovery and the FPS sessions, many participants spoke about the importance of being able to rely on each other to do his or her part. There were several stories that revealed a notable sense of pride and relief among the team members when things went smoother than expected during an otherwise stressful deadline. There was discussion regarding two levels of teamwork: departmental and organizational. Many stories emphasized how certain aspects reflected the reputation of the facility more noticeably than others simply by their contact with the customer. This made the functionality of the team more critical. Several participants stressed the connections between positive relationship, their departmental team success, and the success of the overall facility. Most participants agreed that their successful teamwork was dependant on the support of teamwork by the leadership. It was pointed out that this was not always the case. Most of the participants affirmed that their team work was influenced the most by communication between all levels.

Relationships

Each participant agreed that the current freedom for internal and external relationships were critical. The leadership's efforts were rumored to limit the ability of the employees to be open with one another. Participants talked about how they enjoyed and benefited from these transparent relationships among peers. In most of the stories, the relationship with leadership showed to be the most critical for the success of effective relationship building. Relationships with leaders were mentioned as a factor associated with all other themes and KIFs. While many participants trusted the overall organizational system as well as their own skill sets, everyone agreed that most of the trust they held for leadership and each other derived from day to day communication. Relationships were also found to be especially critical for the long-time employees (tenure over two years). These employees expressed that building healthy relationships among team members both in and out of the facility were beneficial to the success of their jobs. Therefore, the more experienced an employee was, the more accustomed he or she was to nurturing current and potential relationships.

Trust

Participants wanted to trust leadership. Data revealed that large amount of verbal promises and commitments such as incentives, promotions, awards, and recognitions were made to different departments. Much of this would not come to fruition. It was made clear by the participants that when leadership communicates inconsistently or vaguely, employees become uncertain of their tasks and responsibilities, including their own sense of job security. This, in turn, creates scrutiny towards the communicator and his or her message which, if not addressed, results in degradation of trust (Beer & Nohria, 2000; Armenakis et al., 1993; Bouckenooghe et al., 2009). It has also been argued that trust by employees is influenced by a leader's perceived openness, intent and concern for participants projected through verbal and non-verbal cues during social interaction (Nahapiet & Ghoshal, 1996). Trust was clearly the most important value for the employees in almost every aspect of the KIFs and prioritizing. The relationships between the employee and the leaders showed the most desire for opportunities for improvement.

Overall the consensus was to emphasize trust between the employees and the leadership. In retrospect, before the ASK intervention, the staff had only imagined that there was a strong, positive trusting relationship between the leadership and them. This simple fact made the participants realize the relationship of trust between the two had much to be desired.

Recommendations and Plan of Action

The recommendation to senior leadership was to begin with a meeting with the director and the two supervisors to assess the possibility of implementing the ideas proposed in the FPS matrix. Both the KE/KIF matrix and the FPS matrix would be used to determine if these were 'doable' and ideal interventions. The suggested path was twofold: managerial reframing of communication and restructuring the amount of employee participation in the facility.

Based on the FPS matrix, it was clear to see the call for more reliable participation from leadership in the trust and relationship areas. The focus should be to help management develop more employee friendly policies that would make them more visible or transparent to employees. This was due to the shortage of employees and the resulting increased workload. Participants shared that they were beginning to notice that they might have given more concessions to management when certain issues went unanswered. Further, the administration should be de-layered to allow more employee contribution in decision making to enhance organizational cohesion and create more of a team sense. Finally, management should incorporate sharing of knowledge with colleagues and management on an ongoing basis by using the FPS matrix as a template.

PLANNED ACTION

The results of the ASK made the director very aware of the specifics of how employees felt and how to address their concerns. Immediately after the results were handed out to the leadership, the number of meetings increased and, when one had to be cancelled, there was a greater effort to notify everyone involved and to reschedule it for a later time. The recognition and awards meeting were held with consistency. When deadlines did not allow for these ceremonies, the director would pull the staff together to make sure everyone understood why and when the make-up session would be held. Furthermore, he made these awards ceremonies mandatory and would refrain from beginning them until all were present. The director and his deputy are now well known for making weekly rounds to visit with the various departments. The relationship between senior leadership and employees is noticeably more positive and relaxed than in the past. Production has risen and turnover in the past six months has been nearly zero. The director began sponsoring a staff walk around the running track every Friday during the lunch hour. This is a time where any staff member can walk and talk with him while getting a moderate amount of exercise.

CONCLUSION

The ASK project brought the staff and the director closer to knowing and understanding each other than before. The director seemed to have built considerable social capital as a result of this study. The results underscore the need for greater trust between management and leadership; more so towards leadership from the employees. The proposed solutions are the beginning to changing the facility's culture into one that nurtures the true core values of all personnel. Management should seize this opportunity and apply the findings of ASK on a long term basis and vision. Doing so will help them to be on a path to building and sustaining a knowledge sharing culture that has already reduced turnover and increased job satisfaction among staff.

This facility is in a perpetual state of change due to the indicative lifestyle of military and the organizations that support its soldiers and civilian employees. This is more so than traditional, ever-changing corporate industries. A researcher or consultant working in this type of organization may quickly realize that they will have to be flexible. The propositions suggested above have this consideration embedded in them and reveal the complexity of organizational change and the importance of the aforementioned themes.

There is a growing body of research that shows the importance of trust and teamwork in creating high quality connections in the workplace (Dutton, 2003; Stephens, Heaphy, & Dutton, 2011). ASK addresses the specificity and the context of each organization and questions the effectiveness of the problem solving oriented organizational change approaches. There are many factors that are considered to have an impact on the success of organizational effectiveness (Lewin, 1951; Armenakis, Harris, & Mossholder, 1993; Weick, 1995; Schein, 1996; Don & Dennis, 2008; Long & Spurlock, 2008). Those discovered at this facility are unique and specific to its staff. Organizational development research has built a considerable body of research on the dynamics of improving organizational effectiveness. In that context, the key narrative in this chapter, - how leadership can create a positive knowledge sharing culture- is a refreshing approach. ASK methodology provides researchers, consultants, and executives with a meaningful look into what truly creates positive organizational change. The methodology gets to the root of what enables employees and leadership to create trust, teamwork, and high quality connections.

REFERENCES

Armenakis, A. A., Harris, S. G., & Mossholder, K. W. (1993). Creating readiness for organizational change. *Human Relations, 46*(6), 681-204.

Beer, M., & Nohria, N. (2000). Cracking the code of change. *Harvard Business Review*, May/June, 133–141.

Berger, P. L. and T. Luckmann. (1966). *The Social Construction of Reality: A Treatise in the Sociology of Knowledge*. Garden City, NY: Anchor Books.

Bray, D. W. (1994). Personnel-centered organizational diagnosis.

Cameron, K., Spreitzer, G. (Eds.). (2011). *The Oxford Handbook of Positive Organizational Scholarship*. New York: Oxford University Press.

Don, C., & Dennis, W. F. (2008). Success factors in dealing with significant change in an organization. *Business Process Management Journal, 12*(4), 503.

Dutton, J. E. (2003). Energize your workplace: How to build and sustain high-quality connections at work. San Francisco: Jossey-Bass Publishers.

Gergen, K., & Thatchenkery, T. (2004). Organization Science as Social Construction: Postmodern Potentials. *Journal of Applied Behavioral Science, 40,* 2, 228-249.

Gergen, Kenneth. An Invitation to Social Construction. Thousand Oaks, CA: Sage, 1999.

Golden-Biddle., & Dutton, J. (Eds.). (2012). *Using a positive lens to explore social change and organizations: Building a theoretical and research foundation*. New York: Routledge Academic.

Hughes, J. (1994). The philosophy of social research. *Essex.*

Huy, Q. N. (2002). Emotional balancing of organizational continuity and radical change: The contribution of middle managers. *Administrative Science Quarterly, 47,* 31-61.

Jones, E., Watson, B., J., G., & Gallios, C. (2004). Organizational communication: Challenges for the new century. *Journal of Communication, 54*(4), 722–750.

Judge, T. A., Thorensen, C. J., Pucik, V., & Welbourne, T. M. (1951). Managerial coping with organizational change: A disposition perspective. *Journal of Applied Psychology, 84,* 107-122.

Lewin, K. (1951). Field theory in social science.

Long, S., & Spurlock, D. (2008). Motivation and stakeholder acceptance in technology-driven change management: Implications for the engineering manager. *Engineering Management Journal, 20*(2), 242-266.

Nahapiet, J., & Ghoshal, S. Social capital, and the organizational advantage. *Academy of Management Review, 23*(2), 242-266.

Proctor, S. (1998). Linking philosophy and method in the research process: The case for realism. *Nurse Researcher, 5*(4), 73-90.

Roberts., L., & Dutton, J.(Eds). (2009). *Exploring positive identities and organizations: Building a theoretical and research foundation.* New York: Psychology Press.

Schein, E. H. (1996). Kurt Lewin's change theory in the field and the classroom: Notes toward a model of managed learning. *Systemic Practitioner, 9,* 27-47.

Seligman, M. (2011). Flourish: A visionary new understanding of happiness and well-being. New York Free Press.

Stephens, J., Heaphy, E. D., Dutton, J. E. (2011). In Kim Cameron & Gretchen Spreitzer (Ed.), High-Quality Connections New York, NY: Oxford University Press.

Thatchenkery, T. and Chowdhry, D., Appreciative inquiry and knowledge management. A social constructionist perspective, 2007. Cheltenham, UK: Edward Elgar Publishing Limited

Thatchenkery, T. (2005). Appreciative sharing of knowledge: leveraging knowledge management for strategic change. Chagrin Falls: OH: Taos Publishing.

Thatchenkery, T., & Metzker, C. (2006). Appreciative Intelligence: Seeing the mighty oak in the acorn. San Francisco: Berrett-Koehler.

Vakola, M., Tsaousis, I., & Kikolaou, I. (2004). The role of emotional intelligence and personality variables on attitudes toward organizational change. *Journal of Managerial Psychology, 19*(2), 88-110.

Wanberg, C. R., & B., J. T. (2000). Predictors and outcome of openness to changes in a reorganizing workplace. *Journal of Applied Psychology, 85,* 132-142.

Weick, K. E. (1995). Sensemaking in organizations.

APPENDIX A: FINAL KE/KIF/FPS MATRIX

	Knowledge Enablers			
	Trust	**Recognition**	**Teamwork**	**Relationships**
Decision-making	*Employees are brought in to contribute to the decision making process and the final decisions are not undermined by different levels of leadership*	*Employees contribute ideas towards types of recognition, which are put into effect and done in front of everyone.*	*It is common for employees to attend brainstorming session designed to come up with new ideas and solutions for new policy and current or pending issues*	*Group decisions are respected and fellow employees and leadership treat one another with professional courtesy and mutual respect*
Organizational practices and routines	*Management demonstrates faith in employee to competently follow policy and are open to receiving recommendations for improvements*	*The organization practices both positive and negative recognition fairly and evenly across all departments.*	*There are monthly meetings where employees partake in knowledge building and cross training exercises*	*Management encourages building relationships between employees, leadership, and departments through relationship building activates*
Incentives for knowledge sharing	*More experienced personnel are generous with sharing information regarding customer service and system issues: the recipients have faith in their knowledge and experience*	*Management as well as employees recognize each other both formally and informally such as praise for a new employee's progress or acknowledging coworkers for their assistance and guidance*	*Employees learn about different department jobs to make their own jobs more easily accomplished*	*Promotions, salary increases, and monetary rewards are given for employees who go to different sections and learn and perform additional job duties*
Leadership	*Management is trusted to have the employee's best interest at heart and feel that they will stand behind them in any case.*	*Management acknowledges employees not only publically but in some cases with promotions, cash, awards, and or gift certificates*	*Leaders set a good example by visibly working together with mutual respect and are on the 'same sheet of music' with each other including the employees.*	*Management spends time getting to know each employee and are viewed as real people too. They are actively assertive in building stronger relationships both individually and collectively*
Communi-cation	*Members of the organization can rely on what others say regardless if they are management or not without fear of reprisal.*	*Monthly meeting are held for the purpose of recognizing outstanding employees and their accomplishments in view of the others*	*Leadership emphasizes the importance of communication by holding frequent meetings to update employees and team building exercises.*	*Communication is kept open to all employees not just the ones who know each other*
	Future Present Scenarios			

APPENDIX B: PRIORITIZING ("VALENCING") SURVEY

Valencing survey for Propositions from Future Present Scenario session

Knowledge Infrastructure Factors

Trust	1	2	3	4	5
1. How important is it?					
2. How much of it may already be present with your team?					
3. How soon do you want to see the team make this happen?					

Recognition	6	7	8	9	10
1. How important is it?					
2. How much of it may already be present with your team?					
3. How soon do you want to see the team make this happen?					

Teamwork	11	12	13	14	15
1. How important is it?					
2. How much of it may already be present with your team?					
3. How soon do you want to see the team make this happen?					

Relationships	16	17	18	19	20
1. How important is it?					
2. How much of it may already be present with your team?					
3. How soon do you want to see the team make this happen?					

Answer scale

1. How important is it?

5	4	3	2	1
Very Much				Not Much

2. How much of it may already be present with your team?

5	4	3	2	1
Very Much				Not Much

3. How soon do you want to see the team make this happen?

3	2	1
Immediately	Short Term (w/in 6 months)	Long Term (w/in two years)

The numbers in the 'Answer scale' tables allow each participant a Likert selection to rate their preference with each of the above questions.

Nonprofit Board Service: A Qualitative Investigation using Appreciative Inquiry

Tonya Henderson Wakefield*, Alfonso Robertson* and Kenneth Wall*

ABSTRACT

An appreciative-inquiry inspired study was conducted in support of efforts to improve opportunities for young people seeking nonprofit board service in Colorado Springs, Colorado, USA. The authors interviewed nonprofit board members to find out how their boards recruit and assimilate new members. The work was conducted in response to anecdotal evidence that qualified novices often have difficulty finding board service opportunities, while the same group of seasoned individuals populates several local boards. Themes are identified specific to the acceptance of new nonprofit board members and we offer suggestions for facilitating placement. The work identifies needed board member skills specific to this community and explores related topics including training, fundraising, and the recruitment of organizational insiders.

Keywords: Nonprofit, board service, recruiting, volunteers, inclusiveness, board poisoning, appreciative inquiry.

INTRODUCTION

Imagine that you are a young professional with a promising career and demonstrated leadership skills. You want to get more involved in the community. So you contact the executive board of a nonprofit whose mission excites you. You are invited to coffee with a board member and treated politely. You have a sense that, despite rumors that a vacancy on the board exists, they may not be open to accepting an outsider. Since you are not independently wealthy and your social circles tend more toward the nightlife than the golf course, you begin to question whether or not this service opportunity is for you. Nonetheless, you try to remain optimistic and look forward to bringing your enthusiasm and skills to a board in need of new ideas. After three

* Colorado Technical University, Colorado Springs, Colorado, CO, USA.
E-mail: wakefields@me.com, robertson11102@yahoo.com, kwalp@coloradotech.edu

weeks, you realize that the call you have been waiting for will not come. You stop by the organization's offices only to learn that the board position was filled two weeks before. The new member is an older gentleman who serves on three other boards and has a well-known family name. Your disappointment leads you out of the nonprofit sector and instead of volunteering in your spare time, you decide to take up sky diving instead.

Qualified volunteers often struggle to find opportunities for board service, while a handful of experienced individuals populate multiple boards. While the selection of experienced, well-known community members for board service confers the benefits of lessons learned in other contexts, it can sometimes be beneficial to bring in new members. Potential benefits include fresh perspectives, diversity, improved technological savvy and an ability to connect with a younger generation of clientele.If our city's capable young people are unable to make meaningful contributions locally, there is concern among nonprofit and government officials that their energy and positive efforts will be lost to inactivity or relocation.This problem may contribute to the city's documented loss of young professionals in recent years (Colorado Springs Quality of Life Indicators, 2011; Operation 60thirtyfive, 2010). This report describes a studyconducted in support of Leadership Pikes Peak (LPP). The organization is dedicated to promoting civic engagement through training and is seeking to improve placement of its graduates on nonprofit boards. While the work is specific to boards in the City of Colorado Springs, Colorado, USA, it identifies considerations that apply in other contexts.

Leadership Pikes Peak

Founded in 1976, LPP trains adults for civic involvement, serving as a path to community engagement that encourages citizens to apply their talents and visions to community service (Leadership Pikes Peak - 30+ years of History, 2010; Saksa, 2011). Programs are tailored for people of different ages and experience levels(Leadership Pikes Peak: Empowering you to make a difference, 2011). These programs provide training, familiarity with local resources, and networking opportunities for community-minded citizens. Successful placement of LPP graduates is an area of concern for the organization.

Study Description & Scope

This study supported proposed efforts to better facilitate the entry of LPP course alumni into community leadership roles. It specifically targeted nonprofit board service. The work was requested in response to anecdotal evidence that talented individuals sometimes receive training from LPP and find themselves unable to secure opportunities to use these skills. The intent was to find out how qualified volunteers might gain entry into local nonprofit boards, thereby gaining experience and infusing the nonprofit sector with new ideas. To meet this intent, executives from ten nonprofit boards were interviewed, using an appreciative-inquiry inspired protocol designed to elicit explanations of how new members were recruited and selected, along with attitudes about infusions of "new blood." The research question answered was "What does it take to facilitate the acceptance and integration of new members onto nonprofit boards of directors?"

APPRECIATIVE INQUIRY

Appreciative Inquiry (AI) involves seeking out and developing the best in organizations and people through the exploration of the things that bring life into communities and organizations at their best (Cooperrider & Whitney, 2005). AI is a narrative-based mode of inquiry grounded in constructivism, simultaneity, collaborative development of an organization's story, linkages between vision and action, and social ties (Cooperrider & Whitney, 2005). It fosters what Thatchenkery and Metzker (2006) call appreciative intelligence and can also be viewed as a "Shadow process" (Fitzgerald, Oliver, & Hoxsey, 2010). AI is both a method and a philosophy.

METHOD

The method lends itself to action research cycles consisting of the "four D's': Discover, Dream, Design, Destiny" (Cooperrider, 2001, 2002; Cooperrider & Whitney, 2005; Kovaleski, 2008; Royal, 2006). Discovery is accomplished through interviews and group discussions. The dream phase generates a collective vision of the organization, as it should be. Design centers on development of initiatives and prototypes to bring the dreams into being, while destiny involves coming up with action plans to launch initiatives (Kovaleski, 2008). Royal (2006) advocates the use of AI to move beyond past conflicts, emphasizing the careful use of language in framing studies and asking questions. AI has demonstrated success in the airline and shipping industries, and in the formation of religious coalitions (Cooperrider & Whitney, 2005). The method lends itself to large group interventions, although smaller scale applications are not uncommon.

PHILOSOPHY

AI generates a sense of wonder surrounding what works well (Zandee & Cooperrider, 2008), creating enthusiasm throughout an organization by turning its members' collective focus towards shared vision. It represents a shift away from critical thinking and problem-oriented approaches. AI is said to influence cultural influences at all levels of society because circumstances, behaviors, and attitudes affecting inclusion are addressed at all levels (Royal, 2006). Examination of past failures is discarded in favor of identifying and building on strength. Cooperrider (2001) stresses the power of the human imagination and claims that envisioning a desired future enables people to work collaboratively toward shared goals. While some suggest AI overlooks negative issues, its advocates claim most problems correct themselves when we build upon the positive.

METHODOLOGY

The AI method of "Discover, Dream, Design, and Destiny" (Cooperrider, 2001, 2002; Royal, 2006) applies to this study. The discovery portion consisted of discussion with the client, internet and academic research, and interviews. The dream phase began with interview data describing subjects' visions for diverse, inclusive boards that effectively integrate new members and are sustainable over the long term. Diversity and inclusiveness in this context mean that board service is open to people of varying races, ages, and backgrounds. This study identifies key findings that LPP can use to inform the continuation of the dream phase and carry forward into the design phase of the AI methodology, as the organization moves forward with efforts to improve board placement for its graduates. The destiny phase of the AI cycle is left as an area for further study.

PROCEDURES

Table 1 contextualizes the process using the four- D model. Ten interviews were conducted using a six question, AI-inspired protocol designed collaboratively with the LPP Executive Director. The intent was to gain insights concerning each board's diversity,receptivity to new members, needed skills and experience, and any tools or training that might be helpful. Upon completion of each interview, the investigators reviewed their field notes and entered data into an analysis spreadsheet, separated by question and color-coded to facilitate the identification of themes. Themes were grouped according to the frequency with which they featured in the interview results and then examined by question and in aggregate. Consensus between the two investigators was used to improve validity (Rahman, 2008).

Table 1. Research Process

Appreciative Inquiry	Actions	Products
Discover	-Entry -Background Research -Question Formulation	-Interview Protocol -IRB Application -Informed Consent Letter -Permission Letter -Literature Reviews -Confidential interview recordings and notes (begin)
	-Interviews -Notes	-Confidential interview recordings and notes (completed)
	-Analysis	-Themes

| Dream (beginning) | -Final Report | -Final Report
-Preparation of final briefing
-Key knowledge points supporting LPP actions to improve placement |
| Dream (continuation) Design & Destiny | -Follow on actions | -Beyond the scope of this study |

Table contents are the authors' original work

Participants, representing ten different organizations, were chosen with assistance from the Executive Director of LPP. The list included a broad range of nonprofits, chosen to maximize variation in organization size, demographics, mission, and diversity. Of the ten subjects, nine were Executive Directors or CEOs, with one Board President responding. 60% were male and no minority members are believed to be included, although racial demographics were not collected. While the results provide a good starting point for understanding the Colorado Springs nonprofit board service environment, additional work is needed to support any efforts to apply these findings in other contexts.

RESULTS & INTERPRETATION

Findings are presented categorically and in aggregate. This approach accommodates overlap in the responses to different questions. Discussion of the technical skills and talents of prospective members dominates the responses to several questions. Yet when the data is taken in aggregate, it appears social skills are equally if not more important. The following paragraphs address each category of response individually, then explain findings derived from an aggregate data analysis.

Strengths and Training

When asked about board member strengths and efforts to preserve and expand on these strengths, most respondents identified specific technical skills, with passion for themission running a close second. Three respondents indicated prior experience in the organization was a plus. Comments specific to training pertained to effective board member orientation, varying emphasis of training among successive board presidents, and the productive use of consultants. The greatest strengths of local boards are the members' skills and passion for the mission.

Skills and Recruiting

When asked if boards looked for specific skills or representation of various groups and how recruiting was done,70% indicated specific skills and talents were sought. Word of mouth recruiting via social and professional circles was noted, as was diversity-focused recruiting, comprising one organization's entire strategy. Some boards replace departing members with people from the same professions, while others track needed skills, or fill vacancies by word of mouth or referrals. Some religious organizations' bylaws allow only individuals from local churches to serve. The need for specific skills dominates responses to the question of recruiting, although the wide variation among selection methods is noteworthy.

Successful Integration

When asked to give an example of the successful integration of a new member, many respondents spoke with admiration of someone who made a positive difference. In one case, the subject recounted the unique insights of his board's first ethnic minority member, who shed light on the organization's failure to reach a particular demographic. Another subject described someone who brought in leadership skills and shaped the organization to be more professional. Many of the stories reflected serendipitous combinations of new members' skills with organizational needs. Again, skills and talents of the board member in question overshadowed other themes.

Challenges

When asked about challenges for bringing new people into their organizations and for ideas concerning tools or training that might be helpful, respondents identified training as a challenge. Board roles and responsibilities, a closely related topic, were mentioned by three of the ten respondents. Specifically, new member familiarity with expectations and fiduciary responsibilities was helpful. Conducting training at retreats and meetings was also effective. Nonprofit trainingcourses were praised, as were observing meetings prior to becoming a voting member, and orientations for new members. Making sure new board members understand their roles were important.

Prior Service in the Organization

Asking if most board members had previously worked in the organization and how people were recruited yielded responses indicating inclusion of insiders was common. Many members first served on committees or did volunteer work or special studies. Four subjects indicated strong insider participation on their boards, with some preference for recruiting volunteers who understood the mission and/or operations. Yet three of the organizations did not frequently included insiders. Stated reasons inciuded concern for losing talented individuals from the volunteer pool and one organization's very limited use of volunteers due to liability. In some cases, people were directly recruited if they had specific skills or backgrounds, such as legal or financial expertise. Two respondents indicated their boards were a mixture of insiders and outsiders.

Storytelling

Finally, we asked respondents for stories about people who made them feel welcome or sought to get them involved.This question frequently led back to LPP, with several respondents specifically crediting the organization or its Executive Director personally. Figure 1 shows the sources of inspiration described, ordered according to the number of subjects who mentioned them.

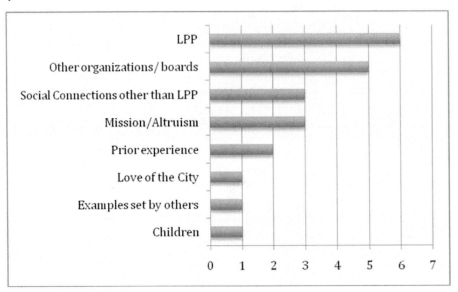

Fig. 1. Sources of Inspiration

Figure is the authors' original work and depicts data from the Study.

AGGREGATE FINDINGS

Aggregation of the responses across all questions suggests the most common topics of discussion were skills and talents, along with prior experience in the organization. Nine of ten subjects mentioned recruiting for specific board member skills. Nine subjects considered prior experience with the organization a plus, emphasizing passion for the mission. Figure 2 summarizes themes identified across all questions and the number of respondents who mentioned each.

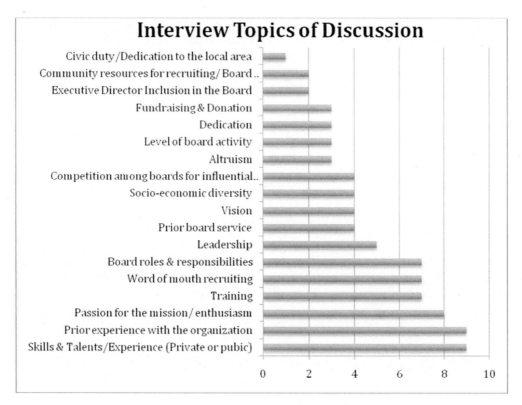

Fig. 2. Number of Interviews Containing Each Theme

Figure is the authors' original work and depicts data from the study.

The Role of Skills in Board Selection

Skills and prior experience with the organization featured in nine of ten interviews. Only one subject indicated his board did not actively seek specific skills. Finance, marketing, and business competence were noted, but social skills were emphasized; board members were expected to have outgoing personalities and get along with others. Social skills in this context did not refer to the extent of one's connections, but rather to personality traits and the ability to work with others. A preference for those with experience serving on other boards was also apparent. Of the four respondents who mentioned prior board service, all considered it beneficial because it facilitated the understanding of expectations or because of associated social connections. Figure 3 identifies specific skills and attributes suggested by respondents.

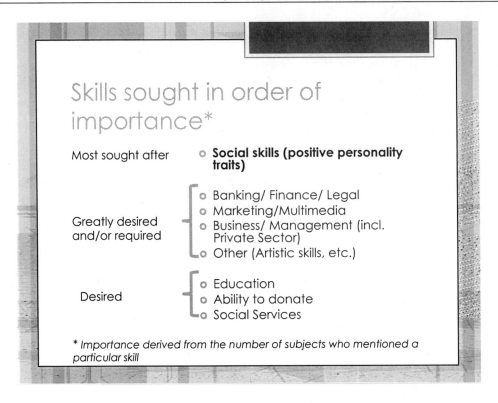

Fig. 3. Skills Identified by Interview Subjects

Figure is the authors' original work and depicts data from the study.

The bulk of board member recruiting in these organizations is done by word of mouth, with seven of ten subjects acknowledging the practice. Members often nominate people whom they know personally. Most subjects indicated board terms of service range from one to three years, emphasizing members' interpersonal skills and commitment. One subject noted how the personality of her board had changed over time as different social circles dominated. Another suggested the need for a more formal mechanism to match vacancies to those with the ability and inclination to serve. While the literature suggests the existence of board banks and placement organizations, we found little evidence of their use in Colorado Springs.

The Mission

Eight of ten subjects emphasized board members' interest in their organization's mission. Applicants are expected to genuinely care about and understand the organization's purpose, something very important to the leaders we spoke with.

Those applying without prior board service or an in-depth knowledge of the mission are often asked to serve on committees first. Some prospective board members work for a year or more on committees or studies before selection. One board only accepts members from local businesses and non-profits in its own industry. Volunteering on a committee allows the new member to gain experience and allows the organization's leadership to determine if the person is a good fit for board service before both parties make a long-term commitment to one another.

Training

As noted above, training is a common topic of interest, with four of ten subjects noting difficulty training new members. One subject noted there is never sufficient time to train new arrivals because board members tend to be very busy people. Some boards conduct retreats, while others offer orientations. When board members lack experience, the Executive Director may even educate them himself.

Money and Influence

Fundraising and individual philanthropy were mentioned in only three interviews, although one subject indicated his organization's board was experiencing a shift from emphasizing oversight to fundraising. Ensuring new members understand cash flow and funding requirements can be challenging. People with the resources to provide financial backing have a clear advantage in gaining placement, as do those whose names are well known in the community. Four subjects mentioned competition among boards for influential community members. Combining the topics of money and influence into a single category suggests money and/or influence is an important consideration for 60% of the organizations considered. This combined result is more consistent with the literature than overt discussions of fundraising alone would suggest.

CONCLUSION & IMPLICATIONS

Two action items were presented to LPP for consideration, one to be undertaken at the individual level, the other in the broader nonprofit community. It is important that individuals seeking service on nonprofit boards of directors adequately assess their own motivations, qualifications, and availability to serve. At the aggregate level, we suggested the development of a more formal process to bridge the gap between boards and qualified applicants. The combination of individual introspection and larger group efforts to improve placement is expected to generate improvements in the ratio of placements to board vacancies when measured over time.

Each person seeking to serve must take an objective, realistic inventory of what he has to offer and consider taking actions to strengthen his qualifications. Such an assessment begins with a series of reflections regarding readiness to serve. Items to be addressed include time commitments, flexibility, accepting less glamorous tasks, accountability, and other aspects of service. If a prospective member is able to answer yes to these kinds of questions, it is appropriate to begin thinking about selection of the path that is most likely to yield positive results. For example, if one is intent on becoming a board member and this assessment suggests readiness to serve, it makes sense to find an organization where one's skills are needed or to volunteer with an organization that recruits from within. We believe that such an exercise will be beneficial in most if not all cases.

Paths to board service vary. Most of the organizations canvassed put incoming members directly on their boards only if they have relevant past experience, financial backing, a needed skill, and/or a name that is highly respected. Some nonprofits allow members to assume board positions only when they have spent significant time in the organization, while others avoid recruiting from their volunteer pools. Those aspiring to board service in a particular organization might be well served by understanding how its current board members were selected. Obtaining such knowledge up front can enable volunteers to select organizations where they are likely to be chosen, rather than spending time volunteering in an organization that recruits outsiders exclusively.

Some findings were surprising. The frequency with which LPP was mentioned as a source of inspiration and/or placement was noteworthy, as was the absence of apparent reliance on existing community resources that list board placement among their functions. We expected fundraising to feature more strongly in the interview data. This dearth of overt concern with financial matters may be the product of how the questions were asked, as AI emphasizes positive material, making it easy to avoid awkward topics. It may also stem from the respondents' relationships with LPP, encouraging more optimistic and inclusive language because of the client's status. It may also be that many of those surveyed were not genuinely concerned about the fundraising aspects of board recruitment. Grouping money and influence into a single category generated results more in line with our expectations, with six of ten organizations making some reference to one or both items. The relationship between name recognition, philanthropy, and fundraising is left as an area for further study.

Though we expected socioeconomic diversity to play a significant role, few respondents specifically mentioned recruiting minorities or efforts to mirror their supported client populations. This finding may stem from the racially and socioeconomically homogeneous nature of the sample or it may reflect a disconnect between nonprofit sector leadership and minority clients. Yet one subject noted diversity as the sole recruiting criterion in effect and another expressed a need to extend his organization's reach beyond its wealthy neighborhood. The role of race, socioeconomic, and geographic diversity in nonprofit board placement is suggested as an area for further study.

The findings of this study can be used to inform individuals seeking appointment to nonprofit boards, increasing their likelihood of selection. They can also be used to inform future LPP efforts to improve placement. As a qualitative inquiry into Colorado Springs' nonprofit board environment, it offers insights specific to this community,suggesting a need for improved board placement mechanisms. During the three months since the completion of this study, LPP has engaged in creative efforts to improve board placement. Chief among these was an event titled "Speed Boarding," wherein current board members seeking new participants engaged in brief exchanges with prospective members, modeled after speed dating, wherein a similar procedure enables unmarried adults to interact with numerous prospective mates in the course of a single evening. This event was very well received, although the number of placements resulting from the effort had yet to be determined.

ACKNOWLEDGEMENT

The authors would like to thank Susan Saksa, the Executive Director of Leadership Pikes Peak, Colorado springs for her support throughout the study in data collection, permission to presents the study at ICMC 2012 and publish in the conference preceedings.

REFERENCES

Colorado Springs Quality of Life Indicators. (2011). Colorado Springs, Colorado, USA: Pikes Peak United Way.

Cooperrider, D. L. (2001). Positive image, positive action: The affirmative basis of organizing. In D. L. Cooperrider, P. F. Sorensen, T. F. Yaeger & D. Whitney (Eds.), Appreciative Inquiry: an emerging direction for organization development. Champaign, IL: Stipes Publishing, L.L.C.

Cooperrider, D. L. (Producer). (2002, 8 March 2011) AI training module - Power Point slides. The best picks of AI tools. PowerPoint presentation retrieved from *http://appreciativeinquiry.case.edu/practice/toolsPackDetail.cfm?coid=1167*

Cooperrider, D. L., & Whitney, D. (2005). Appreciative Inquiry: A positive revolution in change. San Francisco, CA: Berrett-Koehler Publishers.

Fitzgerald, S. P., Oliver, C., & Hoxsey, J. (2010). Appreciative Inquiry as a shadow process. Journal of Management Inquiry, 19(220), 220-233.

Kovaleski, D. (2008). [Meeting Summary]. Associations Meetings, 20-25.

Leadership Pikes Peak: Empowering you to make a difference. (2011) Retrieved 7 July 2011, 2011, from *http://www.leadershippikespeak.org/*

Rahman, M. A. (2008). Some trends in the praxis of participatory action research The SAGE Handbook of action research: Participatory inquiry and practice (Second ed., pp. 49-62). Los Angeles: SAGE Publications.

Reason, P., & Bradbury, H. (2008). Action Research Participative Inquiry and Practice. (2nd ed). Los Angeles. CA: SAGE

Royal, C. L. (2006). Organization development and Appreciative Inquiry: A transformative next step for social justice and diversity practitioners NTL Organization Development Handbook (Author's draft ed.).

Saksa, S. (2011). Possible project for CTU action research class July 2011. Proposed student practicum project. Leadership Pikes Peak. Colorado Springs, CO.

Thatchenkery, T., & Metzker, C. (2006). Appreciative intelligence: Seeing the mighty oak inside the acorn. San Francisco: Berrett-Koehler Publishers, Inc.

Zandee, D. P., & Cooperrider, D. L. (2008). Appreciable worlds, inspired inquiry. In P. Reason & H. Bradbury (Eds.), The SAGE handbook of Action Research participative inquiry and practice (2nd ed., pp. 190-196). Los Angeles: SAGE Publications.

Appreciative Sharing of Knowledge (ASK) Research Case: Undergraduate College (USA)

James T. Colvin, Jr.* and James M. Thorpe**

ABSTRACT

Two research scholars, acting in the role of co-researchers, met with management, faculty and staff members, at an anonymous educational institution, referred to as Undergraduate College, to conduct a Human Resource Management (HRM) intervention. They obtained unprecedented access to conduct face-to-face interviews at all levels. They employed the Appreciative Sharing of Knowledge (ASK) methodology to explore core competencies and to help co-create a shared consensus of a new future at Undergraduate College. Their approach was to affirm what was working in the organization. The researchers briefed, interviewed and surveyed participants to identify organizational competencies based on a positive personal experience or significant accomplishment by each participant. A small groupof 15 participants, six males and nine females, were interviewed using storytelling to leverage knowledge management for the organization.Study outcomes uncovered several areas of improvements including accountability, student focus, retention and communications.

Keywords: Appreciative intelligence, appreciative sharing of knowledge, knowledge management, positive psychology.

INTRODUCTION

The research team offered Undergraduate College, the client organization, processes to help effectively identify opportunities and implementation strategies to reach their desired future state. The researchers intervened to conduct a general appreciative inquiry. The purpose of the project was to conduct an appreciative intelligence (AI) intervention with a client organization to experienceAppreciative Sharing of Knowledge(ASK)as researchers and contribute to the organization. ASK discovers

* Research Scholar, Doctoral Program, Colorado Technical University, Colorado Springs, CO. USA
**Research Scholar, Doctoral Program, Colorado Technical University, Colorado Springs, CO USA.
Email: jamescolvin1122@comcast.net, mark4thorpe@yahoo.com

the talents and competencies at work in the organization, locates knowledge-sharing practices already in existence, and enhances the values and behaviors contributing to collective knowledge (Thatchenkery, 2008). It involves seeing the best of *what is* in order to provide the impetus for imagining *possibilities* that is, the future opportunities. It examines the affirming side of an organization…an affirmation of what is good within the organization itself (Cummings &Worley, 2009).

Organization

An "Open System" view of the organization.

First order of business was to develop a reasonable working knowledge of the antecedent factors before starting process consulting & intervention. Thatchenkery (2008) identifies four characteristics of knowledge sharing organizations:

1. Mutual Respect
2. Norms around knowledge sharing
3. Enthusiasm
4. Appreciation

The researchers found that these values existed at Undergraduate College and had senior management support. They decided that *Human Process Intervention*, at the group level,was the appropriate OD Intervention to employ at the Undergraduate College.

Problem

The challenge was to create a positive knowledge-sharing culture in the client organization. The Knowledge management paradigm can be differentiated as *proactive and reactive* (Thatchenkery, 2008). Traditionally, the *reactive* approach is the dominant approach. It examines what went wrong in the organization. Examples include case studies and after action reports (Thatchenkery, 2008). The *proactive* approach, on the other hand, considers what an individual, group or organization must do to reach a desired state or achieve a specific vision (Thatchenkery, 2008). The researchers chose the proactive approach to *ASK* to value and appreciate *what is*, to affirm what is working, and to identify knowledge enablers (Thatchenkery, 2008).

Need for the Study

Managing organizational change is a process, often very tough to achieve. Yet organizations manage to achieve it every day. What are the cultural characteristics of organizations that are open to change? What are the internal mechanisms that drive organizational change and how can we capture those factors to affect change (Cummings & Worley, 2009)? These are the main questions the researchers set out to answer in their sessions with the President, Dean, faculty and staff ofUndergraduate College.

Objective

The primary objective of the project was to co-create a system where people shared internal knowledge unique to the client organization by identifying those knowledge enablers (KEs) or life-giving forces (core values) and knowledge infrastructure (organizational) factors (KIFs) that leverage knowledge management for strategic change, and then to take that knowledge and create implementation teams to affect desired outcomes in areas such as communications, integrity and teamwork.

Description of the Model

The researchers chose to use the AI knowledge management tools ASK which combines the principles of AI, social constructionism, and knowledge management (Thatchenkery, 2008). "The ASK methodology of organizational analysis typically consists of seven steps:

1. *Setting the stage for appreciative sharing of knowledge.* It comprises of presenting the appreciative knowledge-sharing paradigm and negotiate top management commitment and support.

According to Thatchenkery, the first step involves getting a strong buy-in from top management and involving as many internal staff a spossible to plan and run the ASK process, ...starting with a top-down approach and culminating with "a cadre of knowledge ambassadors within the organization" ... (Thatchenkery, 2008)

2. *Paired Interviews (Interview #1).*The researchers use the story-telling approach to understand what worked in the past. However, instead of paired interviews, they did small group interviews. To accomplish this,the internal researcher sent out email with interview questions, several days ahead of the meeting, explaining the intervention and eliciting positive stories of successful knowledge sharing behaviors already occurring within the organization.

3. *Identify Knowledge Enablers (Interview #2).* Step three of ASK is identifying known and unknown knowledge enablers (KEs) (Thatchenkery, 2008)."A key question necessary for recognizing a knowledge enabler is: *What makes it possible to share knowledge, that is, what "enables" people to be open to participating in this process?*(Thatchenkery, 2008, p. 49)."

The researchers instructed participants on the ASK process and encouraged them to share positive stories with the entire group.

4. *Appreciative analysis(Matrix #1).* This step comprises of thematic analysis of Knowledge Enablers and to analyze the data using Knowledge Infrastructure Factors (KIFs).

Step four is designed to build on the KEs analyzing them with respect to the organization(Thatchenkery, 2008).According to Thatchenkery, a review of knowledge management literature identifies the following KIFs: decision-making, organizational practices and routines, incentives for knowledge sharing, leadership, and communication (Thatchenkery, 2008).

5. *Construct possibility propositions (Matrix #2).* Step five looks towards the future using the ASK approach by constructing future-present scenario (FPS) or possibility proposition statements. Stated as if the future has come to the present, a FPS statement concretely describes with rich details a future desired state happening now (Thatchenkery, 2008).The FPS must meet the following three criteria/tests:

(1) Commitment – Does the data show evidence of a long-term commitment for making the scenario possible?

(2) Inspiration – Is there energy for people to carry out the new possibility?

(3) Groundedness – Is the future-present scenario realistic and plausible?

(Thatchenkery, 2008, p. 76)

6. *Consensually validate and rank the FPS statements.* This step involves exploring, evaluating, and validating the FPS statements. Once participants have written their FPS statements, they check them against the criteria of commitment, inspiration and groundedness in Step 5. "The validation is very much like the voice of the people in the organization and represents their carefully thought-out assessment of where the organization is ready to go and the extent of their willingness to contribute to make each of the future-present scenarios a reality (Thatchenkery, 2008, p. 92)."The researchers validated Step 6 using the criteria in Step 5. They developed an instrument, consisting of all 24 FPS statements,to consensually validate and rank the FPS statements. It included the three valencing questions with Likert scale to measure relative participant agreement or disagreement with the respective FPS statement.

7. *Forming an implementation Team and then execute.* In the final step, participants and knowledge ambassadors take ownership of the process for enacting continuous change. The researchers assigned Action Items from the FPS statements for each department. "advocates or sponsors for action items…take responsibility for the realization of the desired outcome. And senior managers provide input support and/or permission for initiating and/or executing future-present scenarios (Thatchenkery, 2008, p. 97)."The researchers recommended that senior management form implementation teams to act immediately on the findings and to leverage the positive momentum generated by the HRM intervention.

RESEARCH METHODOLOGY

Data Collection Devices/Instruments

The basic ASK paradigm views knowledge management as an opportunity to be embraced not as a problem to be solved. The researchers collected data using interviews, surveys & observations. They decided to collect primary data through small group interviews using the ASK methodology described above. They requested and received permission to record each interview session as it was being conducted.

The researchers began by asking each interviewee to share a positive story of something they did or had experienced. Then the researchers asked how did that particular experience make them feel? What did they learn from that experience? From each individual's story, the researchers asked the interviewees to identify what they believed to be KEs and KIFs. From those they created a list of both the KEs and the KIFs on a white board so all interviewees could see. Once the interviews were completed, the researchers had all interviewees narrow the list down to six KIFs and four KEs. They converted this data into a Matrix for Thematic Analysis of Organizational Data in order to further the process and make it easier for all interviewees to understand.

The group of interviewees began to present FPSs for each of the KEs and for each of the KIFs. From the interviewees responses the researchers built a Matrix for Constructing FPS Statements. From the interviewees FPS Statements the researchers created a twenty-four question survey. The survey was constructed for all employees to consensually validate and rank the FPSs.

With the matrices for Thematic Analysis of Organizational Data and Constructing FPS Statements, and the survey, the researchers thought they had the ideal data collection instruments to present their data in a comprehensive way, which the client organization could easily read and understand.

Sample Size (n) and Sampling

For the study, the researchers decided on a sample size (n) of approximately 15 people. It represented approximately fifty percent of the faculty & staff. These participants were made up of nine females and six males which consisted of the President, Dean, four Department Chairs, with the remaining consisting of faculty and staff. Participation of the college President and Dean being seemed to give validity to our study.

Rationale for Sample Size

The size and make-up of the group was right for the time given. It was ideal for capturing rich and in-depth responses from each participant and it allowed individuals enough time to respond to questions in whatever depth they desired. The group make-up was extremely important, allowing the researchers to encapsulate experiences from President to faculty members. This provided greater coverage of data collection.

Data Collection

The researchers used focus group interviews to collect data. Primary data was collected from face-to-face interviews with the researchers serving as instrument. The researchers asked participants to share a recent *positive* experience they had in the organization and to explain what made it a meaningful positive experience. The researchers also captured what participants learned from that experience.

Interview #1

On Wednesday, July 28, 2010, the researchers conducted their first intervention meetingat Undergraduate College. The focus group consisted of 15 executives, faculty and staff members. The researchers explained AI and that each individual would be participating in the ASK process. The researchers answered questions and ensured everyone understood the process before starting the interviews.

While interviews were being conducted, one researcher wrote the KEs and KIFs on a white board in the front of the classroom so all participants could view. After each interview, the interviewees were asked if they agreed to the KEs and KIFs that were recorded on the white board based. After unanimous agreement, the next participant was interviewed. With participant permission, all interviews were recorded with a digital audio recorder to ensure accuracy of data.The meeting went exceptionally, well.

Matrix #1

The researchers constructed Matrix #1 from the examples given in interview #1. They analyzed the data in Matrix #1 to identify several themes. These themes became the primary KEs. Then the researchers analyzed Matrix #1 using KIFs.

Interview #2

The researchers conducted the second interview meeting on Friday, August 13, 2010. It consisted of the same participants interviewed in the first meeting. The researchers had all participants create 24 FPS statements, which were placed in the second matrix for constructing FPS Statements. The researchers presented the matrix on an overhead projector. Additionally, the researchers constructed an FPS Statement Worksheet to guide andmanually capture responses during interviews.

Matrix #2

Matrix #2 guided construction of the FPS statements. From the FPS statements,the researchers created a survey to consensually validate and rank the FPSs, not only of the participants but also of the entire faculty and staff. The researchers placed the survey in every mailbox of employees who had one, regardless of their position. Once the survey was completed by the respondent, it was placed in the mailbox of the internal researcher.

The researchers had everyone prioritize, rank or rate each FPS Statement. The document, 1) identifies the 24 FPS statements, 2) lists the three questions above to evaluate and explore the potential of each FPS statement and 3) provides a score sheet with scale to measure/rate the importance of each FPS statement.

Results

After successfully collecting the data, the next step was to analyze the data and determine findings. For statistical analysis, the researchers used the electronic quantitative analysis software, Statistical Packages for the Social Sciences (SPSS), Student Version 17.0 for Windows. SPSS enabled the researchers to explore and crunch the numbers, and organize and present the data. The researchers used appreciative analysis to determine their findings.

First, the researchers took the 24 variables from Matrix#2 – created by combining the four KEs and six KIFs. They included:

- Leadership & Teamwork, Leadership & Recognition, Leadership & Integrity, and Leadership & Relevance;
- Communication & Teamwork, Communication & Recognition, Communication & Integrity, and Communication & Relevance;
- Job Placement & Teamwork, Job Placement & Recognition, Job Placement & Integrity, and Job Placement & Relevance;
- Retention & Teamwork, Retention & Recognition, Retention & Integrity, and Retention & Relevance;
- Accountability & Teamwork, Accountability & Recognition, Accountability & Integrity, and Accountability & Relevance; and finally
- Student Focus & Teamwork, Student Focus & Recognition, Student Focus & Integrity, and Student Focus & Relevance.

Then, the researchers constructed three SPSS data files, one for each of the three questions:

1. How much of an *ideal* is it? (How important is it?)

2. How much of it may already be *present*?

3. *How soon* do you want to see this happen?

Then they created "labels" for each variable within the database and coded "values" to identify each measure within the Likert scale. For example, the first variable in the "Ideal data file," was *labeled*,"Leadership & Teamwork," and the Likert scale *values* were coded: 5=Very Much, 4=More, 3=Somewhat, 2=Very Little, and 1= Not Much. The same Likert scale *labels* and *values* were used for Q2 and the "Present Data File."However, for Q3 and the third data file, although the *labels* remained the same, the Likert scale *values* did not. For this database, the *values* were coded: 1=Long Term (within two years), 2=Short Term (within 6 months) and 3=Immediately.Now that the data files were properly constructed and the responses properly entered, the researchers ran a simple Frequency Distribution to analyze the data. They selected descriptive statistics for all 24 variables and used the *summation* function.

The researchers started with an analysis of question#one (Q1), How much of an *ideal* **is** it? They used sampling Tables and Charts of the frequency distribution for the variable *Leadership and Teamwork*. They found that the total number of respondents (n) was 13. They also noted that of the13 respondents, there were only10 responses. The reason is that not everyone replied to the question. Thus, for Q1,"How much of an *ideal* **is** it?" there were three missing responses to all 24 FPS variables.

Looking at the 10 responses to Q1, for the variable *Leadership & Teamwork*,the researchers saw that, of the five values on the Likert scale: 5 = Very Much, 4 = More, 3 = Somewhat, 2 = Very Little, and 1 = Not Much,eight respondents indicated, *Leadership & Teamwork* are **very much** an ideal and two respondents indicated, *Leadership & Teamwork* are **more** of an *ideal* at the Undergraduate College.

Q2. How much of it may already be *present*?

Looking at responses to Q2,"How much of it may already be *present?*" for the variable *Leadership & Teamwork*, against Likert scale values were:5=Very Much, 4=More, 3=Some what, 2 = Very Little, and 1 = Not Much. Analyzing the responses, the researchers saw the total number of respondents (n) is 13. However, there are only12 responses with one missing value to the 24 FPS variables. The researchers noted that one respondent indicated that *very little Leadership & Teamwork* is currently present; three indicates that it is *somewhat* present; four indicates that it is *more* present; and four indicate that it is *very much* present.

Q3. *How soon* do you want to see this happen?

Looking at responses to Q3,"*How soon* do you want to see this happen?"the Likert scale values were 3 = Immediately, 2=Short Term (within six months), and 1=Long Term (within 2 years). Analyzing the data,again the total number of respondents (n) is 13. However, there are six total responses with seven missing to the 24 FPS variables. This is because seven of the eight respondents, who had previously marked the variable, *Leadership and Teamwork,* as either more or very much present, indicated they did not reply to Q3. However, of the six responses,one respondent indicatess/he wanted to see this happen in the *long term*; two indicated they wanted it to happen in the *short term*; and three *indicated* they wanted to see this happen *immediately*.

DIAGNOSIS AND ANALYSIS

Organizational Analysis

The researchers analyzed and interpreted the data, and related findings to the organizational analysis model, ASK. To begin, the researchers looked to the **Summary Frequency Statistics** of all 24 FPS variables for the three-valencing questions:

Q1. How much of an *ideal* is it?

Q2. How much of it may already be *present*?

Q3. *How soon* do you want to see this happen?

By totaling responses to each variable, the researchers could rank and prioritize the FPSs.

Summary Findings for Q1, How Much?

Analyzing responses, the researchers saw the total number of respondents (n) was 13. Of the13 respondents, there were 10 valid responses and three missing responses, indicating 77% (10 of 13) replied to Q1. Looking at the 10 valid responses and using the Likert scale values: 5=Very Much, 4=More, 3=Somewhat, 2=Very Little, and 1= Not Much,the highest possible Sum score is 50. Examining the 24 variables representing the FPSs for Q1, the highest Sum score is 50 and the lowest Sum score is 47, a spread of only 3points. The researchers noted that the difference was very small, which might suggest that generally, respondents felt close to the same about Q1. Additionally, they noted the Sum scores tended towards the high end of the scale for all 24 variables. One may safely conclude that generally, respondents felt that all 24 variables represent *ideals* for the Undergraduate College.

The highest scores (50 of 50 points)from the interview data pertained to the themes *Accountability & Integrity* and *Student Focus & Relevance*.100% said that these two themes were very much an *ideal* at the Undergraduate College.However, the themes around *Communications* and *Student Focus* stood out as themes the Undergraduate College may wish to revisit.

Summary Findings for Q2, Already Present?

Analyzing responses, the researchers saw the total number of respondents (n) was 13. Of the13 respondents, there were 12 valid responses and one missing response, indicating92 % (12 of 13) replied to Q2. Looking at the 12 valid responses and using the Likert scale values: 5=Very Much, 4=More, 3=Somewhat, 2=Very Little, and 1= Not Much, the highest possible Sum score is 60. Examining the 24 variables representing the FPSs for Q2, the highest Sum score is 55 and the lowest Sum score is 33, a spread of 22points. The researchers noted that the difference was very large, which might suggest that generally, respondents hold a wide range of views in response to Q2.

Additionally, they noted the *mode score* was 44 which tended towards the upper two-thirds of the scale for all 24 variables. So one might conclude that generally, respondents felt that most ofthe 24 variables were more presentat the Undergraduate College.

The highest scores from the interview data (55 of 60 points) pertained to the theme *Retention & Integrity.* 85% (11 of 13) said that this theme was **more** *present* or **very much** *present* at the Undergraduate College. Again, the themes around *Communications* and *Student Focus* also stood out as themes the Undergraduate College might wish to revisit. The themes *Student Focus & Recognition* and *Student Focus & Relevance* probably required immediate attention!

Summary Findings for Q3 How Soon?

Analyzing responses, the researchers saw the total number of respondents (n) was 13. Of the13 responses, there are at least six and at most 10 valid responses. Additionally, there are at least three and at most seven missing responses. Looking at the 10 valid responses and using the Likert scale values: 3=Immediately, 2=Short Term (within six months), and 1= Long Term (within 2 years), the highest possible Sum score is 30 (10x3). Finally, examining the 24 variables representing the FPSs for Q3, the highest Sum score is 24 and the lowest score is 14, a spread of 10 points. The researchers noted that the delta was rather large, which might suggest that generally, respondents hold a wide range of views in response to Q3. Additionally, the *mode score* is 19, which tends towards the upper two-thirds of the scale for all 24 variables. Therefore,one may conclude that generally, respondents felt that most of the 24 variables should be implemented in the short term (within six months) at the Undergraduate College.

The highest scores from the interview data (50 of 50 points) pertained to the themes *Accountability & Integrity* and *Student Focus & Relevance.* 100% of the respondents said these two themes were very much an ideal at the Undergraduate College. Again,*Communications* and *Student Focus* stood out as themes the Undergraduate College may wish to revisit.

RECOMMENDATIONS

Organizations are built to change. Without change, industry leaders will lose their competitiveadvantage. "Researchershave identifiedanumberofcontingenciespresent in the change situation that affect intervention success (Cummings & Worley, 2009, p. 152)." These include readiness for change, capability to change, cultural context, and capabilities of the change agent (Cummings &Worley, 2009). To overcome "resistance to change,"the researchers highly recommend obtaining senior management support and getting employees involved. The researchers recommend the following change programs at the Undergraduate College:

Theme 1. Accountability & Integrity

FPS: Our organization maintains 100% compliance in both our internal and external audits.

Action: Appoint an implementation team with trained facilitators and knowledge ambassadors to start the organizational change process.

Time Line: Short Term (within six months)

Program: Techno-structural Intervention: Employee Involvement. "... employee involvement can lead to quicker, more responsive decisions, continuous performance improvements, and greater employee flexibility, commitment, and satisfaction (Cummings &Worley, 2009, p. 350)."

Theme 2. Student Focus & Relevance

FPS: For all subjects, our instructors captivate each student in a way that keeps them coming back to class excited to learn what is next.

Action: Appoint an implementation team with trained facilitators and knowledge ambassadors to start the organizational change process.

Time Line: Short Term (within six months)

Program: Human Resources ManagementIntervention: Performance Management. "Performance management is an integrated process of defining, assessing, and reinforcing employee work behaviors and outcomes.(Cummings &Worley, 2009, p.421)."

Theme 3. Retention & Integrity

FPS: Our organization maintains 100% accuracy in reporting all student drops in the day and month they drop.

Action: Appoint an implementation team with trained facilitators and knowledge ambassadors to start the organizational change process.

Time Line: Immediately!

Program: Human Process Intervention: Organization Process Approaches (Cummings &Worley, 2009)

Theme 4. Communication & Recognition

FPS: We leverage all organizational communication systems to ensure individuals are recognized and that the entire organization is aware of each employee's contributions.

Action: Appoint an implementation team with trained facilitators and knowledge ambassadors to start the organizational change process.

Time Line: Immediately!

Program: Human Resources Management Intervention: Performance Management. "...performance management includes practices and methods for goal setting, performance appraisal, and reward systems (Cummings &Worley, 2009, p. 421)."

CONCLUSIONS

In conclusion, the researchers demonstrated their ability to conduct a general appreciative inquiry with a client organization. They implemented the ASK organizational change process by conducting an HRM Intervention at the Undergraduate College. Their approach affirmed, "what is working" in the organization. They were granted access to conduct face-to-face interviews with management, faculty and staff members. A small group of 15 participants, six males and nine females, were interviewed. Participants shared positive personal experiences or significant accomplishment using story telling to identify four KEs – *Team Work, Recognition, Integrity*, and *Relevance* and six KIFs – *Leadership, Communication, Job Placement, Retention, Accountability*, and *Student Focus*. The group constructed a 4x6 matrix of 24 FPS statements. Then the group consensually validated and ranked the FPS statements using appreciative and statistical analysis with the electronic software SPSS, to determine where the organization should go and its willingness to make each FPS a reality. The FPS statements were ranked and prioritized and the researchers recommended Undergraduate College create implementation teams to achieve its strategic change.Implementation of the recommendations will provide immediate positive change and possibly, instill a continuous change process at Undergraduate College.

REFERENCES

Cummings, Thomas G. & Worley, Christopher G. (2009). *Organization Development & Change* (9th ed.). Mason, OH: South-Western Cengage Learning.

Norušis, Marija J., (2008). *SPSS Statistics 17.0 Guide to Data Analysis.* Upper Saddle River, NJ: Prentice Hall, Inc.

SPSS, Inc., (2009). Statistical Packages for Social Sciences Statistics, Student Version 17.0 for Windows Operating System: 2010 Pearson Education, Inc.

Thatchenkery, Tojo (2008). *Appreciative Sharing of Knowledge: Leveraging Knowledge Management for Strategic Change.* Chagrin Falls, OH: Taos Institute Publishing.

Thatchenkery, Tojo & Metzker, Carol (2006). *Appreciative Intelligence: Seeing the Mighty Oak in the Acorn.* San Francisco, CA: Berrett-Koehler Publishers, Inc.

Simplified Cost-Effective Strategic Artificial and Business Intelligence at Gulf Shores Company

Asma Qureshi* and Jeff Stevens**

ABSTRACT

Business intelligence (BI) has been successful in eliminating the traditional decision support systems at Gulf Shores Company (GSC) to improve efficiency and effectiveness in service delivery and eliminate human errors. Such improved organizations are better prepared to respond quickly to threats and opportunities. Artificial intelligence (AI) supports an organization's BI processes by simplifying them and making them more cost effective so that, under certain conditions, automated decisions and alerts can be used. Introducing AI into GSC processes would also give them the capability of making decisions in real time. GSC could implement the BI/AI combination in complex settings to address a wide range of risks specific to their industry. The case study describes the logic for implementing AI in petroleum industries, based on an intelligent system that helps offshore platforms start up, and explains how it can be applied in other industries such as medical billing.

Keywords: Business intelligence, artificial intelligence, robotics, intelligent system, neuro networks, fuzzy logic.

INTRODUCTION

Gulf Shores Company (GSC) has recently been faced with major budget cuts, downsizing, and acquisitions that have affected research and development as well as its ability to respond to threats and opportunities through business intelligence. Critical reasons for the lack of robust expansion of BI are that the traditional BI approach is not cost effective and barriers exist between IT and other organizational departments. This GSC case study proposes that AI can assist in simplifying BI processes and making them more cost effective. The business case will explain the applicability of AI and

* Colorado Technical University, Colorado Springs, Colorado, USA.
**Jones International University, USA.
E-mail: androidengineering21@yahoo.com

BI in various types of neural networks. The purpose of the case study is to consider the hypothesis (Ha) that implementing artificial intelligence with business intelligence can simplify business intelligence and make it cost effective.

Current trends at GSC make feasible the implementation of a BI-AI link to increase the capability of integrating features ranging from neural networks to fuzzy logic. To simplify discussion of this complex link, the application of BI and AI in the petroleum industry will be focused on separately. A petroleum business plan provides the most complex BI infrastructure in which high-risk solutions must be found for complex problems. The petroleum industry provides the best business case because of the large amounts of data available for use as a learning tool to increase the bottom line. The data are captured through permanent new sensors through which AI captures the data in real time, providing vital information on critical issues inside the wells, thus allowing for real-time analysis and decision making. AI is a cost-effective approach for GSC and other corporations, with low maintenance of a forecasting mechanism to prevent catastrophic events, for example, future oil spills at GSC. Neural processing in AI provides real-time sensory data to determine potential weak points in the system and repair them at the time of discovery. This approach is revolutionary in forecasting problems while addressing issues.

Later sections include the GSC case study outline, including the company infrastructure methodology, data analysis, results, and conclusions from this study. GSC currently does not provide real-time monitoring of oil rigs with reports on damaged oil rig gaskets and oil spills. The company could improve its BI systems by implementing a revolutionary AI infrastructure.

CASE STUDY GSC HYPOTHESIS

H0 = AI cannot be implemented to bring about cost-effective BI at GSC.

Ha = AI can be implemented to bring about cost-effective BI at GSC.

The purpose of this study of GSC is to test the hypothesis concerning implementing the AI-BI link in facility oil rigs. If H0 is supported, the conclusion would be not to implement the simplified cost-effective strategic AI-BI link in the facility rigs.

GSC REVOLUTIONARY AI INFRASTRUCTURE

AI infrastructure is a revolutionary improvement to BI systems in numerous areas. The AI can generate reports on real-time high-level issues, analyzing and predicting the natural gas production in the United States and internationally for the next 10 years or more. Fuzzy logic provides the means to calculate with words and represent any uncertainty caused by the nature of some events. In petroleum industries, fuzzy logic could be used with a neural network to characterize a drilling reservoir analyze it for decision-making purposes (Partridge, 2010). Managers will be able to monitor oil rigs, and AI will deliver the capability to repair any problems in real time. The management level will be able to correct technical issues that concern geoscientists and petroleum engineers in the drilling reservoir and to monitor the deterioration of gaskets and repair or replace them as needed.

AI is subdivided into various expert systems, programs that have the information processing ability of experts in given scenarios. With the proliferation of personal computers and programs for designing AI applications, expert systems are within the reach of many business enterprises. However, some but not all AI applications are costly and energy consuming, but recommendable cost-effective applications for petroleum industries do exist. Professionals in this field need to understand the unique capabilities of expert systems and familiarize themselves with their applications (Turban, Sharda, & Delen, 2011). The primary components of expert systems should be their knowledge bases.

A knowledge base contains various objects with variables in certain fields (Mohaghegh, n.d.). The relation between these variables and objects are defined and coded as rules. For example, if a certain situation occurs, then a given step should follow. To make the knowledge base of an expert system compatible with AI software, each of the processes should be reduced to a more detailed logical sequence consisting of rules and alternatives. Although the simplest processes have decision paths, most alternative sets of logic are essential (Gallant, 1993; Kosko, 1992).

Knowledge bases are considerably complex. An inference engine controls the inner logic relating the facts and rules to user information. The direction of analysis might be either forward or backward, working either from the beginning logic to its conclusion or from the conclusion to the beginning logic. The inference engine prompts the computer to ask the user a question, and the answer determines alternatives to other questions and the results. The inference engine controls the AI speed whereas the knowledge base determines the actual content. The outcome should be expert views and information about a given possibility.

An artificial neural network is an information processing system that uses fuzzy logic. In the petroleum industry, it may be used to assist in accurate analysis of a detailed historical database. These techniques have several attributes of reasoning, such as discovery abstraction and association. According to the research, AI systems can address several issues at GSC that might be classified in two sections. The first is the AI neural network with full knowledge fusion to assist in choosing the best alternatives in complex dynamic cases. The second is optimization of AI, which is demonstrated in the surface facility in response to gas production management, planned maintenance, and temperature changes (Zurada, 1992).

The issue of the rule base could be addressed by using trained neural networks to assist in identifying lithology in learning AI-BI system behavior. Proper log interpretation and provision of best recovery techniques can be viewed as being rule based. Moreover, AI, like any other technology, has its limitations. If GSC does not identify the fundamental problems it needs to solve, then it might not be able to meet its challenges.

AI uses intelligent systems to address various types of scenarios encountered at the GSC. The problems are divided into four categories.

1. Artificial general intelligence (AGI) neural processors are fully rule based in providing real-time log interpretation and identifying recovery methods.

2. AGI provides optimization in locating oil wells in real time to provide reports of the best set of operational conditions to address highly complex nonlinear and dynamic issues. For example, if an oil rig's temperature is rising at dangerous levels, it will generate an alert and begin cool down. The same use can apply in a nuclear plant.

3. AGI includes data-knowledge fusion that will provide real-time data for subject-matter experts to solve complex issues in selecting the best simulation candidate and best practice.

4. The data drives the AI neural processor that will handle the vast amount of data using the empirical approach to model the dynamics of the system.

AGI is limited only by the imagination of the professionals who will be implementing AGI neural processors in monitoring and forecasting. In addition, AI is like any other analytical technique that is limited by budget constraints or the inability to accept change.

It is critical to understand that combining BI and AGI is a smart and cost-effective approach for petroleum and other industries to increase efficiency, for example, in AI neural networks that are strictly implementing existing data before the BI upgrade. The concern is that there could be a data overload. An AI neural processor would probably have the ability to generate new data to replace older data and prevent data mutation.

DESIGN AND METHOD

Implementing AI business processes will provide pilot projects for the GSC's advanced capabilities in IT and increase the functionality and efficiency of BI. The BI processes will be designed as automated and integrated pilot systems. The IT project manager will use the pilot system to run various scenarios and demonstrate the system's functionality and benefits. The scenario is an offshore oil rig located in the Gulf of Mexico and Gulf of Mexico gas platforms that have complex facilities, with a focus on real-time equipment monitoring through a project intelligent asset manager. The real-time monitoring will indicate the level of the oil flow, the speed, and the temperature levels and will alert the manager concerning issues and risk. The real-time monitoring main component is an advanced application that will have artificial neural networks to assist the manager in predictive analysis for potentials risks of an oil spill, making spending a choice between doing proactive or reactive maintenance work on oil rigs.

The current trends at GSC rely on standard tracking. Key performance indicators do not provide real-time tracking for maintenance or the cost of maintenance and do not have AI neural network capability. Using AI will start a new trend by implementing the I-platform application that will provide threshold alerts to the manager and can repair problems without assigning humans to work on dangerous tasks. For example, HRP-3 is a robot that will have the capability of going hundreds of feet below the ocean's surface to repair or replace oil fixtures in situations too dangerous for human oil-rig workers. The cost effect for implementing HRP-3 is not having paid salary or benefits involved with hiring humans, who are paid hazardous-duty pay and medical benefits to go below the ocean's surface hundreds of feet to repair oil rigs. If a human oil-rig worker is killed or injured, it costs the company millions of dollars. However, the one-time cost of the HRP-3 robot is $150,000 (Advanced Industrial Science and Technology, 2009). Petroleum companies spend an immense amount of money for medical and life insurance coverage for employees, whereas robots do not require insurance coverage.

Furthermore, artificial neural networks have the unique ability to detect any deviation in the pressures of the oil gaskets in the ocean's surface (Domaine, 2006). When considering acquiring an intelligent system, a petroleum company should consider the cost of losing humans in tragedies and the cost of covering their medical bills in case of an accident.

Thus, AI simplifies the work system and saves cost in the long run (Simpson, 1990). Some petroleum industries have already implemented AI for rescue-operation assistance on offshore platforms in case of emergencies, to rescue victims through deployment of a rescue craft. The intelligent operation assistant uses heuristic counting and estimation tactics to compute best-and worst-case scenarios for the platform crew location (Simpson, 1990).

METHODOLOGY

AI methodology takes an agile approach, using intelligent neural AI-network deployment platforms that provide real-time maps and monitoring to prevent future oil spills. The system will use streams of SCADA process logic control to collect data from oil rigs and provide alerts to managers. The real-time data will be used to generate a historical file for auditing purposes and preventative tools. The operating envelope's data go from the oil rigs and other components within the organization and feed directly into each layer of the AI neural network. The result is a network with a model nonlinear relationship in the fourth-order hierarchy. The back-end data go through the AI neural network both simultaneously and at different intervals in real time to indicate any error messages from the oil rigs and the financial analysis.

The appropriate approach to implementing AI in BI for GSC has two phases. The first is implementing the functionality of AI into BI. The second is introducing the advanced technology to the IT department.

The manager could introduce the advanced technology in the IT department in a retrospective parallel manner. The phases help identify whether the AI responded well without interfering with normal business operations and whether it is appropriate in data analysis and presentation and detection of anomalies in the system as the temperature or gas level changes. The operations manager could try to connect the robot to countercheck its functionality and reliability. The robots also could assist in opening and closing sensors in the well bore correctly and then alert if there is any change in the sensors normal functioning mode (Domaine, 2006).

Currently, GSC is lacking real-time tracking in maintenance and does not have AI neural-network capability (Liebowitz, 2006). Consider a petroleum company hiring over a thousand employees who go underground a hundred feet to check on pipes and maintain other systems. Doing so might be a risk to both the employees and the company because, if any errors occur, the damage might be more costly that it would be if the company had considered hiring robots to carry out the tasks (Liebowitz, 2006).

The AI methodology will be rapidly developed and offer intelligent neural network offshore platforms for detecting change in pressure of the oil pipes or gas, providing a real-time response in alerting management. It will provide real-time tracking and monitoring to prevent future oil spills. The real-time data could be used to generate a historical file to be used for comparison purposes as a preventative tool. In the operating mode, data will go from the oil-rigs and other components within the organization and feed directly into a layer of the AI neural network. Availability of complex data-processing capability through the introduction of AI in the oil and gas industries might lead to recognition for improving the production of oil and gas. This fact makes it a cost-effective application (Simpson, 1990).

These recommendations are more likely to increase productivity and, ultimately, enhance recovery and promote better and safer operations. The results will be the data constituting a network that contains a model nonlinear relationship in the fourth-order hierarchy. The back-end data will go through the AI neural network both simultaneously and at varying intervals in real time to indicate any error messages from the oil-rigs or the financial information (Kosko, 1992).

SECONDARY DATA ANALYSIS FOR GSC

Data concerning the depth of petroleum and oil wells in the ocean, used to forecast oil leaks, make repairs before a catastrophic event occurs, and forecast annual gas depletion rates, were obtained from the International Journal of Computer Information

Systems. Currently, GSC is implementing AI oil analysis software systems that allow managers to view data in real time to make logical cost-effective decisions and improve the current business trends.

GSC's vision for the future is to improve the current design of real-time AI networks to improve BI systems for detecting any deviation in the pressures of the oil gaskets below the ocean's surface and notify HRP-3 to go hundreds of feet below the ocean's surface to repair or replace the oil fixtures. Upgrading AI oil analysis software system to an adaptive neuro-fuzzy inference system hybrid model will improve prediction of petroleum reservoir properties below the ocean's surface and improve alert system when pressures are above the average temperature of 40°F (Anifowose, Labadin, & Abdulraheem, 2013). The reason for upgrading to the neuro-fuzzy inference system hybrid model is to ensure increased performance in various GSC scenarios.

RESULTS

The artificial fuzzy logic QMA model can forecast in real time the gas production from 2000-2050. Using fuzzy logic would result in saving the cost of hiring 20-30 people at $10 an hour. Instead of wages of $570,00 yearly, the company would make a one-time payment of $300 for artificial fuzzy logic, which takes a nanosecond to break down the employee salary contract bill into bill cost, days, and entropy (in bits). In the petroleum industry, artificial fuzzy logic data can verify blind data sets to forecast gas production from 2000-2050. Ten percent of the data were used to calibrate the QMA model, and the remaining data were not used during the model development phase. Implementing AI will reduce the current cost for GSC by 90% over the 30-year period. Evidence indicates implementing artificial fuzzy logic will reduce human error and provide accuracy in predicting future petroleum production.

The new QMA model performs closer to the WVU Model than the stochastic model and a model developed and used by the U.S. Energy Information Agency. Advanced technology has provided the latest and most accurate model to be implemented in future projects in forecasting production of petroleum, and the U.S. Department of Energy may implement only the latest QMA model. The QMA model is promising in terms of forecasting petroleum production 50 years ahead of other models and can result in a cost savings of $40M because the QMA model is half the cost of competitive models with the same accuracy. In addition, this model will not require manual updates, and the AI component will be autonomous in its ability to repair itself.

The purpose of designing the QMA model was to improve on the current WVU model of neural network architecture by implementing autonomous artificial fuzzy logic in real time with 100% accuracy. The QMA model was designed as a particular neural network architecture to provide flexibility for recurrent networks in real time and the ability to interpret data and input variables. In addition, it has the ability to retrieve the previous year's natural gas production, to forecast petroleum requirements based on the population of a country, to determine the depth of petroleum and oil wells in the ocean, to forecast oil leaks and make repairs before a catastrophic event occurs, and to forecast annual gas depletion rates before a crisis occurs. The secondary analysis concluded that, with AI improving BI, real-time data analysis will free the manager to focus on critical issues across the plant and to strategically improve the program through the development of better management strategies.

GSC SURFACE FACILITY MODELING

The GSC surface facility has approximately 400 producing wells, flowing to eight remote, three-phase separation facilities (flow stations and gathering centers). High-pressure gas is discharged from these facilities into a cross-country pipeline system flowing to a central compression plant. The fuel gas supply (at the flow stations and gathering centers) and artificial lift gas supply for the lift gas compressors at GSC are taken off the gas transit line upstream of the compression plant. Doing so reduces the feed gas rate and pressure at the inlet to the compression plant. Gas feeding the central compression plant is processed to produce natural gas liquids and miscible injectant. Residue gas from the process is compressed further for reinjection into the reservoir to provide pressure support.

Ambient temperature has a dominant effect on compressor efficiency and, hence, the total gas handling capacity and subsequent oil production. The range of daily average temperatures from 1990-2000 and the actual daily average observed temperature variations during a 24-hour period for 2001 and 2002 could be as high as 50°F. The curve fit of total shipped gas rate to the compression plant versus ambient temperature for the year of 2010 shows a significant reduction in gas-handling capacity at ambient temperatures above 0°F. Individual well gas-oil ratios (GOR) range between 600 scf/stb and 25,000 scf/stb, with the lower GOR wells in the water-flood area of the field and higher GORs in the gravity-drainage area. GSC gas compression capacity is the major bottleneck in oil production because the field oil rate will be maximized by preferentially producing the lowest GOR wells. As the ambient temperature increases from 0 to 45°F, the maximum (or "marginal") GORs in the field decrease from approximately 35,000 to 28,000 scf/stb. A temperature swing from 0 to 45°F in one day equates to an approximate oil volume reduction of 40,000 bbls, or 1000 bopd per degree F rise in temperature.

The reduction in achievable oil rate per degree F increase in temperature increases with the ambient temperature, due, in part, to the increase in the slope of the curve of shipped gas versus temperature and to the reduction in limiting or "marginal" GORs as gas capacity decreases. At higher temperatures, larger gas cuts are required at lower GORs to stay within compression limits. As the ambient temperature rises, the inlet pressure at the compression plant increases. High inlet pressure can create backpressures at the separation facilities and can cause flaring. This flaring is not environmentally acceptable and is avoided by cutting gas production. However, sometimes, ambient temperatures change so rapidly that significant gas cuts are necessary to avoid flaring. A similar problem occurs if a compressor experiences unexpected mechanical failure.

The ability to optimize the facilities in response to ambient temperature swings, compressor failures, or planned maintenance is a major business driver for this project. Proactive management of gas production also reduces unnecessary emissions. As part of a two-stage process to maximize total oil rate under a variety of field conditions, it is, first, necessary to understand the relationship between the inlet gas rate and pressure at the central compression plant and the gas rates and discharge pressures into the gas transit line system at each of the separation facilities. Therefore, the first stage of this study was to build an intelligent model capable of accurately predicting the state of this dynamic and complex system in real time.

The accuracy of the predictive models built for the central compression plant and the pressure and rate can be predicted with reasonable accuracy. The field oil rate will be affected by the manner in which gas is distributed between facilities. A state-of-the-art genetic algorithm-based optimization tool will be built based on the neural network models to optimize the oil rate. The goal of the optimization tool is to determine the gas discharge rates and pressures at each separation facility to maximize the field oil rate at a given ambient temperature, using curves of oil versus gas at each facility.

The data were clustered using a fuzzy c-mean clustering algorithm for modeling preparation. In addition, the power of the hybrid intelligent systems made modeling such a complex and nonlinear system possible. Using conventional simulation techniques has been inadequate for a system as large and complex as the one mentioned here. The number of facilities, pipe sizes, and fittings and the rigors associated with modeling each component and combining them at the end make it a difficult task. On the other hand, hybrid intelligent systems, when handled properly and with the right set of software tools, can account for all the intricacies of such a complex system as long as the collected data set is representative of the system and process behavior.

The result will be cost savings for GSC, for example, in terms of workers compensation claims currently being processed via human input. AI will reduce mundane work and be cost effective for GSC. Through AI, the data pipeline for processing oil rig reports will be automated with classification schemes to improve speed and efficiency. GSC contractor employee bills will be categorized to improve processing and determine appropriate adjudication type for bills and disputes. The method to achieve such improvement is using a simple naïve Bayes classifier to train the set class occurrences to provide a 99.99% accuracy rate as opposed to a human accuracy rate of 80%.

For example, given a set of 20,000 GSC employee contractor bills, if the AI component is implemented, it will quickly and accurately determine the correct adjudication type for each bill. The employee contractor bill classification AI methodology will focus on bill adjudication type and variations of possible classification in creating AI learning components for larger information processes in the pipeline exposition of Bayesian and neural net solutions. The AI training and testing data will result in eliminating the cost of humans.

CONCLUSION

In conclusion, the most important role for the petroleum professional is identifying situations that will benefit most from virtual intelligence. GSC will benefit from an integrated, intelligent system as it would from any other technology advancement. The purpose of implementing BI with AI is to reduce costs and help GSC to gain profits and avoid catastrophic events or going out of business. The business implementing AI can act as a pilot project for the petroleum industry's advanced capabilities in IT and increased functionality and efficiency in BI. The BI processes will be an automated and integrated pilot system. The IT project manager will use the pilot system to run various scenarios and demonstrate the system's functionality and benefits.

AI appears to be of use at GSC, and the hypothesis (Ha) is supported concerning AI being implemented to bring about cost-effective BI at GSC. However, virtual intelligence will play a decisive role in moving AI into the world of information technology. Though the digital petroleum field has existed for a decade, AI will help GSC enjoy real interoperability as it awaits the commercial software that will integrate intelligent systems, bringing them into line with the oil and gas industry. Those companies that realize the importance of investing in this mode of technology now will be the pioneers that will reap its benefits sooner.

REFERENCES

Advanced Industrial Science and Technology. (2009). Successful development of a robot with appearance and performance similar to human—For the entertainment industry.

Anifowose, A.F., Labadin, J., & Abdulraheem, A. (2013). Prediction of petroleum reservoir properties using different versions of adaptive neuro-fuzzy inference system hybrid models. International Journal of Computer Information Systems and Industrial Management Applications, 5, pp.413-426.

Domaine, H. (2006). Robotics. Minneapolis, MN: Lerner.

Gallant, S. I. (1993). Neural network learning and expert systems. Cambridge, MA: MIT Press.

Kosko, B. (1992). Neural networks and fuzzy systems: A dynamical systems approach to machine intelligence. Englewood Cliffs, NJ: Prentice Hall.

Liebowitz, J. (2006). Strategic intelligence: business intelligence, competitive intelligence, and knowledge management. Boca Raton, FL: Auerbach.

Mohaghegh, S. (n.d.). Recent development in application of artificial intelligence in petroleum engineering. Retrieved from http://www.pe.wvu.edu/Publications/Pdfs/ 89033.pdf

Partridge, K. (2010). Robotics. New York, NY: Wilson.

Simpson, P. K. (1990). Artificial neural systems: Foundations, paradigms, applications, and implementations. New York, NY: Pergamon Press.

Turban, E., Sharda, R., & Delen, D. (2011). Decision support and business intelligence systems (9th ed.). Boston, MA: Prentice Hall.

Zurada, J. M. (1992). Introduction to artificial neural systems. St. Paul, MN: West.

Virtual Appreciative Sharing of Knowledge for Global Teaming

Ken Long* and Parag Dighe*

ABSTRACT

A group of self-organizing equity market traders created a virtual, global investment community of practice that deliberately applied Virtual Appreciative Sharing of Knowledge (VASK) to develop a mutually supportive learning organization. They usedVASK to shape their routine practice and to recruit new members as part of their mission statement. Thisteaching case study places VASK within the literature of learning organizations. It describes the practical results of an organization applying ASK in a virtual environment to develop their strategic plan. As a teaching case, this provides a rich set of qualitative and quantitative data for analysts to consider within a framework of both organizational history and management literature. Appendices offer ways to apply the material in the classroom.

Keywords: Appreciative sharing of knowledge, learning organizations, networking, digital teaming.

INTRODUCTION

The Trading Mastermind(name changed to protect privacy interests) is a private, self-organizing community of practice dedicated to the idea that a group of like-minded individual traders can come together and share their knowledge to compete successfully in the challenging world of global equity markets. These traders are working hard in a high stakes game that places many obstacles against individual traders. They compete with institutional money managers, sophisticated artificial intelligence programs, and well-connected hedge fund managers. In a recent survey of active members, one participant described the benefits of the Mastermind, saying "this Mastermind …is a real learning laboratory and it makes me a better trader" (Dighe& Long, 2012). That

---

* Colorado Technical University, Calorado Springs, CO, USA.
E-mail: longk@yahoo.com, paragdighe@gmail.com

member described in practice what the Mastermind founders had envisioned years several years earlier. This case examines how the application of Appreciative Sharing of Knowledge in a virtual environmenthelped make the vision a reality. It suggests that the Virtual Appreciative Sharing of Knowledge (VASK) can support a variety of organizational teams, and frames the decisions the Mastermind can make to improve their operations in the future.

Modern organizations are social networks with complex structure where sharing of knowledge, collaboration and team work can be challenging. As a result of rapid globalization, the individuals who compose teams, organizations and industries may be in many different geographical locations and lack the face to face contacts of traditional work places. The increasing virtualization of workspace and social communitiessaves money, adds flexibility, and can integrate skilled resources regardless of their physical location. Opportunities may now be exploited that have previously been infeasible because of the connective power of digital communications that can transcend the barriers of physical separation.These virtual structures however, have their own communication and knowledge sharing challenges due to inadequate infrastructure, technological skills, cultural diversity, non-aligned or unsynchronized individual goals and expectations, inadequate training and difficulty in bringing people sharing common interests and goals together.

This paper begins with the background of the Trading Mastermind, itscommunity and its virtual learning environment followed by the description of problems with virtual learning communities, objectives of this case study and the assumptions made. A literature review on different types of learning communities creates a theoretical context that may be used to place this organization and its experiences in a broader context. An analysis of an internal Trading Mastermind surveywill provide insights into some of the beliefs and experiences, preferences and emerging goals of its members. Survey results and a review of management literature on self-organizing teams and learning organizations will frame the Mastermind's strategic planning choices and will support classroom discussions for business and leadership classrooms.

BACKGROUND

In the late 1990's, digital communications and computing technology created the opportunity for a more globally connected economy. Opportunities for individuals to participate as traders and investors in capital markets expanded at the same time into a more global forum which allowed for many organizations and individuals to collaborate globally. Long term investing is one of the ventures that has benefited from the technology boom.

Dr.John Walters(names changed to protect privacy interests), founder of Global Trading Mastery (GTM) is one of the leading trading coaches in the world. He has consulted on a regular basis with some of the most successful private and institutional money managers in the world andteaches traders to gain a competitive advantage in the markets. At a GTM weekend workshop, a group of Dr Walters' students decided to extend their network of cooperation and coordination beyond the weekend workshop they had attended together.

INTRODUCTION OF PROTAGONISTS

The case study identifies four distinct groups of members of the Trading Mastermind, plus the ASK consultant working with them to develop their plan for the way ahead.

The Owner

An investment and trading professional, who owns the business entity, is responsible for the development, operation and decision-making of the Trading Mastermind. He is responsible for most of the original research that informs the strategies discussed and implemented in various ways by all the members of the Trading Mastermind.

The Founders

They are the group of six students who developed the initial vision and direction of the Trading Mastermind in the prototype years. Three were investment professionals; three were part-time traders supplementing their income. Friends in both virtual and physical space, the Founders have actively participated in the four years of the mastermind's operations and remain committed for at least the next five years.

Subscribers

Subscribers comprised two groups based on their longevity with the Mastermind. Long-term subscribers had been members for more than a year and are active on a regular basis, which is governed by their level of interest, free time and personal inclinations. Long-term subscribers operated on either a daily, weekly or monthly basis. Short-term subscribers had been members for less than a year but who appeared to be committed to regular ongoing contact and interaction with the network based on their expressed interest in personal contributions to group learning.

Observers

These are participants who used a free trial membership period to evaluate the theMastermind environment, and to check the fit between the Mastermind and their objectives. Typically, after three months of contact, the Observer would either move on or decide to become a subscriber for at least an additional year.

THE ASK CONSULTANTS

A doctoral student in organizational development who applied the Appreciative Sharing of Knowledge (ASK) methodology to construct a Web delivered survey to the global Trading Mastermind community. The consultant conducted scholarly research into a variety of modern organizational structures and methods to provide a theoretical context to evaluate the Trading Mastermind situation as well as the efficacy of conducting ASK in a virtual setting. The ASK methodology and survey are described in Appendix 2.

CASE NARRATIVE AND CHRONOLOGY

Year 1: Informal Practice

A web-based repository was created to capture the dialogue between fellow traders. Collaborating via electronic mail seemed too cumbersome, so the students used a Mastermind approach to share trading strategies and build a global learning network. The trading strategies were designed for a variety of world markets, over different time horizons, and at different parts of the market and business cycles. They featured a price-based, top down approach to assessing conditions in the world market, regions, sectors, styles, currencies and commodities. They produced signals to buy and sell specific exchange traded funds and stocks in a risk–adjusted manner, with clear instructions on exits and position sizing.The Founders cooperated informally for a full year, primarily through the use of e-mail. Satisfied with the results of their coordination, they decided to create a more formal organizational structure to expand the network and simplify their cooperation.

Years 2-4: Trading Mastermind Pilot Program

The Founders added more structure and formality to their network. They named their organization the Traders Mastermind and committed to creating a self-sustaining organization focused on their common vision and principles. They drafted a Founders vision document that described the principles for developing and operating the Mastermind(Appendix 1). The vision document was strongly aligned with the principles of Thatchenkery's (2005)Appreciative Sharing Knowledge, a powerful and effective methodology for organizational development based on the positive psychology movement. The Trading Mastermindused a web-based infrastructure to engage globally in synchronous and asynchronous collaboration featuring messaging, live chat, threaded discussions, file-sharing, image sharing and a wiki-based discussion forum. Founders contributed nominal fees to sustain the infrastructure.

One member became the Owner of the Mastermind, and became chief of research and the administrator of the growing digital infrastructure. The Owner created a business entity to manage the day-to-day finances of the community. With the permission of the Founders, the Owner charged a nominal participation subscription fee to support the growth and day-to-day operations of the enterprise. Through word-of-mouth, delivery of educational workshops and industry publications, the Trading Mastermind attracted a set of new members called Subscribers who interacted on a regular basis according to their interests, time schedules, and skills. The founders and the owner informally agreed that the pilot program of the Trading Mastermind was a success and that they needed to consider expanding their operation even more broadly.

Year 5: Self-Assessment and Mapping the Future Direction of the Mastermind

After five years of operations, the Founders and the Owner conducted an internal inquiry into the members' perceptions of the Mastermind. The goal was to check alignment with the principles of the vision document and to shape their plans. They used an ASK survey and an organizational development consultant to provide additional insights from the management literature.

CONSULTANT'S LITERATURE REVIEW

The consultant provided the following insights from management literature. He showed that VASK fits nicely within the broad management literature investigating teams and learning organizations. The Mastermind found that management literature resonated strongly with their direct experience with the Mastermind, and gave them a framework for understanding their choices in strategic planning.

Learning Organizations

Organizational learning, defined by Lipshitz and Popper (1996) as a process through which members of an organization learn by sharing values and knowledge based on their experience. While this definition suggests that organizational learning occurs as a result of individual learning, Lipshitz and Popper elaborate this by proposing that organizational learning is a result of a structured and planned process that allows an organizations to collect, analyze, share and use information relevant to its needs. Organizations which institute these Organizational Learning Mechanisms (OLM) are Learning Organizations (Lipshitz, Popper, & Oz, 1996). Learning organizations are organizations which create structures and values, visions and goals to establisha learning environment by assisting individuals with personal learning and getting feedback and benefits from learning outcomes (Moilanen, 2005).

A plan to transform the Ordnance Corps of the Israel Defense Forces (IDF) into a learning organization based on the principles and metaphors of learning organizations was developed by Lipshitz and Popper (1996). They used defined learning processes consisting of collecting and analyzing information based on causality, OLMs, adopting ideas from organizations which have demonstrated success in building learning environment, and building organizational learning culture and cultural change. The program relied on the principle that learning can be achieved by trying and that this learning would help the organization build the processes which could then be exportedto other areas of the organization. Despite difficulties in the start-up phase due to ineffective team work and flawed intervention methods, management commitment made the transition successful. Based on a different study, Bennett & O'Brien (1994) have argued that learning organizations show increased employee and organizational productivity, better financial results and higher customer and employee satisfaction (Estrada, 2007).

Communities of Practice

Finding, enhancing and retaining intellectual knowledge embedded within organizational resources is gaining importance as a result of globalization and the need to create new capabilities (Krishnaveni & Sujatha, 2012). This requires organizations to develop Knowledge Management (KM) strategies to facilitate the efficient sharing, transfer and exchange of knowledge between organizational resources (Liyanage et al., 2009). The knowledge can be tacit where it is mostly within the person, non-documented and unstructured (Polanyi, 1962) or explicit which can be easily transferred,as it is structured and mostly documented (Koulopoulos and Frappaolo, 1999).

The transfer of tacit knowledge is difficult as it is inside the brain of an individual; once made explicit, it can be shared through collaboration and interaction through a common platform. A Community of Practice (CoP) is a group of people sharing common areas of interest, problems or expertise looking for engaging into a mutual learning process by interacting on a regular basis (Wenger et al., 2002). A CoP provides this common platform for knowledge sharing through reflection, storytelling, and questioning through a continuous interaction between the community members either face to face or through virtual collaboration (Krishnaveni & Sujatha, 2012). While CoP provides a very effective platform for knowledge sharing, it faces certain challenges such as management's commitment,making it visible, motivating participation and building trust between the members.

Self-Organizing Teams

Kane (2008) has defined self-organizing teams as a group of people coming together as an informal team to work on a specific problem or a project. Contrasting with CoP, these teams are unplanned and do not have a permanent existence. They emerge mostly through local interactions amongst people sharing common goals or areas of interest while pursuing individual agendas. The group members in these self-organized teams adapt their roles depending on the needs thus bringing more flexibility to the teams as compared to the traditional teams (Kane, 2008). Ageeth and Eric (1999) have defined self-organizing teams as autonomous task groups, self-managing groups or empowered groups formed to increase organizational efficiency and quality of working life for employees (Ageeth & Eric, 1999).

In case studies, Kane (2008) shows that self-organizing groups appear "...an echo of a greater whole..." terming it has *"holoanticho"* in nature. Her study also showed that these groups show a *"holoallagic"* nature where individuals change for the benefit of larger group or interest (Kane, 2008). This study also showed that within a self-organizing group, the natural ability, creativity, awareness and resiliency is heightened. This helps the teams to manage the chaos and conflicts occurring due to the unorganized structure of such teams.Ageeth and Eric (1999) found that though self-organizing team offer to adapt to the changes and enhance the organizational performance, the barriers in developing these self-organizing teams limit the benefits. Barriers to growth are formed by the opportunities for self-organization provided by management, lack of control, attitude of workers, skills and learning abilities of members involved and team needs.

Self-Directed Teams

Organizations search for ways to increase employee participationand use their individual and group strengths to meet the organizational goals. Self-Directed teams, also known as Self-Managed teams is one socio-technical formation which consists of team members with diverse skills, led by a person from within the group not necessarily from higher ranks. This is a permanent, self-managed group working towards common goals. Beckham has argues that the effectiveness of the self-directed teams is based on the group's ability to complement individual strengths and weaknesses and rely on the group achievements rather than individual contributions (Beckham, 1998).

Equal division of workload and contributions, effective communication, focus on the team goals, open-mindedness, members as effective leaders are the factors that contribute to the success of self-directed teams, as presented by Hickman and Creighton-Zollar (1998). They evaluated the collaborative processes among college level group members from diverse background (Gill Robinson & Creighton-Zollar, 1998). Team building is the biggest barrier to the formation of self-directed teams where managers, supervisors, systems, and unions pose challenges in team building efforts (Beckham, 1998).

Virtual Team (VT), also known as distributed teams (Lyons, Priest, Wildman, Salas, & Carnegie, 2009), can be defined as teams comprising of members working across geographical, temporal, relational boundaries by making use of technology for coordination and communication to accomplish an interdependent task or tasks (Martins, Gilson, & Maynard, 2004). Berry (2011) has defined VT as team consisting of members who may be located within the same office space or across geographical boundaries, using combination of telecommunication and information technologies, working interdependently to accomplish an organizational task. It is a team that has fewer face-to-face meetings, does most of its work through phones, e-mails, electronic bulletin boards, chat groups, electronic databases, teleconferences (Berry, 2011) and webinars. Cohen & Gibson (2003) have defined VT as groups of individual team members working together from different physical locations on interdependent tasks, sharing responsibilities for the results and use technology for coordination, collaboration and communication (Staples & Webster, 2007).

Virtual teams are social systems with their work processes intertwined with technological systems, with high levels of diversity as compared to face-to-face or co-located teams. The communication between the virtual team members is mostly asynchronous, usually happening offline due to differences in time zones where the team members are located. This combined with cultural diversity adds to the complexity in creating effective teams which increases as a function of decentralization and virtuality(Berry, 2011).

Virtual team poses several challenges primarily due to the people spread out across around the globe, belonging to diverse cultural background, with different language, social, political, financial and other personal preferences. A survey of randomly selected employees of multinational corporations by Solomon (2010) has found language barriers, conflict management and decision making, exchanging opinions and innovative ideas, working across multiple time zones, absence of visual communication cues, participation, cultural differences, technology and infrastructure as the most common challenges faced by the organizations working with VTs.

Appreciative Sharing of Knowledge

True organization wealth and strength are found within the knowledge held by its employees which increases whenshared.This drives organizations to search for effective and efficient ways of Knowledge Management (KM) and sharing. KM has two aspects – technical and social (Thatchenkery, 2005). Several strategies have been successfully implemented to manage the technical aspects of KM but the social aspect has posed challenges because of tacit knowledge (Polanyi, 1962). Some individuals resist sharing their knowledge for reasons such as fear of being replaced, remaining individually competitive and lack of time.

Appreciative Sharing of Knowledge (ASK), described by Thatchenkery (2005), is based on the principles of Appreciative Inquiry (AI) (Cooperrider, Whitney and Stavros, 2003), social constructionism, and knowledge management. ASK creates an environment of knowledge sharing by focusing on the positives with a futuristic approach rather than looking backwards to find out what did not work. Thatchenkery's seven step approach finds and unleashes this positive energy.

The first step begins with educating the management about ASK, piloting it in a small project to build momentum and skill. The second step finds success stories from the participants through narrations rather than structured interviews, thus bringing the knowledge out of the natural flow of thoughts. The third step identifies the Knowledge Enablers (KE) such as empowerment, respect, teamwork and building relationships, which are vital for motivating participation. The fourth step analyzes the information using Knowledge Infrastructure Factors (KIF) which includes decision making, organizational practices and routines, incentives, leadership and communication. The fifth step focuses on the future by means of future-present scenarios (FPS) where the participants are guided to think towards the feeling about having attained the goals rather than thinking about attaining the goals. This builds momentum towards an environment where information can flow freely. In the sixth step, the FPS is then ranked based on the validation of the scenarios. The last step forms an implementation team to execute the plan.

SURVEY FINDINGS

Survey Quantitative Summary

The ASK-based survey asked both quantitative and qualitative questions. For a quantitative data set, members ranked the importance of 12 values listed in the vision document and the degree to which they felt these values were being satisfied on a 5-point Likert scale. The ASK valencing technique computes the difference between importance and satisfaction to find areas for improvement and/or reinforcement. The consultant provided data tables for insights as shown in Tables 1, 2 and 3.

Table 1: Rankings by Importance

Value	Importance	Satisfaction	Difference
Effective	4.18	4.05	-0.12
Friendly	4.13	4.34	0.22
Reflective	4.08	4.16	0.09
Community	4.08	4.16	0.08
Humble	4.03	4.26	0.23
Participatory	4.00	4.03	0.03
User-driven	3.97	4.09	0.11
Energetic	3.95	4.12	0.17

Fair Value	3.95	4.22	0.27
Voluntary	3.80	4.26	0.46
Flexible	3.70	4.08	0.38
Efficient	3.63	3.97	0.35

Table 2: Rankings by Satisfaction

Value	Importance	Satisfaction	Difference
Friendly	4.13	4.34	0.22
Humble	4.03	4.26	0.23
Voluntary	3.80	4.26	0.46
Fair Value	3.95	4.22	0.27
Reflective	*4.08*	*4.16*	*0.09*
Community	4.08	4.16	0.08
Energetic	3.95	4.12	0.17
User-driven	3.97	4.09	0.11
Flexible	3.70	4.08	0.38
Effective	4.18	4.05	-0.12
Participatory	4.00	4.03	0.03
Efficient	3.63	3.97	0.35

Table 3: Rankings by Valence Difference

Value	Importance	Satisfaction	Difference
Voluntary	3.80	4.26	0.46
Flexible	3.70	4.08	0.38
Efficient	3.63	3.97	0.35
Fair Value	3.95	4.22	0.27
Humble	4.03	4.26	0.23
Friendly	4.13	4.34	0.22
Energetic	3.95	4.12	0.17
User-driven	3.97	4.09	0.11
Reflective	4.08	4.16	0.09
Community	4.08	4.16	0.08
Participatory	4.00	4.03	0.03
Effective	4.18	4.05	-0.12

SURVEY QUALITATIVE SUMMARY

Members described the features they found most attractive and positive about the Mastermind CoP, and what they would like to see added to the CoP in the future. The top 10 results from the comments are found in Tables 4 and 5.

Table 4: Top 10 most Favorable Features

1	Friendliness of participants
2	Rich source of new ideas
3	Helping atmosphere
4	No ego problems
5	Works across all time-zones
6	Search function in the archives
7	Many case studies shared
8	Using case studies form that week during educational webinars
9	Human social connection
10	Improved accountability through public sharing of ideas

Table 5: Top Areas for Improvements

1	More real time trading examples
2	More people should contribute their ideas
3	Need a trading simulator to test ideas
4	More discussion of trade management while the trade is open
5	More longer term trade ideas
6	Formal feedback system
7	Teaming like- minded individuals together
8	More examples of failed trades
9	How to take professional losses
10	A non-real time discussion area

DISCUSSION QUESTIONS TO FRAME STRATEGIC PLANNING

The consultant prepared the following discussion for the next round of developing the Mastermind strategic plan:

DISCUSSION QUESTIONS ARISING FROM THE QUANTITATIVE DATA

1. Are you satisfied with the levels of satisfaction for the 12 measured areas?
2. Does the rank order of importance offer any insights or surprises?

3. What does a comparison of the most important and least important values and their levels of satisfaction suggest?

4. How can we do better on the most important measures of importance?

5. Should we maintain the same level of support for the least important values or can we reallocate resources to other areas?

DISCUSSION QUESTIONS ARISING FROM THE QUALITATIVE DATA

1. Do you find any of the entries on either list surprising and why?

2. How can some items be on both lists?

3. How do the top 10 findings connect back to the quantitative data insights?

4. What future improvements are suggested by the data?

5. What resource constraints would prevent you from making improvements or leveraging the success stories?

6. Are there any natural groupings of insights?

7. How can we use the data to update and inform all members on the state of the mastermind?

CONCLUSION

The Trading Mastermind is prepared to conduct the next round of strategic planning, with the literature review providing a rich context for sense making. The ASK methodology supported this virtual organization's planning and should be considered for organizations with diverse and globally distributed members accustomed to digital interactions. VASK could be further expanded as a methodology for organizational transformation. The asynchronously gathered insights were as effective as those gathered in the traditional, co-located group session.

ACKNOWLEDGEMENT

The authors would like to express their thanks to Mr Stephen Long, Manager, Research and Operations , Tortoise Capital Management, Leavenworth, KS, USA for support in developing this case and permission for the case to be published in its entirety and without change or limitation by ICMC 2012.

REFERENCES

Per APA, book titles should be in italics. Please change all book titles accordingly.

Ageeth, B., & Eric, M. (1999). Barriers to the development of self-organizing teams. *Journal of Managerial Psychology, 14*(2), 134-149.

Beckham, R. (1998). Self-directed work teams: The wave of the future? *Hospital Materiel Management Quarterly, 20*(1), 48-60.

Berry, G. R. (2011). Enhancing Effectiveness on Virtual Teams. *Journal of Business Communication, 48*(2), 186-206. doi: 10.1177/0021943610397270

Cooperrider, D., Whitney, D., & Stavros, J. (2003). *Appreciative Inquiry: The Handbook.* Bedford Heights, OH: Lake Shore Publishers.

C. Solomon, *The Challenges of Working in Virtual Teams: Virtual Teams Survey Report 2010,* New York, NY: RW3 CultureWizard, 2010.

Dighe, P. & Long, K. (2012). [Mastermind survey narratives]. Unpublished raw data.

Estrada, N. A. (2007). *Learning organizations and evidence-based practice by RNs.* Ph.D. 3267824, The University of Arizona, United States -- Arizona. Retrieved from https://login.ctu.idm/oclc.org/?url=http://search.proquest.com/docview/304895301?accountid=26967 ProQuest Dissertations & Theses (PQDT) database.

Gill Robinson, H., & Creighton-Zollar, A. (1998). Diverse self-directed work teams: Developing strategic initiatives for 21st century organizations. *Public Personnel Management, 27*(2), 187-200.

Kane, L. (2008). *Fostering the emergence of self-organizing work groups.* Ed.D. 3323385, Seattle University, United States -- Washington. Retrieved from https://login.ctu.idm/oclc.org/?url=http://search.proquest.com/docview/304383239?accountid=26967 ProQuest Dissertations & Theses (PQDT) database.

Koulopoulos T and Frappaolo C (1999), *Smart Things to Know About Knowledge Management.*Capstone, Dover, NH.

Krishnaveni, R., & Sujatha, R. (2012). Communities of Practice: An Influencing Factor for Effective Knowledge Transfer in Organizations. [Article]. *IUP Journal of Knowledge Management, 10*(1), 26-40.

Lipshitz, R., Popper, M., & Oz, S. (1996). Building learning organizations: The design and implementation of organizational learning mechanisms. *The Journal of Applied Behavioral Science, 32*(3), 292-292.

Liyanage C, Elhag T, Ballal T and Li Q (2009), "Knowledge Communication and Translation: A Knowledge Transfer Model". *Journal of Knowledge Management, Vol. 13, No. 3,* pp. 118-131.

Lyons, R., Priest, H. A., Wildman, J. L., Salas, E., & Carnegie, D. (2009). Managing Virtual Teams: Strategies for Team Leaders. *Ergonomics in Design: The Quarterly of Human Factors Applications, 17*(1), 8-13. doi: 10.1518/106480409x415152

Martins, L. L., Gilson, L. L., & Maynard, M. T. (2004). Virtual Teams: What Do We Know and Where Do We Go From Here? *Journal of Management, 30*(6), 805-835. doi: 10.1016/j.jm.2004.05.002

Moilanen, R. (2005). Diagnosing and measuring learning organizations. *The Learning Organization, 12*(1), 71-89.

Polanyi M (1962), *Personal Knowledge: Toward a Post-Critical Philosophy.* Harper Torchbooks, New York.

Staples, D. S., & Webster, J. (2007). Exploring Traditional and Virtual Team Members' "Best Practices". *Small Group Research, 38*(1), 60-97. doi: 10.1177/1046496406296961

Thatchenkery, T. (2005). *Appreciative Sharing of Knowledge: Leveraging Knowledge Management for Strategic Change.*Chagrin Falls, OH: Taos Publications. .

Wenger E, McDermott R and Snyder B (2002), Cultivating Communities of Practice. Boston, MA: Harvard Business School Press.

APPENDIX 1: THE TRADING MASTERMIND VISION

Our vision for the Trading Mastermind is of a positive community that reflects these values in action:

1. **Voluntary:** people self-select as subscribers based on perceived value.
2. **Participatory:** participate as the spirit moves them. No pressure to talk, contribute or attend.
3. **Friendly:** A moderator will enforce acceptable public behavior. The community will find its own level of acceptable discourse.
4. **Humble:** we will maintain a spirit of humble cooperation, acknowledging the market is not only unknown, it may very well be unknowable
5. **Energetic:** reliable, frequent engagement so people are eager to participate.
6. **Efficient:** simple and intuitive to operate and maintain.
7. **Effective:** Value is added through sharing, reflection, and discussion
8. **Self-funding:** pay a fair price for good value.
9. **Flexible:** support multiple modes of discourse, allow for storage, support multiple groups, and self-directed work group areas. Security, privacy, storage, asynchronous transcripts, images, text and multiple modes of formatting.
10. Web-enabled and scalable.
11. **Global access:** no limitations based on geography or time of day.
12. **User-driven:** usersshape the direction, mode and content of discourse.

Perceptions of the United States' New Healthcare Reform Law, the PPACA, as Exemplified by the NFIB, a Lobbyist Organization for Small Businesses

Divya Srinivasan*, Tojo Thatchenkery** and Anne L. Washington***

ABSTRACT

This case study will analyze how perceptions toward the US's new healthcare reform law, the Patient Protection and Affordable Care Act (PPACA), are shaped by the National Federation of Independent Business (NFIB) and other lobbyist organizations. The period of analysis is March 2012 when attempts were made to repeal the law by various US organizations. The NFIB, which advocates US small and independent businesses' interests, discusses the influence of the PPACA in the US Supreme Court Hearings based on their interpretation of healthcare reform having a predominantly negative effect on businesses. Using discourse from the Supreme Court hearings, various categories of issues have been developed which show the impact of the PPACA on businesses: 1) changes to Medicare and Medicaid, 2) community rating and guaranteed issue provisions, 3) individual mandate and severability of provisions, and 4) financial issues linked to healthcare, which translate into positive and negative views toward the law. A statistical analysis of the relationship between positive or negative perception and each provision of the PPACA using multinomial logistic regression is tested, followed by a thematic analysis of the reasoning behind these viewpoints.

Keywords: Patient protection, medicare, financial issues, small business interests, reforms.

---

* Divya Srinivasan is Doctoral student, school of Public Policy, George Mason University, VA, USA.

** Tojo Thatchenkery is Professor, School of Public Policy, George Mason University, VA, USA.

*** Anne L. Washington is Assistant Professor, School of Public Policy, George Mason University, VA, USA.

E-mail: dsriniv2@masonlive.gmu.edu, thatchen@gmu.edu, awashi14@gmu.edu

INTRODUCTION

There have been varying interpretations of the ground breaking new healthcare law, the Patient Protection and Affordable Care Act (also known as ACA and PPACA), in the United States. The National Federation of Independent Business (NFIB) filed a lawsuit against the Department of Health and Human Services (DHHS) for upholding the new health care law on the grounds of unconstitutional provisions, due to its negative viewpoints about the law. During the hearing, a friend of the court brief was filed by patient advocacy organizations countering the NFIB's viewpoint, and providing a comparison group in support of organizations representing patients, healthcare providers and physicians associations with a positive discourse on the health care reform law and why it should be upheld. It is important to see how this discourse differed in its positive and negative attitudes.

The viewpoints on healthcare can be categorized by their representation of values, beliefs and portrayal. While other studies(Dranove(1988); Danzon (1988); Deal and Kennedy (2000); Danzon (2004)) have demonstrated how healthcare has an impact on the economy, costs, various industries and the community, this case study takes these factors into consideration through a grouping process which analyzes each of these provisions that were mentioned, and reasoning for why they are positively or negatively portrayed. On one side is the NFIB who is against healthcare reform. On the other side are health care organizations, such as the American Hospital Association, American Cancer Association and more who submitted friend of the court or amicus curiae briefs in favor of the new provisions. The positive and negative attitudes toward the healthcare law are present in the following major provisions of the PPACA: 1) changes to Medicare and Medicaid, 2) community rating and guaranteed issue provisions, 3) individual mandate and severability of provisions, and 4) financial issues linked to healthcare. These provisions are defined as follows. The community rating and guaranteed issue provision focuses on adverse selection issues that have impacted the community before healthcare reform, as defined by the glossary of health insurance terms in a report by the National Association of Insurance Commissioners (NAIC) and the Center for Insurance Policy Research (CIPR). There has been a tendency for insurance companies to limit coverage based on preexisting conditions and characteristics of the individual, so the above provisions have guaranteed a blind review process of individuals who want to have access to health insurance. To define the individual mandate, it is a provision in the PPACA which requires minimum coverage of health insurance for all individuals in the nation. There is a severability clause in the hearing that proposes that all other healthcare provisions are tied to the individual mandate, so they must fall, if this provision falls. Financial issues in healthcare have to do with those aspects impacting small businesses such as employer-mandated healthcare, tax credits, and insurance premiums (NAIC and CIPR Report: Glossary of Terms).

The highly polarized discourse about healthcare reform in the United States is shaped and influenced by equally diverse political beliefs and core values that are prevalent in American society (Crowley, 2009). In this case study, we consider five of them: 1) public choice model, 2) the role of government (limited versus expansionary), 3) American exceptionalism, 4) internal versus external locus of control, and 5) American freedoms and liberties. The public choice model has been developed in detail by Kingdon(1984). The concept supports interest in utility maximization for the community using game theory over incentivized decision making, with a focus on healthcare as a commodity. The role of governments has long played a role in development of public policies and has a role in healthcare as well. Americans have debated a public choice model but perceive health insurance coverage as a choice, rather than a necessity. For this reason, the individual mandate that requires every American to have health insurance has been seen by some as a restriction on American freedoms, especially for small businesses who are required to purchase health insurance for their employees under the new law (PPACA). At the same time, there are provisions such as community rating and guaranteed issue, which state that there should be practices to eliminate discrimination in health insurance policies by age, race, preexisting conditions and comorbidities, which represent American individualism and the value of American exceptionalism as well. Not all of the new law is contested by the NFIB, which is why it is important to analyze the hearing by the NFIB to extrapolate which portions are seen in a positive versus a negative light.

American exceptionalism is a term coined by French political thinker and historian Alexis Tocqueville (1835 & 1840) and further elaborated by political theorists such as Lipset (1997). The core argument behind the exceptionalism thesis is that the United States possesses certain unique cultural characteristics that are deep rooted such as belief in free markets, risk-taking, high entrepreneurship, and philanthropy. Tocqueville visited the U.S. in 1831 to observe the American political system and wrote two books about what he believed was American uniqueness (1835 & 1840). He noted the flourishing democracy in America at a time (1830s) when true democracy was not present anywhere else in the world. He observed various characteristics of American culture and called it American exceptionalism. For example, unlike the aristocratic ethic prevalent in Europe, the American society was founded on opportunity whereby anyone could rise to the top, acquire any amount of wealth, and enjoy autonomy and freedom. Lipset (1997), too, observed various uniqueness of American culture such as high levels of religiosity, high participation in voluntary associations, generous philanthropy, but very low turnout in elections. Lipset pointed out that the U.S. was the only industrial country in the world that had never produced a major socialist party. Such fundamental beliefs in the supremacy of the individual and free choice will have significant implications in the healthcare discourse as healthcare in the US has been a choice and a luxury rather than a mandate. A way of describing the American exceptionalism principles in healthcare reform is through potential long run cost savings, elimination of discrimination toward the most unhealthy, and tax incentives to small businesses that provide employee health insurance. Small businesses also will be allowed a less restrictive platform to choose health insurance through access to information and resources in what is known as a health information exchange (HIE), keeping a streak of the traditional American spirit, blended with the new reforms. This HIE is another example of American exceptionalism. The health information exchanges have a heavy role in the debate because they represent a blend of the public and private sector values. The HIEs incorporate the public sector's need for transparency of information and records, including the numbers and names of insurance companies, plans and cost of the plans, while also including a private sector component of a free market where incentives such as tax credits are provided to those companies who provide their employees with insurance. Through the presence of this new market, the exchanges could impact supply and demand of insurance markets as they will be able to gauge the economics for Medicare, Medicaid, private plans and the demand elasticity of consumers who need to be covered for multiple health abnormalities versus those who need minimal coverage.

Originally proposed by Julian Rotter (1954), locus of control is a popular construct in psychology. It refers to the extent to which individuals believe that they can control events that affect them. Individuals with internal local control believe that they are in control of their lives and therefore feel responsible for both successes and failures. Individuals with external locus of control believe that events in the environment have more influence on their lives than individual decisions that they may make about life choices. In general, people from individualistic societies such as the United States have higher internal locus of control while those from collectivist cultures such as Japan may have higher external locus of control. Internal locus of control is also connected to entrepreneurship. Most entrepreneurs believe that they are responsible for their success. In collectivist countries, success is seen as a social product made possible by the network of people a person is part of. When it comes to the healthcare discourse, high internal locus of control individuals may believe that they alone (and not the government) are responsible for their well-being and health. High external locus control individuals may believe that a mature society has a collective responsibility to take care of one another and provide for the wellbeing of all. A free market driven model of health insurance provided largely by the private sector is typically present where societies have high internal locus of control (as in the case of United States. On the other hand, public models with national health care systems are typically present where there is high external locus of control (such as in the UK, France, etc.). For this reason, there are more public and tax payer funded health programs with a focus on public health and preventative care which can reduce costs on the overall health system in countries with high external locus of control (Basu et al, 2012).. This concept has been debated in the healthcare hearing, where an individual mandate was proposed, suggesting each and every individual carry health insurance of a public (government) or privately (individual) funded nature.

Finally, American individualism plays a role in individual needs and innovation, where progressivism, a combination of creativity and idealism, is more important than following a traditional mindset , as portrayed by President Herbert Hoover in his role as the executive in the 1920s (Zeiger,1974). He believed in principles of promoting individual progress over a collectivist mentality in society, which had carried on many generations in the private healthcare market. Amartya Sen (1999) has also proposed his thoughts on liberty, democracy and the intersection of healthcare in his book, Development as Freedom. His views provide for the importance in a public health system that has compassion for the underprivileged while teaching lessons of the importance of awareness and gratitude for one's individual freedoms; these freedoms tend to be restricted and/ or portrayed differently in various developed and developing countries (Sen, 1999).

This point of this case study is to analyze the healthcare debate in a multidimensional way. The subject of healthcare in the United States becomes significant because it actually involves many other traditions and values inherent to the American culture, including the role of government, trust and confidence in government, progressivism, and more. There are two specific levels of analysis. The discourse is first studied to see which provisions were the most likely to be depicted positively or negatively by the NFIB and its comparison group. Then, the concept or theme that this provision represents was coded to provide a philosophical "theme" or reason. The purpose of the grouping into provisions and then themes is to provide examples of US values, historically represented in the US's privatized health model that may differentiate it from other nations. The paper takes on the following format: a literature review of other papers in the field of discourse analysis, reasoning for new contribution to the field, methods of the study, results and interpretations, and a discussion of the policy implications of the study.

LITERATURE REVIEW

Literature about the debate on healthcare in the US and abroad has been discussed by many authors to date, but little literature exists on the discourse analysis of healthcare issues. Other fields like public policy and business have analyzed marketing techniques and organization building using positive and negative discourse. One recent example includes an inductive analysis by Yildiz and Kurban (2011) who wrote a paper on electronic government and discourse, analyzing how electronic government has changed the type of information and presentation of conversations and discourse from various information channels. They present topics of discourse from various newspapers and study equality, government reforms, security breaches, participation and more. Another example is that of Zirn, Neipert et al (2011) who report on the use of sentiment analysis for lexicon analysis. Thatchenkery (2001) also provides the basics on discourse analysis in business organizations, emphasizing how the power of language can impact societies, organizations, communities, global economies. For example, he shows the impact of words such as "irrational exuberance" used by Alan Greenspan, the top banker of U.S at that time, in moving financial markets around the world. It is a reminder that language can be just as powerful as any other kind of action in both its impact and consequences.

Other papers in the field of health care discuss topics such as health care costs through discourse (Cheek, 2004). Typical healthcare discourse analysis has covered doctor-patient interactions, chronic condition awareness, or clinical procedures. There is more to be discovered in the field of health policy as public policies can be brought to the forefront at the intersection of legal and health reform issues in 2012. For this reason, this paper analyzes the most recent hearings of the NFIB on their perceptions of healthcare and reasoning for primarily negative attitudes toward healthcare reform.

NEW CONTRIBUTION TO THE FIELD

This paper also presents a different way of analyzing the discussion of healthcare reform, beyond cost/ benefit analyses or qualitative analysis of issues in the law. The analysis provides a contribution to the healthcare literature, as it provides provisions of the ACA in a positive or negative light by the NFIB but also by including a philosophical backing for these issues, using justifications derived from theories of renowned authors in the public policy field (e.g. Lipset, Kingdon, Sen, etc.) The paper also presents a mixed methods approach of analysis with a qualitative and quantitative perspective of the health reform hearing discourse.

METHODS

This was a cross sectional study, with an analysis done on one day of Supreme Court arguments in the case NFIB vs. Health and Human Services. The case was heard on March 28, 2012.The discourse analysis was limited to 100 pages of the hearing, within which there is a portion for the NFIB's statement as well as an almost equivalent number of pages of discourse and perspective from the amicus curiae, or friend of the court brief, that provides the opposite perspective. The NFIB statements are compared against the statements of other healthcare organizations, such as the American Hospital Association (AHA), American Cancer Association (ACA) and Small Business Management (SBM).These organizations are in favor of the new additions – community rating, minimum coverage, etc. and see healthcare reform as a necessity. The research design consists of quantitative and qualitative analysis of the data from the two contrasting groups of lobbyist coalitions.

The study had coders who were instructed to categorize the data in three ways. First coders reviewed the text and labeled it as positive discourse or negative discourse or neither. Positive discourse was viewed as favorable perception towards healthcare reform. Negative discourse was viewed as unfavorable perception. Second, coders identified healthcare reform provisions that the discourse represented. Finally, coders identified philosophical theme linked to the healthcare reform provision.The analysis is mixed methods in nature, considering both statistical and inductive approaches. The statistical portion consists of a multinomial logistic regression analysis of the differences in the attitudes on healthcare reform. The independent variable being measured is the healthcare reform provision and the dependent variable is favorable or unfavorable perception toward that provision. Since the dependent variable is either 0 or 1 for unfavorable or favorable attitude, the regression conducted is a multinomial logistic regression analysis, as each provision has a varying perception identified to it. Coding for the healthcare provisions (independent variables) were as follows: 1 for issue on health care issues regarding Medicare/Medicaid expansion through healthcare reform, 2 for issues on adverse selection (community rating and guaranteed issue or solving disparity issues through healthcare including issues pertaining to the health information exchanges which help the information asymmetry problems), 3 for individual mandate (necessitating all to buy health insurance) and severability clause provisions (stating that all provisions are tied to each other) and 4 for insurance premiums, tax credits, and financial issues relating to healthcare.

Finally, a qualitative technique was used to inductively code the hearing on the basis of philosophical theme, including 1) public versus private choice theory (taking a collective versus individualistic perspective on healthcare), 2) the role of government in setting the agenda, 3) American exceptionalism, and 4) an internal versus external locus of control and 5) liberties, freedoms and free markets. For coding purposes, any reference to Paul Feldstein's definitions of public and private choice theory included words or definitions relating to a public health care system or private health care system with characteristics that define each. A public health care system portrays healthcare as a commodity, where every individual pays into the health care system through taxes (Feldstein, 250). On the other hand, a private health care systems typically provide the following: "1) offer a simplified set of flexible medical savings account options to all Americans; 2) provide a tax credit option for taxpayers who choose to purchase health insurance that is not sponsored by their employers; 3) expand consumer choices that increase market-based accountability of health plans; and 4)improve access to health care through incentives to purchase less comprehensive insurance, expand high-risk pool coverage, finance charitable safety net care, and deregulate state insurance regulation" as discussed by the Cato Institute in its policy recommendations (The Cato Handbook, 283-294). The role of government is a theme captured by government initiated actions, government instigated health care initiatives, or federally mandated provisions to access or provide healthcare. This is defined in a general sense by Kingdon as the presence of governmental agenda- "the list of subjects or problems to which governmental officials, and people outside of government closely associated with those officials, are paying some serious attention at any given time" (Kingdon,3). Understanding and coding for an internal and external locus of control is best done by using Rotter's definition of locus of control and searching for terms that referenced or implied the use of either self-help and individualism (internal locus) versus use of a government program or plea for help from a public agency (external locus). Finally, individual liberties, freedoms and markets were depicted through coding for references to the markets, and healthcare being depicted either as a luxury or a necessity and how it should be sold in the markets-with a government or private entity as having majority control.

RESULTS

The following were results found from the quantitative statistical analysis of the data. It appears that while financial considerations are important to small businesses, when placed as the base category of the analysis, two other provisions were statistically significant in the analysis: the individual mandate and community rating. The community rating provision prevents adverse selection, while the individual mandate requires health insurance be bought by all Americans. Both of these provisions were slightly more likely to impact a negative attitude toward healthcare reform for the NFIB than the base category, financial provisions (tax credits, higher insurance premiums, etc.). Since this is a multinomial logistic regression, a relative risk ratio was conducted in place of an odds ratio to portray the relationship between theme and perception. The base category was financial issues because small businesses were typically influenced by their financial situation in policy changes. The community rating provision was 25 percent more likely than the financial issues within health care to initiate a negative perception, whereas individual mandate as a minimum provision was about 13 percent more likely. Medicare and Medicaid expansion and redistribution policies were not a statistically significant issue in the analysis.

Table 1: Provisions Impacting Attitudes on Health Reform for the NFIB versus other Lobbyist Organizations

	Number of observations = 77			
	Likelihood Ratio chi2(3) = 8.47			
	Probability> chi2 = 0.0372			
	Log likelihood = -95.113973			
	Multinomial Logistic Regression of Provisions and Attitudes on Health Reform Policies	Likelihood of Negative Attitude		
Provision #	Title or Concept of Provision	RRR (likelihood ratio)	Std. Error	P>|z|
1	Medicaid/Medicare provisions	0.235	0.232	0.143

2	Community Rating & Guaranteed Issue clause	0.25*		0.183	0.058
3	Individual Mandate as a minimum provision	0.1323529**		0.101	0.008
4	Tax Credits, Premiums and Financial Issues in Healthcare	Base category			
	Statistical significance is starred above as p<.10* ; p<.01**				
	*Base category was provision #4				

An inductive thematic analysis of the data suggests why these categories have negative perceptions. The data indicates that locus of control and American exceptionalism are statistically significant in importance. Other philosophies such as democracy as freedom, the role of government, and public choice theory were less significant overall in the qualitative analysis. A few examples of the thematic analysis are shown below, while the complete analysis is in the Appendix.

Table 2 A: Examples of Classification of Provisions as Themes

	Title of Hearing: National Federation of Independent Business (NFIB) Vs. Department of Health and Human Services (DHHS)			*Date: March 28,2012 Time: 10:19 am Supreme Court Hearing No. 11-400*
	Examples of how the NFIB portrays various themes in a positive or negative light			
Page found	*Provision/Issue*	*Positive/ Negative Perception*	*Interpretation*	*Presentation of theme in relation to a philosophy: 1.Public choice; 2.Government;3. American exceptionalism; 4. Internal/external locus of control;5. Individualism*
12	"Is half a loaf [of bread] better than no loaf? On something like the exchanges, it seems there are situations [where exchanges are involved] where half a loaf is actually worse."	negative	exchanges may be problematic	Distrust in government and government presence. Exchanges that involve too much government influence are problematic and could hurt big business.
17	"Surely there are provisions that are just looking for the next legislative vehicle that is going to make it across the finish line."	negative	Just because some provisions want to make it into a legislation don't make them germane or even necessary to the rest of the act	Distrust in government; problems with provisions being added that aren't necessary.
42	What would happen to the insurance industry, which would now be in the in the hole for $350 billion over 10 years?"	negative	May become more expensive for insurance companies	American values of limited government and greater individualism/freedom for entrepreneurship. Insurance companies are hurt, especially private corporations.

| 48 | "Two-and-a-half million people under 26 have gotten insurance by one of the insurance requirements [in anticipation of the minimum coverage]" | negative and positive | For better or for worse, some expected action and risks have already been taken to get ready for health reform | Anticipated changes are already in effect from banks and people preparing to get coverage; especially impacts youth |
| 54 | "And if you took the minimum coverage provision out and left the other two provisions in....it would make the adverse selection in that market problem even worse." | negative | Risks that were anticipated coupled with no min. coverage could be very hurtful and have serious economic consequences | Presence of severability and adverse selection problems |

More examples of NFIB statements are found in the Appendix.

Table 2 B: Examples of how the Amicus Curiae brief (Opposing view point)Classification of Provisions as Themes

	Amicus Curiae for National Federation of Independent Business (NFIB) Vs. Department of Health and Human Services (DHHS) *Comparison group for the study Amicus Curiae –Opposing views on healthcare by Mr. Farr within the same hearing*			*Date: March 28,2012 Time: 10:19 am Supreme Court Hearing No. 11-400*
Page found	*Provision/ Issue*	*Positive/ Negative Perceptions of Healthcare reform*	*Interpretation*	*Presentation of theme in relation to a philosophy: 1.Public choice, 2.Government 3. American exceptionalism, 4. Internal/external locus of control 5. Freedoms*
56	"It will for millions of people lower prices, which were raised high under the old system because of their poor health."	positive	possibility to lower prices	Public choice; contradicts American value of individualism through risk sharing ; lowering prices for people by reducing adverse selection
57	Premiums do not apply accurately to everybody.	both positive and negative	Premiums could help some while hurting some.	Contradicting American value of individualism; public choice model
62	"For people below 250 percent of the Federal poverty line, Congress also picks up and subsidizes the out-of-pocket costs, raising the actuarial value."	positive	Positive impacts of government involvement.	Role of government and an external locus of control; American values of giving back: helps those in poverty.

67	"In the first 3 years of the operation of the exchanges those insurance companies that get sort of a worse selection of consumers will be given essentially credits from insurance companies that get better selections."	positive	Incentives from Indiv. Mandate in stimulating insurance companies even when they are initially hurt by provisions.	Expanding government's role - could help insurance companies; may be helped by getting credits back for the hurt business
78	"Severability is by necessity a blunt tool."	negative	Severability clause can be debated in its usefulness.	Severing the provisions from the heart of the act could be very problematic.
82	Community rating and guaranteed issue are the crown jewels of the act.	positive	Without these, the entire act falls.	Prevents adverse selection by promoting American exceptionalism in reducing disparities. Provides patient protection, promotes freedoms.

More examples of this table are found in the Appendix.

Table 3: Count of Reasoning/ Thematic Classification for American Healthcare Perceptions

Theme	Total Count	Total Negative	Total Positive
Public choice	5	2	3
Government's role	16	11	5
American exceptionalism	7	4	3
Internal/external locus of control	7	3	4
Liberties/freedom/individualism	6	3	3

Theme	Total Count
Public choice	5
Government's role	16
American exceptionalism	7
Internal/external locus of control	7
Liberties/free markets/individualism/entrepreneurship	6

Discourse analysis of verbatim text can be found in the Appendix. This data demonstrates perceptions of the role of government being the most important driving factor of both those opposing and in favor of healthcare reform. Government's role was mentioned 16 times out of the 41 total count, primarily in a negative connotation.

The government's role is perceived as limiting choice and causing big business to suffer, which is why the NFIB seems to have grievances with it. One example of this is the quote: "If you take the mandate out, the subsidies that the government provides to any individual will increase, and they will be less efficient (61)." This discourse suggests that without the individual mandate requiring all individuals to purchase health insurance, there are consequences that could result in an inefficient system due to the presence of government. Another example of the distrust in government is the following: "Is half a loaf [of bread] better than no loaf? On something like the exchanges, it seems there are situations [where exchanges are involved] where half a loaf is actually worse (12)." To elaborate, this represents the lack of satisfaction toward the government's role in the health information exchanges (HIEs) and government presence, as even a half loaf, or the preliminary role of government in the exchanges, is less useful than no role at all. The NFIB perspective suggests that taking a laissez faire approach of letting the markets play their part free of government intervention is better than involving them in the HIEs.

On the other hand, about five counts of positive attitudes toward government were brought up in discourse. These attitudes include more transparent government policies, reducing information asymmetry through the health information exchanges, catering healthcare access and resources to the underprivileged, pooling risk, and reducing the age differential for those who are covered with health insurance. For example, "In the first 3 years of the operation of the exchanges those insurance companies that get sort of a worse selection of consumers will be given essentially credits from insurance companies that get better selections (67)." Here, there is some positive discourse about a benefit to the health information exchange and health insurance selection process. The NFIB advocates the presence of positive change for small business and insurance intermediaries that are represented by tax credits and support with the presence of government and reducing adverse selection issues. "The exchanges in turn are critical to the tax credits, because the amount of the tax credit is key to the amount of the policy price on the exchange (24)." Again, tax credits may be an offshoot of the health information exchanges because pricing policies are based on the amount of tax credits present. The number of tax credits is actually dependent on the number of businesses who are involved in the health insurance market, which is why public-private interactions have such a large role in this discussion. So, the government provides tax credit incentives to those employers willing to purchase insurance for their employees on the exchange, which in turn allows a HIE to thrive.

Based on the count that was coded in Table 3, such themes as American exceptionalism, an internal locus of control, and American liberties and freedoms also represent a great deal of the reasoning for the perceptions toward healthcare reform. A positive perception of the HIEs (health information exchanges) drives many of the American values, as these HIEs are viewed as a way to provide the nation with greater resources to compare health insurance, improve information asymmetry issues, and even provide cost saving incentives. Looking at Table 2 and the Appendix, claims such as: 1) "The exchanges...are a cost saver" (6); 2) "Surely there are provisions that are just looking for the next legislative vehicle that is going to make it across the finish line."(17); 3) "What would happen to the insurance industry, which would now be in the in the hole for $350 billion over 10 years?"(42); and 4) "Community rating and guaranteed issue are the crown jewels of the act" (82). The reason why these represent American exceptionalism is that the statements seem to advocate taking control of one's problem and not being dependent on government to bail the organization out. The insurance industry is not going to wait as a catastrophe is in the making, but instead, wants to work now to see definite change, using the cost saving mechanism of the exchanges. At the same time, there is some distrust that by asking government to take a lead in health care reform, it may become ineffective and act in vain. The statement discussing using the PPACA as a vehicle to drive other provisions down the finish suggests a way to muddle and overpopulate the original purpose of the act- to make healthcare more efficient and effective for the nation. The negative attitudes toward government's role in health care are depicted by an American sense of internal locus of control and a free markets-heavy, private sector focused approach. A belief that American liberties and equality should play a role in health insurance is represented by the presence of community rating and guaranteed issue provisions, the "crown jewels" of the health reform act (82). This buttresses the argument that eliminating adverse selection is an important goal of the NFIB, even though it may perceive some of the health reform provisions negatively.

Looking at this discussion from anAmerican viewpoint, the legality of various healthcare reform provisions may be differently perceived than views of health reform in other nations, both developing and developed (Feldstein, 235). Many of these philosophies- American individualism, internal locus of control, a focus on free markets and laissez faire values would not be viewed in the same way in "public programs- heavy" nations. Such countries (France, United Kingdom, Canada) have a community based mindset, with values that place importance on charity and equality, and an external locus of control. It seems as though the use of an external locus of control creates positive views toward healthcare, possibly through expansion of government's role and public programs. This is the fairly prevalent viewpoint that is present in European countries that have a bigger role for government, higher taxes and acceptance of public choice theory (Feldstein, 240). On the other hand, a focus on freedom and individualism in the US has remained important, which is why government control should not overshadow the presence of individualism, the ability to choose one's health plan and choices present in making a decision on the best healthcare solutions for ones needs. For this reason, the presence of many of these solutions should be beneficial to the US: a reduction in discriminatory practices (adverse selection) that allows more individuals to be covered in healthcare, information gathering throughthe health information exchange, financial incentives for small businesses in the US, and Medicare and Medicaid expansion provisions. These different provisions were provided a positive perception in the analysis and may provide a balance between American exceptionalism and a move toward a national healthcare system. American values of exceptionalism and progressivism will remain intact if the new public healthcare program protects freedoms, improves information availability, spreads awareness, and provides greater access to all in society.

CONCLUSIONS AND POLICY IMPLICATIONS

It is important to analyze how a positive or negative discourse and attitudes can impact policy making. It is also interesting in gaining a comparative perspective of major healthcare issues and how the US compares to the world in these areas. This paper analyzes thematic content of the hearings in the Supreme Court of the NFIB's dissatisfaction with various health care reform provisions. It takes into consideration a number of themes, from positive and negative attitudes to the philosophies and reasoning underlying these themes. The basis for this analysis included both quantitative and qualitative reasoning, which is presented in the Appendix in greater detail.

From a policy perspective, such attitudes can actually have a direct impact on the mood of the nation, depending on the economic times, presence of free markets, public programs and globalization. As shown, limiting government is still of utmost consideration for the NFIB as business has reason to believe it will be negatively impacted if government takes on too much power. The role of government and its hand in the revamping of the healthcare system may directly impact the attitudes of small businesses, as portrayed through findings in this research and through the Small Business Majority 2011 survey results. This has links to the economy and state of the nation's markets. This also could have implications on other nations through world markets and financial trade networks. At the same time, public choice theory and an external locus of control thrives in many nations across the globe. During this period of globalization, transitioning to a public choice model may help the US find itself comparable to other nations in public health prevention and health improvements. There is hope for improvements to its current health status as it is the highest spender on healthcare but lower in the ranks than many nations for health outcomes(The Commonwealth Fund). Portrayed by the results, small businesses tend to value workethic and disparity reduction through two provisions: 1) community rating and guaranteed provision, as well as 2) focus on individual mandate. These are of greater importance than financial implications to businesses. Using guaranteed issue and community rating provisions, the emphasis in an HIE market and eliminating adverse selection in healthcare will be important in policy initiatives going forward(Small

Business Majority Survey, 2011). Adverse selection was a recurring theme in the analysis, so this seems to be one of the greatest hindrances in the US's pre-healthcare reform strategies. Individualism and freedom are important to small businesses as well as the role of government and trust in government. Financial issues alone have not been found to be a statistically significant priority on the minds of typical NFIB small businesses. This may be because the individual mandate will provide a mandated supply and demand for insurance, impacting financial / taxation policies, as well as many of the other provisions and economic considerations which are tied to the lifestyle and socioeconomicvalues of US residents.

What will work for the US may be different from other nations, based on the set of values inherent in the nation's history. This is described by the focus on American values in this paper. From the presence of adverse selection policies to tax credits, the US has focused on the individual's needs, and a universal mandate should not change that entirely. For this reason, accepting a balance between the new presence of universal health care reform with many traditional American valuesand goals is important for the US if it wants to ensure a satisfied community at large.

WORK CITED

Basu S, Andrews J, Kishore S, Panjabi R, Stuckler D (2012) Comparative Performance of Private and Public Healthcare Systems in Low- and Middle-Income Countries: A Systematic Review. PLoS Med 9(6): e1001244. doi:10.1371/journal.pmed.1001244

Cato Handbook for Congress. Policy Recommendations to the 108th Congress. Pp 283-294.

Cheek. (2004). At the Margins? Discourse Analysis and Qualitative Research. Quality Health Research, 1140-1150.

Crowley, Mary (2009). Values, Health Care Reform, and Universal Participation. New England Journal of Medicine 361:10.

Currie, Janet, and John Fahr. "Hospitals, managed care, and the charity caseload in California." Journal of Health Economics (Elselvier B.V.) 23 (2004): 421-442.

Danzon, Patrick Munch. "Hospital Profits - The Effects of Reimbursement Policies." Journal of Health Economics (North Holland Publishing Company), 1988: 29-52.

De Tocqueville, A. (2000). Democracy in America. University of Chicago Press.

Deal, Terry, and Allan Kennedy. Corporate Cultures: The Rites and Rituals of Corporate Life. Basic Books, 2000.

Dranove, David. "Pricing by Nonprofit Institutions: The Case of Hospital Cost-Shifting." Journal of Health Economics (Elselvier Science Publishers B.V. (North Holland)), 1988: 47-57.

Feldstein, Paul. (2011). Health Policy Issues: An Economic Perspective, Fifth Edition.

Kingdon, J. W. (1984). Agendas, Alternatives, and Public Policies. Boston: Little, Brown.

Lipset, S. M. (1997). American Exceptionalism: A Double Edged Sword. W.W. Norton & Company.

National Federation of Independent Business, ET Al.,Petitioners v. Kathleen Sebelius, Secretary of. (March 28, 2012). (pp. 1-100). Alderson Reporting Company.

Rotter, J.B. (1954). Social learning and clinical psychology. NY: Prentice-Hall.

Sen, A. (1999). Development as Freedom. Oxford: Oxford University Press.

Small Business Majority Survey (2011). Opinion Survey: Small Business Owners' Views on Key Provisions. Sausalito: Small Business Majority.

Squires, D. (2012). Explaining High Health Care Spending in the United States: An International Comparison of Supply, Utilization, Prices, and Quality. The Commonwealth Fund. Retrieved from http://www.commonwealthfund.org/ Publications/Issue-Briefs/2012/May/High-Health-Care-Spending.aspx

Thatchenkery, T. J. (2001). Mining for Meaning: Reading Organizations using Hermeneutic Philosophy. The Language of Organization, 113-131.

Yildiz, M., & Kurban, A. (2011). Discourses of E-Government: An Inductive Analysis. Hacettepe University, Turkey.

Zieger, Robert H. "Labor, progressivism, and Herbert Hoover in the 1920's" Wisconsin Magazine Of History. Volume: 58 /Issue: 3 (1974-1975).

Zirn, C., Niepert, M., Stuckenschmidt, H., & Strube, M. (2011). Fine Grained Sentiment Analysis with Structural Features. Proceedings of the 5th International Joint Conference on Natural Language Processing, (pp. 336-344).

APPENDIX

Examples of how the NFIB perceives various provisions as "themes"

	Title of Hearing: National Federation of Independent Business (NFIB) Vs. Department of Health and Human Services (DHHS) Examples of how the NFIB portrays various themes in a positive or negative light			Date of Hearing March 28,2012
Page found	Provision or Issue	Positive/ Negative Perceptions of Healthcare Reform	Interpretation	Presentation of theme in relation to a philosophy: 1.Public choice, 2.Government 3. American exceptionalism, 4. Internal/external locus of control 5. Individualism
5	Guaranteed issue and community rating provisions	negative	The two provisions together will cause premiums to skyrocket	Individual mandate is tied to these issues; without the mandate, these two issues actually exacerbate healthcare problems.
6	"The exchanges...are a cost saver"	positive	Exchanges will be a cost saver	American exceptionalism principle alleviating info asymmetry; People having freedom to decide; promoting awareness and knowledge
10	The severability clause	negative	the court does not necessarily need the entire act to stand if the heart is gone	Internal locus of control; Other provisions should be given a fair chance. Severability should not impact other provisions which may remain.
11	Individual mandate is essential to the operation of the exchanges.	no positive/negative	individual mandate is the heart of the entire act	Individual mandate has a large government presence. The act itself is mainly based on the individual mandate as a minimum provision.
12	"Is half a loaf [of bread] better than no loaf? On something like the exchanges, it seems there are situations [where exchanges are involved] where half a loaf is actually worse."	negative	exchanges may be problematic	Distrust in government and government presence. Exchanges that involve too much government influence are problematic and could hurt big business.
16	"You can't possibly think that Congress would have passed that hollow shell without the heart of the Act."	negative	These issues and provisions 1- 4 are connected and severing one severs all the rest.	legislative intent; severability; many issues are interconnected

17	"Surely there are provisions that are just looking for the next legislative vehicle that is going to make it across the finish line."	negative	Just because some provisions want to make it into a legislation don't make them germane or even necessary to the rest of the act	Distrust in government; problems with provisions being added that aren't necessary.
24	Individual mandate is tied, as the government suggests, to guaranteed-issue and community rating, but the individual mandate, guaranteed-issue, and community rating together are the heart of this Act. They are what make the exchanges work.	Neither positive/ negative	Together these are tied and linked to the heart of the act	Government's interest
24	The exchanges in turn are critical to the tax credits, because the amount of the tax credit is key to the amount of the policy price on the exchange.	Neither positive/ negative	links between business decisions and government	The intersection of government and big business; How business is impacted by exchanges
24	The exchanges are also key to the employer mandate, because the employer mandate becomes imposed on an employer if one of the employees gets insurance on the exchanges.	Neither positive/ negative	links between business decisions and government	The government's impact plays a role on business through exchanges which have an indirect effect on employer mandated insurance.
25	Medicare provisions in DISH won't work without Indiv. Mandate.	negative	tied to Indiv. Mandate	There is lack of flexibility of Indiv. Mandate as its severability issue impacts many provisions.
26	"We've struck the heart of this Act, let's just give Congress a clean slate."	negative	There is no longer need to have any of the other provisions if you cut out the heart .	Internal locus of control; Taking responsibility in providing Congress a fresh start for the law rather than keeping old issues in the mix.
28	"Without the Indiv. Mandate provision, people would wait to get insurance, and therefore cause all the adverse selection problems that arise."	positive	There is no longer need to have any of the other provisions if you cut out the heart.	American exceptionalism; adverse selection is prevented through Indiv. Mandate.

41	Without minimum coverage, there is adverse selection.	positive	Adverse selection issues are alleviated.	American exceptionalism
42	Economists' view point: "They say that the insurance reforms impose 10-year costs of roughly $700 billion on the insurance industry, and that these costs are supposed to be offset by about 350 billion in new revenue from the individual mandate and 350 billion from the Medicaid expansion."	negative	Expensive undertaking that needs to be financed by Medicaid expansion and Indiv. Mandate.	Liberty as freedom principle; Indiv. mandate is expensive and takes away American liberties/freedoms and imposes a tax.
42	What would happen to the insurance industry, which would now be in the in the hole for $350 billion over 10 years?"	negative	May become more expensive for insurance companies	American values of limited government and greater individualism/freedom for entrepreneurship. Insurance companies are hurt, especially private corporations.
48	"Two-and-a-half million people under 26 have gotten insurance by one of the insurance requirements [in anticipation of the minimum coverage]"	negative and positive	For better or for worse, some expected action and risks have already been taken to get ready for health reform	Bankruptcy is possible without the Indiv. mandate and min. coverage because of anticipated changes that are already in effect from banks and people getting coverage
54	"And if you took the minimum coverage provision out and left the other two provisions in....it would make the adverse selection in that market problem even worse."	negative	Risks that were anticipated coupled with no min. coverage could be very hurtful and have serious economic consequences	Presence of severability and adverse selection problems
	Amicus Curiae for National Federation of Independent Business (NFIB) Vs. Department of Health and Human Services (DHHS) **Comparison group for the study** **Amicus Curiae –Opposing views on healthcare by Mr. Farr within the same hearing**			**Date of Hearing March 28,2012**
56	"The community-rating and guaranteed-issue provisions ought to be struck down is an example of the best driving out the good."	positive	These two provisions are fairly important in the reform, with or without the Indiv. Mandate.	Dependence and need for public/government programs.

56	"Even without the minimum coverage provision, those two provisions, guaranteed-issue and community-rating, will still open insurance markets to millions of people that were excluded under the prior system."	positive	The system is still helping the community even without min coverage	External locus of control. Dependence on public programs. Health reform could be the answer to reducing disparity if some provisions remain.
56	" It will for millions of people lower prices, which were raised high under the old system because of their poor health."	positive	possibility to lower prices	Public choice; contradicts American value of individualism through risk sharing ; lowering prices for people by reducing adverse selection
57	Premiums do not apply accurately to everybody.	both positive and negative	Premiums could help some while hurting some.	Contradicting American value of individualism; public choice model
57	"Their rates will be lower under the system, even without the minimum coverage provision. Their rates are going to be lower than they were under the prior system because they are going into a pool of people, rather than having their rates set according to their individual health characteristics."	positive	pooling risk	American exceptionalism through reduction of adverse selection but contradicts individualism
59	"While the min coverage has worked for some states, it has crashed and burned in others."	both positive and negative	pooling risk	External locus of control; possible that expansion of government programs could have different impacts.
60	The Act authorizes annual enrollment periods, so people can't just show up at the hospital.	positive	Reducing unfair advantages and trying to beat the system.	Public choice theory, but uses American exceptionalism; act has provisions that make sure people are paying attention to their healthcare
60	"For people below 200 percent of the federal poverty line, the subsidy will cover 80 percent, on average, of the premium which makes it attractive to them to join."	positive	Helps those in greatest need through dependence on public programs.	External locus of control; people who need help will get it.

60	"This is important in adverse selection because if you do have a change in the mix of people, and average premiums start to rise, the government picks up the increase in the premium."	positive	Helps those in greatest need through dependence on public programs.	External locus of control; government provides a great deal of help to the underinsured
61	If you take the mandate out, the subsidies that the government provides to any individual will increase, and they will be less efficient.	negative	Without the mandate, there is a worse situation present.	Role of government could cause an ineffective system without the individual mandate.
61	"The overall amount of the subsidies that the government will provide will decline, as the government notes itself in its brief, because there will be fewer people getting them."	negative	Without the mandate, there is a worse situation present.	Possible neg. effect- the overall amount of subsidies reduces.
61	Some people will opt out of the system even though they are getting subsidies.	negative	Without the mandate, there is a worse situation present.	Role of government could cause an ineffective system without the individual mandate.
62	"For people below 250 percent of the Federal poverty line, Congress also picks up and subsidizes the out-of-pocket costs, raising the actuarial value."	positive	Positive impacts of government involvement.	Role of government and an external locus of control; American values of giving back: helps those in poverty.
62	Instead of charging $4000 for a 26 yr old and $12000 for a 60 yr old, now the insurance companies will be charging the same for both.	positive	establishing an age differential of nearly 3 to 1	American exceptionalism; age discrimination is reduced
63-65	Debating how "essential" is used according to Congress in providing requirements that are "essential to an effective health insurance."	positive	Essential could mean useful versus meaning necessary.	The entire goal of the act is tied to the indiv. mandate which is important in reducing guaranteed issue and community rating problems.

67	"In the first 3 years of the operation of the exchanges those insurance companies that get sort of a worse selection of consumers will be given essentially credits from insurance companies that get better selections."	positive	Incentives from Indiv. Mandate in stimulating insurance companies even when they are initially hurt by provisions.	Expanding government's role - could help insurance companies; may be helped by getting credits back for the hurt business
68	Now, I agree that there is a risk and the significance of it people can debate.	negative	The reforms remain risky.	The reform as a whole has its risks.
69	"The minimum coverage provision wasn't something that everybody was bragging about. It was something that was meant to be part of this package. "	positive	Possibility that minimum coverage is not necessarily beneficial but needed for other provisions.	Role of government and the definition of essential again being debated.
72	"The States have tended to change that because they've found that having too narrow a band worked against the effectiveness of their programs."	negative	Lack of flexibility can stifle effectiveness	Flexibility and liberty is necessary in a democracy; one step at a time approach also may be useful.
78	"Severability is by necessity a blunt tool."	negative	Severability clause can be debated in its usefulness.	Severing the provisions from the heart of the act could be very problematic.
78	Economists predict in the year 2020, they are expected to be over $100 billion in that 1 year alone.	negative	Public choice theory and government expansion could be expensive.	Government impacts and public choice theory. Subsidy programs within health reform rack up high costs.
68, 82	Community rating and guaranteed issue are the crown jewels of the act.	positive	Without these, the entire act falls.	Prevents adverse selection by promoting American exceptionalism in reducing disparities. Provides patient protection, promotes freedoms.

Data Conversion for Electronic Medical Records: A Case Study of SGN

Yaw M*, Parag Dighe*, Monty Miller* and Kenneth Wall*

ABSTRACT

Healthcare organizations around the world are recognizing the benefits of maintaining electronic medical records for patients by improved quality of service, free flow of information (multiple locations), reduced cost of operations resulting in cost efficiencies, better health, and efficient utilization of resources. Recognizing these benefits as opportunities, healthcare providers have or are in the process of migrating paper medical records to electronic medical systems. This migration is not always free from challenges. This study presents recommendations for managing challenges with data conversion from paper form to electronic database based on a case study done by students from Colorado Technical University, Colorado Springs, CO, USA for Shri Ganapati Netralaya (SGN), Jalna, India, a prominent eye hospital in the region, using appreciative inquiry.

Keywords: Electronic medical records, data conversion, eye hospitals, quality of service.

INTRODUCTION

Farmer Ashok Singh arrives at the Shri Ganapati Netralaya (SGN) hospital complaining of pain in his right eye. Ashok has been there some years ago and was diagnosed with Glaucoma but since he had not had any symptoms of problems, he has not been back. Upon arrival, he describes his symptoms to the hospital receptionist and explains he had been there before. The receptionist requests his records be brought to the glaucoma clinic where Ashok is escorted. To no real surprise, the records cannot be found among the several thousand records filed in the basement. His history of glaucoma and the results of tests are nowhere to be found so the testing and medical history forms began again. Should there be a better system for finding patient records?

An electronic medical record (EMR) is a computerized medical record rendered or created in a medical institution that provides systematic processing of files and

* Colorado Technical University, Colorado Springs, Colorado, CO, USA.
E-mail: paragdighe@gmail.com , monty@ipsltd.info, kwall@coloradotech.edu

proper organization of timed data for future use (Davis & Garets, 2005). Hospitals generate large amounts of paper based data which results in growing cost of printing and publication, besides making it difficult to retrieve information. Hospitals embraced EMR to address this problem, which would improve the data organization, communication, recording, retrieval, and modification of medical records. In India, the importance of maintaining medical records and following the process and documenting the processes is at a nascent stage.

The success of EMR relies largely on how correctly and effectively the paper based data is converted to electronic database. This adoption requires thorough analysis in data conversion to prevent data loss and interchanges and also to maintain data security during and after conversion. While bigger institutions and hospitals are adopting procedures to follow documentation and record maintenance, smaller clinics and hospitals are yet to follow suite (Thomas, 2009), thus leaving minimum to no medical records for the patients. Electronic medical records would help small as well as larger clinics and hospitals in India to fill the void in maintenance of medical records and simultaneously reduce the vulnerability of unauthorized access or loss due to improper storage.

This paper will show the processes involved in data adoption from about 500,000 paper based data files to electronic medical record for SGN, an eye hospital in Jalna, Maharashtra, India. The study evaluates the methods of data conversion and makes recommendations in context of the resources available with the eye hospital. Appreciative inquiry is used for determining the expectations from the EMR in general, desired goals and strengths of resources available with SGN.

BACKGROUND OF THE STUDY

The success of implementing EMR at SGN depends on how paper based data is converted to electronic database within a reasonable amount of time and cost. The effectiveness of this data conversion also determines whether the converted data is searchable and meets the requirements of the EMR being developed. The amount and type of data to be transferred would require significant resources that need to be managed following a process in order to meet the goals. Apart from financial investments, this SGN initiative would require time to carry out the project, information technology infrastructure which includes servers, user workstations, IT personnel, data security considering online hacking and data leakage. The proposed EMR should be able to secure the data by providing authorized access through the interfaces for the users (Marcus, 2009), to protect confidential files such DNA tests and HIV test results. SGN estimates that the financial investment made will benefit the organization by reducing the operating cost such as reduced paper work, data transfers, mails, test results and physical storage.

STATEMENT OF THE PROBLEM

At SGN patient records are maintained manually in a paper based record system. As a result of several years of operations, the number of records has become huge which is posing difficulties in maintaining and retrieving patient records. SGN is considering EMR to make medical records management more efficient. The implementation of EMR system offers several advantages which outweigh the challenges posed by the adoption. For the project of this size and complexity, it is important for any organization to evaluate the challenges and risks associated with the implementation of EMR and data conversion. This study seeks:

1. To examine the implementation and data conversion challenges

2. To evaluate the methods of data conversion and make recommendations

Purpose and Objective of the Study

The general purpose of the study is to evaluate the methods of converting paper based data into electronic database after considering the type, volume, quality and form of data to be converted. This study also aims to provide general guidelines of implementing a software system in an organization. The recommendations made by this study would benefit the healthcare organizations considering transition to EMR. It would also benefit the managers who can adopt the process guidelines from this study in situations involving system implementation in general.

From the interviews and group discussions with the Human Resource Director and Hospital Director, this study found that SGN is expanding its operations by developing five new regional centers. Their goal is to meet or exceed the patient expectations by providing excellent services. Converting to electronic medical records (EMR) system is one of the several initiatives being undertaken by SGN to meet these goals.

In order to be prepared to face the challenges posed by converting to EMR, the Colorado Technical University (CTU) team was asked to gather information and provide guidance on converting the SGN medical record to EMR. The purpose of this study was to help SGN identify the processes involved to successfully implement the EMR system and also to identify the methods of converting paper based data into searchable electronic database. CTU carried out the study with the following objectives to meet the purpose of the study:

1. Gather information about the present and future state of the operations

2. Recommend methods of data conversion from paper based records to the electronic database

Assumptions and Limitations

This study assumes that the participants have provided accurate information about the estimated amount of data to be converted. It is also assumed that SGN has done the feasibility study for the implementation of EMR and the needs of the hospital and patient care has been incorporated into the system. While evaluating the challenges and limitations of data conversion methods, this study was limited due to the limited availability of English speaking participants.

LITERATURE REVIEW

Introduction to EMR

An electronic medical record (EMR) is a computerized medical record rendered or created in a medical institution that provides systematic processing of files and proper organization of timed data for future use (Davis & Garets, 2005). Medical institutions have been working with a combination of manual and electronic systems to reduce the net operating costs for the hospitals (Garets, 2006).The EMR will stand as the legal record created for hospitals and ambulatory environments thus being a source of statutory reporting and inpatient's or outpatient's needs.

EMR has made significant inroads in various health facilities. An EMR is an automated environment that manages function such as order entry, clinical documentation and clinical support roles (Garets, & Davis, 2006). Others define EMR as electronic records containing the patient's information captured during medical visits.

Role of EMR

The primary role of EMR is to provide and maintain patient medical records. Other scholars argue that EMR are also useful in reducing errors in healthcare and promoting cost reduction strategies essential in limiting exhaustion of healthcare resources (Fraser et al., 2005). EMR is also vital in promoting exchange of information that can allow evaluation of care in remote sites. Furthermore, EMR can also streamline the management of drugs and other communication need within a healthcare environment. These roles situate the need of electronic medical records in healthcare facilities such as hospitals.

Implementation of EMR

EMR implementation consists of modules such as laboratory reporting that provide reporting services to clinicians. In addition, EMR can be implemented to combine data from various services such as radiology and pharmacy into usable services. This model of EMR implementation allows the integration of administrative, radiology, laboratory services, pharmacy, clinical documentation, and computerized physician order entry. The modules work together as a single EMR system.

Benefits of EMR

A wealth of literature indicates that EMR's have many significant incentives. EMR allows sharing of patient's records and their use for research work, unlike paper record. EMR also streamlines management of hospital functions and process such as inventory of resources such as drugs (Fraser et al. 2005). Other benefits of EMR include reduced errors and improve the quality of service in health centers (MacKinnon & Wasserman, 2009). Improved patient participation is also another incentive of EMR use in healthcare cents (Ved et al. 2011).

Challenges and Conclusions of EMR implementation

Despite its usefulness, various challenges have marred the implementation of EMR by healthcare providers. In developing worlds, scarcity of resources has placed a limit on the implementation of EMR systems (Fraser et al., 2005). In addition, prioritizations of need and environment conditions have made EMR implementation lag in some countries (Fraser et al., 2005; Sood et al., 2008). More precisely, lack of developed infrastructure, workforce turnover, incompatibility, and limited training continue to curtain EMR adoption (Ferreira et al. 2004).

There is no doubt that EMR have more benefits to healthcare providers. With EMR mainly made of modules that execute various functions that avail healthcare process, its use allows the automation of process. Therefore, EMR provides exchange of information, along with promoting safety and quality of care. Various implementation of EMR combine various functions into a system that healthcare providers rely to store and retrieve data. EMRs have immense benefits despite challenges such as lack of resources and training. Nonetheless, providers can address these challenges for them to enjoy the full potential of EMRs.

Appreciative Inquiry

Appreciative Inquiry (AI) is the organizational development method that searches for the qualities that enhances the functioning of an organizational system (Thatchenkery, 2005). It focuses on the effects that increase the over-all development in a certain project, office, systems, methods, works, publication and laws (Hall, 2012). Since it is focused on the positive effects, it simply focuses on the terms "what will be" or "what could be". This will help to determine the total effects of the system in an institution. Through an inquiry, it will search with full appreciation on the positive traits in all levels of organization and thus circling its advancements on those things

According to Richard Seel (2008) his impression of appreciative inquiry can be focused on four ways of reporting: Discover, Dream, Design and Deliver. Miller et. al. (2005) also advocated a variant method of Discover, Dream, Dialog and Design to place emphasis on concrete plan when distinguishing the AI processes (Miller, Fitzgerald, Murrell, Preston, & Ambekar, 2005). The AI process focuses on intervention activities, which work for the betterment of the organization. It is not to forget the limitations and liabilities rather consider them to be the opportunities of the work thereof. This is also called the opposite of problem solving: aims to find better ways not the right way. A polarity map compares AI to problem solving results in building the strengths of both methods to deal with the opportunity and the realities of the situation (Miller et al., 2005). The AI approach recognizes the role of the entire workforce in institutions including the president down to the lowest position in the organization. The AI intervention is used to augment trust, develop organizational alignment, and meet expectation of plans. The method aims to create meaning by drawing from stories of concrete successes and lends itself to cross-industrial social activities. It is enjoyable and natural to many managers, who are often sociable people (Hall, 2012).

Project Management

Project Management Institute (PMI) has identified initiating, planning, executing, monitoring and controlling, and closing as the main processes within a project (PMI, 2004). A set of guidelines which includes inputs and outputs of each of these processes and the relationship between these processes has been clearly described. This study has evaluated the applicability of these guidelines to develop the process guidelines for EMR implementation at SGN.

METHODOLOGY

This study used Action Research (AR) and Appreciative Inquiry (AI) to understand the needs, objectives and challenges of implementing an EMR system at SGN. These methods helped the research team in discovering the scope of the EMR system, user concerns and expectations from the EMR system. The AI process revolves around finding what the strengths are, dialoguing where participants may answer questions like "What should be?", and innovating where the participants would try to answer, "What will be?" It follows a 4D cycle comprised of Discovery, Dream, Design and Destiny (Whitney & Cooperrider, 1998). A case study on building a trans-cultural strategic alliance between a U.S. multinational and an Indian family business by Miller et. al. (2005) have shown that Appreciative Inquiries are uniquely suited to deal effectively with challenges in building relationship, understanding, trust and collaboration. Due to time limitation, this study completed the Discovery process and only conducted limited Dream and Design phases of the 4D cycle with hospital participants.

The CTU team comprised of 18 students and 2 professors. Out of these, 3 students and 2 professors were at the hospital in India for five days. The process began with interviewing the HR Manager and Director of the Hospital. They were asked to explain the vision behind converting to EMR. They were asked to identify the departments and key positions within those departments who would either be involved in this conversion or will be affected by this change. The researchers did not have any influence in picking these participants. There was no pre-determined demographic preference for these participants other than asking for people who could speak and understand English. As a result, the participants were picked due to their ability to communicate with the researchers with or without the help of an interpreter. The researchers were still able to collect rich data in spite of the language barrier between them and the participants.

After considering process consultation and Action Research, Action Research (AR) through intervention using AI was chosen as the methodology for this case study. AR was chosen because of the need for actionable knowledge, which was to develop guidelines for implementing the EMR system and recommendations for converting paper data to EMR. AI was kept in mind while framing questions, where focus was more towards the strengths and positive aspects of the current and future state. Based on the assumption that an organization changes in the direction of the studies, use of positive topic for inquiry helps construct positive social realities and collaboration. The team uses group discussions, interviews, evaluation of existing processes and documentation with a goal to bring a positive change thus help preparing the concerned departments to embrace technology in carrying out their activities, which currently depends on manual and paper based processes.

DATA COLLECTION AND ANALYSIS

CTU students worked with ten different departments within SGN to provide information on EMR and the vendor working with the hospital to get the necessary infrastructure including hardware and software to implement the EMR system. The India based research team gathered information about the existing manual process of collecting and maintaining patient records and designed features of the proposed system. In addition, interviews and discussions with the participants were focused on obtaining information on the plans for migrating to the EMR system, transferring data to the EMR from paper based record, amount of paper based records to be converted, data entry skills, quality control and other resources available with SGN and/or its vendor.

It was found had SGN had an estimated number of 50 or more users who saw and/or supported the large patient volume. On a daily basis, 100 new patients and 200 returning patients were seen in the following departments: registration, clinics (glaucoma, cornea, retina, and pediatrics), consultation, the ward, operation theater, optical/pharmacy counters, administration, business office, purchasing, and the gift shop/store.

INTERPRETATION

The study discovered some of the major concerns mostly related to conversion of paper based patient records to electronic database. The analysis was based on the amount of data to be converted and how far back did the hospital want the records to go in the EMR. The study addressed the type of records to be converted and the basis of classifying/identifying the records which would be converted. Also reviewed was how the system could be brought online before all the paper based data was converted.

PRESENT STATE

Since the start of SGN eye hospitalin Jalna in December 1992, patient medical records are maintained manually using a non- electronic record keeping system in the form of paper records. Many of these paper based records are in the form of handwritten script in Devanagari, a script used by many Indian languages such as Sanskrit, Hindi and Marathi (Malik & Deshpande, 2010). Over a period of time, the size of these paper-based records has reached challenging limits, causing delays and in some cases failure to retrieve records. This has resulted in inefficient usage of employee time, loss of productivity and more importantly it has created a bottleneck in improving the level of service to the patients. Figure 1 shows the present file storage system at SGN.

Fig. 1:

Due to lack of time, the CTU team could not gather information which would have helped the research team know if the paper- based system had any impact in the quality and cost of health care being provided to the patient.

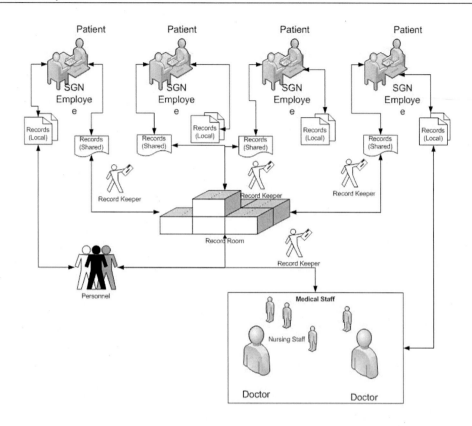

Problems with the present state
- Decentralized data, information about the same patient not shared within the organization
- Slow process of collecting, recording, storing and retrieving paper data
- Needs more people to complete simple task such as retrieving patient records
- Risk of loosing data due to disasters, ageing of paper data, legibility, misplaced documents, manual errors
- Delays in providing information to the patient / SGN departments

Fig. 2:

FUTURE STATE

SGN is acquiring an EMR system from Dewsoft Solutions (DS), which will allow SGN to maintain patient records in an electronic database. The level of services provided to the patient will improve by reducing the time required to retrieve patient information and providing accurate present and historical information of the patient to the medical staff. The service to patient is also improved by facilitating collaboration between multiple functions within the hospital.

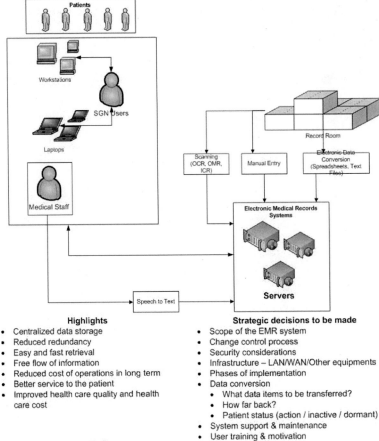

Highlights

- Centralized data storage
- Reduced redundancy
- Easy and fast retrieval
- Free flow of information
- Reduced cost of operations in long term
- Better service to the patient
- Improved health care quality and health care cost

Strategic decisions to be made

- Scope of the EMR system
- Change control process
- Security considerations
- Infrastructure – LAN/WAN/Other equipments
- Phases of implementation
- Data conversion
  - What data items to be transferred?
  - How far back?
  - Patient status (action / inactive / dormant)
- System support & maintenance
- User training & motivation

Challenges

- Capital investment
- Resources
- EMR System – Scope, quality of the system
- Vendor and system reliability
- System support & maintenance
- Security
- Data conversion – difficult and expensive, error prone
- User training

Fig. 3:

RECOMMENDATIONS

After carefully analyzing the information gathered at SGN and understanding the resources available to SGN, the needs and goals of transitioning to an EMR system and the current state of the initiative, the CTU team has made the following recommendations. Since the focus of this study is to determine the methods of converting data from paper-based records to the electronic database, the recommendations for data conversion are elaborated, while only guidelines (PMI 2004) are presented for other areas of system implementation. Additional site analysis is required for providing detailed recommendations on these areas.

General Guidelines

1. Define scope
2. Determine an experienced project
3. Define core and non-core features of the system
4. Define phases & implementation plan – It is recommended that a system with such widespread impact should be implemented in phases. Components should be categorized under core components, add-on components (that can be added in phases) and optional (discretionary) components. The phases may also be defined based on the department priorities and needs.
5. Identify risks and risk management plan – SGN and DS should work together to identify risks associated with every stage of the implementation, categorized by the likelihood of occurrence, impact across the system and organization and any other category seen to be relevant. A risk mitigation plan should be developed for each one of the risks identified.
6. Change control process –All changes should go through a change control process, which may determine the impact, dependencies, feasibility and risks before approving the change.
7. Identify project team
8. System testing and quality assurance –A dedicated team comprised of quality assurance engineers and users should be involved in thoroughly testing the system.
9. System support – The system support and maintenance plan should be laid out and a contract signed with the vendor. It is recommended to have an in-house team, which should be trained to meet the support and minor needs of changes in the system.
10. Communicating change – SGN executive leadership should clearly communicate the purpose, need and benefits of EMR systems to the SGN employees. This communication should include details on how it affects the employees, which departments are affected, what they should expect, timing and the direct benefits for the employees and the organization.
11. User training –The users should be provided appropriate training and support tools such as user manuals, quick reference guides, cheat-sheets, etc.

EMR System Implementation Recommendations for SGN

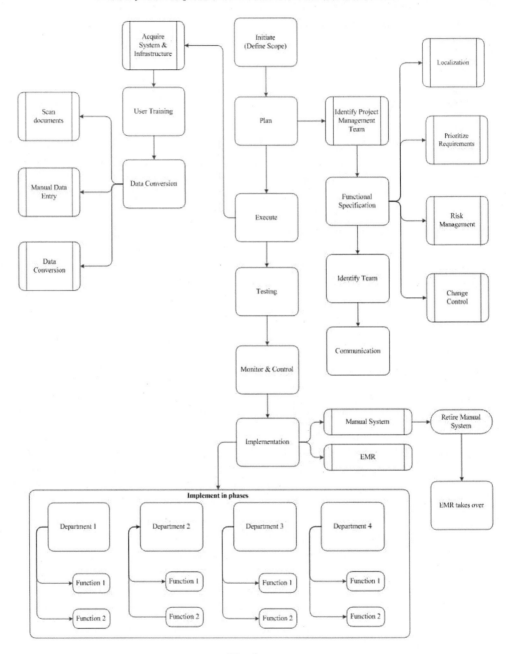

Fig. 4:

Data Conversion Recommendations for SGN

Based on the interviews with the software vendor DS and SGN's IT staff members, this study has made some recommendations for this data conversion process. These recommendations will help SGN achieve its goals with minimum cost, training, support and time, but at the same time be able to feed quality data into the system.

Scoping (AHIMA, 2012)

Scoping the data to be migrated is one of the most important strategic decisions SGN will need to make.It should take into account the purpose of the system, feasibility of transferring data into EMR and reports required from the system. Benchmarks and criteria for the data to be included in conversion should be clearly laid down before picking the method of data conversion and estimating the efforts required. Some of the common criteria on which candidate data can be identified are patient status, the possibility of patient returning to SGN, patient's medical condition, and number of years of past data to be captured, etc.

Methods of data conversion

Manual entry, scanning, speech to text (medical transcription) and electronic conversion are the four methods of data conversion from one system to another.

Manual entry is more time - consuming, and costly, but the benefits of quality of data conversion considering the challenges in automated conversion of handwritten scripts in Devanagari and availability of skilled data entry operators(Kaka & Sinha, 2005), manual entry may be justified in selective areas.

Scanning is easier, faster and depending on cost of resources, sometimes cheaper (Dubiel, 1999). However, in context of cost of resources in India, acquiring scanning software may be more expensive, as compared to hiring temporary workers to do the data entry(Kaka & Sinha, 2005). The cost varies by the quality of original data and language. Acquiring scanning software to scan handwritten script in Devanagari may be challenging. For SGN, scanning can be used for data items, which do not require inclusion in text searches, as they can be stored as images. It may also use a combination of using electronic scanning with manual review of data converted to improve accuracy of automated data conversion.

Electronic conversion (Outlook Associated, 2012) is a preferred method of data conversion, especially when data from one system has to be transferred to another system. However, in the case of SGN, since the data comes from non-electronic sources, hybrid conversion methods can be used where data from paper can be entered into easy to use electronic document management systems such as spreadsheets, text files etc., and then imported into the new system. This will require minimal training and most of the data entry error can be fixed by implementing data validation processes.

Medical transcription and speech-to-text (Bikman and Whiting, 2007, Hurley, 2008) is another non-traditional data conversion method, which is recommended to capture data such as medical reports by the doctors once the system goes live.

Resourcing (Brooks 2004)

This study recommends that SGN hire a vendor to provide an EMR system with the ability to import data from sources such as text files and spreadsheets, with validation routines for capturing errors in electronic and manual data entry. The data conversion process may be expedited and resource requirements can be minimized by filtering the data to be imported into the system based on patient status, location and time, then classifying the data for manual entry, scanning and electronic conversion. In order to support these efforts, it is recommended that SGN hire temporary staff in combination with outsourcing data conversion to meet the strategic goals.

CONCLUSION

Transforming to an EMR system from a manual record keeping and processing system involves challenges due to large financial investments, scope, building or acquiring the system, implementing the system and converting the historical paper based data to the electronic system. This study found that following defined processes minimizes these challenges. This study also concludes that depending on the quality, form and volume of data to be converted, a combination of data conversion methods comprising of manual data entry, scanning, speech to text and electronic conversion would help in effectively converting paper based data to electronic database. Healthcare providers planning for such data conversion should consider filtering the data to be converted based on patient status, amount of historical data required and cost of manual entry versus cost of acquiring software to scan or import data into the electronic database.

This study was carried out by a group of CTU students and faculty as part of an Action Research course.Appreciative inquiry methods helped the research team motivate participation and as a result the study was able to collect information which was used to develop recommendations.

This study provides the guidelines, processes and methods of data conversion based on the information available. Due to lack of time and other resources, a cost analysis for the methods of data conversion could not be done. This study can be extended to include an empirical examination of cost of data conversion based on the specific information about the volume of data to be converted. Also, a detailed examination of features supported by the proposed EMR system may be carried out to determine if the reporting needs are met following the recommended data conversion methods.

REFERENCES

AHIMA, retrieved from http://library.ahima.org/xpedio/groups/public/documents/ahima/bok1_047676.hcsp?dDocName=bok1_047676

Bikman, J. and S. Whiting (2007). "medical transcription outsourcing greased lightning?" hfm (Healthcare Financial Management) 61(6): 94-97

Brooks, G. (2004). "WHAT IS OUTSOURCING?" New Media Age: 4-4

Davis, M., & Garets, D. (2005). Electronic patient records: Emrs and ehrs. *Healthcare Informatics*, 1-4. Retrieved from http://www.providersedge.com/ehdocs/ehr_articles/Electronic_Patient_Records-EMRs_and_EHRs.pdf

Dubiel, B. (1999). OCR scanning system saves time and money, insures good first impression. *Health Management Technology, 20*(5), 42-3

Ferreira, A., Corria, R., Antunes, L., Palhares, E., Marques, P., Costa, P., & Pereira, A. (2004). *Integrity of electronic patient records reports*. IEEE Symposium on Computer-Based Medical Systems.1063-7125/04

Fraser, S.F. H., Biondich, P., Moodley, D., Choi, S. Mamlin, B.W. and Szolovits, P. (2005). Implementing electronic medical record systems in developing countries. *Informatics in Primary Care*, 13:83–95

Garets, D. & Davis, M. (2006). *Electronic Medical Records vs. Electronic Health Records: Yes,There Is a Difference*. Ohio: HIMSS Analytics

Hillestad, R., Bigelow, J., Bower, A., Girosi, F., Meili, R., Scoville, R., & Taylor, R. (2005). Can Electronic Medical Record Systems Transform Health Care? Potential Health Benefits, Savings, And Costs. *Health Affairs, 24*(5), 1103-1117. doi: 10.1377/hlthaff.24.5.1103

Holbrook, A., Keshavjee, K., Troyan, S., Pray, M., & Ford, P. (2003). Applying methodology to electronic medical record selection. *International Journal of Medical Informatics*, (71), 43-50. Retrieved from *http://square.umin.ac.jp/DMIESemi/y2003/20030901/SC.pdf*

Hurley, B. J. (2008). "Dictation Best Practices for Quality Documentation." Journal of Health Care Compliance 10(1): 21-74

Kaka, N., & Sinha, J. (2005). An upgrade for the Indian IT services industry. [Article]. *McKinsey Quarterly*, 84-89.

Kazmin, A. L. (1999). Learning curve gets a boost: TRAINING IN INDIA by Amy Louise Kazmin: NIIT, one of India's leading software companies, has more than 700 computer training centres across the country, *Financial Times*, pp. 03-03. Retrieved from https://login.ctu.idm/oclc.org/?url=http://search.proquest.com/docview/248660719?accountid=26967

Malik, L., & Deshpande, P. S. (2010). RECOGNITION OF HANDWRITTEN DEVANAGARI SCRIPT. [Article]. *International Journal of Pattern Recognition & Artificial Intelligence*, 24(5), 809-822. doi: 10.1142/s0218001410008123

Marcus, D., Lubrano, J., & Murray, J. (2009). Electronic medical record:the link to a better future .*www.physiciansfoundation.org*, *2nd edition*, 1-105. Retrieved from *http://home.smh.*

com/documents/forPhysiciansDocs/documents/EMR_Implementation_Guide_2nd_Ed.pdf

Miller, M. G., Fitzgerald, S. P., Murrell, K. L., Preston, J., & Ambekar, R. (2005). Appreciative Inquiry in Building a Transcultural Strategic Alliance. *The Journal of Applied Behavioral Science, 41*(1), 91-110. doi: 10.1177/0021886304273060

Nikravan, L. (2012). Back to Class. [Article]. *Chief Learning Officer, 11*(1), 18-21.

Outlook Associates, Retrieved from *http://www.outlook-associates.com/docs/MedicalRecordsConversion-quicktips.pdf*

PMI. (2004). A Guide to the Project Management Body of Knowledge. [Book]. *Third Edition,* 341.

Seel, Richard (2008). Introduction to Appreciative Inquiry. New Paradigm Consulting. Retrieved from *http://www.new-paradigm.co.uk/introduction_to_ai.htm*

Sood, S. P, Nwabueze, S. N., Mbarika, W.A, Prakash, N., Chatterjee, S., Ray, P., Mishra, S. (2008). *Electronic Medical Records: A Review Comparing the Challenges in Developed and Developing Countries.* Proceedings of the 41st Hawaii International Conference on System Sciences

Thatchenkery, T. (2005). Appreciative sharing of knowledge: Leveraging knowledge management for Strategic Change. Chagrin Falls, Ohio: Taos Institute Publishing.

Thomas, J. (2009). Medical records and issues in negligence. *Indian Journal of Urology, 25*(3), 384-388. doi: 10.4103/0970-1591.56208

Times, F. (1999). A growing force and going places: The region, especially India, is beginning to realise its potential as a software development powerhouse in the IT sector, says Paul Taylor, *Financial Times,* pp. 01-01. Retrieved from https://login.ctu.idm/oclc.org/?url=http://search.proquest.com/docview/248710154?accountid=26967

Ved, V., Tyagi, V., Agarwal, A., & Pandya, A. S. (2011). *Personal Health Record System and Integration Techniques with Various Electronic Medical Record Systems.* EEE 13th International Symposium on High-Assurance Systems Engineering

Whitney, D., & Cooperrider, D.L. (1998). The appreciative inquiry summit: Overview and applications. *Employment Relations Today, 25*(2), 17-28. doi: 10.1002/ert.3910250203

PART II: Cases in Knowledge Management, Talent Management, and Education

Resource driven organizations depend largely on technology and knowledge for value addition. The knowledge represents the accumulation of experience in the organization which is the result of costly trials, experimentation, and enduring transformation processes. The modern day organization faces challenges to store the tacit knowledge so gathered and retain the talent that delivered it. The cases covered in this section highlight the strategies, methods and practices followed in some of the most successful organizations in managing knowledge and talent. Mohammed Arshad Khan and Santanu Roy in the first chapter reflect upon the innovative steps by the IT major Sapient Corporation. The analysis is geared towards understanding the impact of such initiatives on organizational performance. Jaya Gupta and Megha Singh Tomar analyse the effectiveness of Talent Management practices at Grasim Industries of the Birla Group. The authors refer to creation of talent pool and the intricacies of managing it. Their analyses bring to surface the realization that many of the non-talent pool members feel that the transparency in the talent management process is low. In the next chapter, Geeta Rana and Alok Goel examine the talent retention practices in Bharat Heavy Electricals Limited (BHEL), a massive knowledge intensive public sector organization in India. Their findings are of significant value not just to BHEL but to the hundreds of similarly large public sector entities in India.

Ramkrishnan Tenkasi and George Hay next elucidate the basic principles and key competencies underlying integration of theory and research knowledge to the realm of practice in the context of a study of scholar-practitioners. Their case study suggests employment of six strategies for interrelating theory and practice and two meta-strategies.

Tero Montonen and Päivi Eriksson next analyse how innovation and entrepreneurship have been taught at one Finnish higher education institution. The case study demonstrates success story of a new model of teaching to initiate and enhance a more open and practice oriented innovation process as part of the business degree curriculum. As a nation, Finland has been lauded very positively for their innovative educational system.

Noted case writers Lamy Erwan and Lapoule Paul in the final chapter in this section highlight the complexity of management situations when it comes to using case studies as a teaching tool.

The reality is always more complicated than the classroom and yet the case writer should strive to maintain a deep embeddedness to the real world. The authors share various fine tuning of the pedagogy of case studies in management educationbased on their long years of practice in this area and present a survey of current trends to choose a topic for a case.The half a dozen cases here portray the dynamic world of tacit knowledge sharing, talent management and the field of education.

Enhancing the Edge: Innovative Management of Knowledge at Sapient Corporation

Mohammed Arshad Khan and Santanu Roy**

ABSTRACT

This case study reflects upon the innovative steps by the IT major Sapient Corporation to enhance the knowledge management competencies of the enterprise and of the employees so essential for a company's survival and growth in today's turbulent times. In August 2010, Sapient was named the 45th fastest growing company by Fortune Magazine. The case refers to the steps taken by the company to develop knowledge generation and assimilation tools on its own as well as in partnership with Google such as the Google Enterprise Professional Program and Sapient' s Enterprise Professional Practice that was the core implementation engine of knowledge initiatives at Sapient. The case details the evolution of the major components of this initiative – the People Portal, the Result Space for use the Global Distributed Delivery Model for project development, and the Vox- Internal Networking Platform.

Sapient was also instrumental in developing dedicated e-learning programmes both on Domain and Technology fronts primarily to tackle the twin problems of making the new employees equipped to handle their job assignments as well as to tide over attrition-related issues with the help of a couple of external specialized enterprise learning firms and academic institutions working in the training domain. The case also highlights the strategic thrusts and initiatives driven by Sapient apart from taking internal organizational steps and collaborating with outside partners to develop and nurture knowledge management practices and e-learning environment within the enterprise. The case attempts to fulfil a gap that exists in the case literature, that is, knowledge management initiatives in an information technology firm in the Indian context with a strategic perspective. The analysis is geared towards understanding the impact of such initiatives on organizational performance, and the challenges faced by the management while going ahead with these decisions.

Keywords: Knowledge management, performance, innovation, Sapient, e-learning, information technology.

* Sapient Corporation, NOIDA Oxygen Boulevard, NOIDA, India.
** Institute of Management Technology, Dubai International Academic City, Dubai, UAE.
E-mail: mkhan11@sapient.com;ask_arshad@hotmail.com, sroy@imtdubai.ac.ae; sroy@imt.edu

'Sapient embodies as part of its culture, agile and limber execution of its mission, embracing a spirit of both adaptability and innovation' [1]   **KMWorld, April 2009**

INTRODUCTION

The case takes us through a journey through various knowledge management initiatives undertaken by Sapient Corporation (NASDAQ: SAPE) [2]. The case refers to the steps taken by the company to develop knowledge generation and assimilation tools, developing dedicated e-learning programmes on domain and technology fronts and other strategic thrusts on its own as well as in partnership with other organizations and institutions, and challenges faced by the management in going ahead the way it did and also in the implementation phase.

In March 2009, Sapient Corporationa Boston based global integrated marketing and technology services firm was one of the winners in the *KMWorlD*'100 Companies that Matter in Knowledge Management'* [3]. KMWorld reported that amid the tough economic and credit crisis situation, *'Each company embodies the resiliency and wisdom to identify and act upon their own areas requiring improvement and more importantly, those of their customers. They have the ability to not only survive a potential catastrophe but also thrive and deliver solutions to help their customers succeed, as well'*[3].

In August 2010, Sapient Corporation was named the *45th fastest growing company* by *Fortune Magazine*, a 43-spot improvement over the 2009 rank of 88. Sapient was also ranked #2 in terms of profit growth among the 100 companies, based on a three-year EPS*growth of 188%.[4].

HISTORY OF SAPIENT CORPORATION

Sapient was founded by Greenberg and Moore in 1990 with their own initial capital of $80,000 and got incorporated in 1991; they worked out of a small office in a building owned by Moore's father in Beverly Farms, Massachusetts. Sapient developed and integrated complex client-server applications in the initial years of their existence. By 1994 the revenue rose to $9 million. In 1996, Sapient went public at $21 per share; in the next four years the company attained tremendous growth and the market capitalization increased by almost 25 times its initial offering value. The revenues steadily rose to $502 million.

During the period of recession in US between 2000 and 2002, Sapient witnessed a downfall in headcounts by almost 50% and stock price by $1 per share, but they kept offering competitive services despite the adverse economic situation thanks to its Global Distributed Delivery model***. Sapient kept building a strong client list across different vertical like aviation, financial services, retail,telecommunications, and government services, some of the prominent clients being American Airlines, Merrill

Lynch, Verizon, United States Marines Corps, and Wal-Mart. Sapient kept expanding its capabilities to include personnel with multiple skill sets that included information system architects, web designers and brand strategists. Sapient's headcount increased steadily to 6217 and the service revenues were $546.4 million, a 35% increase from service revenues of $405.6 million for 2006, and a 74% increase from service revenues of $313.6 million for 2005 [5].

In October 2006, Alan J Herrick was named the new President and Chief Executive Officer of Sapient. He succeeded former Co-Chairman and Chief Executive Officer Jerry A. Greenberg who resigned from the company and its board.

In 2007, Verizon, one of the clients of Sapient and a global leader in telecommunications, awarded Sapient with Supplier Excellence Award****. Sapient executed over 50 projects during the past seven years of association with Verizon from 2000 till 2007. The services included business and IT strategy, business applications, business intelligence and outsourcing[6]. In August, 2008, Sapient acquired Derivatives Consulting Group Limited (DCG), a London-based international financial advisory firm which was a provider of derivatives consulting and outsourcing services to institutional players and market participants like investment banks, hedge funds, asset managers and commercial banking clients. The DCG acquisition expanded the TRM capabilities in derivative processing, local and offshore operations support, operations benchmarking and technology services [7].

In January 2009, Sapient acquired Planning Group International, Inc. (PGI), to enhance thestrength of the company in advertising, digital and direct marketing, and brand development. The acquisition expanded their service offering to online, offline and multi-channel marketing strategies and programs [8]. In July 2009, Sapient acquired Nitro Group Ltd., a global advertising network operating across North America, Europe, Australia and Asia. The acquisition expanded the digital commerce and marketing technology services of Sapient to traditional advertising services. The acquisition also added 330 employees to Sapient. [9].

In February 2010, Sapient re-aligned the organization structure consisting of three divisions: Sapient Nitro, Sapient Global Market, and Sapient Government Services. As of now Sapient had over 9000 employees in North America, Europe and the Asia-Pacific region, including India and the annual revenue was over $850 million.

A snapshot of the current revenues can be seen in Annexure, Exhibit 1 – Sapient Revenue [10].

SAPIENT INITIATIVE 1: DEVELOPING KNOWLEDGE GENERATION AND ASSIMILATION TOOLS

As Sapient business grew and expanded into new markets at both domestic as well as global fronts, the leadership considered scattered operational data and knowledge as a key challenge and a big risk to productivity and organizational efficiency. They sensed a compelling business need for a system which had centrally-located data that will help the employees with the information they need to be more productive and drive the bottom line. The idea was to effectively connect with both in-house employees and customers spread across various geographies and to enable them to create and foster a collaborative environment in the organization. In May 2006, a serious push to this effort was given when Sapient partnered with Google to join the Google Enterprise Professional Program to further their success in finding innovative solutions to complex business problems of their own and that of their customers. *'Companies want to find new ways to extract value from the massive amounts of information stored within their organizations. With Google's enterprise search technology, we are further strengthening our ability to help our clients unlock the value in their information and make decisions in a timelier manner'*, said Sapient Executive Vice President Alan Herrick. [11].

Sapient established the Enterprise Portals Practice (EPP) in order to create necessary information infrastructure that allowed organization to effectively connect with in-house employees and customers. It included the development of systems web content management, intranets, document management and digital asset management systems. The very idea was to give the employees an engaging, intuitive and useful tool that not only creates a collaborative community experience but had the potential for further growth and expansion.

COMPONENTS OF SAPIENT ENTERPRISE PORTALS PRACTICE (EPP)

The EPP was the core implementation engine of knowledge initiatives at Sapient consisting of many tools and programmes. The below mentioned tools were the major components of EPP.

People Portal

The People Portal was the new face of the corporate intranet of Sapient. It actedas a pivot along which all the knowledge sharing activities revolved. It was an online portal based on Microsoft SharePoint Server 2007. Prior to People Portal Sapient had a corporate intranet which was plagued by couple of problems of Information sharing, communication hindrances and stale Information. Due to these very issues employees spent huge time in searching for answers on the corporate intranet. The absence of a unified place for up-to-date corporate information resulted into huge loss of time for the helpdesk resources for answering trivial policy or process related queries of the employees. The employee headcount was growing rapidly and spread across geographies. It was, therefore, imperative for the business to provide a central place of access for all corporate Information and company policies as it became very critical for their success. Keeping these points in mind Sapient went on to upgrade their corporate intranet with the objective of increased team collaboration, smooth information flow and knowledge sharing. The quest was to make an online community which was centralized and provided organizational information which was relevant, organized, current and reliable, improving communication and be time efficient.

In mid-2007, Sapient started the development of its new corporate intranet based on Microsoft SharePoint server 2007 with the help of Microsoft consultants. They leveraged on the out-of-box features of SharePoint to reduce their development effort and better the future maintenance. Sapient took six months to create the new portal. The initial version of the portal contained more than 1500 plus pages, 1000 plus documents and around 45 community sites. Since Sapient had a corporate collaboration with Microsoft so this became a cost efficient solution [12].

The challenges faced during the development of People Portal were even more diverse in nature, from the fresh content development to managing stakeholders' expectations and from maintaining the excitement and awareness towards the people portal among employees to keeping end user needs in view. When the People Portal was launched the benefits were evident from improved usability and accessibility of information along with enhanced performance. Sapient conducted an internal survey of employees which revealed some key metrics [13]:

- 97% employees were aware of People Portal;95% have visited it.
- 42% employees visited it a minimum of once per week; 36% visited it daily.
- 59% employees used People Portal to get information; 44% did visit it when sent a link.
- 70% employees believed the site organization was better than the old Intranet.
- 59% employees believed that the ease of finding relevant information and the functionality were superior.
- 56% employees believed that the content quality was better.

Overall, 69% employee found the new portal an improvement over the old intranet.

It seemed that the primary objectives of providing a unified online platform for information sharing and communication, enabling improved usability and accessibility etc. had been achieved. As of now the People Portal acts as a knowledge portal which contains comprehensive information regarding the organization, people, project and its practices [14].

A snapshot of the people portal can be seen in Appendix, Exhibit 2 – People Portal.

Result Space

ResultSpace was a project management and collaboration tool based on agile lifecycle management. In early 2000 when Sapient started using Global Distributed Delivery model for project development, it was increasingly tough for the project team, which were scattered across the globe, to be on the same page and collaboration across the scattered team members became a real challenge. A compelling need was sensed for an organized, secure, centralized and accessible repository for all the various project artifacts that made the team collaboration easy, robust and scalable to meet the business needs.

The ResultSpace was a web application so it was accessible from all the places. It was based on subversion; a source control mechanism which made sure that the critical project information was never lost and always is available at hand. It was accessed via a secured mode which made the sharing of project document and code remotely very safe and easy.

The Result Space came with various features like agile project estimation and planning, progress tracking and reporting metrics, defects, issues, and risk management, custom trackers, document sharing, collaborative content development, traceability, notification services and role-based access control etc. due to these features it brought certain key business benefits like increased productivity for project teams transparency for client stakeholders and resource visibility to the managers to monitor and drive down costs.

The success of ResultSpacein internal project management prompted Sapient to launch it in the market as a project management and collaboration tool based on agile methodologies. It was believed that the end clients will be benefitted by optimized delivery distribution, reduced cycle time of iteration, cost effectiveness and improved coordination between the project team for the clients [14].

A snapshot of the Project Dashboard can be seen in Appendix, Exhibit 3 – ResultSpace.

Vox – Internal Networking Platform

Sapient principally believed that every employee was a potential source of knowledge which he would have acquired either by experience or formal learning. The employee, therefore, was both a creator and a consumer of the knowledge. This very idea prompted Sapient to create and imbibe a learning culture wherein every employee was able to share his ideas and experiences.

The crux behind Vox was to increase the collaboration and facilitate idea sharing among the employees in real-time. This was a very unique organizational initiative at Sapient. It provided the platform using which the employeeswere able to actively participateand share ideas. The employees were able to create their own specific groups and forums to discuss their ideas, problems and get the answers which were specific to their domain, practice and verticals.

In August 2011, Business today published an article regarding few companies, about their innovative ways of encouraging their employees to think and innovate.

Sapient was commended for Vox, the in-house networking platform. *'Like Facebook, the platform includes special forums and groups which enable engineers and technical professionals to post and resolve queries'*, said Anand Bhaskar, Vice President, People Success at Sapient India[15].

Sapient Initiative 2: Developing Dedicated E-Learning Platforms

Sapient was working under three different division named Global Markets, Nitro, and Government services. All these divisions were having diverse nature of work. Global Markets worked on capital and commodities market technology services. Nitro worked on Digital Advertising and allied areas and Government services worked with the Federal Government to undertake their technical projects. As new employees joined, there was a need for rapid ramping up of these employees both on domain and technology fronts so that they can be staffed on the projects at the earliest and get billable. Although Sapient had a very good and robust hiring process in place but then it was still not able to full fill the need for required level of advanced domain and technological skills that would make the new employees suitable for their new job assignments. The attrition rate was also a key concern, which has been hovering around on an average of over 20% consistently. The attrition rate was much higher than the industry norms and with each employee leaving the organization the acquired knowledge dissipation was all the more evident. The other challenge was to de-alienate employee training platforms from class room based training modules as thesewere not scalable across the geographies.The trainers were not easily accessible to all geographic locations and travelling for them was fast becoming hugely expensive. The set-up of other allied classroom infrastructureat all office places for learning and development was tough and expensive. Keeping these issues in consideration, Sapient wanted to establish dedicated e-learning platforms both on domain as well as on technology frontsthat were scalable, easily accessible, and updateable. Given the unprecedented change and advancements happening at very fast pace at global market places there was a constant pressure for new training initiatives and update the existing ones to be in line with the current market needs. These e-learning programs were intended for both augmenting and enhancing a skill-gap of the existing and new employees of the organizations and were used to rapidly ramp up the necessary skills.

Sapient roped in couple of external specialized enterprise learning firms and academic institutions in working in the training space to initiate these platforms at the organizational level. Although Sapient had to pay a phenomenal cost towards the setup and as license fees for these initiatives but the management envisioned the benefits were far greater and compelling than the capital investments needed for these kinds of initiatives. Moreover,it was realized that these initiatives were the need of the hour as the class room mode was just not feasible.

Acumen was roped in to augment and enhance the Domain skills in Finance. The Acumen provided integrated enterprise training with the state-of-art learning management. The eLearning for Financial Markets was highly recognized in the Industry. The training contents were created by a highly reputed professional having vast industry experiences in global financial markets. To top it all, Acumen used latest online learning techniques like simulations to re–enforce and enrich the process of knowledge transfers. The programmeswere very intuitive, easy-to-use and the interactive content brought a compelling online experience of blended learning in finance domain. The flexible structures of the training programmes combined with new learning techniques delivered fast and quantifiable results [16].

Inner Working was another firm which was roped in to upgrade the technology skills in the area ofsoftware development based on Microsoft technologies as this was one of the major technologies used in development of software projects. The learning platform was based on SharePoint which gave out-of-box features of collaboration and content sharing. The programme was designed to be configured at individual level with the help of personal software and gave ample scope for personalized, self-paced .NET training with lots of examples and design challenges that was expected to enable the employee to hone and augment their technical skills [17].

The Oxford Princeton Programwas a world class training programme in the dynamic energy and derivative market. It included trading, hedging, risk management, and the physical markets. All these training initiatives were internet-based which made them accessible from anywhere, anytime. The trainings were customized to the organizational needs. Sapient collaborated with the Oxford Princeton Programand after extensive surveys, charted out courses which were specific to their commodities business. It was open to all the employees of Sapient Global Markets who wanted to enhance their domain skills [18].

All these programmes were augmented by the regular in-house communication and collaboration tools like Communicator (a peer to peer communication tool), Outlook (a mail server), WebEx(a web conferencing, online meeting, desktop sharing and video sharing tool) etc. to facilitate knowledge sharing.

Sapient Initiative 3: Launching a Journal and a Derivative Handbook

Sapient Global Market, a division of Sapient which workedin Capital and Commodity market offers advisory, analytics and technology solutions to institutional players and market participants. They floated 'Crossing'. This was a journal of Trading and Risk Management. It was a very classic case of promulgation of acquired knowledge and brand awarenessshowcasing the depth of understanding of the domain knowledge and competencies. It also exhibited the thought leadership of the Company giving it an edge over the competitors. The journal contained articles on the contemporary issues of trading, risk, regulatory issues and compliance in the current global market [19]. In October 2010 Sapient launched an'Over the Counter' handbook for the derivative market that contained consolidated references to all the OTC regulatory commitments and market utilities available for 2010 [21]. Initially this was meant for the clients of Sapient but later this handbook was made available to the public at large. *'The purpose of the handbook is not to justify Industry Initiatives, but to raise awareness and create a better understanding of how market participants can meet them successfully. Ultimately, we compiled them into one convenient handbook to provide clients with a one-stop reference point for these initiatives. We are happy now to offer this handbook to thePublic for free download from our website'*said Chip Register, SVP and managing director of Sapient Global Markets.

Apart from this Sapient also regularly publishes whitepaper and case studies on wide variety of topics and area of operations to put their perspective and understanding. All these initiatives helpedSapient consolidate its position and brand as a premier player in Capital and commodity market services space.

THE ROAD AHEAD

Sapient so far has done quite well to setup these e-Learning initiatives in the organization but now the crux lies in to increase the knowledge awareness and sharing among the employees, to promote and motivate people to contribute to the knowledge processes. Considering the ever increasing employee base it will also be a challenge of some sort to continuously check the existing knowledge artifacts for its current business relevance, update/add new artifacts and to enhance the efficiency of accessibility to all the employees. Sapient has to augmentthese initiatives with somekind of mechanism to measure the effectiveness of these programs. What remains to be seen is how well Sapientwill act upon these challenges and imbibe in its culture the quest for knowledge management excellence and they better do. As Aristotle rightly said, *'We are what we repeatedly do; Excellence then is not an act but a habit'.*

ACKNOWLEDGEMENT

The authors which to thank Deborah Overdeput Director and Head of Marketing, Sapient Global Market for support provided in development of this case and permission to present and publish the same at ICMC 2012

Notes

*   KMWorld is the leading information provider serving the Knowledge, Document and Content Management systems market. It is the publishing unit of Information Today Inc.

**   EPS – Earning per share indicates a company's profitability. It is the portion of a company's profit which is allocated to each outstanding share of common stock.

***   Global Distributed Delivery is a one model where in a project is executed with the help of multiple project teams scattered across several different physical locations.

****   Supplier Excellence Award was established by Verizon to recognize its most valuable partners for outstanding service and exceptional performance.

REFERENCES

http://www.sapient.com/Assets/AssetHandler/ArticlePdf/1041.pdf, accessed on 11 Nov 2011

www.sapient.com, accessed on 11 Nov 2011

http://www.kmworld.com/articles/editorial/feature/kmworld-100-companies-that-matter-in-knowledge-management-52787.aspx, accessed on 12 Nov 2011

http://www.bloomberg.com/apps/news?pid=conewsstory&tkr=SAPE:US&sid=aEIw9Ddb8nDE. Accessed on 11 Nov 2011

http://edge.sapient.com/assets/ImageDownloader/156/YaleSOMSapient.pdf, accessed on12 Nov 2011

http://www.4-traders.com/SAPIENT-CORP-10740/news/Sapient-Corp-Verizon-Honors-Sapient-with-Supplier-Excellence-Award-374287/, Accessed on 12 Nov 2011

http://uk.reuters.com/article/2008/08/07/idUS249664+07-Aug-2008+BW20080807, Accessed on 12 Nov

http://www.businesswire.com/news/home/20060104005786/en/Sapient-Completes-Acquisition-Planning-Group-International, Accessed on 12 Nov

http://www.adweek.com/news/advertising-branding/sapient-buy-nitro-50-mil-99479, Accessed on 12 Nov

http://www.nasdaq.com/symbol/sape/revenue-eps, Accessed on 12 Nov

http://www.bloomberg.com/apps/news?pid=newsarchive&sid=aWvyoSUvNI0M, Accessed on 12 Nov

Microsoft case study on People Portal, accessed on 13 Nov 2011

http://www.expresscomputeronline.com/20090420/management01.shtml, accessed on 13 Nov 2011

http://edge.sapient.com/assets/ImageDownloader/176/SapientPeoplePortal.pdf, Accessed on 13 Nov 2011

http://www.sapient.com/resultspace/, accessed on 14 Nov 2011

http://businesstoday.intoday.in/story/companies-are-encouraging-employees-to-think-and-

innovate/1/17119.html, accessed on 14 Nov 2011

http://www.acumennet.com/EnterpriseLearningArena.htm, accessed on 14 Nov 2011

http://www.innerworkings.com/, accessed on 14 Nov 2011

http://www.oxfordprinceton.com/, accessed on 15 Nov 2011

http://www.4-traders.com/SAPIENT-10740/news/SAPIENT-Global-Markets-Examines-Financial-Reform-Legislation-in-Crossings-The-Journal-of-Trading-13441067/, accessed on 22 Nov 2011

http://www.sapient.com/Assets/AssetHandler/ArticlePdf/1519.pdf, accessed on 22 Nov 2011

Talent Management Practices and its Effectiveness at Grasim Industries

Jaya Gupta* and Megha Singh Tomar**

ABSTRACT

This research was undertaken to analyse the effectiveness of Talent Management practices implemented at Grasim. A questionnaire was designed highlighting the key areas of the Talent Management practice executed in the organization. A sample survey was performed with the help of this questionnaire targeting staff employees of Grasim. The survey intended to find the perception of the employees with respect to the Talent Management process and the level of satisfaction for the process. The study revealed that the employees' perceived Talent Management process as effective for most of the themes defined. But major disagreement existed over the selection parameters for getting into the talent pool. Most of the non talent pool members felt that the transparency in the Talent Management process was low and the awareness regarding the Talent Management process should be increased.

Keywords: Talent management, Grasim, perception, effectiveness, talent pool.

INTRODUCTION

In today's global market, 'people success' consists of aligning the company's vision, values and strategy with the Talent Management process so as to form a coherent whole. It is also important to align the Talent management process to the expectation of the employees and the employer so as to reap collective benefits out of it. To declare a process to be successful, it is essential to know the perception of the people involved in it. Designing a good process and implementing it successfully is important but it is equally important to evaluate the process to find out if the desired outcome was accomplished.

* Faculty, Birla Institute of Management Technology, Greater Noida, India
** PG Scholar, Birla Institute of Management Technology, Greater Noida. India
E-mail: jaya.gupta@bimtech.ac.in, meghas.tomar13@bimtech.ac.in

BACKGROUND OF THE PROBLEM

The study focuses on Talent management practices in the context of Grasim Industries Limited, Nagda. Talent Management practices of the Aditya Birla Group are considered to be the best in the industry. So it is expected that employees should perceive Talent Management practices at Grasim as effective. The Grasim Industries under Aditya Birla Group is one of the major conglomerate of private sector industries in India and a major Indian multinational. The company has a well-defined structure and system for Talent management, which was put in place in 2003. The study intends to throw some light on the effectiveness of the Talent Management practices implemented in Grasim. The major motive is to identify areas of improvement in terms of Talent Management, if any, and provide recommendations for the same.

NEED FOR THE PRESENT STUDY

Although there is a talent review process in place to monitor the progress of the talent pool members, there was no process to study the perception of the employees in relation to Talent management and to know engagement level of the employees with the Talent management practices at Grasim. With this study, it is expected to get a measure of the awareness of the employees and to what extent they relate themselves to the Talent Management process.

OBJECTIVES OF THE RESEARCH

The study aims at analysing following facts in context of Talent management practices:

1. To assess the perception of employees at Grasim regarding the effectiveness of Talent management practices in the company.
2. To compare the perception of the employees and the senior management on effectiveness of Talent management practices.
3. Compare the perception of the talent pool members and other employees.

LITERATURE REVIEW

Traditionally, Talent management is referred exclusively to the development and replacement of top executives. However today, it is realized that attracting and retaining talented employees should take place at all levels within the organization. This idea leads to a shift from the idea of one single ladder (i.e. one talent pipeline focused only on potential leaders) towards the idea of multiple talent-ladders or pipelines (i.e. talent pipelines for different kinds of people in the organisation, not exclusively leaders). Talent management aims at improving the potential of employees who are seen as being able to make a valuable difference for the organisation, now or in the future. Moreover, Talent management leads to improved organisational performance.

A talent is an individual with special competencies. In a business context these competencies are of strategic importance to the organisation. The absence of these competencies would pose an actual situation of crisis for the organisation. Furthermore, they are hard to copy for other organisations and can rarely be developed here and now. (Marieke, 2009).

In order to manage these talents, organisations are thinking about special ways to attract, develop, and retain talented employees. These initiatives are constituents of Talent management. Talent management aims at improving the potential of employees who are seen as being able to make a valuable difference for the organisation, now or in the future. Moreover, Talent management should improve organisational performance. According to Croteau (2011), perception means everything and the way to manage this is to learn as much as you can about your employees, build up their skill sets, plan for succession and recruit additional talent to your organization. Furthermore, Talent management does not necessarily mean moving talents upwards in organisations. The most important task for organisations is to make sure talents are situated at the position that suits them best. Also, it is deemed important that Talent management is embedded in the organisational culture.

TALENT MANAGEMENT

Definition

In the early 2000s, Talent Management was expected by some to be an HR buzzword that would come and go (Stainton,2005; Sullivan, 2004). However, Talent Management has proven itself to be more than just a buzzword, as the importance of Talent Management has been receiving increasingly greater attention in academic and professional spheres. Upon reviewing definitions of Talent Management, one thing becomes evident; there is no universal definition of the term and no universal consensus of the activities that should be included under its umbrella (Blass, 2007; Suvillan, 2004). But there seems to be consensus on one fundamental goal of Talent Management: *Finding the right person, at the right time, to put in the right position.*

DEFINING THE PROCESS

Talent Identification

Before Talent Management programs can begin, companies must identify the employees who will take part in these activities. Different companies have different identification and selection processes for identifying talent as well as different criteria regarding which individuals are regarded as talent(Blass,2007;Stainton,2005). When companies search for talent, one approach is to look for competencies within individuals which are regarded as most important. These differ across companies based on companies' priorities and values. Another indentification process that has emerged is known as an Organizational Talent Review (OTR). During an OTR, high potentials go through an evaluation of a number of different criteria such as their potential, learning agility, people skills and their ability to drive change. An OTR can be conducted both by internal resource or outsourced for a third-party assessment (Watkin, 2007).

Talent Development

Once talents have been identified and selected within organisation, the next major process is developing those talents. Learning and performance development are corner stones in Talent Management. Additionally, Barlow (2005) notes that difference in current talent skills and abilities result in different learning and development potential based on the approach adopted. Barlow argues that in addition to each individual's unique capacity to learn and develop in different ways, development should also be dependent upon that individual's likely career trajectory. Literature suggests that while the identification and development of talent are important functions of HR department, there are many different approaches to both these processes.

Recent Developments

Small (2012), argues that what employees feel about their organization is not dependent on the outcomes they get but the processes implemented in the organization. If the employees perceive that processes are handled in a fair way, they are most likely to stick to the organization even if they don't get the best of everything. Understanding the mindset of the employees is essential to get the fruitful outcomes from processes like Talent management. Capelli (2011) argues that instead of blaming the education system for not producing the 'Industry Ready' candidate, the companies should find people capable of doing a job with training and practice. The whole idea of attracting and developing talent rotates around finding candidates eligible to be called as 'Talent' and then to develop them. Perrin (2010), concludes, that organizations are focused on the value of Talent management practices to an unprecedented degree. As Talent management systems stretch the visibility of managers to better understand and manage people, workforce trends; it also helps employees to seek opportunities to climb up the career ladder. In this way, HR becomes the strategic enabler of Talent management processes that empower managers and employees and the employer. ADP(2010) highlights that like any other strategy which requires investment of time, money and resources, it is essential to measure the effectiveness of Talent management programs implemented in the organization.

In a study conducted by SHRM India to understand how the Indian corporate are dealing with the war of talent (2008), various HR directors, vice presidents were interviewed across 8 industry sectors and it was found that it had become difficult to find talent because of competition from global firms, mindset of employees to switch jobs frequently and unrealistic employee expectations. Also to develop the talent in the right manner the focus should be on tapping talents from varied groups-young people, managers, etc; customized training; emphasis on a learning culture, education up gradation schemes, etc.

THE ORGANIZATION - ADITYA BIRLA GROUP (ABG)

The Aditya Birla Group is India's first Global Multinational Corporation with turnover of more than US $ 35 billion Corporation ,with more than 1,00,000 employees across nation and presence in 25 countries all across the world. Over 60% of the revenues flow from overseas operations. Recognized as 'The Best Employer in India & amongst top 20 in Asia', global rankings of the group are no 1 in Viscose staple Fibre, 3rd largest producer of primary aluminium in Asia with largest single location of copper smelter and the 4th largest producer of Insulators & Carbon Black.

THE COMPANY - GRASIM INDUSTRIES LTD., NAGDA

Grasim Industries Limited was incorporated in 1948; Grasim is the largest exporter of Viscose Rayon Fiber in the country, with exports to over 50 countries. Grasim is headquartered in Nagda, Madhya Pradesh and also has a large plant at Kharach (Kosamba,Gujarat).

Grasim Industries Limited, a flagship company of the Aditya Birla Group, ranks among India's largest private sector companies, with a consolidated net revenue of Rs.216 billion and consolidated net profit Rs.22.8 billion (FY 2011)Starting as a textiles manufacturer in 1948, today Grasim's businesses comprise viscose staple fibre (VSF), cement, chemicals and textiles. Its core businesses are VSF and cement, which contribute to over 90 per cent of its revenues and operating profit.

Key HR Initiatives

Human resource practices at Grasim Industries and all over ABG group are considered as best HR practices. HR initiatives taken by ABG are world class initiatives and the advanced initiatives undertaken by ABG are regarded as best HR practices.

Some HR initiatives at Grasim rated high include: Recruiting & staffing, Employee Engagement , Nurturing Talent, Development Assessment Centres, Talent revives, Talent engagement, Career moves & succession plans,Education & Training

Talent Management at Grasim

Watkin's (2004) offers one of the simplest explanations of the concept. Chris suggests replacing the word "talent" with "potential" and the word management with the words "identification" and "development". The identification and development of potential is what Talent management is all about. At ABG, Talent management initiative was formally launched in November 2003 to provide a common framework of for all the group companies. The challenge for the group is to identify and develop the explicit as well as latent talent of individuals, to optimize individual and business performance. As such, talent that is relevant to a business context needs to be identified earlier & developed.

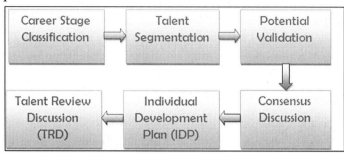

Chart 1: ABG Talent Management Framework

ABG Talent Management Framework

To be effective at each career stage, people are required to develop and sharpen different competencies and behaviours. Over all there are nine behavioural competencies which

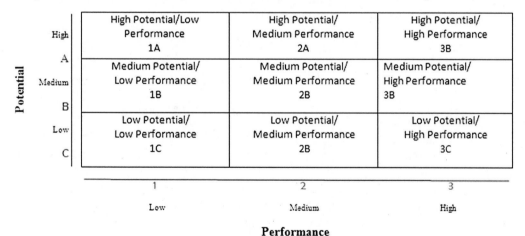

Chart 2: The Nine Box Performance Potential Matrix

the individual needs to develop throughout the career at different career stages. The two criteria on which the talent pool is segmented are Performance and Potential.Using the Nine Box Matrix, every individual must be rated on his/her performance and on his/her potential to move to the next two career stages. This rating on performance and potential is the basis for identifying the individual with one of the nine boxes in the matrix

Annual Talent Review

To ensure that the collective efforts on the Talent management processes yield results for the benefit of the business, it is important to record, measure and systematically monitor the outcome of the process over a period.

METHODOLOGY

Research Design

The research relies mainly on primary data collected from 80 respondents who were staff cadre employees from Officer, Engineer, and Assistant Manager to Assistant General Manager, Deputy General Manager and General Manager ranks. This has been collected with the help of questionnaire on Talent Management practices based on three themes – (a) reasons for Talent management, (b) approach of organisation and (c) characteristics of Talent management. The questionnaires have been tested for reliability through T-Test and Cronbach's Alpha. The data was statistically analysed using graphs and t-test to derive at conclusion.

An exploratory research was designed to collect data from respondents and to analyse it. The exploratory research helped to select the best-suited options in the design, data collection methods, etc.

QUESTIONNAIRE DEVELOPMENT AND SCALING TECHNIQUES

The questionnaire development work included developing a questionnaire to cover the main parts of the Talent management process. Several interactions were carried out with HRD employees to understand the practical application of Talent Management process and how was the talent reviewed. After discussions with key officials at Grasim and considering the relevance of the same in the company's context, 12 questions were shortlisted for the questionnaire.

The whole questionnaire was divided into three themes:

- Reason to implement Talent management practice at Grasim
- Approach adopted by the organisation towards implementing Talent management practices
- The characteristics of Talent management practices

Each theme comprised of 4 questions and employees were asked to rate each question on the 4 point Likert scale, with the format - 'Strongly Agree', 'Agree', 'Disagree' and 'Strongly Disagree' was used.

Sampling Techniques

The research intended to collect the responses from employees of various departments, designations, age, and tenure. 'Purposive' sampling based on these aspects was employed in the 'Convenience' method. The survey covered more than 10 departments. Only the staff employees working in general shift duties were included in the sample. The employees of shift duties working in morning and night shifts were excluded because of timing constraints. A sample size of more than 70 was decided to get a proper representation of the staff employees of Grasim. The departments represented includes Shares Department, Staple Fibre Division, E&DD, Accounts, Spinning, Grasim Staple Fibre, IT, Purchase, PC4,Excel Fibre Division, MCHP, Auxiliary. The employees from all the Designation like Officer, Engineer, Assistant Manager, Deputy Manager, Manager, Assistant General Manager, Deputy General Manager, General Manager. The work experience of respondents varied from 1 to 20+ years. The age of respondents ranged from 21 to 50+ years

DATA ANALYSIS AND RESULTS

T-Test

To ensure the reliability of the data considered, a two tailed T-Test was conducted on all 80 responses. The t-test reflects whether the factor was able to map the perception of the respondent such that he /she could agree or disagree clearly.

Hypothesis H0: *There is no significant difference between people who wish to agree and who wish to disagree.*

Hypothesis H1: *There is a significant difference between people who wish to agree and who wish to disagree.*

Table 1: Table for p-value for each of the item

Q1	Q2	Q3	Q4	Q5	Q6	Q7	Q8	Q9	Q10	Q11	Q12
6.66E-21	5.10E-19	5.51E-17	2.41E-24	1.16E-15	1.82E-10	1.02E-14	1.27E-12	2.23E-16	1.10E-10	7.51E-07	0.004

After doing the T-test for all the items, the p-value for the items was found to be less than the value at 0.05 level of significance, so we rejected the Null Hypothesis. Therefore, there is a significant difference between the people who wish to agree and who wish to disagree on effectiveness of Talent Management at Grasim.

Reliability Test

The reliability test was performed on all the 12 questions, which were included in the main survey for Talent Management. A Cronbach's alpha value of 0.852 was obtained assuring a strong reliability.

Table 2: Reliability test for scale of questionnaire

Cronbach's Alpha	N of Items
.852	12

The scale was reliable which assured consistency in future use. It will provide consistent results for repeated testing.

Perception of Employees Regarding Effectiveness of Talent Management Practices

The mean response for each item was evaluated in response to reference constant of 2.5. Mean value higher than 2.5 indicated positive mean responses. Responses lower than 2.5 are indicative of misalignment of perception of employees regarding the effectiveness of Talent Management practices.

Table 3: Mean result of T-test

	t	*Mean*	*Std. Deviation*	*p-value*
Q1.desire to improve business results	12.771	3.30	.560	6.66E-21
Q2.enhance behavioural competencies	11.750	3.29	.599	5.10E-19
Q3.desire to manage internal talent	10.676	3.29	.660	5.51E-17
Q4.manage talent for business growth	14.716	3.39	.539	2.41E-24
Q5.org. goals are linked to IDPs	9.987	3.12	.560	1.16E-15
Q6.open and transparent sharing of assessment reports	7.319	3.01	.626	1.82E-10
Q7.accelerate employee's career growth	9.502	3.10	.565	1.02E-14
Q8.behavioural competencies are clearly defined	8.429	3.12	.663	1.27E-12
Q9.purpose and result of TALENT MANAGEMENT is well communicated	10.360	3.10	.518	2.23E-16
Q10.IDPs help TALENT MANAGEMENT pool members attain desired level of competencies	7.431	3.10	.722	1.10E-10
Q11.result of TALENT MANAGEMENT program are clearly evaluated	5.376	2.88	.624	7.51E-7
Q12. nine box matrix should be the only parameter for identification of TALENT MANAGEMENT pool	2.997	2.76	.783	.004

It is evident from the table above that the mean responses for all the questions are towards agreement which indicates effectiveness of Talent Management practices at Grasim as perceived by the employees. However, amongst the 12 items least agreement is on Q11 and Q12 being 2.88 and 2.76 respectively. This shows that considerable amount of respondents feel that the result of Talent Management program are not evaluated properly and there should be other parameters to select members in talent pool.

Theme Wise Results

Perception of employees at Grasim regarding the effectiveness of Talent management practices in the company.

Theme 1: Purpose of using Talent management practices at Grasim

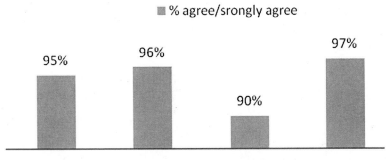

Graph 1: %agreement on Theme 1

The responses showed that 97% of the employees agreed that Talent management practices implemented at Grasim to manage Talent for Business growth while 96% agreed that it is implemented to enhance behavioural competencies.

The Talent management process implemented at Grasim is aimed at building leadership skills of the employees by strengthening the behavioural competencies.96% of the respondents agreed to this fact. This shows that the purpose of Talent management process is well communicated amongst the employees.

Theme 2: Approach of organization towards implementation of Talent management practices

There was least agreement on the fact that there is open and transparent sharing of assessment reports in this theme. 13% of the respondents felt that behavioural competencies are not clearly defined. Although percentage of agreement on the following theme is high, the implementation can be made more effective by increasing the transparency in sharing assessment reports.

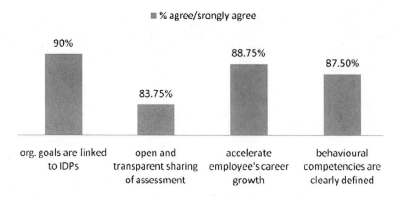

Graph 2: %agreement on Theme 2

Theme 3: Characteristics of Talent management practices

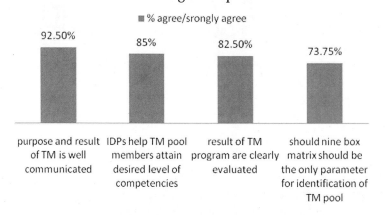

Graph 3: %agreement on Theme 3

Characteristics of Talent Management practices at Grasim include stages in Talent Management process in which 92.50% of the population agreed that purpose and result of Talent Management is well communicated between employees.

Majorly there is disagreement on nine box matrix being the only parameter of identification of talent pool members. The disagreement is 27%. Suggestions were given to include other parameters such as qualification, work experience, conduct aptitude tests, weekly assessment of performance. Around 18% of the respondents were not satisfied with the evaluation of the results obtained after the action plan was executed. Proper evaluation would help the talent pool members improve their performance based on the action plan designed and this would also help to check if the action plan is being followed properly by the talent pool member.

Perception of the employees and the senior management on effectiveness of Talent management practices.

Theme 1: Purpose of using Talent management practices at Grasim

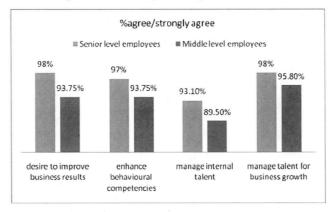

Graph 4: %agreement on Theme 1 by Senior and Middle Level Employees

The level of agreement is quite similar for all the items of this theme. This shows that employees at senior level and middle level perceive the reason of implementing Talent management process in similar way.

Theme 2: Approach of organization towards implementation of Talent management practices

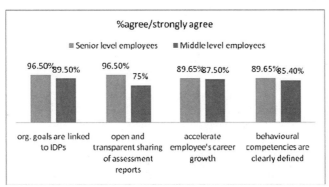

Graph 5: %agreement on Theme 2 by Senior and Middle level Employees

Around 97% of senior-middle management felt the assessment reports were shared openly whereas 25% of the middle level employees disagreed on the same. This shows that the reports are not shared openly at middle level.

Theme 3: Characteristics of Talent management practices

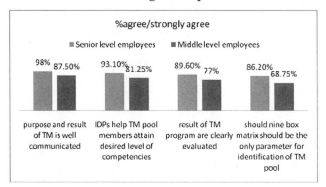

Graph 6: %agreement on Theme 3 by Senior and Middle Level Employees

Only 2% of the senior level employees disagreed to the fact that purpose and result of Talent management was well communicated whereas 14% of the middle level employees disagreed to it. Result of the Talent Management process needs to be openly shared at middle level.

The difference in agreement on nine box matrix being the only criteria for selection of talent pool members was 18% between the senior level and middle level employees. Almost 32% of middle level employees showed disagreement on this question whereas it was 14% for senior level employees.

Perception of talent pool members and other employees on effectiveness of Talent Management practices

Theme 1: Purpose of using Talent management practices at Grasim

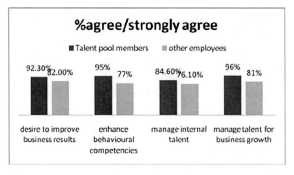

Graph 7: %agreement by Talent Pool Members and Other Employees

95% of the talent pool members agreed that Talent management practices were implemented to enhance behavioural competencies whereas only 77%

on other employees agreed to it. This shows that the talent pool members are more aware about the process then other employees.

Theme 2: Approach of organization towards implementation of Talent management practices

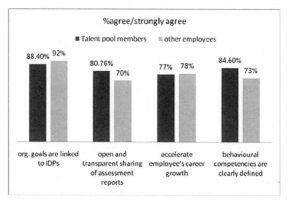

Graph 8: %agreement on Theme 2 by Talent Pool Members and Other Employees

The areas of disagreement were open and transparent sharing of assessment reports and whether Talent management helps in accelerating employee's career growth. 23% of talent pool members felt that Talent management did not help in accelerating the career growth. This indicates that talent pool members are not satisfied with their Individual Development Plans. Action plan should be made more effective aiming at career growth.

Also 27% of non talent pool members felt the competencies were not clearly defined. This indicates that these employees are not aware of behavioural competencies at each level.

Theme 3: Characteristics of Talent management practices

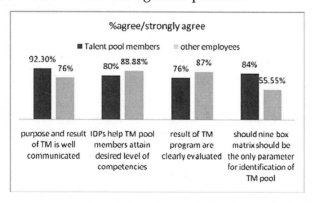

Graph 9: %agreement on Theme 3 by Talent pool Members and other Employees

Result of this theme had some interesting facts. Firstly 24% of non talent pool members felt that the purpose and result of Talent management was not well communicated. Again the transparency and openness of the process needed to be increased.

Secondly, only 80% of talent pool members felt that Individual Development Plans (IDPs) helped them attain desired level of competencies whereas agreement on the same was 88% by non-talent pool members. Other employees perceived that Talent management practices were good but on the other hand the talent pool members who were part of it were less satisfied with the process.

Thirdly, 24% of talent pool members were not satisfied with the evaluation of the result of Talent management process. Lastly, almost 45% of non talent pool members were not satisfied with the selection process of talent pool members. This indicated that employees were interested to get into talent pool, but were highly dissatisfied with the selection process which might take off their interest over Talent Management.

RECOMMENDATIONS

Talent management requires a talent culture to be developed to make talent conversations acceptable throughout the organisation and individuals are encouraged to expand their networks.

Selecting the right talent is important and recognition of right talent is even more essential for that. With the compulsion of bell curve, most of the employees are given a rating of 3 or 4. But they may have high experience or potential to grow. So to select them into talent pool, other criteria can be introduced. This will highly motivate them and they will feel highly related to their job which will improve the performance in turn adding to the growth of the organization.

Nine box matrix is a good tool to judge the performance and potential of the employees   but other criterion such as qualification, experience, aptitude test can also be used to judge the performance of employees having appraisal rating of as 3 and 4 for 2 consecutive years.

They should be given a chance to compete. The selection process can be made harder for them compared to employees in very good and excellent range of appraisal.

First parameter for selection can be qualification followed by experience.

If employee meets the above requirements, an aptitude test can be conducted to check on conceptual and logical skills of the employee followed by a personal interview.

The result obtained from the above selection process should be combined with the nine-box matrix result to get the final selection done.

If the desired level of proficiency is achieved by the talent pool member then he/she can share his experience with other members so that will they can build competencies according to their Individual Development Plans (IDPs).

Experts from the industry can be invited to guide talent pool members to build on their competencies and achieve the desired level of proficiency required according to the Individual Development Plan (IDP) designed.

Talent management leads to segmentation and which would lead to conflict with diversity and inclusion initiatives. Talent management systems can complement diversity initiatives in Talent management system can be ensured by equal opportunity to enter the talent pool and transparency over selection criteria.

Discussion forums can be organised where talent pool members can explain the selection process to other employees and clear the doubts.

CONCLUSION

The study and research shows that Talent management at Grasim is effective. The Talent management process at Grasim is good and it can be improved further by increasing awareness about Talent management among employees. The process can be improved by working on key aspects – generate more awareness among employees, introducing other criterion for selection of Talent pool members, more involvement of junior level employees, discussion forums for employees to increase the knowledge of employees about Talent management.

ACKNOWLEDGEMENT

The authors would like to express their sincere thanks to Grasim Industries Ltd. for its support in developing this case, the consent to present the same at ICMC2012 and publish the same in ICMC2012 proceedings.

REFERENCES

ABP (2010), 'Effective Talent management Has Become an Essential Strategy for Organizational Success', White Paper, ADP Inc.,2010. Retrieved on 28th June, 2012 from http://www.adp.com/tools-and-resources/case-studies-white-papers.

Barlow, L. (2005): Talent development: The new imperative, *Development and Learning in Organizations*, 20(3):6-9

Blass, E. (2007): Talent management: Maximising talent for business performance, *Chartered Management Institute and Ashridge Consulting Limited*, Retrieved on 13th June,2012 from http://www.ashridge.org.uk.

Croteau, P. (2011): Talent management 2011- Perception means everything, *Legacy Bowes Articles*. Retrieved on 15th june,2012 from http://www.legacybowes.com/latest-blog-posts/entry/talent-management-2011-perception-means-everything.hTalent management.

Capelli, P. (2011): Why Companies Aren't Getting the Employees They Need, *The Wall Street Journal*. Retrieved on 21ˢᵗ July, 2012 from http://online.wsj.com/article/SB100014 240 5297020442240457659630897409182.hTalent management

'Corporate Indian Companies: Forging New Talent Pipelines and Creative Career Pathways', Article, SHRM India, November 2008.

Marieke, B. (2009): Talent Management- Alternatives to the single-ladder approach, Faculty *Report, Danish Business Research Academy (DEA)*. Retrieved on 28ᵗʰ June, 2012 from http://dea.nu/sites/default/files/Report_EHRM.pdf

Small,D. (2012): Declining Employee Loyalty- A Casualty of the New Workplace, Knowledge@Wharton. Retrieved on 15ᵗʰ july,2012 from http://knowledge.wharton. upenn.edu/article.cfm?article=2995

Stainton, A. (2005): Talent management: latest buzzword or refocusing existing processes? *Competency & emotional intelligence*, Vol. 12, No. 4

Sullivan, J. (2004): Talent management defined: is it a buzzword or a major breakthrough,*ere. net* http://www.ere.net/articles. Accessed on 13ᵗʰ June,2012.

Perrin. (2010): Tower Perrins Global Workforce Study 2010. Retrieved on 16ᵗʰ July,2012 from www.towerwatson.com.

Watkin, C. (2007): How to manage leadership talent strategically, *People Management*, 13(22): 44-45 http://www.ashridge.org.uk/

http://www.forum.com/_assets/download/c5a3677e-5e9e-4cf8-a3bb-e27480f90891.pdf

http://www.grasim.com/about_us/index.hTalent management

APPENDIX

Questionnaire – condensed version

Survey to assess the effectiveness of Talent Management Practices at Grasim

Please indicate the extent to which you agree/disagree with the following statements by placing a (X) in the appropriate box.

Employee details: Name of employee [optional] –

Designation –

Department –

Age	21 - 30	31 – 40	41 - 50	50 +
Years of Experience	0 - 5	6 – 12	13 - 20	20+

Questions:

Theme 1: Talent Management practices are used at Grasim for following reasons:

Sr no.	Particulars	Strongly Disagree	Disagree	Agree	Strongly Agree
1	Desire to improve business results				
2	To enhance behavioural competencies of employees				
3	Desire to manage internal Talent effectively				
4	Better management of Talent for business growth				

Theme 2: Approach adopted at Grasim towards implementation of Talent Management practices:

Sr no.	Particulars	Strongly Disagree	Disagree	Agree	Strongly Agree
1	Organisation goals are linked to IDPs				
2	Open and transparent sharing of assessment reports				
3	To accelerate employees career growth				
4	Behavioural competencies required at each level are clearly defined				

Theme 3: The Characteristics of Talent Management practices:

Sr no	Particulars	Strongly Disagree	Disagree	Agree	Strongly Agree
1	The purpose and desired results of TM is well communicated				
2	IDPs helps talent pool members attain desired level of Competencies				
3	The results of TM program are properly evaluated				
4	Do you think nine box matrix (Performance – Potential) should be the only parameter for identification of talent pool				

Retaining Talent in Bharat Heavy Electricals Limited: An Indian PSU

Geeta Rana* and Alok Goel**

ABSTRACT

This case examines the talent retention practices in Bharat Heavy Electricals Limited (BHEL), a Navratan public sector undertaking(PSU) of Government of India. It analyses the extent, strategy and imperatives of talent retention practices in BHEL. This case explores in detail the unique talent retention practices followed by BHEL. It demonstrates a number of practical tools HR professionals can utilize for talent retention within their organizations. The talent retention practice ensures that the turnover rate is as low as possible and the available workforce is suited for all needs. BHEL is a knowledge intensive organization whose survival or success is highly dependent upon knowledge-based-activities, processes, skills and talented employees. The purpose behind selecting this company is due to BHEL's reputation on focusing towards employees' development specially through innovative HR practices. This is an organization where not only the management is supportive but the employees also are engaged in various assignments in rapidly changing technology area. The results indicate that more government organizations need to consider the strengths of talent management system and implement a formal talent management strategy.

Keywords: Talent management, human resource management, organization development, talent retention, public sector management.

INTRODUCTION

Employees are one of the most important stakeholders in an organization and are the major enablers for the achievement of aspirations of other stakeholders. They are in fact the medium through which the vision and mission of an organization can be realized and greater goals can be attained. In this context, it is important to ensure that the factors that adversely impact employee morale are identified and addressed.

* Research Scholar, Department of Management Studies, Indian Institute of Technology, Roorkee.
** Research Scholar, Department of Management Studies, Indian Institute of Technology, Roorkee.
E-mail: mauli.sharma870@gmail.com, alok goel @gmail.com.

The first plant of BHEL was established more than 50 years ago at Bhopal and was the genesis of the heavy electrical equipment industry in India. BHEL is today, the largest engineering and manufacturing enterprise of its kind in India, with a well recognized track record of performance, earning profits continuously since 1971-72. BHEL caters to core sectors of the Indian economy viz. power generation, transmission, industry, transportation, telecommunication, renewable energy, defense etc. BHEL has a wide network consisting of fourteen manufacturing divisions, four power sector regional centres, over hundred project sites, eight service centres and fourteen regional offices which enable the company to be closer to its customers and provides them with suitable products, highly efficient systems and services and competitive prices. Having attained ISO 9000 certification, BHEL is now well on its journey towards Total Quality Management (TQM) on the environmental management front. Major units of BHEL have acquired the ISO-14001 certification also. The company's inherent potential coupled with its strong performance over the years, has resulted in it being chosen as "Navratna" PSU. BHEL statements of Vision and Mission, as well as the Values, and list of publicly stated policies are given above in Table 1.

Table 1: BHEL's Vision, Mission, Values and Policies

Vision	A World-Class Engineering Enterprise Committed to Enhancing Stakeholder Value		
Mission	To be an Indian Multinational Engineering Enterprise providing Total Business Solutions through Quality Products, Systems and Services in the fields of Energy, Industry, Transportation, Infrastructure and other potential areas		
Values	1. Zeal to Excel and Zest for Change	2. Integrity and Fairness in all Matters	3. Respect for Dignity and Potential of Individuals
4. Strict Adherence to Commitments	5. Ensure Speed of Response	6. Foster Learning, Creativity and Team-work	7. Loyalty and Pride in the Company
Policies			
1. Works Policy	5. IT Policy	9. Corporate Governance Policy	
2. Purchase Policy	6. Information Security Policy		
3. Quality Policy	7. Energy Management Policy		
4. Knowledge Management Policy	8. HSE Policy		

HUMAN RESOURCE ACCOMPLISHMENTS AT BHEL

Beginning from 1980 till date, BHEL has witnessed a phenomenal growth in personnel. At BHEL human resources are planned, managed and improved. It is reflected in corporate vision, mission & values and HR pole star statement "Enhancing value to employees and society resulting in committed and highly motivated human resource for effective achievement of business objectives and striving for better quality of life to the society". These policies are issued as personnel manual and are reviewed and revised based on strategic plans, business policy and various feedbacks including surveys.

At BHEL, employees' feedback is an essential part of policy related decisions. HR policies are developed and executed through established three tier participative management forums viz. joint committee at corporate level, plant council at unit level of management-union body and shop councils at function level management-union body. As a policy matter, the company also involves employees and unions in developing HR policies/plans.

HUMAN RESOURCE DEVELOPMENT INSTITUTE (HRDI)

Guided by the HRD Mission statement of the company "To promote and inculcate a value-based culture utilizing the fullest potential of Human Resources for achieving the BHEL Mission", the HRDI, Noida a training wing of BHEL, has revitalized the whole system through a step by step strategic long term training process and several short term need based programmes based on comprehensive organizational research which enable the human resources to unearth and hone their potential. In a major advancement, an integrated Human Resource Management system was implemented during the year 2010-11, which aims at reaching out to the internal stakeholders on real time basis and redefining the role of HR functions as a strategic partner in business, through process standardization, optimization and seamless enterprise integration. Some of the core programmes include Strategic need based programmes; Competency based programmes and Functional programmes like Advanced Management Programmes (AMP), General Management Programmes (GMP), Senior Management Programmes (SMP), Middle Management Programmes (MMP), Young Managers Programmes (YMP) and Self Starter Programmes (SSP) for budding managers. In addition, the HRDI provides professional support to Corporate HR and HRDCs at Units/Divisions. HRDI is also accepting consulting assignments from other organizations in a selective manner. During the year 2011-12, HRDI conducted 69 programmes spread over 352 days. A total of 1544 participants have been covered giving 7286 training man-days.

OBJECTIVES OF THE STUDY

This case study illustrates the key dimensions for talent management in BHEL. This study first examines the theoretical understanding of talent management followed by review of qualitative and quantitative studies on talent management to uncover the manifestation of talent retention and reveal its antecedents and consequences at BHEL.

This study addresses following key questions. What model can help HR professionals to identify and address the key issue of Talent Management System? How human resource professionals implementing this model for organization excellence? It seeks to answer the question: what are the innovative practices adopted by BHEL for improving talent retention in Indian public sector? These include the following:

1. To analyze the key drivers for talent retention and to understand the variables influencing talent management in BHEL.

2. To ascertain employee satisfaction levels of the employees in BHEL and to identify the areas in which BHEL is lagging.

3. To suggest ways to improve the talent retention at BHEL.

RESEARCH METHODOLOGY

An exploratory, inductive approach using grounded theory as described by Glaser and Strauss (1967) is adopted for this study. Grounded theory is a well-established inductive process for developing theoretical models with a high level of rigour. This inductive approach is being used to gain an understanding of the concerns of stakeholders involved in establishing the process of talent management under the ambit of grounded theory. Interviews conducted with the stakeholders are the primary mode of data collection. A short set of 'why' questions revolving around why and how the talent management system in BHEL is used in each interview. In addition, the researchers were able to gain data from other sources, such as direct observation via on-site visits to BHEL, Hardwar.

This research study included interviews with BHEL HR managers, HR executives, line managers and employees to get a better understanding of the talent retention practices in BHEL context. The data for this case study includes analysis of interviews with a range of stakeholders. The paper is based on the practical experiences. The authors' experiences are transferable and there are a number of key messages which will be of use to HRD managers.

TALENT RETENTION PRACTICES AT BHEL

BHEL has recruited more than 20,000 highly talented and competent personnel at all levels during the last five years. At BHEL in the process to reorient human resources and focus to develop not only employees' competencies, but also their performance and potential in alignment with their ongoing business challenges like leadership development competency mapping and succession planning initiatives are in various stages of implementation. The recruitment is planned and done through a defined process to maintain a balance of youth & experience to meet the future challenges.

Executives are recruited through campus recruitment and all India entrance examination at Corporate level. Recruitment of non-executives is done at unit level. To bring transparency in recruitment process, the undertaking shares the criteria /

guidelines with unions. Govt. regulations/ guidelines are also complied with. The general process of recruitment is shown as in Figure 1.

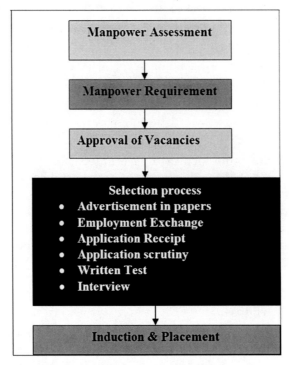

Fig. 1: Recruitment Process

BHEL fully adhere to the reservation policy of the Government of India and implements it in letter and spirit in making recruitment of its employees by keeping certain percentages of reservation in direct recruitment as well as promotion in specified posts and for specified reserved category of candidates, viz. SCs, STs, OBC's and physically challenged. Besides, rules regarding provision of certain concessions and relaxations in direct recruitments, promotions and reservation for housing for specified category of employees are also complied with. The Presidential Directives on the subject issued from time to time are being strictly complied with and reservation percentages are ensured through maintenance of Post Based Roster system as prescribed by Govt. The overall representation of SC/ST/OBC[1] employees

---

[1.] These represent Scheduled Castes, Scheduled Tribes and Other Backward Classes in the cast ridden Indian society. The reservations are ordained by constitution and sanctioned by the highest court of the country and are justified in the name of uplift to be provided to certain section suppressed by the society since generations.

in total manpower was 19.59%, 5.40% and 18.28% for SCs, STs and OBC respectively as on 31.12.2011. BHEL have a total of 755 Physically Challenged employees in BHEL as on 01.01.2012.

Employee retention refers to the ability of an organization to retain its employees. However, some people consider employee retention as relating to the efforts by which employers attempt to retain employees in their workforce. For talent retention, competency assessment has remained an area of focus at BHEL. The employees are assessed through competency framework. The methodology used for the assessment and development manpower is e-map cycle. This e-map is the foundation for an outstanding talent management program. A systematic method of alignment of individual and team objectives with company's targets has been ensured through the implementation of e-map performance cycle. Figure-2 illustrates the cascading of company level targets vis-à-vis individual targets with reference to finances, stake holders, internal process and strategic capability perspectives outlined in balanced score card. Identification of talent is directly related to the higher motivation and performance of an employee. A realistic target for an individual employee must be in line with the organizational goals. Employees need a periodic feedback to check their performances. Effective performance appraisal program is a vital part of the overall talent management system. A proper balance between evaluation of present performance and the reward system within the organization helps the employee remain motivated towards attaining personal and organizational goals. In this sense, retention becomes the strategies rather than the outcome.

For the senior leadership, development centers are organized for assessment of leadership competencies based on BHEL's leadership competency framework. Around 160 senior executives at the level of GM and AGM are covered through this exercise every year. Based on the assessment, competency gaps have been identified and individual development plans have been created to bridge the gaps. Competency requirements are drawn from Strategic Plan whereby every function identifies its competency needs. Based on identified needs, employees in different categories are inducted. All employees on induction undergo comprehensive induction training programme. On cadre change from worker to supervisor and from supervisor to executive, orientation training of two weeks is provided to all of them. Technical, managerial & leadership competency requirements of the executives are identified through e-MAP. Identified competency gaps are met through internal/external training, participation in the in-house technical meets, seminars, workshops and on the job training etc.

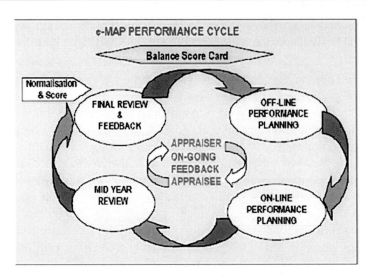

Fig. 2: E-Map Performance Cycle at BHEL

All HODs/ DROs identify the training needs of their employees for the year and get it incorporated in the annual training calendar through their respective training coordinator. On-line personnel training database is also available. To develop managerial and leadership competencies, AMP (Advanced Management Programme) for GMs, GMP and SMP for middle management and YMP for young executives' up to Manager level are organized on regular basis. The faculty for these programmes is drawn from Corporate Apex Mgmt, Industry leaders, IIMs and other professional bodies. Training needs of workmen are also identified to ensure their effective redeployment. To enhance the effectiveness of training with regard to usefulness, content of programme, duration, trainer's capability etc., BHEL has introduced a system to evaluate effectiveness of training at different stages namely input, process & output (post training evaluation). This will help in aligning training needs with organizational needs & meet the emerging challenges.

At BHEL succession planning and career development exercise are the thrust of talent retention programme. The process followed for succession planning at BHEL is depicted in Figure-3. Training and other growth opportunities including promotions are the avenues also available for career development (Figure- 4). Executives can rise to the highest office in the organization. Meritorious workers are promoted as supervisors and supervisors as executives as per the policy. Performance appraisal system for executives is continuously reviewed based on feedback from online survey & performance plan audit workshops.

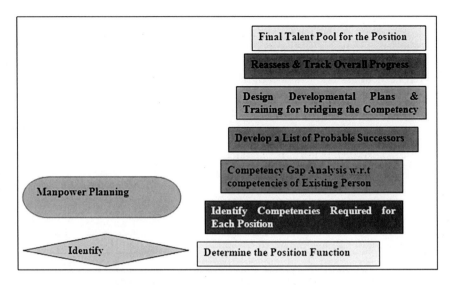

Fig. 3: Succession Planning Process at BHEL

BHEL CONDUCTS VARIOUS INTERVENTION EXERCISES REGULARLY FOR TTALENT RETENTION

Employees are also encouraged to participate in seminars/ conferences and to become the members of various professional bodies. Executives are routinely sent to collaborators'/ equipment manufacturers' sites to enhance their technical knowledge & skills. Selected executives are trained for development of their assessment/ audit skills (Figure-4). Through succession planning and career development employees are trained to realize their full potential. Besides, several approaches to realize full potential of the employees are also in vogue.

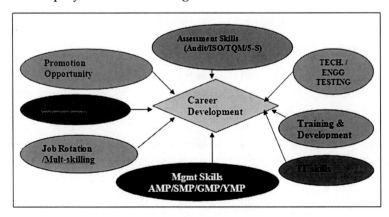

Fig. 4: Career Development Opportunities at BHEL

THRUST ON MENTORING

Mentoring has been made compulsory for every Engineer Trainee / Executive Trainee since the year 2008-09. During the year 2011-12, 368 Mentors were trained in 13 training programmes held at HRDI and other units. Engineer Trainees (ETs) were provided one year training according to Dakshata-2007.

During the year, 634 ETs were successfully absorbed and Common Induction Learning for additional 1000 ETs has also been successfully completed.

Additionally, 900 ETs joined BHEL in February 2011 at various units. Their corporate induction training has also been successfully completed at various units. All employees are imparted training at induction level as well as at cadre change. Learning opportunities for individuals & teams are created through various modes as listed in Figure 5.

Learning Opportunities		
Individual learning	*Team Learning*	*Organizational Learning*
Class Room Training- Internal & External	Teams for improvement projects	Assessment & its feedback based on CII-EXIM Bank Model for Business Excellence
On the job-positional	Tasks Forces/groups for specific task	Intranet knowledge management web-site
Modular Training for various engineering Trades	Seminars/conferences	
Learning through experience-Working as an ISO 9001, 14001, OHSAS 18001, TQ Assessors/Functional coordinator/MAP coordinator etc.	Syndicate workshops	Knowledge sharing with customer/Vendor
	RCA Committees-29 Nos.	Benchmarking with Sister units
	Quality Circles & OEE	Learning Missions to Benchmark companies-Tisco, M&M, BEL, TVS, Ricoh, Tata Motors
Internet facility at all computer terminals	Various Plant level committees like plant standards committee, HSE committee, FTQC, ATQC etc.	
Books/periodicals at technical information centre		External consultants-Hewitt Associates, IBM, Mckinsey, Kaizen Institutes, CII, CSMM, GN consultant

Fig. 5: Learning Opportunities at BHEL

INNOVATIVE METHODOLOGIES

BHEL a forerunner in implementing innovative methodologies for retaining the employees which have helped in improving team work and promoting mutual understanding among the workers. Many promotional schemes are invoked at BHEL like improvement projects rewards scheme (IMPRES) , Quality Circles, operation equipment efficiency (OEE), e-MAP, BHEL excel awards, effective communication through HR query-online, employees corner on intranet, display best work of the day/week/month and monthly e-bulletin on business excellence, celebration of "Utpadakta Utsav" for enhancing employees' morale while retaining them for long duration etc. "Integrity and fairness in all matters" is one of the BHEL values being practiced for retaining employees. The unit provides fairness in employment by ensuring implementation of documented HR policies. Growth opportunities like promotions are implemented through well laid criteria and transparent performance appraisal systems.

DEVELOPING PERSONNEL THROUGH EXPERIENCE

Developing personnel through experience is encouraged by action learning & redeployment for retaining talent. Learning experiences are shared through monthly functional communication meetings and special HRD lectures by internal faculty. To ensure transfer of skills, on the job training is provided to new workmen by associating them with experienced workmen. Under e-MAP, "skill development for subordinates in key technological areas" is one of the key result areas (KRAs), which helps in personnel development. Participation of Quality Circle teams in National & International Conventions, papers presentation by executives in seminars help in learning through experience sharing. Beside this, in-house conferences and inter-unit conventions are regularly organized at BHEL. The process not only enhances a sense of belonging but also encourages employees to perform and excel with a high sense of team achievement. Employees are encouraged for social activities also like blood donation, tree plantation, cultural meets, environmental rallies, support for national calamities, community projects etc.

RECOGNIZING MERITORIOUS EMPLOYEES

Various forums to involve employees in improvement activities provide opportunities for stimulating involvement and support for innovation and creativity. Employees excelling in improvement activities are recognized at company level through Excel Awards. BHEL employees have won a large number of awards at national level also. Timely recognition of individuals and teams both at unit and corporate levels helped in improvement in satisfaction index for "Reward & Recognition". For contribution in various improvement initiatives nominations of employees are forwarded for "BHEL Excel Awards" at Corporation level and "PM's Shram Awards" & "Vishwakarma Rashtriya Puraskar" at National level. This has been possible due to well established structured system of awarding BHEL employees internally. Prime Minister's Shram Awards are given to workmen in Public Sector of Central & State Governments in recognition of their distinguished performance, innovative abilities, outstanding contribution in the field of Productivity and exhibition of exceptional courage and presence of mind. As regard the coveted Prime Minister's Shram Awards: Shram Shree Award 2010 was won by an employee from BAP-Ranipet. Shram Bhushan Award 2011 was won by four employees from HPBP-Trichy. The rewards were announced on 5th July 2011 and handed over personally by Hon. The Prime Minister on 13 October, 2011.

EMPOWERING PEOPLE TO TAKE DECISIONS

Delegation of powers is well documented in various manuals & work instructions at BHEL. People are encouraged to take decision within their area of operation. Special training programs are organized to enhance awareness on empowerment. A common task force (CTF) is formed to look into various aspects of empowerment. Implementation of their recommendations, training & communication helped in improvement in employee satisfaction index for empowerment.

COMMUNICATION POLICY AND PLANS

Corporate communication policy helps in formulating strategies and plans for meeting communication needs of the people. Communication channels which provide wide communication network in terms of hardware and software are used for effective top-down, bottom-up and lateral communication. HR information is accessible to employees on Intranet Departmental web-pages and on-line systems are utilized for effective communication. Notice boards including electronic boards are used to share first hand information and plans. Major IT based initiatives like e-mail access to all executives, networking of PCs, Intranet and Internet facilities strengthen the communication system. Additionally, daily shop visits and Open Forums by GMs & senior executives facilitate the bottom up communication.

SHARING BEST PRACTICES AND KNOWLEDGE

Knowledge Base website, web pages of Quality & TQM, OEE & Product Profile and various Departmental Web-sites are available on intranet for sharing best practices and knowledge. Annual conferences/ specific theme based events provide platform for knowledge sharing. Knowledge management and benchmarking are the effective tool for talent retention.

REWARD AND RECOGNITION

Remunerations at BHEL are one of the best in similar organizations. This is ensured through participation of trade unions at the time of

wage revision and revision of other benefits. Right sizing being one of the strategies practiced at BHEL, redeployment and restructuring is a continuous exercise. Employees are provided opportunity for job-rotation within as well as outside the unit. The redundancy of manpower is managed through precise manpower plans and horizontal transfers from areas where the operations have become redundant e.g. Motors & Hydro-generators business.

MEDICAL FACILITIES FOR EMPLOYEES & THEIR FAMILIES

Some of the imporant facilities are noted as under:

- Well equipped 200 bed hospital and eight sector Dispensaries
- Free medical treatment to employees and their families
- 75000 photo identity medical cards issued
- Serious cases warranting care by Super Specialists are referred to AIIMS, Escorts, Ganga Ram Hospital at Delhi and elsewhere etc.
- Computerized registration cell for Patients.
- TMT (Treed mill test) & Dialysis Units recently installed
- Special Clinic: Cardiac, Diabetic, Asthma, T.B. etc.

SAFETY & ENVIRONMENT RELATED ISSUES

BHEL has been certified for Environment Management System ISO 14001 and Occupational Health and Safety management System OHSAS 18001. An Apex level Safety Committee (HSE Committee) regularly reviews the aspects of plant safety. Regular Safety awareness training programmes and competitions are organized. To provide immediate medical help, there is Main Gate Dispensary inside the Plant and First-Aid boxes have been provided in different areas. Preventive measures are taken to avoid road accidents in the campus.

To gauge the satisfaction level of the employees the Employee Satisfaction Survey (ESS) was conducted during May-June 2011 to receive feedback on work related issues and work environment. The feedback was sought on nineteen parameters, which impact employee motivation and satisfaction in the company. Parameters like career development, performance appraisal, succession planning, employment conditions and facilities at work were studied. To provide thrust for improving employee satisfaction, the parameter wise picture for BHEL as a whole is shown in figure 6.

The parameters that have been rated high are Peer Relationship, Employment conditions & Job Security, Organization's role in community and society and Empowerment. Incidentally these parameters were also the ones rated high during the previous Employee Satisfaction Survey exercise in 2009-10. All these parameters have been rated high in all the units and are close to or above seven on the measurement scale of ten.

- Safety, Training & Development, Career Development, Health, Rewards & Recognition, Management of Change and Pay & Benefits have been rated low by the respondents. Further, none of the parameters fall below the score of 6, with the least score being attributed to safety.

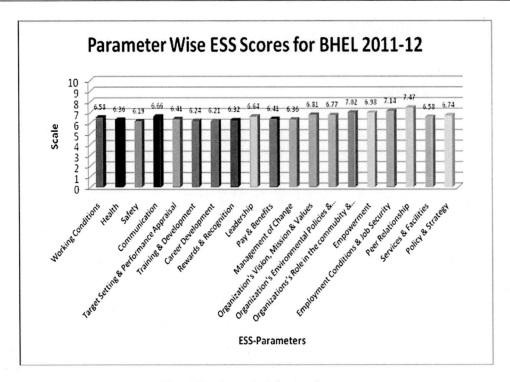

Fig. 6: Employee Satisfaction Survey

- Peer Relationship has scored high in all the survey units. Barring Rudrapur and EMRP this aspect has been rated in high 7s and even 8s, which is a good sign for the health of the company. This generally will result in mutual trust and respect, a fact corroborated by high score on the values of Respect and Team work captured in organizational Vision, Mission and Values parameter.

- HFI also presents an opportunity to the management of low HFI units to work and address these aspects and see its impact directly on the improved ESI of the unit.

- Safety, Rewards & Recognition, Career Development, Training & Development and Management of Change are rated the lowest in all the units. Certain other aspects which have been rated low include Health which shows a very peculiar trend. For smaller units like HERP, CFP, Piping Center, IVP, EMRP, Health has been rated very low in the range of 2.5-4 or even below and is a serious aspect which needs to be addressed.

- Safety being perceived as 'low' is a matter of concern. The Units should look into the reasons and take measures for improvement.

CONCLUSION

This case contributes to the understanding of talent management among managers and HRM professionals especially in Indian public sector. This case study will be of value to anyone seeking to better understand talent management or to improve employee recruitment and retention. It is suggested that HR professionals should begin to think about the nourishing and grooming the talent that is required to any given solution to problems and attempt to recruit the optimal people for the endeavor. At BHEL talent retention is being taken as a business priority and not alone a HR intervention. BHEL use unique development processes geared to build the competencies linked to future success as this is a best practice to identify and narrow developmental gaps, and measure readiness. Talent Management System at BHEL is dedicated to attracting, developing and retaining talented people. Though BHEL has implemented various exercises for talent retention but employee satisfaction survey results depict that at BHEL employees are not satisfied with prevailing practices on career development, rewards and recognition, safety, training and development and many more. The research findings indicate that talent management system could improve organizational and managerial as well as financial aspects of an organization.

ACKNOWLEDGEMENT

The authors wish to thanks Mr. A. K. Upadhay, Sh. Deputy General Manager, Bharat Heay Electrical Ltd, Human Resource Development Centre, Hardwar, for support to develop this case and full permission for the same to be published in its entirely and without change or limitation by BIMTECH in ICMC-2012 proceedings in the form of edited books.

REFERENCES

BHEL Annual Report 2010-11

BHEL Performance Highlight 2010-11

Position Report of BHEL for Sustainability, 2011

Understanding the Essential Principles for Integrating Theory and Research Knowledge to the Realm of Practice: Lessons from the Scholar-Practitioner

Ramkrishnan (Ram) V. Tenkasi* and George W. Hay**

ABSTRACT

The quest for integrating theory and research knowledge into practice has intrigued philosophers since the time of Aristotle. Our study of eleven scholar-practitioners, which follows their efforts in organizational projects to generate actionable scientific knowledge suggests that they employ six strategies for interrelating theory and practice: 1). Framing the problem; 2). Conjecturing the appropriate pathway to resolve the problem;3). Influencing and Legitimizing the chosen pathway; 4). Activating the conjectured pathway; 5).Making sense of the activated pathway; and, 6). Demonstrating impact of the chosen pathway in achieving change. Two meta-strategies that cut across all six strategies were Turns and Scaffolding. We discuss implications from our findings to elucidate the basic principles and key competencies underlying integration of theory and research knowledge to the realm of practice

Keywords: Theory and research knowledge, integration, competencies, practice, pathway.

INTRODUCTION

The need to bridge knowledge and action has been a recurring theme in the management discourse (Lawler, Mohrman, Mohrman, Ledford and Cummings, 1999; Astley and Zammuto, 1993; Mohrman and Lawler, 2011). For example, Rynes, Bartunek and Daft

*Ramkrishnan (Ram) V. Tenkasi is with PhD Program in Organization Development and Change College of Business, Benedictine University, Lisle, IL. USA.

**George W. Hay, Chicago School of Professional Psychology, Chicago, IL .

E-mail: rtenkasi@ben.edu or tenkasi@msn.com, geowhay@hotmail.com

(2001) describe the gap between theory and practice as a "great divide" that has and continues to characterize most of the history of academic knowledge production. These observations are not new and can be traced back to the Greek philosopher Aristotle to the second century BC. Although initially Aristotle distinguished between the spheres of scientific knowledge and of craft in his writings in Book VI of the *Nicomachean Ethics (Aristotle, 1962) as two separate and distinct domains (Parry, 2003), he later questioned the separation of theory and practice* in his subsequent reflections on the nature of knowledge in the classic work *Metaphysics.* (Aristotle, 1961).Here inspired by ideas of his mentors Socrates and Plato, Aristotle presents a radically different image of what it means to create true knowledge of events and situations. And in this second, less known 'image' presented by Aristotle, we find compelling claims that the bedrock of true understanding emanates from the creative integration of knowledge based on theory, practice, and experience. True knowledge, and understanding, according to Aristotle has a basis in the integration of experience (*empeiria*), craft (*techne*), and theory (*episteme*).

Traditionally the challenge of connecting academic theory and research to practice was seen as the exclusive responsibility of the research-scholar. The academic was asked to devise clever ways to make such bridging possible through the contextualization of their research results so that it can provide enhanced meaning for practitioners (Tenkasi, Mohrman and Mohrman, 2007); write in a compelling and interesting style that captures the minds, hearts, and consciences of practitioners (Bartunek, Rynes and Ireland, 2006; Green, 2004; Van De Ven and Schomaker, 2002); and contribute to an evidence based management infrastructure that builds evidence based practice capabilities among managers (Rousseau, 2006).

Recent decades, however, have seen several intermediates emerge between the world of research knowledge and its application. These intermediates have changed society's perception of the research-scholar, who has gone from the primary or sole agent responsible for translating and applying scholarly knowledge to one of several agents involved in the process. Several intermediate bundlers and co-producers of knowledge, including scholar-practitioners, consulting firms, and professional groups, now serve as alternative pathways for translating and integrating scholarly knowledge to practice (Mohrman and Lawler, 2011).

One such intermediate bundler is the Scholar-Practitioner. Astley and Zammuto (1993) called for the creation of an intermediate cadre of professionals who by virtue of membership in both the academic and practice worlds can play the role of "semiotic brokers" and thus act as effective bridges between the otherwise incommensurate communities of scholars and practitioners and enable the translation of research and theory to inform practice. Similarly, several scholars have noted the emergence of Executive Doctoral programs as offering a renewed opportunity to more closely study ways and means by which this divide may be bridged. For example, Huff and Huff

(2001) advance the perspective that the executive doctoral student/graduate promises to be a "boundary-spanner" who [can] "potentially close the relevance gap from both ends" of science and business (p. S50). It is these semiotic brokers and boundary-spanners that we loosely call scholar-practitioners, actors who have a foot in both worlds and are broadly interested in advancing the causes of both theory and practice.

There is agreement that one sign of a successful spanning of science and business is the production of actionable scientific knowledge (Hay, 2003). According to Adler, Shani and Styhre (2003, p. 84), Actionable scientific knowledge refers to the knowledge creation processes that meet the criteria of the scientific community and the business needs of the organization. Whether from the fields of organization development with its dual emphasis on social practice and knowledge of change (Alderfer, 1977), management science with its calls for "rigor and relevance" (Hodgkinson, Herriot & Anderson, 2001, p. S42), or modes of knowledge production that describe the rise of scholarly knowledge from the practical problems of business (Gibbons et. al., 1994), there is agreement that useful research must both advance the theoretical understanding of the phenomena as well as provide for a better resolution of business problems.

It has been only recently that works such as Adler and Shani (2001), and, Adler, Shani and Styhre (2003) have begun to document the tasks and activities of scholars-practitioners. In general most of the literature on theory-practice linkages has not systematically investigated the nature of these bridging dynamics; the focus has been on building the case for theory-practice linkages. Even in the few studies that have attempted to do so, the primary reliance has been on anecdotal evidence (Lawler, et.al., 1999; Huff and Huff, 2001; Werr and Greiner, 2008). Further, the limited studies in this arena have focused on variance models (Mohr, 1982) without much reference to the processes and the sequence of activities entailed in creating such linkages. Our interest was in taking a temporal look at the organizational projects of scholar-practitioners in order to identify the elements of theory and practice, their linkages through the course of these projects and the sequence of actions they undertake in bridging the knowledge-action gap. Process models attempt to understand discrete states/events and not variables. Furthermore, as in a story, there is an order to events in a process theory. In contrast variance theories are often less, or not at all, concerned with the causal ordering of variables (Mohr, 1982).

The thrust of this study is on the scholar-practitioner and how he or she applies theory and research knowledge to practice to produce outcomes for an organization while advancing scientific knowledge in the process. We focus on three questions concerning scholar-practitioners as intermediate agents and alternative pathways in the research-to-practice translation value chain (Bartunek and Schein, 2011). The questions are: (1) Who are scholar-practitioners?; (2) How do scholar-practitioners translate and apply theoretical and research knowledge to resolve organizational problems and what is the underlying process?; (3) What are the key competencies that a Scholar-practitioner needs to have in order to effectively integrate theory with practice that holds relevance for advancement of organizational causes while at the same time advancing theory and research that can contribute to generalizable knowledge. In understanding the strategies of theory-practice translation and the key competencies underlying successful theory-practice, we rely on the analysis of 11 in-depth case studies of scholar-practitioners and their organizational projects as they went about creating actionable scientific knowledge that had both effective theory and business outcomes.

Who are Scholar-Practitioners?

Scholar-practitioners are actors who have received traditional academic training, and who apply their knowledge of theory and research to an organization's particular challenges to resolve business problems. Unlike traditional academics, scholar-practitioners are full-time organizational employees, and thus are primarily committed to practical concerns and advancing organizational causes. Only as a secondary consequence do they feel responsible for advancing a theoretical and empirical understanding of the phenomenon of concern (Tenkasi and Hay, 2004; 2008). Astley and Zammuto (1993) label scholar-practitioners an intermediate cadre of professionals who, by virtue of belonging to both the practice and academic communities, can effectively bridge the incommensurate worlds of scholars and practitioners. Huff and Huff (2001) label scholar-practitioners intermediate boundary spanners who have one foot in the world of practice and the other in the world of theory and research.

The mode 2 knowledge producer, as described by Gibbons and Nowotny (Gibbons Limoges, Nowotny, Schwartzman, Scott, P. and Trow, 1994; Nowotny, Scott, and Gibbons, 2001; Nowotny, Scott & Gibbons, 2005), is a prototype of the scholar-practitioner who combines theoretical knowledge with applied practice knowledge to solve particular organizational problems. As opposed to mode 1 knowledge producers, who seek to find generalizable laws across contexts in a non-engaged, basic scholarship way (Gibbons, et.al., 1994; Van De Ven and Johnson, 2006; Van De Ven, 2007), mode 2 knowledge producers are closely tied to applied contexts. They are charged with achieving concrete results by creating actionable knowledge that can advance organizational causes. Their point of contact is closer to practice and involves investigating problems of high interest and practical import that sometimes cut across disciplines (Van De Ven, 2007; Mohrman and Lawler, 2011).

In mode 2 knowledge environments, theoretical knowledge is tested not in the abstract but rather under concrete, local circumstances. This is to ensure that the theoretical knowledge is socially robust and produces consequential outcomes. The mode 2 knowledge producer's primary concern is solving problems, since that is what their organizations reward them for (Wasserman and Kram, 2009; Tinnish and O'Neal,

2010). They produce generalizable knowledge only as a byproduct. Examples of mode 2 knowledge producers are traditionally trained Ph.D.'s in the life sciences who work for pharmaceutical firms to develop drugs. Their main interest is producing effective drugs to combat the disease area they work in; their secondary interest is contributing to the body of literature on scientific theories on their particular concerns. In bringing it to the organizational sciences, graduates of executive doctoral programs who continue working in organizations post education are an example of these intermediate cadre of "boundary spanners" who can close the "relevance gap from both ends of business and science" (Huff and Huff, 2001; p. 50). Scholar-practitioners can also be classified as a subtype of the "engaged scholar," as defined by Andrew Van De Ven (Van De Ven and Johnson, 2006; Van De Ven, 2007). They can simultaneously play the role of the detached outsider and the attached insider (Evered and Louis, 1981; Mahoney and McGahan, 2007). Knowing outside research can provide evidence of the persuasiveness and boundary conditions of the problem, while knowing the inside situation and its contingencies can concretely ground the research in a particular situation (Mahoney and Sanchez, 2004).

The idea of the scholar-practitioner as an important intermediate agent between the scholar and practitioner—one with both outside and inside knowledge—goes back to Aristotle. The second century (B.C.) Greek philosopher initially taught the need to separate theory and practice, and treated the spheres of scientific knowledge and those of experience and craft as separate, distinct domains (Aristotle, 1962). This divide became the primary assumption underlying Western scientific thought (Parry, 2003; Chalmers, 1999). But in later writings, Aristotle suggested that only by combining theory and practice can people solve consequential problems of science and society (*Metaphysics*; Aristotle, 1961; Tenkasi and Hay, 2008). He labeled the combined knowledge of theory and practice *phronesis*, or practical wisdom (Peters, 1967; p. 157; Dunne, 1993). The person who is able to combine and apply such knowledge is the *technites*, or master craftsperson.

The scholar (*lógios*) appeals to scientific knowledge. Her strength is finding generalizable principles and explanatory reasons underlying a situation by invoking the larger scientific discourse of cause and effect (*episteme theoretike*) drawn from multiple contexts. However, the *lógios* lacks specific knowledge about and experience in particular contexts. In contrast, the practitioner (*cheirotechne*) derives her knowledge from experience (*empeiria*) with the specifics of a situation. She has the craft (*techne*) of getting things done in her context. But she does not know the general principles of cause and effect that underlie the situation, and engages in local activities as mostly unreflective, habitual forms of practice (Bourdieu; 1977; Bunge, 2004; Schon, 1995).

To truly change situations, such as helping a patient afflicted with disease, one needs both kinds of knowledge, concluded Aristotle—such as a physician who understands both the general principles of medicine and also the particulars of the patient's situation. This combined knowledge, or *phronesis*, mirrors the integrated knowledge and pluralism suggested by contemporary scholars (Pettigrew, 2001; Van De Ven and Johnson, 2006; Van De Ven, 2007). This integration is required to yield the kind of actionable knowledge that can address complex and wicked problems.

HOW DO SCHOLAR-PRACTITIONERS APPLY THEORETICAL AND RESEARCH KNOWLEDGE TO RESOLVE ORGANIZATIONAL PROBLEMS AND WHAT IS THE UNDERLYING PROCESS?

We see that the scholar-practitioner's intermediate role has both historical and contemporary precedent in Aristotle's concept of *phronesis* (*Metaphysics*; Aristotle, 1961) and Van De Ven's (2007) notion of engaged scholarship. But less is known about the specific ways the mode 2 knowledge producer (*technites*) successfully integrates knowledge of the general with the particulars of an organizational context in order to inform practice. To understand this integration, we turn to an inductive qualitative study reported in some detail in earlier publications (Tenkasi and Hay, 2004; 2008, Hay, Woodman and Tenkasi, 2008). The study sought to understand not only the theory and practice the scholar-practitioner brings to the table, but also how he or she goes about linking theory to practice in organizational projects.

The eleven scholar-practitioners surveyed were graduates of Benedictine University's executive Ph.D. program in Organization Development and Change, the program that first author has worked with as a core faculty member since 1998. Typical Benedictine students are skilled practitioners in a senior-level position who want to bring meaningful change to their organizations. They come from diverse industries and positions: presidents and chief officers of large and small firms in technology, finance, nonprofits, and so on; vice presidents who manage human resources and organizational effectiveness; doctors who lead medical departments and hospital systems; and consultants with major and minor consulting firms. Their common interest (beyond the status and career advancement that a Ph.D. brings) is, in most cases, to gain theoretical and research knowledge in order to improve their organizations or client systems.

Interviews were completed with eleven scholar-practitioners, whom the first author was associated with as the chair or active member of their respective dissertation committees. We also had continual contact with them as they pursued additional projects related to their dissertations or post-doctoral projects unrelated to their dissertations. The scholar-practitioners represented a purposive sample and were asked to recount organizational projects in which they had applied their theory and research knowledge to achieve business outcomes. Typical outcomes were customized business models and new techniques or processes that were implemented as a result of the project. Theoretical outcomes were mostly academic presentations, conference proceedings, and, in a few cases, journal publications and books written independently by the scholar-practitioner or coauthored with a Ph.D. program faculty member.

The eleven cases were analyzed using an iterative approach of going back and forth between the data and the emerging theory to develop a process model (Yin, 1994; Eisenhardt, 1989; Elsbach and Sutton, 1992; Silverman, 2001). Six contrast interviews completed as part of an earlier project were also enfolded in the systematic case analysis (Tenkasi and Hay, 2004). Four of the interviewees were business researchers with no scholarly affiliation, and two were academics who had little experience in organizations but who had engaged in organization-based projects.

The cornerstone of our analyses were; 1) to develop a narrative sequence of events for each case (Elsbach and Sutton, 1992; Silverman, 2001); 2) employ a within and across case analysis of all cases to identify similarities and differences across events (Eisenhardt, 1989); and, 3) systematically develop and employ an emergent coding system to methodically discern and elaborate on the common dynamics of theory-practice integration observed across the cases based on the logic of replication (Yin, 1984). The logic of replication treats a series of cases as a series of experiments with each case serving to confirm, or disconfirm, an emergent relationship, where the emphasis is on retaining the common relationships found across all the cases (Yin, 1994; Eisenhardt, 1989)

The analysis broadly revealed that scholar-practitioners use both their theory and research knowledge and their familiarity with local cultural conventions to approach organizational projects. They combined their formal knowledge of theory and research principles from articles, books, and expert opinion with local knowledge of the organization's power relationships and cultural norms to manage and move projects forward (Tenkasi and Hay, 2004).

Of more pertinence to this paper, however, were the subjects' strategies for integrating theory and research knowledge to produce outcomes while achieving academic results and the underlying process. To illustrate these dynamics, we will rely on two of the eleven cases that best illustrate the dynamics of theory-to-practice integration. The first case involves creating self-managing teams at a cable production firm to achieve manufacturing excellence. The second case involves improving the effectiveness of the research and development function at a high-tech firm. Scholar-practitioners tended to use theory and research to inform practice in four key ways. Their chosen way depended on whether their respective projects were in the definition and planning stage, the implementation stage, or the realization/closure stage of the project life cycle (Pinto and Prescott, 1988).

Three key and interdependent dynamics compose the project definition and planning stage: framing the problem, conjecturing an appropriate pathway to resolve the problem, and influencing and legitimizing the pathway as the right course of action. Two key dynamics compose the implementation stage: activating the conjectured pathway, and making sense of the pathway. Demonstrating the impact of the conjectured pathway was most commonly associated with the project realization/completion stage. The scholar-practitioners also used two meta-strategies—turns and scaffolding— to inconspicuously embed theory and research into the background of the organizational projects across all stages.

PROJECT DEFINITION AND PLANNING STAGE

Framing the Problem

The scholar-practitioners frequently used theory and research findings to frame and give direction to a broadly expressed change mandate from the organization's leadership looking for the resolution to a perceived organizational crisis or the realization of a desired future state. They typically used framing to structure an otherwise equivocal phenomenon in more concrete, precise terms (Weick, 1979). In interviews with the scholar-practitioners, it was clear that CEOs and other top-management members expressed the desire for a future state and sometimes mandated a resolution to an organizational crisis, but not with clear specifics. This is frequently where the scholar-practitioner steps in, using her theory and research knowledge to analyze the situation and frame and define the problem in more precise terms (Van De Ven, 2007).

One scholar-practitioner took the CEO's vision to make his manufacturing plant a center of excellence by defining the program as one of bolstering the aging workforce's effectiveness and productivity through principles of motivation and employee involvement (Lawler, 1986). In a second case, the scholar-practitioner framed the CEO's mandate to make the research and development organization more effective as better systems and processes for knowledge management.

Conjecturing the Appropriate Pathway to Resolve the Problem

After top management accepted the scholar-practitioner's framing as an appropriate problem definition (Van De Ven, 2007), the scholar-practitioners used their theory and research findings to conjecture a pathway (Bunge, 2004) most suitable for resolving the problem in light of the local contingencies. In the first case of the CEO's mandate for the manufacturing plant to become a center of excellence, the scholar-practitioner could have addressed the issue using various mechanisms, including better manufacturing processes or materials management, both scientifically validated pathways to achieve manufacturing excellence (Best Manufacturing Practices Report, 1998). But the scholar-practitioner saw that the real issue was motivating an aging workforce and enhancing their effectiveness through principles of employee involvement. She thus chose self-managing teams as the best mechanism to involve employees and increase their productivity.

She made this choice based on several local considerations. First, the older work force had high levels of camaraderie and a collective identity as a group distinct from their supervisors. The scholar-practitioner saw that the best way to heighten awareness of quality, cost, and schedule was to let the employees take ownership of these issues through self-governing teams instead of relying on supervisory mandates, which had been ineffective in the past. Second, the scholar-practitioner chose the team-based design to allow for multi-skilling and job rotation, which would give team members variety and challenge in an otherwise routine environment. Pathways such as technological enhancements to the old assembly-line format or better material management techniques would not have alleviated employee boredom or solved quality problems, since these pathways didn't take into account the company's specific social dynamics.

This was also evident in the case of the second scholar-practitioner, who framed the problem of enhancing R&D effectiveness as one of better systems and processes for knowledge management. After reviewing several models for knowledge management, she found that the Socio-Technical Systems (STS) approach was most suitable. STS addressed the interface of knowledge elements pertaining to the social, technical, and environmental systems, and also engaged the workforce in designing such a system—a wise strategy given the CEO's desire to involve a large swath of the R&D function in the change. The scholar-practitioner skillfully matched the CEO's practical requirement of broad employee engagement with a theoretical model that allowed for the same. Asking managers from several R&D functions to join the central design team was attributed to the CEO's mandate, although it was also clearly required by the STS approach.

Influencing and legitimizing the chosen pathway

Conjecturing the pathway and considering why one mechanism works better than others also helps to legitimize the pathway, since it is based on both theoretical and practical considerations. Influencing and legitimizing frequently involved distributing articles and books from practitioner sources that carry legitimacy in the business world, such as the Harvard Business Review or Sloan Management Review, and readable article summaries from academic sources like the Academy of Management Journal and Organization Science, condensed by the scholar-practitioner. Occasionally, the scholar-practitioner also brought in experts, including practitioners with hands-on experience implementing the conjectured pathway in similar environments, and scholars who had written practical books or articles on the topic. Sometimes the experts were hired as consultants to guide the project, but in most cases we observed, they came in as additional sources to influence and legitimize the chosen pathway and acceptance of it among concerned stakeholders.

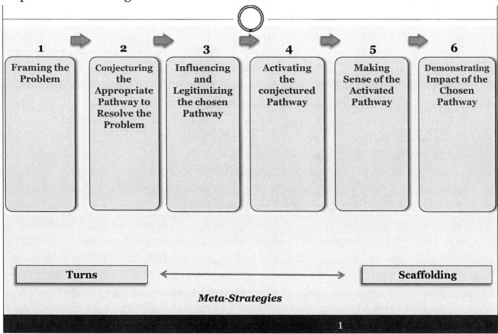

Fig. 1: A Process Model of Strategies for Interrelating Theory with Practice

Project Implementation Stage

Activating the conjectured pathway: Once the causal pathway or preferred strategy for change was established and accepted by relevant stakeholders, the fourth function of theory and research in informing practice was in activating the conjectured pathway. To activate the project, the scholar-practitioner often used the theoretical, research, and practice literature, including expert opinion on the chosen platform (whether self-managing teams or non-routine STS), as guiding frameworks. This frequently meant creating training programs for the community to enact the details of the chosen pathway for change that preceded implementing the intervention. Often scholar-practitioners also used training programs as pre-assessment forums, using survey instrumentation, qualitative interviews, or in several cases, both, to create baseline information before enacting the change.

Making Sense of the Activated Pathway

Scholar-practitioners used surveys, interviews, systematic observations, and, in one case, personal diary recordings to monitor and assess the pathway's ongoing progress. Sometimes the scholar-practitioners used the same instruments as during the pre-intervention stage. In other cases they created new surveys and interview questions based on the ongoing assessment of the activated pathway's implementation. For example, the self-managing team project used a constant comparison qualitative design. The scholar-practitioner compared the evolution of six self-managing work groups as they transitioned into effective self-managing teams at different speeds over a six-month period. Her use of triangulated methods (Jick, 1979) over six time periods included surveys, interviews, and analyzing the team members' diary entries. These methods helped her develop new insights and create questions that aided her in the ongoing assessment process. They also enabled her to design appropriate interventions for the lagging teams to catch up.

Likewise, for the STS knowledge management project, the scholar-practitioner used systematic research methods such as surveys and interviews to assess whether the quality of internal deliberations—an intervention created within the teams—helped them meet monthly goals in cost, quality, and schedule over one year. In this case, she used the systematic research methods to test a hypothesis instead of finding evolutionary insights, as with the self-managing teams. Whether hypothesis-driven or based on evolutionary insights, the scholar-practitioners' hallmark was using systematic research methods to gauge the efficacy of the conjectured pathway. Scholar-practitioners on the whole engaged in fact-based decision making (Pfeffer and Sutton, 2006), paying attention to the data, rather than getting trapped by ideologies, beliefs, or conventional wisdom.

Project Realization/Closure Stage

Demonstrating Impact of the Chosen Pathway in Achieving the Change

Finally, the scholar-practitioners applied research knowledge to demonstrate impact. Applying systematic research methods to activate and make ongoing sense of the conjectured pathway also helped demonstrate that the organizational project successfully achieved practical results, whether that meant changing mindsets, behavior, or other hard metrics. A selection bias is clearly at work in the successful projects we chose to study. Nonetheless, for these projects, demonstrating business impact required collecting data and analyzing it using systematic research designs in the project execution phase. Scholar-practitioners frequently used quantitative evidence to indicate behavior and attitude change both before and after implementing the program. They also used quantitative evidence to show shifts in hard performance measures before and after change. Likewise, the scholar-practitioners used qualitative data, particularly context-sensitive quotes or verbatim comments, to show changes in perspective or behavior. For example, the scholar-practitioner who set up self-managing teams used many quotes from team members to demonstrate that they were engaged in the kinds of behaviors involved in team self-management.

Turns: a Meta-strategy for Relating Theory to Practice

In a majority of cases, what was most salient and needed attention in the minds of management was the business problem. Our interviews with scholar-practitioners suggest that consulting is seen as adding value to the organization's business problem, while research is seen as an abstract act that is not practically relevant. For many scholar-practitioners, *research* was a term they preferred not to use but rather to integrate into the process. As one aptly summarized,

> *My CEO wants us to become a center of manufacturing excellence. . . . I have convinced him that the best way to achieve it is to create self-managing teams. He wants them to happen, and if I tell him I want to conduct a research project on testing a theory of self-managing team effectiveness, I will probably be out of the door tomorrow. We don't have the luxury of presenting a research proposal but have to build research principles into the way we consult. But if I do write a few articles from this project, he is okay with it as long as I show practical results. That is what is most important to him. If I gain research knowledge that is fine, as long as it does not come in the way of organizational needs.*

Turns are reframing moves and tools that help make an element more familiar, legitimate, and palatable to the concerned audience. Turns achieve this by locating the element in a community's "systems of meaning" (Fleck, 1957). In our observation, successful scholar-practitioners used theory-to-practice turns to make the unfamiliar familiar to the practitioner community during all stages of the project. We found several instances of theory- and research-to-practice turns that helped a community accept theoretically informed and research based activities. Self-evident examples of theory-to-practice turns include: (1) turning knowledge of current literature into information from best practices in the industry and other organizations; (2) turning representative sampling across level, function, and gender into a strategy for broader employee involvement; (3) turning action-research processes of implementation into learning from experience; and (4) turning principles of valid and reliable research (systematic data collection, comparative research designs, and rigorous analytical strategy) into fool-proof strategies to assess bottom-line impact.

Scholar-practitioners used these turns to influence a business, not an academic, audience. Reframing for a business audience carries a more pragmatic goal: not to change the academic import of the theoretical action, but rather to present it in a way that is intelligible to the business audience, who will be motivated to construe and continue with the research for being practically relevant. Framing research activities in terms similar to familiar corporate activities exemplifies the underlying logic of scholar-practitioners who use turns to legitimate activities informed by theory and research principles. Translating in this way helps the organizational community to accept theory- and research-driven activities.

Scaffolding: A Meta-strategy to Achieve Theoretical and Research Outcomes

In a few cases, scholar-practitioners used another, less common meta-strategy known as *scaffolding* across a project's life cycle. Commonly associated with construction, the word *scaffolding* typically means a "platform made for workers to stand on when they want to reach higher parts of a building to add on to or modify the structure of the building" (Cambridge Dictionary, 2003). For scholar-practitioners, scaffolding means carefully selecting a theory-based platform that helps frame the problem at hand, guides practice, and, has the potential to realize subsequent theoretical and empirical outcomes by seeking to answer new research questions. For example, the scholar-practitioner who framed the CEO's vision to make the manufacturing plant a center of excellence used scaffolding in reorganizing the workforce into self-managing teams. She used the theory-based platform of self-managing teams to direct action and conduct systematic research on the gap she identified in the teams' research literature (i.e., what is the evolutionary pathway in becoming a self-managing team?; why can some teams but not others successfully transition into self-management; and why are some faster at it?).

The scholar-practitioner who applied principles of STS theory to knowledge work in the R&D organization also used scaffolding. Her platform held practical ramifications in terms of guiding the process and also theoretical ramifications in potentially charting new territory for socio-technical theory. It assessed how an R&D project team's deliberations affect the team's success, and how they affect knowledge transfer and assimilation processes in and between multidisciplinary teams. In doing so, she was able to extend STS's application from routine to non-routine work.

One of scholar-practitioners' defining qualities was reflecting on appropriate causal mechanisms in ways that accounted for both the general and the local. Doing this enabled them to produce outcomes for the organization and to add to the larger body of knowledge. Considering both the general and the local distinguished scholar-practitioners from practitioners, who often mimic the latest technique or fad and apply it indiscriminately to their local environment without fully grasping the underlying theory or conducting research to direct their efforts. The scholar-practitioner's approach also differed from the scholar's approach. The scholar applies her theoretical understanding of organizations and conducts research on an abstract problem without fully considering local dynamics or how useful the findings may be for improving the organization's causes (Tenkasi and Hay, 2004; 2008).

WHAT ARE THE KEY COMPETENCIES THAT A SCHOLAR-PRACTITIONER NEEDS TO HAVE IN ORDER TO EFFECTIVELY INTEGRATE THEORY WITH PRACTICE?

Scholar-Practitioners, clearly appreciate using scholarship and the principles of systematic research design for approaching organizational problems. Frequently they use academic research to frame problems and to conjecture appropriate pathways to resolve them. The practitioner-scholar applies both theoretical and research knowledge to activate the pathway and to make sense of its progress, as well as to demonstrate the conjectured pathway's impact. In this sense, the scholar-practitioner is a sound theory and research-to-practice translator, and an effective intermediate agent. Their research- and theory-driven practical projects sometimes lead to policy and practical changes in their concerned organizations. So what essentially are the key competencies that these scholar-practitioners hold that enables them to successfully integrate theory and practice to produce actionable scientific knowledge?

Our observations indicate that while they use theory and research knowledge to inform practice and produce outcomes of dual relevance, we also see that theory and research knowledge, a critical component of the scholar-practitioner's repertoire, is just one of a set of "know that" (knowing about something) and "know how" (knowing how to do something) (Ryle, 1949) in successfully impacting organizational practice. In connecting with organizations, the scholar-practitioner brings certain kinds of "know that" (current literature, social science theory, principles of research design), and certain kinds of "know how" (designing research and data analysis). But he or she also understands the importance of merging this knowledge with the "know that" (contextual conventions, norms, rules, power relationships, routines, and established procedures) and "know how" (influencing, legitimizing, project management) specific to the organization. Further, the practitioner-scholar reframes her research ideas and methods in terms palatable to a practitioner audience. In particular, using devices like turns and scaffolding to translate academic and research elements for the practitioner audience is useful in this regard. Likewise, when a scholar-practitioner presents a research proposal on academic problems that he or she wants to investigate in a practical setting, they present the research question in a way that appropriately frames and defines the problem at hand, and also shows how the investigative or intervention process is the suitable pathway for resolving the problem. They are also able to demonstrate impact on intended outcomes. Firms are most interested in reaching practical outcomes.

In summary, Scholar-Practitioners demonstrate distinct competencies to effectively bridge theory and research knowledge with practice that invoke different sets of "know how" and "know that".

First, they are familiar with the *universals* (the larger scientific discourse pertaining to theory and research) and can articulate what is known and what needs to be known to advance knowledge from a theory and research vantage. Second, they are familiar with the *particulars* of the organization—local theories of action, organizational history, social dynamics, norms, and power relationships—a unique competency that successful scholar- practitioners are adept at. When these two sets of competencies unite, scholar-practitioners are able to find appropriate causal mechanisms that can move the system to its desired state, achieving practical outcomes while enhancing scientific theory. Third, to put causal pathways into motion, scholar-practitioners need credibility, legitimacy, and influence in the organizational system, particularly among top management and other stakeholders. These actors have deep practical knowledge of how to move projects in the organization. Fourth, a critical skill of scholar-practitioners is the ability to adeptly translate theory regarding its practice implications, and can frame practice contingencies in terms of their theoretical potentials. Fifth is the competency to interrelate theory and research to practice that can help in mutual sensemaking. Scholar-practitioners frequently use theory to activate and make sense of practice. And when executing practical organizational projects, scholar-practitioner's evolving practice insights re-enable them to make sense of the theory at hand. This important reciprocal dynamic often leads to relevant outcomes for practice and theory.

CONCLUSION

The growing number of executive Ph.D. programs in the United States and worldwide, as well as the number of working professionals from diverse positions who are enrolling in these programs, show that scholar-practitioners play a key role in organizations today (Tinnish and O'Neal, 2010; Wasserman and Kram, 2009). Further, they can play the role of effective intermediaries in the knowledge-to-practice value chain. From an Aristotelian legacy, practitioner-scholars are the modern representation of the *technites*, who carefully blend the traditions of theory and practice to address problems of scientific and social concern (Tenkasi and Hay, 2008). Keeping in mind the unique competencies of the scholar-practitioner would well serve the scholar who wants to impact organizations and in refrain the casual practitioner.

REFERENCES

Adler, N., Shani, A.B.., & Styhre, A. (2003) *Collaborative research in organizations.* Thousand Oaks, CA: SAGE Publications.

Adler, N., & Shani, R. (2001). In search of an alternative framework for the creation of actionable knowledge: Table-tennis research at Ericsson. In R. Woodman, W. Pasmore, and A. B. Shani (Eds.), *Research in organizational change & development* (vol. 13, pp. 43–79). Greenwich: CT. JAI Press.

Alderfer, C. (1977). Organization development. *Annual Review of Psychology,* 28, 197-233.

Aristotle. (1961). *Metaphysics* (Vol. 1, Bks. 1–9; Vol. 2, Bks. 10–14). (H. Tredennick, Trans.). Loeb Classical Library. Cambridge, MA: Harvard University Press.

Aristotle. (1962). *Nicomachean Ethics* (M. Ostwald, Trans.). Englewood Cliffs, NJ: Prentice-Hall .

Astley, W., & Zammuto, R. (1993). Organization science, managers, and language games. *Organization Science, 3*, 443–460.

Bartunek, J. M., Rynes, S., & Ireland, R. D. (2006). What makes management research interesting, and why does it matter? *Academy of Management Journal, 49*, 9–15.

Bartunek, J. M., and Schein, E. H. (2011). Organization Development Scholar-Practitioners: Between Scholarship and Practice. In Mohrman, S. A. and Lawler, E. E. (Eds). Useful Research: Advancing Theory and Practice. San Francisco: Berrett-Kohler, pp. 233-250.

Best manufacturing practices report. (1998). Retrieved October 1, 2006, from http://www.bmpcoe.org.

Bourdieu, P. (1977). *Outline of a theory of practice.* Cambridge: Cambridge University Press.

Bunge, M. (2004). How does it work? The search for explanatory mechanisms. *Philosophy of Social Sciences, 34*(2), 182–210.

Cambridge dictionary of American English. (2003). Cambridge: Cambridge University Press.

Chalmers, A. F. (1999). *What is this thing called science?* Indianapolis, IN: Hackett.

Dunne, J. (1993). *Back to the rough ground: 'Phronesis' and 'Techne' in modern philosophy and in Aristotle.* Notre Dame, IN: University of Notre Dame Press.

Eslbach, K., & Sutton, R. (1992). Acquiring organizational legitimacy through illegitimate actions: A marriage of institutional and impression management theories. *Academy of Management Journal, 35*(4), 699–738.

Eisenhardt, K. (1989). Building theories from case study research. *Academy of Management Review, 14*(4), 532–550.

Evered, R., & Louis, M. R. (1981). Alternative perspectives in the organizational sciences: "Inquiry from the inside" and "Inquiry from the outside." *Academy of Management Review, 6*, 385–395.

Fleck, L. (1979). *Genesis and development of a scientific fact.* Chicago: University of Chicago Press. (Original work published in German in 1935).

Gibbons, M., Limoges, C., Nowotny, H., Schwartzman, S., Scott, P., & Trow, M. (1994). *The new production of knowledge.* London: Sage.

Green, S. E. (2004). A rhetorical theory of diffusion. *Academy of Management Review, 29*, 653–669.

Hay, G. W. (2003). The nature and significance of the executive doctoral scholar-practitioner of organizational development and change: A morphogenetic account of theory-practice linkages for the achievement of scholarly knowledge and business results (Benedictine University, 2003). *Dissertation Abstracts International, 64*, 1747A.

Hay, G. W., Woodman, R. W., & Tenkasi, R. V. (2008). Closing the ODC application gap by bringing ODC knowledge closer to ODC practice. *OD Practitioner, 40*(2), 55–60.

Hodgkinson, G., Herriot, P., and Anderson, N. (Special Issue, 2001). Re-aligning the stakeholders in management research: lessons from industrial, work and organizational psychology. *British Journal of Management, 12,* S41-S48.

Huff, A., & Huff, J. (2001). Refocusing the business school agenda. *British Journal of Management, 12,* S49–S54.

Lawler, E. E. (1986). *High-involvement management: Participative strategies for improving organizational performance.* San Francisco: Jossey-Bass.

Lawler, E. III, Mohrman, A. Jr., Mohrman, S., Ledford, G., Cummings, T., & Associates (Eds.) (1985). *Doing Research That is Useful for Theory & Practice.* San Francisco, CA: Jossey-Bass.

Jick, T. M. (1979). Mixing qualitative and quantitative methods: Triangulation in action. *Administrative Science Quarterly, 24,* 602–611.

Mahoney, J. T., & Sanchez, R. (2004). Building management theory by integrating products and processes of thought. *Journal of Management Inquiry, 13,* 34–47.

Mahoney, J. T., & McGahan, A. M. (2007). The field of strategic management within the evolving field of strategic organization. *Strategic Organization, 5,* 79–99.

Mohr, L. (1982). *Explaining Organizational Behavior.* San Francisco: Jossey-Bass.

Mohrman, S. A. and Lawler, E. E. (2011). *Useful Research: Advancing Theory and Practice.* San Francisco, Berrett-Kohler.

Nowotny, H., Scott, P., & Gibbons, M. (2001). *Re-thinking science: Knowledge and the public in an age of uncertainty.* London: Polity Press.

Nowotny, H., Scott, P., & Gibbons, M. (2005). Re-thinking science: Mode 2 in societal context. In E. Carayannis & D. Campbell (Eds.), *Knowledge creation, diffusion, and use in innovation networks and knowledge clusters: A comparative systems approach across the United States, Europe, and Asia* (pp. 39–51). Westport, CT: Praeger.

Parry, R. (2003). *Episteme* and *Techne.* In E. N. Zalta (Ed.), *The Stanford encyclopedia of philosophy.* Retrieved from http://plato.stanford.edu/archives/sum2003/entries/episteme-techne.

Peters, F. E. (1967). *Greek philosophical terms: A historical lexicon.* New York: New York University Press.

Pettigrew, A. (2001). Management research after modernism. *British Journal of Management,* 12(Special Issue), S61–S70.

Pfeffer, J., & Sutton, R. I. (2006). *Hard facts, dangerous half-truths, and total nonsense.* Boston: Harvard Business School Press.

Pinto, J., & Prescott, J. (1988). Variations in critical success factors over the stages in the project life cycle. *Journal of Management, 14*(1), 5–18.

Rousseau, D. M. (2006). Is there such a thing as "evidence based management"? *Academy of Management Review, 31*, 256–269.

Ryle, G. (1949). *The concept of mind.* London: Hutchinson.

Rynes, S., Bartunek, J., & Daft, R. (2001). Across the great divide: Knowledge creation & transfer between practitioners & academics. *Academy of Management Journal,* 44, 340-355.

Schon, D. A. (1995). Causality and causal inference in the study of organizations. In R. F. Goodman & W. R. Fisher (Eds.), *Rethinking knowledge: Reflections across the disciplines.* Albany, NY: State University of New York Press.

Silverman, D. (2001). *Interpreting qualitative research* (2nd ed.). Thousand Oaks, CA: Sage.

Tenkasi, R. V., & Hay, G. W. (2004). Actionable knowledge and scholar-practitioners: A process model of theory-practice linkages. *Systemic Practice & Action Research, 17*(3), 177–206.

Tenkasi, R. V., & Hay, G. W. (2008). Following the second legacy of Aristotle: The scholar-practitioner as an epistemic-technician. In A. B. Shani, N. Adler, S. A. Mohrman, W. A. Pasmore, & B. Stymne (Eds.), *Handbook of collaborative management research.* Thousand Oaks, CA: Sage. pp. 49-72.

Tenkasi, R. V., Mohrman, S. A., & Mohrman, A. M. (2007). *Making knowledge contextually relevant: The challenge of connecting academic research with practice.* Paper presented at the Third Organization Studies Summer Workshop on Organization Studies as Applied Science: The Generation and Use of Academic Knowledge about Organizations, Crete, Greece.

Tinnish, S., & O'Neal, R. (2010). *Building on the scholar-practitioner legacy: An investigation into the publishing rates, enablers and obstacles to publishing in the OD field.* Lisle, IL: Working Paper, PhD program in Organization Development, Benedictine University.

Van De Ven, A. H. (2007). *Engaged scholarship: A guide for organizational and social research.* Oxford: Oxford University Press.

Van De Ven, A. H., & Johnson, P. E. (2006). Knowledge for theory and practice. *Academy of Management Review, 31*, 902–921.

Van De Ven, A. H., & Schomaker, M. S. (2002). The rhetoric of evidence-based medicine. *Health Care Management Review, 27*(3), 88–90.

Wasserman, I., & Kram, K. (2009). Enacting the scholar practitioner: An exploration of narratives. *Journal of Applied Behavioral Science, 45*(5), 12–38.

Weick, K. (1979). *The social psychology of organizing.* New York: McGraw-Hill.

Werr, A., & Greiner, L. (2008). Collaboration and the production of management knowledge in research, consulting and management practice. In A. B. Shani, N. Adler, S. A. Mohrman, W. A. Pasmore, & B. Stymne (Eds.), *Handbook of collaborative management research.* Thousand Oaks, CA: Sage.

Yin, R. (1994). *Case study research: Design and methods.* Thousand Oaks, CA: Sage.

Open Innovation Space

Tero Montonen* and Päivi Eriksson**

ABSTRACT

The main objective of the article is to describe and analyse how innovation and entrepreneurship have been taught at one Finnish higher education institution, the University of Eastern Finland (UEF) during 2009-2012. The UEF case study shows how a new model of teaching innovation and entrepreneurship was developed and implemented to guide teaching. More specifically, the case study shows how teaching can be used to initiate and enhance a more open and practice oriented innovation process as part of the business degree curriculum. The results of the new model have been encouraging: interest in innovation and entrepreneurship has accelerated and, in particular, the number of student established start up companies has clearly increased.

Keywords: Innovation, open innovation, innovation practice, entrepreneurship, teaching.

ORGANIZATION, PROBLEMS AND ISSUES

The University of Eastern Finland (UEF) is an active player in the Eastern Finland regional innovation system, which refers to how innovation, learning and competitiveness evolve in specific places (see e.g. Doloreux and Parto 2005). In its current form, the university was established in 2010 as the result of the merger of the University of Joensuu and the University of Kuopio. In its own webpages (www.uef.fi/english), the UEF describes itself in the following way:

'With approximately 15,000 students and 2,800 members of staff, the University of Eastern Finland is one of the largest universities in Finland. The university's campuses are located in Joensuu, Kuopio and Savonlinna. The University of Eastern Finland is a multidisciplinary university, which offers teaching in more

* Tero Montonen is with University of Eastern Finland, Kuopio Campus, Finland.
**Päivi Eriksson is with University of Eastern Finland, Kuopio Campus, Finland.
E-mail: tero.montonen@uef.fi, paivi.eriksson@uef.fi

than 100 major subjects. The university comprises four faculties: the Philosophical Faculty, the Faculty of Science and Forestry, the Faculty of Health Sciences, and the Faculty of Social Sciences and Business Studies. The well-being of students is among the primary concerns of the university and, in addition to the high standard of teaching, the university offers its students a modern study environment, which is under constant development. With its extensive networks, this multidisciplinary and international university constitutes a significant competence cluster, which promotes the well-being and positive development of eastern Finland.'

When it was established, the new university formulated its main strategic goal to be among the best 200 universities in the world by 2015. In the 2011 QS World University Rankings of the world's top 500 universities, the UEF was ranked 305[th.] In 2012 the same organization ranked the UEF among the 100 best universities in medicine, among the 150 best in English language and literature, and among the 200 best in geography and pharmacy.

While the UEF has clearly advanced on its way to become a world class university when measured by research publications and quality of teaching, there are still challenges ahead. One of the big challenges of the UEF concerns the third task or third role of the higher education institutions, referring to the wider benefits that the university produces for the society. As Srinivas and Viljamaa (2006, pp. 3) note, media and policy discussions in Finland, Europe, and worldwide refer to the pressures on universities to take on economic development mandates in addition to teaching and research.

In the Finnish context, universities located in the periphery (outside the southern Finland economic centres) have experienced the pressure to perform the third task better that the universities located in the prosperous south. The ability of the Eastern Finland universities (University of Eastern Finland, Savonia University of Applied Sciences and Karelian university of Applied Sciences) to perform their third role has been evaluated and re-evaluated several times (see e.g. Goddard, Asheim, Cronberg and Virtanen 2003). Every time, there have been some recommendations on how to improve the situation. Overall, the recommendations have remained administrative or rather general in nature.

THE NEED FOR STUDY

We argue that one of the central issues concerning the ability of higher education institutions to contribute to the economic development and the production of innovation at the regional, national and international contexts, is the question of how to teach innovation and entrepreneurship to university students and researchers? As Hampden-Turner (2009, pp. 1-6) notes there are good reasons to be sceptical about teaching innovation and entrepreneurship and not least because they both are, by definition, indefinable. Both break out from the limits that we have set earlier, just because the main idea is to generate new combinations outperforming the old ones.

At the UEF, innovation and entrepreneurship are taught at the Department of Business, which belongs to the Faculty of Social Sciences and Business Studies and confers business degrees at the Bachelor, Master and Doctor levels. The department has 900 students and 50 employees, working in four different theme areas: Accounting and Finance, Business and Law, Innovation Management, and Service Management.

The Innovation Management theme area, in particular, focuses on teaching innovation and entrepreneurship to business students as well as any other students interested in the subject. When establishing this theme area we had to ask ourselves questions such as: How is it possible to teach innovativeness? How teaching can inspire young business students to be entrepreneurs? Starting with these types of questions, we have been developing a new model of teaching innovation and entrepreneurship, which we call Open Innovation Space (OIS). Central to the OIS-model is an increased practice orientation in business education (see e.g. Vermeulen 2005; Tushman Tushman, O'Reilly, Fenollosa, Kleinbaum A. and McGrath (2007), Gulati 2007), openness of the innovation process (see e.g. Elmquist, Fredberg and Ollila (2009) and intensive co-operation with the key players of the regional innovation system (see e.g. Doloreux and Parto 2005). These players include companies and public organizations, higher education institutions as well as innovation policy makers and innovation financiers.

The OIS-model has now been evolving for three years (2009-2012) and, therefore, it is time to analyse how this model has been working and what are the main results. Furthermore, we wish to share our experiences and lessons learned and give other higher education institutions a chance to benefit from them.

OBJECTIVES

The main objective of the case study is to explore how innovation and entrepreneurship have been taught at one Finnish higher education institution, the University of Eastern Finland, and more specifically, at the Innovation Management theme area in the Department of Business. Furthermore, we will analyse how the practice oriented Open Innovation Space (OIS) model adapted at the UEF Department of Business operates. We will explore, in particular, how the ideas of practice orientation and open innovation (see e.g. Elmquist, Fredberg and Ollila 2009) have been injected into the curriculum and course designs, and how they have been implemented during 2009-2012.

RESEARCH METHODOLOGY

Research methodology draws from a combination of the intensive case study strategy (Eriksson and Kovalainen 2008, pp. 119-122) and the action research strategy (Eriksson and Kovalainen 2008, pp. 193-208). The intensive case study strategy refers to the interest of understanding one case (teaching of innovation and entrepreneurship at the UEF) and learning from the unique aspects of the case. Methodologically, our aim is to tell a good story worth hearing (Dyer and Wilkins, 1991) rather than test hypothesis or develop new conceptual constructs, which would be the goal of an extensive case study based on several case and their systematic comparison (Eriksson and Kovalainen 2008, pp. 122-125). The action research strategy refers to the fact that both of the authors of this article work and teach at the organization in question. Therefore, we are studying our own actions and activities, which is typical to action research Eriksson and Kovalainen 2008, pp. 193-197).

In the analysis, we have used various types of materials including documents, minutes of meetings, feedback reports from teaching as well as our own notes from formal and informal discussions with the innovation management teaching group at the UEF and the co-operating partners. The analysis of the material follows the guidelines of qualitative content analysis.

DIAGNOSIS AND ANALYSIS

In 2008 the UEF was requested by the Ministry of Education to develop new type of business education and research as a precondition for further funding and the right to confer business degrees. The solution was to integrate the traditional business disciplines (e.g. marketing, entrepreneurship, management, accounting, finance etc.) into four theme areas: Accounting and Finance, Business and Law, Innovation Management, and Service Management. At that time, Innovation Management (INNO) represented a more radical change from the past compared to the other theme areas. The INNO theme area combined elements of management, marketing, entrepreneurship and international business to form a clear focus on innovativeness, renewal and change in business contexts. In addition, there was an increase emphasis on innovation as concrete practice, which can be taught and learned (cf. Ellström 2010).

The establishment of the Innovation Management theme area at UEF in 2009 was based on the analysis of the future needs of innovation and entrepreneurship oriented business education. The analysis was made by the lead of the current Head of the Department, professor Päivi Eriksson. When looking back, she summarizes the main points of the analysis through three issues: 1) problems of the Finnish university education in the area of innovation and entrepreneurship, 2) new solutions and 3) key benefits (see Table 1).

Table 1: Analysis of the problems, solutions and benefits of teaching innovation and entrepreneurship

Problem	Solution	Benefit
Competence produced at the university does not renew practice (business or other)	Teaching the renewal of practice in addition to traditional academic topics	Intensifying the relationship between the university and the society (Third Task)
Scientific knowledge does not contribute enough to the development of new products and services	Broad based innovation view: not only commercialization of scientific research, but also social innovation	Broad based innovators: all university students and researchers can innovate in different ways
Technology transfer is product oriented and demands resources, results are uncertain	More emphasis on the development of services and service businesses	Provides opportunities for innovation in other than traditional science disciplines (e.g. sociology, education)
Traditional ways of enhancing academic entrepreneurship have failed	Multidisciplinary co-operation, customer orientation, practice based learning-by-doing	Entrepreneurial doing becomes familiar to a wide range of university students
Innovation is difficult to learn and understand, it can only be done by qualified experts	Practical innovation projects, co-operative team work among students, teachers and stakeholders	Innovation practice becomes familiar to a wide range of university students

Based on the analysis presented in Table 1, the Innovation Management teaching group, including approximately 15 teachers and researchers lead by Professor Päivi Eriksson, started to develop the new model of teaching innovation and entrepreneurship at UEF in 2008. After one year of intensive period of rethinking and revising the starting points of the business study curriculum at the bachelor and master levels, the new practice oriented OIS model started to take form.

To speed up and support the implementation of the new model, UEF and Savonia University of Applied Sciences had applied for some external funding. The funding was granted for a joint project in which both universities develop their own models but in an integrated way. According to the goals of the project, the two universities co-operate to develop an operating model, which brings together students, teachers and outside co-operators. According to these goals, the students of the two universities also have some joint courses. With the joint project in the background, this article focuses on primarily on the OIS model developed for the purposes of UEF Department of Business. The new study programmes based on the UEF OIS model started in autumn 2009.

The OIS model developed at the UEF Department of Business, Innovation Management theme area is built on six interlinked guiding principles.

1. Innovators as key actors. The teaching of innovation and entrepreneurship brings and initiates intensive co-operation between students, teachers and practitioners. These actors become innovators who are interested in combining academic knowledge and competence with practical problems and solutions.

2. Innovating through practice. Besides reading academic texts on innovation and entrepreneurship the students will be offered the chance to do concrete projects. Innovating through practice projects is open to anyone and the main goal is to inspire the participants to become more innovative. Innovating through practice is based on a methodology and pedagogy that forces the combination of analytic and creative work.

3. Real life projects. Working in real life projects which have been initiated by the students or by the co-operating business companies accelerates the learning process. The projects can last for some hours or for several months. Concrete results inspire to learn more.

4. Customer orientation. The students learn to know the needs of the users or customers of the new products and services that will be developed. Meeting with the users or customers personally, virtually, or through stories and like increases the understanding of their problems and needs.

5. Co-operation without limits. The teaching of innovation and entrepreneurship utilizes the expertise of a multitude of actors (teachers, supervisors, students, practitioners) in creative ways. Opening up the innovation process emphasizes the value of diversity of people and ideas, different points of views, and creativity.

6. Management and reflection. The teachers, students and other co-operating partners learn how to work in diverse teams, how to lead co-operative processes and how to reflect upon the innovation process. The main goal is to become more knowledgeable about the strategies that the participants can use for guiding the innovation process into a desirable direction.

Based on these interlinked guiding principles, we designed and implemented the new innovation management curriculum. At the bachelor level (and doctoral level), the curriculum has been integrated into the general business degree program. At the master level, however, there is a specialist degree program focusing on innovation management in particular.

At the bachelor level, issues of innovation and renewal have been integrated into all management, marketing and entrepreneurship courses. Therefore, these courses emphasize the importance innovativeness in business and the course work focuses on real life projects. The courses also embrace some ideas of open innovation (see e.g. through company co-operation and team work).

In addition to the integrative courses, the bachelor degree includes two specialist courses on innovation management. The first course, the basics of business and entrepreneurship, focuses on exploring innovative business models in various industries. The course work includes a real life project in which the students analyse the business models of specific companies and give recommendation of how to make them even more innovative. The second specialist course, Innovation Management, focuses on customer oriented innovation, in particular. The whole course is an extended hands-on exercise in which the students innovate new products and services for specific co-operating companies and other organizations (public, third sector).

At the master level, the innovation management curriculum comprises of two compulsory courses, three selective courses and a master's thesis. The first one of the two compulsory courses, Innovation cultures, focuses on organizational innovation and learning as well as solutions, processes and practices resulting from human co-operation. The course work deals with the development of the innovation culture of business students.

The second compulsory course, Commercialization of knowledge, develops the students understanding about how knowledge and competence can be commercialized and new businesses developed, particularly in customer-centred ways drawing on the ideas of design thinking. The course work includes intensive co-operation with the companies whose knowledge and competence the students aim to commercialize.

The selective courses of the master program focus on managerial work and leadership, change management, management of the future, social innovation and strategy, and consumer behaviour. All these courses have been designed with the six guiding principles of the OIS-model in mind. The most innovative of the selective courses in Living Lab, which allows the students to develop their own real life projects (individually or in a group). This course is very much student led and the teacher acts as a personal or team coach. The most popular self selected project in the Living Lab course is the students' own start up company.

In addition to courses, the master's degree includes master's thesis and related research course and thesis seminar. The research course is a reading seminar in which students analyse scientific innovation management articles and present their findings to the class. Master's theses are most often done in close co-operation with business companies and other organizations. It is also possible for the student to do action research in his/her thesis: to study and develop his/her own (or somebody else's) start up company in his/her master's thesis.

After three years of operation, the results of the UEF OIS model are very encouraging: level of interest and understanding of the students towards innovation and entrepreneurship have clearly increased. Particularly, the interest towards start up companies is high both during the courses and outside of them. The course work has increased interest in entrepreneurial and innovative activities, but it has also lowered the threshold to start up a company during studies at the university.

RECOMMENDATIONS

We have been working with the OIS-model and the new curriculum based on this model for about three years now. Based on the experiences from the OIS-model, we recommend in particular that the teaching of innovation and entrepreneurship should be oriented towards real life practice through the pedagogy of learning by doing.

In addition, involving companies and other organizations as 'customers', supervisors, coaches and intensive co-operators of real life projects open up the innovation. In addition, it brings out the diversity of the innovation and entrepreneurship process and gives a better chance to discuss and reflect upon the process together with all parties.

It can be challenging at first to get companies and other organizations involved because of old stereotypes of lecture based university teaching. All the companies that we have worked with have been positively surprised about the pedagogical solutions on our courses which are very much based on increasing the activity of the students and encouraging them to take lead of their own learning processes.

Another recommendation is to be very open and innovative with the curriculum development and course work design and let the students to be involved in decision making and course management. Becoming the master of your own studies paves way to the increased interest in entrepreneurial and innovative modes of action.

CONCLUSIONS

In this article we have the case of teaching innovation and entrepreneurship at the University of Eastern Finland, Department of Business, Innovation Management theme area. While we have concentrated on the building and implementation of a new model that guides the development of the curriculum and course design, further research should be focused on the actual learning processes that take place among the students, teachers and other co-operators.

The teaching model presented in this article combines elements of open innovation (e.g. sharing innovative ideas among the co-operators) with strong practice orientation (concrete doing, real life projects, learning by doing). In general, the learning results have been very good. In conclusion and based on our experience, the element of open innovation and practice orientation feed each other in a dynamic and synergistic way and their combination is more valuable than the simple sum of the two.

ACKNOWLEDGEMENT

The authors wish to thank Prof. Päiri Eriksson, University of Eastern Finland for suport provided in development of this case and permission to publish the same in its entirety in ICMC 2012 proceedings in the form of edited book.

REFERENCES

Doloreux, D. and Parto, S. (2005). Regional innovation systems: Current discourse and unresolved issues. Technology and Society 27, 133-153.

Dyer and Wilkins (1991), Better stories, not better constructs to generate better theory: a rejoinder to Eisenhart. Academy of Management Review, 16(3), 613-619.

Ellström P-E (2010). Practice-based innovation: a learning perspective. Journal of workplace Learning, 22(172), 27-40

Elmquist, M., Fredberg T. and Ollila, S. (2009), Exploring the field of open innovation. European Journal of Innovation Management, 12(3), 326-345.

Eriksson, P. and Kovalainen, A. (2008) *Qualitative Methods in Business Research*. London: Sage.

Goddard, J., Asheim, B., Cronberg, T. and Virtanen, I. (2003). Learning Regional Engagement. A re-evaluation of the Third Role of eastern Finland Universities. Publications of the Finnish Higher Education Evaluation Council 11:2003.

Gulati R. (2007). Tent Poles, Tribalism, and Boundary Spanning: The Rigor-Relevance Debate in Management. Academy of Management Journal, 50(4), 775-782.

Hampden-Turner, C. (2009). *Teaching Innovation and Entrepreneurship, Building on the Singaporean Experiment*. Cambridge: Cambridge University Press.

Srinivas, S. and Viljamaa, K. (2005). Economic institutionalization in practice: Development and the 'Third Role' of universities. Publications of the Massachusetts Institute of Technology. MIT-IPC-LIS-O5-002.

Tushman M., O'Reilly C.,Fenollosa A., Kleinbaum A. and McGrath D. (2007). Relevance and Rigor: Executive Education as a Lever in Shaping Practice and Research. Academy of Management Learning and Education, 6(3), 345-362.

Vermeulen F. (2005), On rigor and relevance: Fostering dialectic progress in management research. Academy of Management Journal, 48(6) 978–982.

Case Studies and Research in Management Science

Lamy Erwan* and Lapoule Paul**

ABSTRACT

To highlight the complexity of management situations and reveal the processes which underlie them, any meaningful scientific analysis should encompass not only quantitative approaches, but also qualitative methods. It is notably through case studies that managerial situations can best be understood, and this method of investigation should be encouraged and developed. Indeed, even if case studies are used differently in teaching and research, this does not stop the method from being fully deployed.

Keywords: Management situations, scientific analysis, case method, ECCH.

INTRODUCTION

The case study method is an important pedagogical tool in the field of management science (Abdessemed, 2005). The production of "pedagogical case studies" for teaching purposes is a part of well established institutional and corporate system, which largely defines their form, quantity and even content. In Great Britain, the leader in the case studies publishing sector is the ECCH (European Case Clearing House), while its French counterparty is the CCMP (Centrale de Cas et de Médias Pédagogiques), run under the aegis of the Paris Chamber of Commerce and Industry. The number of case studies lodged at and published by these bodies is steadily increasing in number, and, as a result, these organizations, which now sell turnkey products (case studies, teaching notes, debriefing slide presentations, and videos) are becoming ever-more demanding and selective. The authors' of pedagogical case studies are obliged to follow precise norms, which can be either formal (where case studies must be accompanied by "teaching notes", for example), or informal (for example, care must be taken to ensure

---

* Lamy Erwan, NOVANCIA, Business School Paris, France.
**Lapoule Paul, NOVANCIA, Business School, Paris, France.
E-mail: elamy@novancia.fr, plapoule@novancia.fr

that case studies are "lively"). It is, above all, a question of providing a key to the understanding of a phenomenon or a particular situation for learners who are highly sensitive to the concrete nature of what they are presented with, and who particularly appreciate elements that emphasize that concrete nature, such as films, advertisements, dialogues between employees, quotes from business people, and so on.

When they are used in a scientific perspective, case studies are not subject to the same normative constraints as they are when they are used for teaching purposes. Whereas pedagogical case studies have to be attractive and capable of retaining the attention of students, articles generally adopt a "neutral", academic vocabulary couched in a distant, factual style designed to reveal the essence of the phenomena described while ensuring that contingent factors do not detract from clarity of exposition. Nor are the objectives the same: scientific articles must provide a demonstration, while pedagogical case studies must make it possible to understand a situation. But it is here that the two approaches can coincide: "understanding", in the sense outlined by Max Weber, is, evidently, an essential aspect of articles based on the use of one or more case studies. A scientific article must enable the reader to understand a particular phenomenon in exactly the same way as a pedagogical case study must make it possible for students to understand a specific situation.

However, for a long time, the case study method applied in the realm of teaching remained separate from the method applied to scientific articles. The writing of case studies did not feed any scientific ambitions on the part of their authors, and the use of the case study method within the framework of scientific projects did not lead to the production of pedagogical case studies but, rather, to academic books or articles. Furthermore, their reception in the field of management studies varied greatly. While the role of "pedagogical case studies" in teaching is well known (Bonoma, 1989), the scientific value of articles based on case studies still has a questionable status, notably in Britain and the United States, where quantitative approaches to management phenomena are dominant. Authors including Yin (1994) posit a "nomothetic modelization" based on series of case studies, from which a number of generalizations can be derived. Others prefer an "idiographic modelization" (La Ville, 2000) focusing on revealing the rich and singular history of a specific situation, and underlining the particular conditions of its development. Regardless, while the case study method has long been the object of a good deal of scepticism in the scientific field (Yin, 1981; Scholz, 2001), it is fully recognized in the sphere of teaching, at least in management science.

But the gap between the two is breaking down (Jenkins, 2011). Business schools, which must today position themselves on an increasingly globalised education market and whose academic reputations are meticulously evaluated in both national and international classifications, are subject to growing pressure to develop their scientific output (particularly in terms of the publication of articles in peer-reviewed journals).

Teacher-researchers have to meet publication objectives, while at the same time – naturally enough – continuing their teaching activities, an area which includes the production of case studies. Again according to Jenkins (2011), teacher-researchers are being put under increasing pressure to combine teaching and research. In this regard, cases studies are the most efficient way of exploiting research data and communicating effectively with a class of students. After having written and applied a case study in a teaching situation, authors are entitled to suppose that their subject is worthy of further exploration and that it may lead to a publication in a scientific journal. Indeed, pedagogical case studies dealing with subjects as diverse as international management (Schmid and Grosche, 2008), international trade (Hampton and Rowell, 2011), strategic innovation (Bourdon and Lehmann-Ortega, 2007), multi-channel retail strategies (Colla and Lapoule, 2011), and the launch of a new product (Mayrhofer and Roederer, 2009) have been expanded into research articles. Meanwhile, Netzley (2011) considers the kind of groundwork required to develop case studies as an opportunity to improve teaching and research methods.

The question thus arises of potential synergies between approaches to teaching and research, notably in terms of the articulation between pedagogical case studies and research articles. Here, we pose the question of potential synergies by examining the ways in which the transition from one sphere to the other can be made. The importance of a strong articulation between teaching and research activities is now widely recognized, as is the role of case studies in that articulation. For example, Quinn (1994) initiated each of his research articles by writing and teaching one or more pedagogical case studies. But, beyond statements of a general nature, the way in which the articulation between teaching and research functions concretely has not yet been adequately described. This is the question to which we intend to provide an answer in this empirical study.

METHODOLOGY

Our study, which is still ongoing, is divided into three major stages. The first, an exploratory stage, consisted in a series of unstructured interviews with a number of teacher-researchers working, like us, in business schools. Rather than introduce our own *a priori* on the question of the articulation between teaching and research practices and the role of the case study method therein, we preferred instead to listen to colleagues with experience in the area.

We carried out nine interviews, recording and transcribing them from beginning to end. Using the interviews, we were able to identify the three main ways in which pedagogical case studies and research articles can mutually enrich one another.

The first corresponds to taking certain elements from a pedagogical case study (verbatims and other components) and using them as the basis of a research article. The second is based on extracting elements from an article and using them to develop a pedagogical case study. The third situation consists in using points raised in debates with students about the case study in a classroom situation simultaneously to clarify the problematic and provide the bases of future research articles.

We will also examine the role of teaching notes (Hermant, 1980), which are published alongside case studies and represent an "explicit bridge" between research and teaching. Teaching notes can clearly serve as prolegomena to scientific articles based on material deriving from pedagogical case studies.

For the second phase of the study, we developed a questionnaire containing the various elements described above (see appendix). The questions mainly focus on the way in which case studies and teaching notes can be used in research articles and, inversely, the way in which articles can be used in case studies and their teaching notes, as well as the way in which the use of a case study for teaching purposes can improve research practices.

This questionnaire was sent to 7,467 researchers and teachers throughout the world. This sample of the academic population was extracted from the Social Science Citations Index (SSCI) database. We started by identifying 6,646 articles published between 2005 and 2012 in journals indexed on this database, of which either the title, or the abstract, or the list of key words contained the phrase "case study" or "case studies", and which were categorized in the fields of management, finance, business science, economics or sociology.[1] From this database of articles we identified the 7,467 email addresses of the principal authors and sent the questionnaire to them. We received 964 replies, or a rate of reply of approximately 13%.

At the same time, a French version of the questionnaire was also drawn up and sent to 687 teacher-researchers active in major business schools in France. We received 93 replies, or a reply rate of approximately 13.5%.

In the final analysis, we received a total of 1,057 replies. These replies were entered into a database and the names were rendered anonymous after the nationalities and disciplines of the respondents had been added with a view to identifying any differences of a cultural nature.

The distribution of nationalities and disciplines of this population are as follows:

Table 1: Distribution of Respondents by Nationality (57 Nationalities, 15 of which Provided over 20 Respondents each)

USA	187	17.7%
France	127	12.0%
England	107	10.1%
Australia	46	4.4%
Canada	44	4.2%

Spain	43	4.1%
Netherlands	43	4.1%
Italy	39	3.7%
Sweden	39	3.7%
Brazil	31	2.9%
Germany	28	2.6%
Denmark	27	2.6%
Norway	25	2.4%
Finland	23	2.2%
Switzerland	20	1.9%
Others	228	21.6%

Table 2: Distribution by Discipline (the total is Superior to 1,057 since Individual Authors May be Involved in More than One Discipline)

Business & Economics	823	51.0%
Sociology	156	9.7%
Operations Research & Management Science	100	6.2%
Social Sciences - Other Topics	82	5.1%
Engineering	74	4.6%
Public Administration	66	4.1%
Environmental Sciences & Ecology	60	3.7%
Others	254	15.7%

In the third phase of the study, using an analysis of the results of the questionnaire, we intend to conduct a series of semi-structured interviews focusing on the various aspects of the articulation between research and teaching practices.

RESULTS OF THE SURVEY

A large majority of respondents to the questionnaire (72.4%) had produced at least one pedagogical case study, while over a third (36%) had produced at least three.

Table 3: Number of Case Studies Undertaken by the Respondents

0	292	27.6%
1	112	10.6%
2	129	12.2%
3-5	262	24.8%
6-10	118	11.2%
10 and over	144	13.6%

A substantial majority considered that it is increasingly important to combine teaching and research (only 0.8% of respondents strongly disagreed with this idea).

Table 4: Replies to the question: "In your view, is it increasingly important to ensure that there is a close relationship between teaching and research?"

No, not at all	8	0.8%
No, not really	69	6.5%
Yes, to a certain degree	416	39.4%
Yes, absolutely	564	53.4%

We also found that a substantial majority of respondents considered that case studies are a particularly suitable tool for combining teaching and research.

Table 5: Replies to the Question: "Are case Studies Particularly Suited to Associating Teaching and Research?

No, not at all	13	1.2%
No, not really	108	10.2%
Yes, to a certain degree	531	50.2%
Yes, absolutely	289	27.3%
NR	116	11.0%

Lastly, a majority of respondents had already combined teaching and research practices by using the results of a survey to write up a case study and a research article.

Table 6: Replies to the question: "Have you already used the results of an empirical investigation to write both a pedagogical case study and a research article (for an academic journal)?

No	367	34.7%
Yes	571	54.0%
NR	119	11.3%

These early results confirm the initial hypotheses of this study: the question of the rapprochement between teaching and research is considered to be increasingly important, and case studies are viewed as offering a means of promoting it. The modalities of this rapprochement, or at least the respective importance the various ways in which the case study method can be used to affect a rapprochement between teaching and research, have yet to be defined.

The exploratory surveys that we conducted with nine European teacher researchers helped us to identify three main approaches: incorporating elements from pedagogical case studies or the accompanying teaching note into the article; incorporating elements from an article into a case study; and using scientific elements gleaned from the use of a case study in a teaching context.

We used our exploratory interviews to distinguish a number of different aspects of each approach.

For the transition to the case study (and its teaching note), we envision the possibility that the following elements can be incorporated into an article: the description of the situation, the verbatims, the results of the analysis, the theoretical contributions, the bibliography.

In the opposite configuration – the transition from an article to a case study (or its teaching note) – we envision the possibility of the following elements being incorporated: the conclusions, the theoretical considerations, some extracts from interviews, the quantitative analyses (if there were any), the theoretical developments or the bibliography.

Lastly, the use of case studies in a teaching context (in a classroom) could have the following advantages: it could help to clarify managerial contributions (practical aspects, recommendations), it could lead the authors to return to the field, it could enable to better define the research problematic, it could help to reveal certain weaknesses in the theoretical approach, to identify a number of interesting theoretical perspectives, to clarify certain concepts, to organize the literature review more effectively. We have also envisioned the possibility that the use of case studies may have no scientific value.

Below, we examine empirically the respective importance of the various kinds of synergies between teaching and research practices.

FROM THE ARTICLE TO THE PEDAGOGICAL CASE STUDY

The table below shows that the elements most frequently taken from articles and used in case studies are conclusions and theoretical developments, as well as, unsurprisingly, verbatims (quotes from interviewees). Conclusions and theoretical developments are incorporated into both the case study and the accompanying teaching note. It should be observed that bibliographies from articles are only relatively rarely used in teaching notes.

Table 7: Respective Weighting of Different sorts of use of Scientific Articles in Case Studies or Teaching notes, Expressed as a Percentage of Respondents

Use of conclusions in the teaching note	41%
Use of theoretical developments in the teaching note	37%
Use of conclusions in the case study	36%
Use of extracts of interviews from the case study	35%
Use of theoretical considerations in the case study	34%
Use of any quantitative analyses in the teaching note	20%
Use of the bibliography in the teaching note	16%
Other uses of the article in the teaching note	13%
Other uses of the article in the case study	11%

Table 8: Distribution of Various Synergies in Terms of Elements from Articles used in case Studies in Function of Respondents' Experience of the case Study Method. (Results Significantly Lower than average Highlighted in pink, Results Significantly Higher than Average in Blue)

	Experience of case study method				
	Weak	Average	Strong	Average	Fisher
Use of extracts of interviews from the case studies	23%	43%	51%	35%	38.76
Use of theoretical developments in the teaching note	27%	41%	52%	37%	27.81
Use of conclusions in the teaching note	30%	51%	53%	41%	27.66
Use of the bibliography in the teaching note	11%	14%	26%	16%	15.83
Use of theoretical considerations in the case study	26%	39%	45%	34%	15.67
Use of conclusions in the case study	29%	44%	42%	36%	12.62
Potential use of quantitative analyses in the teaching note	15%	23%	28%	20%	10.84

In differentiating between respondents with a good deal of experience of case studies (those who had produced at least 6) and those with average (3-5) or little (at most 2) experience (no more than 2 case studies), we were able to observe that the most experienced subjects distinguished[2] themselves from the other respondents, on the one hand because their use of extracts from interviews is more systematic, and, on the other, because they tend to add conclusions and theoretical developments from research articles to their teaching notes. Similarly, it can be observed that, although they are in a small minority, experienced respondents make a more extensive use of bibliographical elements from research in their teaching notes. This result demonstrates the importance of teaching notes in terms of linking research to teaching practices, especially amongst specialists in the case study method.

FROM CASE STUDY TO ARTICLE

In terms of the use of elements of pedagogical case studies in research articles, it is, unsurprisingly, not only descriptive features, but also results that are most frequently incorporated. There is an unexpected contiguity, or even a continuity between pedagogical and scientific approaches. While the objective of analyses of case studies is, above all, to deliver a concrete reality to students, it can be observed that such analyses can also contribute to the development of research issues. The problematic of a specific organization thus becomes a scientific problematic, with the case study providing support to the publication of research articles in the form of a theoretical system that not only satisfies internal validity criteria, but also has a more general application (Yin, 1994). Consequently, it does not come as a surprise that theoretical considerations developed for the case study are often incorporated into the article. It can also be observed – but this is less unexpected – that verbatims from case studies are infrequently used in research articles.

Table 9: Respective Incidence of Different Kinds of use of the Case Study in the Teaching note or the Article as a Percentage of Respondents

Use of descriptive elements	38%
Use of an analysis of the case	35%
Use of theoretical consideration	26%
Other elements used	15%
Use of the bibliography	13%
Use of verbatim	12%

The analysis of the distribution of these synergies in function of the experience of the respondents in terms of the case study method does not substantially modify these observations. It is, however, possible to observe that experienced respondents use verbatim and bibliographical elements significantly more often than their less experienced colleagues, which suggests that, for the former, there is a greater proximity between case studies and research articles.

Table 10: Distribution of Various Synergies in terms of Elements from articles used in case Studies in Function of Respondents' Experience of the case Study Kethod. (Results Significantly Lower than Average are Highlighted in pink, Results Significantly Higher than Average in blue).

Type	Experience of case study method			Average	Fisher
	Weak	Average	Strong		
Use of the results of the analysis of the case study	23%	44%	48%	35%	32.95
Use of descriptive elements	27%	48%	50%	38%	30.31
Use of verbatim	6%	14%	21%	12%	19.22
Use of theoretical considerations	20%	27%	38%	26%	15.05
Use of the bibliography	8%	13%	21%	12%	13.04

FROM THE USE OF THE CASE STUDY TO THE RESEARCH ARTICLE

Teaching with case studies is also a way to get some scientifically useful lessons from students' reactions. In effect, case studies used for teaching make it possible to test information acquired in the field on various groups of learners with a view to defining situations which are not, initially, sufficiently clear to either the students or the author. Indeed, they can prompt researchers to return to the field in order to rework the case or find new elements of proof. Getting learners to draw conclusions from a case can help to anticipate certain theoretical and conceptual limits. Students can also help to point out empirical gaps that can only be filled thanks to additional fieldwork. Writing a research article based on a pedagogical case study presupposes a more critical perspective. Using case studies for teaching purposes can help to develop a critical stance of this kind. Authors like Bonnafous-Boucher, Redien-Collot and Teglborg (2010) think that pedagogical case studies are inherently optimistic, that they give students the impression that there is always an answer to everything; but student reactions can always help to reveal weaknesses that need to be corrected or, more simply, points that need to be better explained. It is these various approaches to exploiting case studies scientifically that we have examined in our study. The table below shows the respective incidence of each of these approaches amongst the respondents.

In our survey, only a small minority of respondents – 26% – considered that pedagogical case studies contributed nothing scientifically. Even more worthy of note, as is shown in the following table, even fewer of the most experienced respondents considered that pedagogical case studies were of no scientific interest.

Table 11: Respective Incidence of Different Kinds of use of Case Studies in Articles as a Percentage of Respondents

Clarification of concepts	29%
Clarification of managerial contributions	27%
No contribution to the article	26%
Improved definition of the problematic	21%
Identification of interesting theoretical perspectives	20%
Identification of theoretical weaknesses	12%
Improved organization of the literature review	9%
Other contributions	8%
Leads to additional fieldwork	6%

We then observed that the main contributions made by pedagogical case studies were to clarifying concepts and problematics. This is where the articulation between teaching and research, and the place occupied by case studies in that configuration, acquires all its meaning. What might seem obvious to the teacher-researcher becomes decidedly less so when presented to the critical gaze of the student body. And the approach consisting in never being satisfied with superficial clarity is at the heart of scientific practice. However,

Table 12: Distribution of Various Synergies in Terms of Elements from Case Studies used in Articles in Function of Respondents' Experience of the case Study Method. (Results Significantly Lower than Average Highlighted in Pink, Results Significantly Higher than Average in Blue).

Type	Experience of case study methods			Moyenne	Fisher
	Weak	Average	Strong		
Clarification of managerial contributions	17%	35%	37%	26%	25,86
Clarification of concepts	22%	31%	42%	29%	16,47
Improved definition of the problematic	16%	22%	31%	21%	12,69
Identification of interesting theoretical perspectives	15%	19%	29%	19%	11,87
No contribution to the article	32%	17%	21%	26%	11,56
Identification of theoretical weaknesses	9%	15%	15%	12%	4,76
Improved organization of the literature review	7%	10%	12%	9%	2,95
Leads to a return to the field	5%	6%	9%	6%	2,37

it should be pointed out that case studies make only a small contribution to the task of identifying theoretical weaknesses. That is probably due to the superficial nature of the theoretical dialogue between teachers and students, who have not yet mastered theoretical tools.

Case studies can also be used, although to a lesser degree, to identify interesting theoretical perspectives. This is probably more an indirect effect of outlining the case to students than the result of a theoretical dialogue with them. On this point, it would be better to focus on the teacher-researchers themselves in order to gain a better understanding of how they are able to identify these theoretical perspectives.

An analysis of the distribution of responses between experienced teacher-researchers and their less experienced counterparts in the writing of case studies reveals no notable discrepancy from the preceding observations.

CONCLUSIONS

The table above recapitulates the principal initial conclusions of our study by showing the most current interactions and synergies between pedagogical case studies and research articles. Again, the importance of the teaching note as a kind of bridge between teaching and research is apparent, as the conclusions of research articles are often incorporated in them. More interesting is the role played by case studies in terms of providing clarification. This is one of the most frequent sources of synergy (over 22% of respondents mention it) and, as such, it is a point that should be further examined in the following stage of this study. Moreover, it can also be observed that exchanges between pedagogical and scientific practices are balanced: amongst the main synergies there are not significantly more contributions to articles than contributions to teaching notes.

Table 13: Respective Incidence of Various Synergies Envisioned and Direction of the Exchange (from the Article to the Teaching note: AT; from the Article to the case Study: AC; from the case Study and the Teaching note to the Article: CTA ; from the Pedagogical Treatment of the Teaching note to the article : PTA)

Use of conclusions in the teaching note	AT	41%
Use of descriptive elements	CTA	38%
Use of theoretical developments in the teaching note	AT	37%
Use of conclusions in the case study	AC	36%
Use of extracts of interviews in the case study	AC	35%
Use of analysis of case study	CTA	35%
Use of theoretical considerations in the case study	AC	34%
Clarification of concepts	PTA	29%
Clarification of managerial contributions	PTA	27%

Use of theoretical considerations	CTA	26%
Average		22%
Improved definition of the problematic	PTA	21%
Identification of interesting theoretical perspectives	PTA	20%
Use of any quantitative analyses in the teaching note	AT	20%
Use of the bibliography in the teaching note	AT	16%
Use of the bibliography	CTA	13%
Identification of theoretical weaknesses	PTA	12%
Use of verbatim	CTA	12%
Improved organization of the literature review	PTA	9%
Leads to additional to fieldwork	PTA	6%

Of course, for the moment this is only the first phase of a survey on the potential synergies between pedagogical case studies and research. This first phase should enable us to explore a number of avenues to get a better idea of this emerging problematic. In effect, there are more questions than there are answers in the preceding paragraphs.

Making better use of research carried out in management schools on pedagogical and exploratory case studies should contribute to narrowing the gap between theory and practice, and between testable theories and empirical observations, and to enrich management research. Without wishing to be exhaustive, this survey may encourage teacher-researchers to apply this as yet still little recognized method of investigation in terms of both practice and theory.

Our research has a certain number of limits. Some elements of the relationship between teaching and research were not discussed, for example the choices made and ways of addressing a subject or a field, and the possible articulations in terms of form and content between research articles and pedagogical case studies. In particular, we have neither mentioned the modifications that can be made to a teaching note in order to transform it into a more academic form, nor focused on the style of writing employed (MacNair, 1971; Cova & de la Baume, 1991), a style on which structure and tone depend. Nor have we dealt with the question of the generalization of pedagogical case studies, or that of the choice of field in which they are carried out. All these question and a number of others should be developed in the wake of this study.

BIBLIOGRAPHY

Abdessemed, T. (2009). Les conditions du renouveau de la méthode des cas dans la formation au management. Gestion 2000, March-April, 167-191.

Bonnafous-Boucher, M.; Redien-Collot, R.; and Teglborg, A. (2010, March). Comment favoriser l'innovation par la participation des salariés ? Une approche complémentaire de l'intrapreneuriat : les leçons tirées d'études de cas français. Paper presented at the 3èmes Journées Georges Doriot « L'Intrapreneuriat : Au-delà des discours, quelles pratiques ? », March 4-5, Caen, France.

Bonoma, T. (1989), *Learning with cases*. Boston: Harvard Business School.

Bourdon, I. and Lehmann-Ortega, L. (2007), Systèmes d'information et innovation stratégique : une étude de cas. Systèmes d'Information et Management, March (12).

Colla, E. and Lapoule, P. (2011), Facteurs -clés de succès des cybermarchés : les enseignements du cas Tesco.com. Décisions Marketing, January-March (61).

Cova, B. and de la Baume, C. (1991). Cas et Méthode des Cas : fondements concepts et universalité. Gestion 2000 (3)

Hampton, A. and Rowell, J.W. (2010). Leveraging Integrated Partnerships as a Means of Developing International Capability: An SME Case Study. International Journal of Knowledge, Culture and Change Management, 10, 6, 19-30. Common Ground Publishing LLC USA.

Hermant, J. (1980). *La note pédagogique, un outil de stratégie éducative*, Paris: Enseignement et gestion, Nouvelle série n° 15.

Jenkins, M. (2011). Cité dans *Research vs. Teaching – achieving synergies with cases, www.ecch. com/educators/casemethod/resources/features/rvt*

La Ville (de), V. (2000, September). La recherché idiographique en management stratégique : une pratique en quête de méthode ? Finance Contrôle Stratégie, 3, 5, 73-99.

MacNair, M. (1971). *McNair on cases*, Harvard Business School Bulletin, July/August

Mayrhofer, U. and Roederer, C. (2009). Levi Strauss Signature : une nouvelle marque pour la grande distribution. Gestion 2000, 5, 15-25.

Netzley, M. (2011). Quoted in *Research vs. Teaching – achieving synergies with cases, www. ecch.com/educators/casemethod/resources/features/rvt*

Quinn, J.B. (1994), *L'entreprise intelligente*. Paris: Dunod.

Schmid, S. and Grosche, P. (2008). From assembly plant to center of excellence. The rise of Audi's subsidiary in Györ, Hungary. In Bertelsmann Foundation (eds.), *Managing the International Value Chain in the Automotive Industry - Strategy, Structure, and Culture*. (pp.104-127). Bertelsmann Stiftung, Gütersloh: Bertelsmann Stiftung.

Shmid, S. (2011). Die Fusion der Hypovereinsbank mit der UniCredit Group 2005 – Grenzüberschreitende Akquisitionen und Fusionen in der Bankenbranche. In Burhop, Carsten/Scholtyseck, Joachim (2011, Hrsg.): *Weichenstellungen der deutschen Banken- und Finanzgeschichte*, 2011 (in press).

Scholz, R. and Tictje, O. (2001). *Embedded Case Study Methods: Integrating Quantitative and Qualitative Knowledge*. Thousand Oaks, CA: Sage Publications

Yin, R-K (1994), *Case study Research: Design and Methods*, Sage

APPENDIX: QUESTIONNAIRE

How many pedagogical case studies have you written?

- 0
- 1
- 2
- Between 3 and 5
- Between 6 and 10
- More than 10

In your view, is it increasingly important to ensure that there is a close relationship between teaching and research?

- No, not at all
- No, not really
- Yes, to a certain degree
- Yes, absolutely

Is there an increasingly close relationship between your teaching and research approaches?

- No, not at all
- No, not really
- Yes, to a certain degree
- Yes, absolutely

Are case studies particularly suited to associating teaching and research?

- No, not at all
- No, not really
- Yes, to a certain degree
- Yes, absolutely

Have you already used the results of an empirical investigation to write both a pedagogical case study and a research article (for an academic journal)?

- Yes
- No

How did your use of a case study in a teaching situation contribute to the writing of the article?

- It made no contribution
- It helped to clarify managerial contributions (practical aspects, recommendations)
- It led me to return to the field

- It enabled me to better define the research problematic
- It helped to reveal certain weaknesses in my theoretical approach
- It helped to identify a number of interesting theoretical perspectives
- It helped to clarify certain concepts
- It helped me to organize my literature review more effectively
- Other (please explain)

After writing a research article, which of the following elements did you use later, either partially or in their entirety, in the case study?

- The conclusions
- Theoretical considerations
- Extracts from interviews
- Other (please explain)

After writing a research article, which of the following elements did you later use, either partially or in their entirety, in the teaching note of your case study?

- Quantitative analyses (if there were any)
- The conclusions
- The theoretical developments
- The bibliography
- Other (please explain) 313761

After writing a case study and its accompanying teaching note, which of the following elements did you later use, either partially or in their entirety in writing the research article?

- The description of the situation
- The verbatims
- The results of the analysis
- The theoretical contributions
- The bibliography
- Other (please explain)

1. The key used is as follows: TS=("case study") or TS=("case studies"). Refined by: Web of Science Categories=(MANAGEMENT OR BUSINESS FINANCE OR BUSINESS OR ECONOMICS OR SOCIOLOGY); Timespan=2005-2012. Databases=SSCI.

2. The Fisher test reveals a very significant gap with the average. The gap is also significant for other synergies, only less so.

PART III: Cases in Human Capital Development

A twenty first century organization deeply embedded in the economic environment of globalizationand free trade, an explosion of information technology, and access to real time data is under enormous stress to meet competition, changing customer preferences, emerging societal concerns, and still creates innovation in products and processes. Such organizations are called upon to discover new rules of doing business, maintain an edge in sustainable business practices, and be accountable to stakeholders. In the final diagnosis it is the human capital which is both called upon to discover new solutions and methodologies to implementation. Human resource is also the carrier of intellectual capital. The management of human capital thus emerges as the biggest challenge and opportunity.

The four cases in this section explicate some of these issues facing the management of human capital. The cases cover the success stories and lessons learned from failures, both in anengaging narrative format. The reader benefits from seeing how things work in the real word when it comes to leveraging human capital. The first such exploration is by Shuchi Agarwal and Manosi Chaudhuri who present a study conducted at Jindal Steel and Power Limited (JSPL), the largest in India today after the public sector SAIL, with presence in steel, mining, power and infrastructure sector. The study recognises factors of retention as Work Atmosphere, Growth Opportunities, Non-monetary incentives, and Flexibility and Clarity in work.

Parameswar Nayak and Sanjana Tyagi next discuss a financial services company's learning and development programs to address the problem of absenteeism.The case brings out both strengths of learning continuum and weaknesses of classroom training. Pooja Misra, Shreya Jain and Abhay Sood present an exploratory studyin Indian Retail Industry. The study seeks to analyze the impact of compensation components in terms of financial and non-financial rewards and organizational justice on motivation, job satisfaction, and turnover intentions. In the final case study in this section, Sakshi Puri and Manosi Chaudhuri discuss an exploratory study of initiatives of competency assessment at ADIDAS India to change the way its franchisee stores managed their human resources. The analysis used in-depth interviewing and observations and brought out insightful findings. Overall, the four chapters present a convincing case for human capital development in organizations of all sorts.

Employee Retention at Jindal Steel and Power Limited

Shuchi Agarwal* and Manosi Chaudhuri**

ABSTRACT

Jindal Steel and Power Limited (JSPL) is a company with presence in steel, mining, power and infrastructure sector. A study was conducted at the corporate office located in Gurgaon to determine the factors which help in reducing attrition. Analysis of exit interview forms was done to find out the key factors which caused employees to leave the organization. Along with that, after studying the literature, a questionnaire was designed. The questionnaire was administered to employees with the aim to determine the factors with which employees were satisfied. Broadly, the factors of retention were as follows: Work Atmosphere, Growth Opportunities, Non-monetary incentives, and Flexibility and Clarity in work. These are the factors the company must focus on to formulate retention strategies.

Keywords: Jindal Steel and Power Ltd., employee retention, flexibility, non-monetary incentives, attrition, growth, clarity in work

OVERVIEW OF THE COMPANY

Jindal Steel and Power Limited(JSPL) is one of the major producers of steel with significant presence in other sectors like Mining, Power and Infrastructure. The company has plants at Chattisgarh, Raigarh, Raipur, Tamnar, Angul, Barbil, Tensa and Patratu. The company has its presence internationally also in Bolivia, Africa, South Africa, Mozambique, Madagascar, Zambia, Tanzania, Oman and Australia. The company has taken a lot of CSR initiatives in the areas of environment, healthcare,

* Shuchi Agarwal is pursuing post graduate studies in management at Birla Institute of Management Technology, Greater Noida, India.

**Manosi Chaudhuri is Associate Professor,OB & HR at Birla Institute of Management Technology, Greater Noida, India.

E-mail: shuchi.agarwal13@bimtech.ac.in, manosi.chaudhuri@bimtech.ac.in community development, education and other social issues. JSPL pioneered the production of 121 meter long railway track and it also built a facility to factory weld these rails in welded lengths. Other products manufactured by JSPL include parallel flange beams and coils, plates and coils, angles and channels, TMT Re-bars, Wire rods, fabricated sections, etc.

JSPL aims at inclusive growth and not profits. Its key areas of focus are Health, Education, Women Empowerment, Livelihood, Livestock Care, Drinking Water and Sanitation, Youth and Sports and Infrastructure Development. JSPL is equally concerned about environmental issues. JSPL has taken appropriate measures at plant locations to control air pollution and water pollution. The company believes in the principle of "Wealth from waste". The company has been also awarded with several Environment Management Awards, Energy Conservation Awards, Safety Awards, Corporate Social Responsibility Awards and various HR Awards. JSPL received Asia Pacific HRM Congress 2011 Awards for "Organization with innovative HR Practices." It was also among Top 20 "Best Companies to Work for" by Business Today in 2009.

The HR function at JSPL is commendable. It values its employees and has well defined HR Policies. The HR Policies are fair and clearly mentioned and communicated. The HR department at JSPL strives to provide its employees with the work culture wherein best out of each employee comes out. JSPL realizes that the knowledge and experience of its employees is very crucial for its survival and competitive advantage. It does not want the existing talent to leave the organization.

OBJECTIVES

The study is aimed to determine the factors which cause employees to quit the company. In addition to that, the objective of the study is to determine the factors on which the organization is doing well and factors on which further improvement is required. With a proactive approach in mind, a study has been conducted to determine the factors which help in retaining employees. Analyzing exit interview forms is a good way to determine the loop holes, if any, existing in the system. So the exit interview forms of employees who left the organization in the past one year were analyzed. In order to capture the view point of the existing employees, a questionnaire was designed and administered to employees and the data thus collected was supplemented to the exit interview data.

After determining the factors on the basis of the participants perception, the aim is to suggest measures to overcome the shortcomings, which would help in increasing retention.

LITERATURE REVIEW

Hiring good people is tough but retaining them can be even tougher. Employee turnover and employee retention are inextricably linked; to control turnover is to enhance retention (McConnell, 2011). Direct and indirect costs occur when an employee leaves the organization. Enough attention is not paid to this factor. This is because so much of it is indirect and thus not readily visible (McConnell, 2011). A study done by the Saratoga Institute, Saratoga, California, and the Society for Human Resource Management, McLean, Va., as cited by Wille (1994) placed the average cost to hire a non-exempt employee at $1,023 and an exempt employee at $7,839. A similar study done by the Bureau of National Affairs, Washington, D.C., as cited by Wille (1994) places the cost of hiring a non-exempt employee at $1,283. These figures do not include the cost of training. With an annual average turnover rate of approximately 15 to 18 percent in credit unions, those costs can add up quickly. High turnover creates other hard-to-measure negative effects. The morale of remaining employees can be diminished by a constant outflow of co-workers. Employees begin to wonder if they would be better off leaving the organization themselves; especially if there are a large number of terminations (Wille, 1994).

RETENTION STRATEGIES

The first strategy which any one would cite for retaining employees is money. Leading organizations - including those on Fortunes "100 Best Companies to Work For" list - are increasingly using a number of nonmonetary strategies to increase employee retention, which include: Create and leverage your brand, Establish formal recognition programs,Partner with training or teaching organizations,Provide family-friendly benefits,Conduct exit interviews (Abrams, 2004).

Factors to be considered for developing employee retention strategies are needs of the employee, work environment, responsibilities, supervision, fairness and equity, effort, employee development and feedback (Ramlall, 2004).

Needs of the Employee – Different employees will have different needs. Needs depend on individual, family, and cultural values. It also depends on the current and desired economic, political, and social status; career aspiration; the need to balance career, family, education, community, religion, and other factors; and a general feeling of one's satisfaction with the current and desired state of being.

Work Environment – A productive, respectful, work environment which provides a feeling of inclusiveness and offers a friendly setting is preferred.

Responsibilities – Having shown competency previously, the employee may desire more challenging work and more responsibilities.

Supervision – Managers and other leaders more frequently than others feel a need to teach, coach, and develop others. As a result they would want to influence the organization's goals, objectives and the strategies designed to achieve the mission of the organization.

Fairness and Equity – Every employee wants to be treated and rewarded in a fair and equitable manner regardless of age, gender, ethnicity, disability, sexual orientation, geographic location, or other similarly defined categories. An employee who contributes more would definitely expect a better reward than his counterpart who performed less.

Effort – An employee may put in a lot of effort keeping in mind the reward, but it can be short-lived if the work is not satisfactory.

Employees' Development – Employees prefer to function in environments that provide a challenge, offer new learning opportunities, significantly contribute to the organization's success so that they feel their task significant, offer opportunities for advancement and personal development based on success and demonstrated interest in a particular area.

Feedback – Timely and open feedback from supervisors is what is preferred by all employees. The feedback should not be only once a year during performance appraisals, but must be a continuous process.

Adhikari (2009) finds that there are significant effects of four dimensions in retaining an employee. Work related issues have the highest effect on attrition. Factors pertaining to employer related issues and skills of employees have almost the same effect. Interestingly, the compensation has the lowest effect on attrition. It means that employees give more importance to the quality of job and employer's treatment than salary. It implies that employers should be more careful in assigning tasks to particular employees and a work group, based on the employee's interest.

A chapter "Job Sculpting: The Art of Retaining your Best People" by Timothy Butler and James Waldrop (1999) in Harvard Business Review on finding and keeping the best people describes "The Big Eight". It says that employees are motivated by deeply embedded life interests and emotionally driven passions for certain kind of activities. Hobbies or enthusiasm about something is not life interest. Passion is life interest.

Application of Technology: Some people whether or not they are trained to be engineers or happen to be engineers are curious about finding better ways of using technology to solve business problems. They do this because they love to do this. Application of technology people are the ones who want to know how a clock works because the technology excites them – as does the possibility that it could be tinkered with and perhaps improved.

Quantitative Analysis: Though core or routine work of employees may not be linked with numbers but they might love numbers. They must have chosen a different field because of better career prospects.

Theory Development and Conceptual Thinking: People having this type of interests enjoy talking and thinking about abstract ideas.

Creative Production: People with such interests are out of box thinkers. They like brainstorming or inventing unconventional solutions. They show little interest in things already established.

Counseling and Mentoring: Some people derive interest in guiding others. Reasons may be different. They may get satisfaction seeing others succeed or may get a feeling of being needed.

Managing People and Relationships: Such people enjoy dealing with people on a day to day basis. In contrast to people having counseling and mentoring interests who focus on the success of people, these focus on the success of business.

Enterprise Control: These may or may not like to manage people but people with such interests find satisfaction in making decisions that determine the direction taken by a work team, a business unit, a company division or an entire organization.

Influence through language and ideas: People with this interest love expressing ideas. They enjoy storytelling, negotiating or persuading.

Most common pairs of life interests found together are:

- Enterprise control with Managing People and Relationships
- Managing People and Relationships with Counseling and Mentoring
- Quantitative Analysis with Managing People and Relationships
- Enterprise Control with Influence Through Language and Ideas
- Application of Technology with Managing People and Relationships
- Creative Production with Enterprise Control

RESEARCH METHODOLOGY

Retaining employees is a very challenging job. In order to determine the factors which lead to employee retention and other factors which must be focused on to decrease employee attrition at JSPL, a primary research was conducted at JSPL, Gurgaon. Exploratory research as well as descriptive research was carried out. Exploratory research aimed at determining the factors responsible for employee retention. This was done through reading various journals, research papers, books, etc. Also informal discussions with the employees of the organization helped in determining the factors. The questionnaire was designed covering all the 12 areas which were found and the perception of employee's in each of those areas was captured. The 27 questions were related to roles and responsibilities, work atmosphere, support from supervisors and colleagues, performance management system, mentoring and buddy system benefits, satisfaction with other benefits like Own Your Car Scheme, Transfer Benefits, etc. The questionnaire was found to be reliable with a Cronbach's Alpha value of 0.767. The questionnaire was administered on employees of seven departments, namely Sales and Marketing, IT, Finance and Accounts, JPL-EPC, HR, Oil and Gas and Hydro. Out of approximately 300 employees working at Gurgaon location, the questionnaire was administered to 118 employees. Statistical tools were then applied on the data collected. In addition to this, exit interview forms of employees who left the organization in the past one year were also analyzed.

FINDINGS

Results of the research showed that the company enjoys a good brand value and is one of the major factors of attracting employees. 73% of the employees joined the company because of the brand image it enjoyed. Factor analysis was performed on the data. KMO was found to be 0.713 and thus indicated that factors were correlated and thus factor analysis could be applied. Also probability associated with the Bartlett's test of sphericity was less than the level of significance thus validating the applicability of factor analysis.

Factor analysis yielded four factors. The four factors found were Work Atmosphere, Growth Opportunities, Non-monetary incentives, and Flexibility and Clarity in work. Work Atmosphere constituted support from supervisors, support from colleagues, and team work. Growth Opportunities composed of opportunity to showcase talent, opportunity for personal development, opportunity for professional development, and job rotation. Non monetary incentives comprised of promotion and work appreciated. Flexibility and clarity in work constituted of roles and responsibilities and work environment hindrance. Satisfaction of employees with the benefits provided to them by the organization helps in reducing employee attrition. As per the results, employees were satisfied by the benefits provided to them. However, employees were not satisfied with the non-monetary incentives (recognition).

Analysis of exit interview forms showed that more than 65% employees were satisfied with the Compensation and Benefits, Task significance, Organization culture and Interpersonal relationships at the workplace. But the input of employees who left the organization suggested some improvements in areas of professional development, delegation/autonomy and implementation of Performance Management System. Certain areas where JSPL appeared to be needing focus were training and development, role clarity and process of self-review during annual reviews. The above three factors were found to be the most repeated ones while performing content analysis on the open ended question of exit interview forms. The results showed that the organization had a good Mentoring scheme and employees really get benefitted from the scheme. 60% of the employees shared that they had really benefitted from the mentoring scheme. However, the organization can consider a buddy scheme also and this can help employees a lot.

Other factors which the organization must consider are flexi-work timings, work from home, picnics and team/project parties, to name a few. Another factor, though not leading to attrition, but which can lead to increased performance, is a work week of five days instead of six.

RECOMMENDATIONS

Approach of "One reward/recognition does not fit all"

Each individual is different and so are the rewards they desire. For one a pat on the back for a work well done may be motivating, whereas for another some formal acknowledgement is required for motivation. The kind of rewards that the company may consider are acknowledgments in meetings, mentions in company's monthly magazine "Tabloid", increments, gift vouchers, team/project parties, and trophies. The research found out that employees preferred monetary rewards; but then employees come and go and preferences change. So this cannot be taken as a benchmark and the boss of every employee must try to figure out which kind of rewards his subordinates are interested in.

Create Work-Life Balance

An employee has to face indefinite number of demands of work and home which causes stress. The company must organize stress buster sessions and must encourage employees to attend them. Other ways of reducing stress are to help them manage logistics of their life. The company may introduce the concept of 'Genei', a personal assistant, private shopper, entertainment guide, travel planner, etc. located within the premises of the office to take requests of all employees. Also, the company must continue the policy of assigning mentors as the study done indicated that employees who were assigned mentors were benefitted from this. The company must also start assigning buddies who will help employees to settle at the work place easily and quickly. Another factor which came in the research was that though only 5 percent employees felt that a long work week causes them to look for another job, a large percentage felt that a five day week instead of six can help them increase their efficiency. So the company can introduce the concept of flexi timings, as either work for 6 days per week, with 8 hours per day or 5 days with 9.5 hours per day. In addition to that, work from home facility for the designations possible must be introduced. Also, the company must organize small events and parties on festivals and also picnics and project/team parties.

Employee Engagement

- Employees can be said to be engaged if they have the following:
- Emotional attachment to the organization, their job and their work;
- Rational Understanding of the organization's goals, values and how they contribute; and
- Motivation and willingness to invest discretionary effort to perform better.

On the emotional front, the company needs to focus on clarifying roles and responsibilities of work and ensuring fair practices. On the motivational front, the company must give due recognition for work. For the rational aspect, the company must make employees aware about the strategies, mission, vision and core values. This should not be done once only during induction but this must be a continuous process as reinforcement is necessary.

Growth Opportunities

One of the important factors responsible for retaining employees is their growth and development. The company must focus not only on the professional development but also on personal development. After the completion of four-six months in the organization, an interview must be conducted with the employee to determine his training needs and accordingly training must be provided.

Exit Interview

The company already conducts exit interviews in case of employee separation. Yearly or half yearly analyses of these forms must be done to find out the loopholes in the system. In addition to this, it is suggested that exit interview forms must not require any personal information like name, age, designation, department, etc. These forms must not be handed over in person, instead it is suggested that a drop down box be placed where the employee, after filling the form, can drop the form there. This is suggested to ensure honest feedback from employees. Moreover, another method which can be practiced in order to ensure fair responses from employees leaving the organization is that, employees must not be asked to fill the exit interview form just before they are leaving the organization. This is because separation of an employee from the organization might be triggered because of different reasons. An employee may be extremely happy or extremely sad while leaving the organization and this may result in biased responses as 'Halo Effect' might also play a role.

Induction

During the induction program, the roles to be performed by each employee must be detailed out. Moreover, whenever job rotation, promotion or transfer takes place, roles must again be clarified. Also, even if the designation remains same, whenever new work is assigned then tasks to be performed must be clarified so that there is no confusion regarding who is responsible for what and also there are no accountability problems.

CONCLUSION

The study revealed that the areas in which the company could consider further improvement are: professional development, employee engagement like more reward and recognition, autonomy, performance reviews, and role clarity. Broadly, the factors of retention as a result of factor analysis were as follows: Work Atmosphere, Growth Opportunities, Non-monetary incentives, and Flexibility and Clarity in work. Approach of mass customizing the rewards; creating work life balance through the concept of "genei", stress busting sessions; employee engagement through clarification of roles and responsibilities, providing due recognition for work; determining growth needs of every employee and thus catering to the needs by providing training; and a changed approach in getting the exit interview forms, were suggested as the measures for increasing employee retention.

ACKNOWLEDGEMENT

The authors wish to express their sincere thanks to Mr. Shishir Sinha, Sr. General Manager- HR, Jindal Steel and Power Ltd. for the total support provided by the organization to develop this case, to make presentation of the case at ICMC2012 and publish the case in the conference proceedings.

REFERENCES

Abrams, Michael N. (2004). Employee retention strategies: Lessons from the best. *Health Care Executive*, 19(4), 18-22.

Adhikari, Atanu. (2009). Factors affecting employee attrition: A multiple regression approach. *IUP Journal of Management Research, 8(5)*, 38-43.

Butler, Timothy & Waldroop, James. (1999). Job sculpting: The art of retaining your best people. *Harvard Business Review*, September-October, 144-152.

McConnell, Charles R. (2011). Addressing employee turnover and retention: Keeping your valued performers. *The Health Care Manager, 30(3)*, 271-283.

Ramlall, Sunil. (2004). A review of employee motivation theories and their implications for employee retention within organizations. *Journal of American Academy Business, Cambridge, 5(½)*, 52-63.

Wille, Glenn. (1994). Employee retention: A positive force. *Credit Union Management, 17(12)*, 34-36.

www.search.proquest.com

Branding the Training at Finfare Limited

Parameswar Nayak* and Sanjana Tyagi**

ABSTRACT

The case is about a leading financial services company's learning and development programs with a focus on branding the training to address the problem of absenteeism and achieving 100 per cent attendance in classroom training. It is based on a perception study of 100 sample employees about the importance & relevance of training programs and employees' satisfactions on the supervisor's awareness and support, training content, facilitators, delivery mechanisms and logistic arrangement. It presents the picture of both strengths of a framework of learning continuum and weaknesses of classroom training along with a problem situation of low turn- out of trainees before the management students who can analyze and find more appropriate and innovative solutions. A branding approach suggesting a paradigm shift from a Push strategy to a Pull strategy is presented for critical analysis and for evolving more rational and sustainable model for the company.

Keywords: Branding, learning continuum, absenteeism, training relevance, employee's satisfaction, push & pull strategy, Finfare Limited.

INTRODUCTION

Finfare Ltd. is a leading financial services company, operating for last 18 years in India. Four years back, its human resource functions were reinvigorated with on boarding of the Head- Human Resources and subsequent talent acquisition of HR professionals at varied levels. The company aims at ensuring strategic alignment of learning and development efforts with the organization's goals. The company believes and invests continuously in building the capability of their workforce to enable them to effectively perform their current roles and to prepare some of them for leadership roles. The training function is given high priority in the company in building culture, workforce capability and performance orientation. The company's Learning Academy is the holistic learning and development brand which focuses on four key areas:

---

* Professor, Birla Institute of Management Technology, Greater Noida, India
** PGDM Scholar. Birla Institute of Management Technology, Greater Noida, India
E-mail: parameswar.nayak@bimtech.ac.in

(a) Behavioral Skills Development; (b) Product/Functional Training; (c) Talent & Leadership Development and (d) Organization Development. The Academy designs and conducts both the classroom training and e-learning development programs for the employees who relate the brand with skill, knowledge and behavioral development initiatives of the company. The classroom training platform is leveraged for behavioral capability building and disseminating the values in the organization. Around 130 classroom training programs were conducted during the last financial year. However, about 17 per cent of the employees who were identified and invited for the training did not attend the programs. The company is concerned about understanding the reasons for the low turn –out and finding the measures to bring the absenteeism rate to zero per cent. But question is what did go wrong and how to improve the branding of the classroom training to attract 100 per cent participants? How do the employees perceive the training programs and how much importance they give to the training? In order to find answer to these questions, a study was conducted by a professor and his student from a reputed B-School in India

RESEARCH DESIGN

The study is based on mostly primary data, collected from a sample of 100 employees through survey and observation methods. A structured questionnaire is used for gathering perceptual information on the importance and relevance of training, the level of employee's satisfaction and views on branding of training from a sample of 80 out of total 1076(881 executives and 195 managers & senior managers) training participants(7.4 per cent) who received training during December 2011 and April 2012. Of 80 sample participant-respondents 56 (6.3 per cent of 881) are executives and 24(12.3 per cent of 195) are managers and senior managers. A semi-structured in-depth interview method is used with a sample of 20 absentees in order to understand the reasons of high absenteeism. Sample size for both categories is decided as per the number of programs organized for them. The study team also referred to the relevant official documents in order to learn about the background, learning & development philosophy of the company, its various training programs and participant's details. Some of the branding initiates taken by the company are understood through discussions with the key HR officials. The communication mechanisms, key messages and participants' views for creating a brand for classroom training, displayed through visual-aids such as standees, hangings and information bulletins etc. are studied and analyzed.

LEARNING PLATFORMS

The classroom training is the first learning platform. The e-learning is the second platform, used for building knowledge and awareness of financial services products as well as functional skills. The third platform for Leadership Development and Talent Management involves making differentiated investment of resources in identifying and developing the talents of future leadership at senior and top management levels through an 18 months phased intervention. The intervention comprises of classroom discussions, peer learning forums, 360 degree feedback, feedback on leadership style and organizational climate created and action learning projects[2].These platforms are supported by an online library and an online web-portal.

CLASSROOM TRAINING PROGRAMS

The classroom training programs are designed internally using the instructional design and experiential learning techniques with a mix of group activities, role plays, videos etc. A learning continuum is maintained to ensure that employees not only recapitulate on the trainings imparted earlier but also develop on higher order skills and competencies in the subsequent training program. Classroom training programs are facilitated by a mix of internal and external trainers. The deployment of internal trainers helps in contextualizing the programs, relating to participants better, cost reduction and employee development. There are two training programs for executives and deputy managers. The objective of the first program is to enable them to demonstrate greater energy, enthusiasm and sense of ownership at work, enhance customer relationship and selling skills for achieving operational excellence, while the second program aims at building the competencies of the front line executives who are in individual contributory roles. Similarly, there is a separate training program for managers & senior managers with objectives to help them understand their strengths, learn the concepts and techniques of conflict resolution identify areas of improvement and implement the combination of tasking and tending in becoming more effective managers. Another program was launched about four years back for the selected employees who had attended the above program for improving managerial effectiveness, with main purpose to help them at the second level intervention to:

- identify the factors that affect building of a good professional image;
- be able to use the concept of visibility & credibility & networking to enhance professional image;
- be able to take back a usable model for networking;
- realize that effective day to day transactions are very important to enhance productivity;
- identify various ego states & their impact on day to day transactions;
- enhance their interpersonal effectiveness through the understanding of transactional analysis concepts;
- learn the concepts of parameters of good teamwork; and
- be able to effectively plan, manage resources & evaluate performance of teams.[3]

EMPLOYEES' PERCEPTIONS ON THE TRAINING PROGRAMS

The overall employees' perceptions about the training programs, as per the study conducted by the authors for the purpose of writing this case, are presented at Graphs 1.1 to 1.2. About 55 per cent of the employees give high importance to the Supervisor's support to attend training program (Graph 1.1). The relevance of training for improving the job performance of the employees and the quality of trainer are other important attracting factors for the employee's participation in the training programs. 90 per cent of employees feel that the training should help them in personal and professional development. *"Training is only worth investing time, if it is relevant to our present job and helps us grow as a person and a professional";* says one of the employees who attended a recently conducted in-house training program. An employee expects the facilitator/ trainer to be knowledgeable, a person who connects and has good communication skills.

Creating and maintaining a learning culture with very high level of awareness of the training programs amongst employees is very crucial in branding of the training programs and attracting more employees to attend the same. But the study reveals that about 45 per cent of the employees are not aware of the training programs being offered by the company. Even a few employees are found not knowing the name of the program meant for them. A few employees say that they have no zeal and enthusiasm for attending the training program as they have no knowledge about the benefits of the training programs. Among the absentees, most of the respondents are found reluctant to share the actual reasons due to some inexplicable constraints. In many occasions they hesitate to take call further. Most employees cite personal reasons like family engagements, health issues while others give official engagements for not being able to attend the training programs. Another important aspect is the grouping of the employees for a training program. In this regard a corporate trainer, working for the company says:

> "Having employees from the similar background and level in a training program is important. As the organization being a place of people with diverse backgrounds, positions and needs, connecting with people of similar background and needs is easier. Different level of understanding stops the employees to open up. As they feel shy and uncomfortable".

Though the employees at different grades differ in their perceptions towards training, the most important aspect of training for both the executives and senior managers is *knowledgeable trainer*. The least important aspect for executives is relevance of training content while for senior managers it was availability of pre training reading material (Graph 1.2).

Importance of Training for Employees

The employees percieve five parameters as most important in training:

(a) Knowledgeable & experienced Trainer

(b) Supervisor's support to attend the training

(c) Personal & Professional Evolvement

(d) Relevance and Benefits of the Training for Job Performance and

(e) Supervisor's Support for Application of Learned Skills.

The highest score (4.46 on a 5 point scale) of importance is given to knowledgeable & experienced trainer(Exhibit 1; Graph 1.3).92 per cent of the employees expects the facilitator/trainer to be knowledgeable, a person who connects and has good communication skills. Supervisor's role in the training program is perceived to be most important by 55 per cent of the respondents. Their participation, to a large extent, depends on their supervisor/head (Exhibit-1; Graphs 1.3 - 1.5). Awareness of the benefits of the training is also found to be one of the determining factors for participation of executives in a training program. Training is successful only if the employees apply the learned skills at work or for his/her personal development. 84 per cent of the respondents perceive the support from the senior is most important motivating factor for them to apply the learned skills at work more effectively. Training has no meaning if it does not add any value to the performance of the employees. 87 per cent of respondents feel training brings more job satisfaction. However, most of the parameters rated by managers, at different levels and with different scores, are same as rated overall by the employees (Graph 1.5).

EMPLOYEE SATISFACTION FROM TRAINING

The employees' satisfaction from training was assessed by using 16 rating parameters, grouped under the broad three factors- *Training Relevance, Training Awareness and Supervisor's Role.* The overall employees' satisfaction level is highest on the relevance of training, followed by supervisor's role and training awareness in the organization (Graph 1.6). More specifically, highest satisfaction level of 84 per cent of the respondents/employees is with the parameter- *knowledgeable facilitator* and least satisfaction is with the parameter-*branding of training programs in the company* (Graph 1.7). The level of satisfaction of Executives and Senior Managers assessed on 16 rating parameters are found to be different (Graph 1.8). Over all employees' satisfaction level on 5 top parameters(Graph 1.9) indicates highest score with knowledgaeable & experienced trainer (4.13). "The trainer was knowledgeable who could connect well with the audience... The flow maintained throughout the training was good. It was a good experience attending this training", says an executive after attending the training. However, executives and deputy managers are highly satisfied with supervisor's support to attend the training (Graph 1.10), whereas the satisfaction level of the managers and senior managers is highest on two parameters- supervisor's training awareness and their support to subordinates for attending training programs(Graph 1.11). The level of satisfaction of employees from the training programs is highest with the training relevance to the current jobs, followed by supervisor's role in strengthening learning culture. They are least satisfied with the training awareness in the organization. Both the senior managers as well as executives give due importance to the tangible as well as intangible benefits of training. Most of the employees feel that the need of internal trainers is less important than external trainers. Employees give due importance to other factors like training content, infrastructure and facilitator's knowledge. Executives are least satisfied with the branding of the training programs followed by self awareness of all the programs. Areas of overall dissatisfaction of both Executives and Sr. Managers are same but with different levels of intensity (Graphs 1.12 & 1.13). Thus, branding of the training programs is a matter of great concern for the company. They want to have a massive drive to improve the branding of its training, especially the in-house classroom training.

BRANDING OF TRAINING

The above issue brings forth the importance of branding of classroom training amongst employees. Creating awareness about the programs is very important to make the employees understand the importance of training, for their growth and satisfaction at work place. 76 per cent of the respondents feel the need for re-strategizing the branding of training programs in the company. "Till now the company has been using push strategy to overcome the absenteeism in the training programs. But more than pushing, motivating the employees to attend the training program is beneficial in the long run", says a senior member of the HR Team.

About 50 per cent of the respondents are satisfied with the initiatives of the company for branding the training. Respondents were asked to rate the best branding strategies to create awareness about training on a scale of 1-5(5=Outstanding and 1= Poor). Enhancing training content scored highest rating (Graph 1.14). Most of them are in favor of enhancing relevant training content, sharing of training videos and feedback with the participants.

"Regularly revising the training content as per the job requirements makes training programs more useful and attractive for the employees", says a manager who has attended a few of the training programs. One of the respondents says, "We stay motivated after training only for a few days...". " Our senior expects us to do work even if we are deputed for training. Since, work is our priority and we have responsibility towards them, we remain absent....training doesn't help unless it leads to a good performance appraisal"; says another respondent. The frontline executives suggest minimizing the lecture time and increase activities and interactive sessions by a good facilitator. They prefer external trainers with whom they can share their views and clear their doubts without any fear. They also suggest that the training should be conducted on weekdays and outside the company premises as far as possible.

Some trainers of the training programs are of the views that participants of a training program should be of the same level and there should be more involvement of higher authorities to bring seriousness of the training among the employees.

Re-strategizing the Branding of Training

The branding is one of the techniques of *pull strategy*. It assumes the training as a product and an employee as its customer. Thus branding of training is quite similar to the branding of a product. It is a tool for creating awareness among the employees and increase visibility of the training programs. It aims at establishing a significant presence in the minds of the employees by providing information about the training programs and their benefits. It creates a motivating environment for training and attracts the employees towards it.

With an objective to improve the branding for classroom training, a tentative *Strategic Model of Branding of Classroom Training* is suggested by the authors of this case, based on their study and understanding of the needs and concerns of the company, for implementation on experimental basis in the company. The company has started implementing this model very recently which involves following four key strategies:

Building Awareness and Reach

- In order to build awareness and reach to employees across the organization, the training team would visit the branches along with the training calendar. This would bring a sense of seriousness amongst employees and business heads towards training.
- Training Catalogue is designed for the branch visits. The catalogue consists of the training overview, an insight into the classroom training, the learning continuum, list of training programs and brief profile of the trainers (both external as well as internal).
- A web-portal of training for the employees to access, where in they will have access to all the information regarding the training.
- Branding Aids, such as the following, are developed to increase awareness and reach amongst employees.

  (a) *Visuals:* The visual aids such as *Standees* to be displayed at the entrance of Café and outside Lifts, in the Lobby area and *Hangings* in all the departments at all floors. This may be a cost-effective tool for increasing visibility of the programs, maximizing employees reach and creating awareness of the programs in terms of methods and benefits.

(*b*) *Feedback Display Board:* With a belief that word of mouth works most effectively, trainees' feedback is captured on huge designed display board. It is displayed in the Cafe for a week so that other employees can read the feedback of their fellow employees about the training programs.

(*c*) *Advertisement on company's intranet portal:* An employee during his working hours is most of the time on his work station and exposed to computer for maximum time. And to mark attendance he is ought to login at the company's intranet portal. Thus, putting an advertisement of the upcoming training program would be initiated.

(*d*) *Catalogues /Pamphlets/Brochures:* Currently, only training invitations and reminder mails are being sent to the prospect trainees. In order to make the target trainees more aware of the training program, pamphlets would be distributed to the target employees a week before the training. The pamphlet content would include a brief about the training program, agenda, the profile of the trainer(s) and benefits for the employees. Such aids benefit by giving a sneak peek into the training program, to position training in the mind of employees to be a formal and a serious affair. It creates interest and enthusiasm towards training and a better way to connect to employees.

Making Learning Inspirational

As a step forward to make learning inspirational for the employees following measures are taken as branding techniques:

(a) *Revamping Training Material* to suit the needs of employees.

(b) *Rebranding EDMs, mailers:* In order to catch employee's attention towards training programs, attractive mailers (Electronic Direct Mailers) are designed and sent to the target audience. A formal invitation from the supervisor is sent in advance to the trainee and a reminder mail is sent a week before the training program. In these mailers, a brief about the agenda of the training along with the hint of activities to be conducted are listed. EDMs of all behavioral programs are designed and floated in the organization. This technique benefits in terms of attracting the employees towards the program, creating awareness of the programs and reminding them to attend the training.

Creating Pull and Interest through Reward & Recognition:

Currently, the employees are pushed to attend the training and absentees are penalized for not attending the programs. This is a step to initiate a shift from the culture of *push* to *pull* strategy. Thus, as a measure to pull the employees, focus is put on the gap between the invite and the program date to lure participants through various initiatives like quizzes, games, prizes etc. Small quizzes would be developed to engage employees in the content of the training program. These quizzes, if sent a week before the program, will serve the purpose of pre-testing of training programs. In order to rope in employees in these quizzes attractive prizes or gifts would be distributed on the basis of results.

Feedback

It is a process in which views of the trainees about the past or the present training programs are passed on to their peers and significant others who play an important role in influencing their behavior. It uses the powerful technique of communicating the messages through word of mouth. Feedbacks would be sent in following two forms and at a time interval of 3 months.

(a) Post-Training Follow up Feedback: Feedbacks of employees are captured through regular feedback forms after the training. Out of the lot, four best feedbacks are mapped and are floated throughout the organization. Specific feedback mailers are designed as per the brand guidelines of the company to publish the feedbacks.

(b) Success Stories: Trainees would be asked to share their success stories after attending the training program. Any skill they learnt from training program and incorporated successfully in their work is to be shared with others in the organization. This initiative will spread the message of the effectiveness and benefits of training for employees.

However, success of the above Branding Model is yet to be seen as its implementation started very recently.

QUESTIONS FOR DISCUSSION

1. Find out the main areas of improvement in Training at Finfare Ltd. What are the key drivers of Branding the Training programs? Can you suggest any new driver(s) for improving the branding of their training programs?

2. Critically analyze the New Model of Branding the Training at Finfare Ltd and find out its strengths and weaknesses? What should be the role of the Training

Department in implementation of the New Model to achieve 100 per cent attendance in the classroom training?

3. Based on the current problem situation (as in the case), can you suggest a Model better than the one given in the case, for improving the branding of their training programs?

ACKNOWLEDGEMENT

The authors wish to thank the management of Finfare Ltd.(name under disguise as requested by the organization) for the support provided to develop the case, permission to present the same at ICMC2012 publication in the conference proceedings.

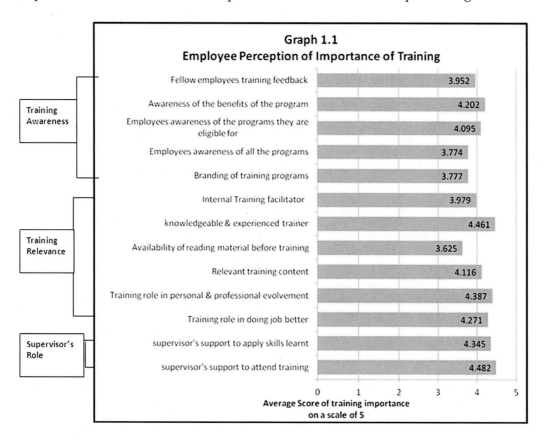

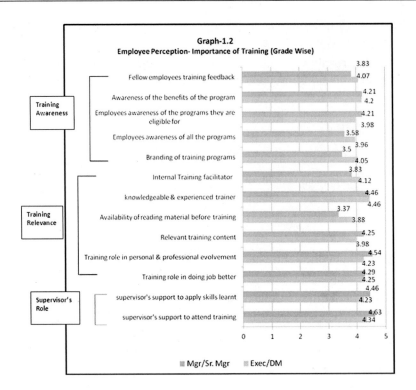

Graph-1.2
Employee Perception- Importance of Training (Grade Wise)

Training Awareness
- Fellow employees training feedback: 3.83 / 4.07
- Awareness of the benefits of the program: 4.21 / 4.2
- Employees awareness of the programs they are eligible for: 4.21 / 3.98
- Employees awareness of all the programs: 3.58 / 3.96
- Branding of training programs: 3.5 / 4.05

Training Relevance
- Internal Training facilitator: 3.83 / 4.12
- knowledgeable & experienced trainer: 4.46 / 4.46
- Availability of reading material before training: 3.37 / 3.88
- Relevant training content: 4.25 / 3.98
- Training role in personal & professional evolvement: 4.54 / 4.23
- Training role in doing job better: 4.29 / 4.25

Supervisor's Role
- supervisor's support to apply skills learnt: 4.46 / 4.23
- supervisor's support to attend training: 4.63 / 4.34

■ Mgr/Sr. Mgr   ■ Exec/DM

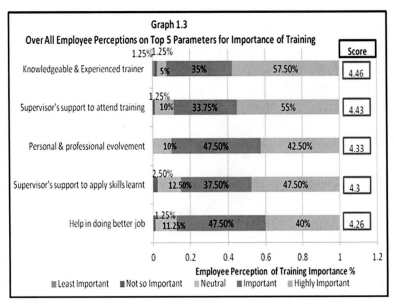

Graph 1.3
Over All Employee Perceptions on Top 5 Parameters for Importance of Training

Parameter	Least Important	Not so Important	Neutral	Important	Highly Important	Score
Knowledgeable & Experienced trainer	1.25%	1.25%	5%	35%	57.50%	4.46
Supervisor's support to attend training		1.25%	10%	33.75%	55%	4.43
Personal & professional evolvement			10%	47.50%	42.50%	4.33
Supervisor's support to apply skills learnt		2.50%	12.50%	37.50%	47.50%	4.3
Help in doing better job		1.25%	11.25%	47.50%	40%	4.26

Employee Perception of Training Importance %

■ Least Important   ■ Not so Important   ■ Neutral   ■ Important   ■ Highly Important

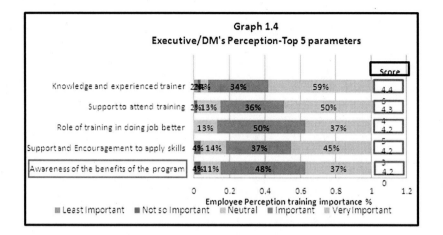

Graph 1.4
Executive/DM's Perception-Top 5 parameters

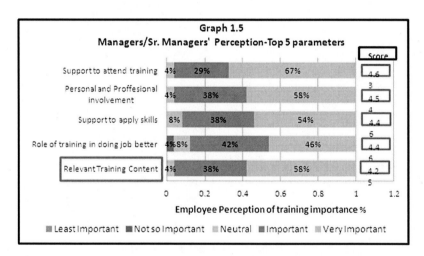

Graph 1.5
Managers/Sr. Managers' Perception-Top 5 parameters

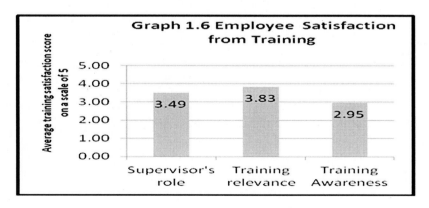

Graph 1.6 Employee Satisfaction from Training

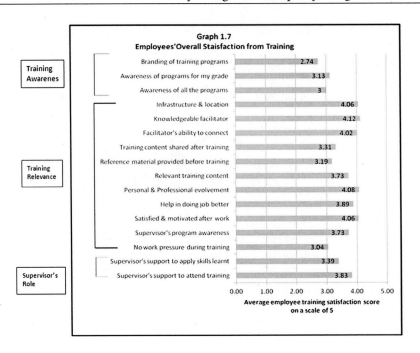

Graph 1.7
Employees' Overall Staisfaction from Training

Training Awarenes
- Branding of training programs — 2.74
- Awareness of programs for my grade — 3.13
- Awareness of all the programs — 3

Training Relevance
- Infrastructure & location — 4.06
- Knowledgeable facilitator — 4.12
- Facilitator's ability to connect — 4.02
- Training content shared after training — 3.31
- Reference material provided before training — 3.19
- Relevant training content — 3.73
- Personal & Professional evolvement — 4.08
- Help in doing job better — 3.89
- Satisfied & motivated after work — 4.06
- Supervisor's program awareness — 3.73
- No work pressure during training — 3.04

Supervisor's Role
- Supervisor's support to apply skills learnt — 3.39
- Supervisor's support to attend training — 3.83

Average employee training satisfaction score on a scale of 5

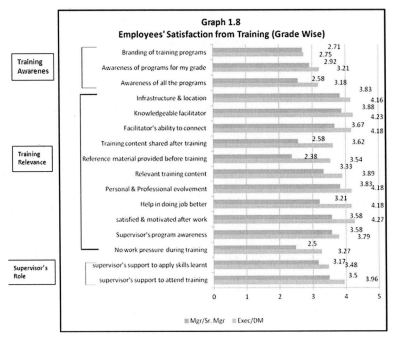

Graph 1.8
Employees' Satisfaction from Training (Grade Wise)

Training Awarenes
- Branding of training programs — 2.71 / 2.75
- Awareness of programs for my grade — 2.92 / 3.21
- Awareness of all the programs — 2.58 / 3.18

Training Relevance
- Infrastructure & location — 3.83 / 4.16
- Knowledgeable facilitator — 3.88 / 4.23
- Facilitator's ability to connect — 3.67 / 4.18
- Training content shared after training — 2.58 / 3.62
- Reference material provided before training — 2.38 / 3.54
- Relevant training content — 3.33 / 3.89
- Personal & Professional evolvement — 3.83 / 4.18
- Help in doing job better — 3.21 / 4.18
- satisfied & motivated after work — 3.58 / 4.27
- Supervisor's program awareness — 3.58 / 3.79
- No work pressure during training — 2.5 / 3.27

Supervisor's Role
- supervisor's support to apply skills learnt — 3.17 / 3.48
- supervisor's support to attend training — 3.5 / 3.96

■ Mgr/Sr. Mgr   ■ Exec/DM

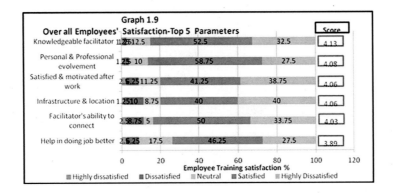

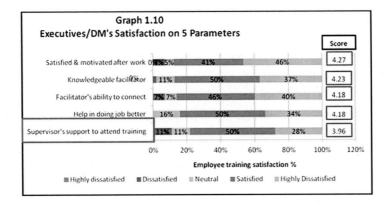

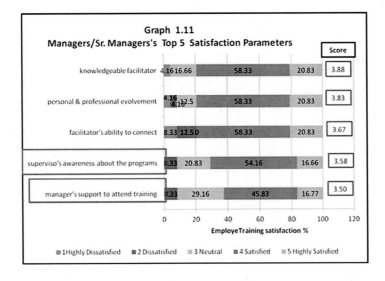

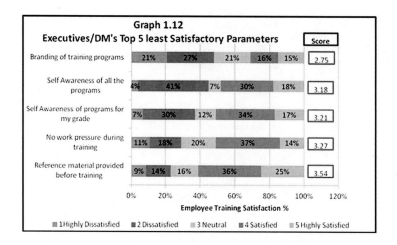

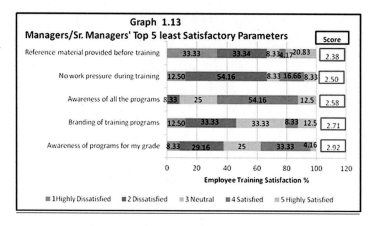

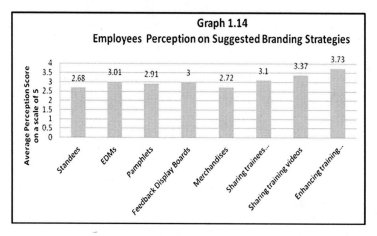

Impact of Compensation on Motivation, Job Satisfaction and Turnover Intentions in the Retail Industry: A Study of NCR

Pooja Misra*, Shreya Jain** and Abhay Sood**

ABSTRACT

In today's dynamic work environment, retention and motivation of personnel has become a major concern for HR especially in the Indian Retail Industry. Compensation, used as rewards for excellent job performance affect an employee's morale and job satisfaction. An effective and just compensation policy can help an organization achieve and sustain a competitive advantage. Employees, on receiving rewards and recognition from their organization, feel obliged to respond with higher levels of engagement. The case study seeks to analyze the impact of compensation components in terms of Rewards (financial and non financial rewards) and Organizational Justice (Distributive and Procedural Justice) on motivation, job satisfaction and turnover intentions in the Indian Retail industry with special reference to Retail Store Operations. It is an exploratory research case and has the objective to understand if compensation in terms of financial and non financial rewards and organisational justice have an impact on motivation, job satisfaction levels and turnover intentions in the Indian Retail industry.

Keywords: Compensation, rewards, organisational justice, turnover intentions, indian retail industry

INTRODUCTION

The Indian Retail Industry is the fifth largest shopping destination in the world and is experiencing an annual growth rate of 30%. This industry, today, accounts for over

---

*   Asst. Professor, Birla Institute of Management Technology, Greater Noida, India.
**   PG Student, Birla Institute of Management Technology, Greater Noida, India.
E-mail: pooja.misra@bimtech.ac.in, shreya.jain13@bimtech.ac.in, abhay.sood13@bimtech.ac.in

10 per cent of the country's GDP. It has come forth as one of the most dynamic and fast paced industries and is gradually inching its way towards becoming the next booming industry. It is one of the most highly manpowered industries in today's times. According to Team Lease, India's leading staffing company, the Indian Retail industry has nearly 70 percent attrition rates (Deccan Herald Report 2008) with attrition levels being the highest for the entry level and front end jobs which in turn is a cause of concern for the management. Compensation & benefits have been ascribed to be one of the factors responsible for high attrition rate. Under the present circumstance, retention and motivation of personnel has become a major concern for Human Resources. As per Singh and Mishra (2006), few studies have been done on analyzing HR challenges in the India retail sector (Chella 2002, Chakraborthy 2007, Abraham & Kumudha 2007); however, there are gaping holes in the existing research. Compensation used as rewards for excellent job performance affects an employee's morale and job satisfaction. In view of the Social Exchange Theory, employees on receiving rewards and recognition from their organization feel obliged to respond with higher levels of engagement. Employees' with perception of higher levels of procedural and distributive justice are more likely to feel obliged and perform their roles by putting in discretionary effort. Many retail companies are trying to deal with the challenge of attrition by introducing innovative human resource initiatives, becoming employee sensitive and using strategic tools to retain employees like incentive based targets, non-financial incentives and raising salaries. Some of the challenges of this industry are increased work stress, ample work load, staff shortage, high turnover rates and long working hours.

The term compensation includes base salary, merit pay, incentives and benefits offered by the employers of the company. Compensation plays an important role in maintaining and retaining an effective workforce (Bergmann and Scarpello 2001). Benefits such as medical insurance, recreational, retirement, etc, represent indirect compensation (Phillips L and Fox MA 2003). Employees expect a certain kind of compensation for their contribution to the organisation and that goes beyond the pay provisions (Rosen C and Shaw S 2004). In order to provide a deeper insight into how does total compensation affect managerial attitudes and behavioural intentions, different forms of total compensation have been assessed: cash compensation, incentive bonuses, medical plan premium, medical plan cost sharing, pensions, post –retirement medical, and employment security provisions (Lawler 1990; Verbeke and Rhoads 1996).

Organisational Justice

It is fundamental to compensation systems. Compensation is formulated based on internal consistency and pay level relative to the market. Organisational justice is the extent to which the employees perceive the interactions amongst peers, the work culture and outcomes to be fair in nature. These kinds of perceptions can affect the attitudes or behaviour of the employees and thereby have a positive or negative influence on the employee performance and success of the organisation. Research has shown that employees examine three components of justice; the justice of consequences (distributive justice), the justice of the process by which the allocation is done (procedural justice) and the justice of interpersonal interactions they have with others (interactional justice). Distributive justice is concerned with the belief that not all workers are treated equally. As per Adam's equity theory (Adams 1965) employees are more interested in the outcomes, relative to the contribution they make, that is, the inputs. Procedural justice refers to what employees perceive as the fairness of the process used to evaluate the outcomes or rewards the employees receive. A process is considered just when it is consistently applied to all. It is free from any kind of biasness and is accurate and in line with the ethical norms (Lambert 2003).

Motivation

Motivation is a psychological attribute that drives a human towards a desired goal, eliciting pleasure. Money in the form of salary is related to control and in form of commission is related to motivation. Luthans (1998) states that, "motivation is the process that arouses, energizes, directs, and sustains behaviour and performance. Job satisfaction is that pleasant state of mind where an employee is appraised for his/her work thereby leading to contentment and happiness. The happier are employees with their work, the more content or satisfied they are (Wright and Cropanzano 1998).

RESEARCH OBJECTIVES AND FOCUS ISSUES

The literature review shows the importance of compensation as one of the factors that affect turnover intentions. Compensation in terms of financial, non financial rewards and benefits and organisational justice could be a factor affecting motivation and job satisfaction levels in this industry. These factors could also be a determining factor of high turnover intentions in the Retail Industry. The scope of the study would be the Retail industry in India with specific reference to Retail Store operations in Delhi and NCR(National Capital Region).

- To analyse the impact of compensation components of Rewards and Benefits and Organisational Justice - Distributive and Procedural Justice on turnover intentions in Retail Store operations.
- To investigate the influence of compensation components of Rewards and Benefits on Motivation and Job Satisfaction in Retail Store operations
- To investigate the influence of Organisational Justice - Distributive and Procedural Justice on Motivation and Job Satisfaction in Retail Store operations

- To investigate the relationship between job satisfaction and motivation in Retail Store operations

LITERATURE REVIEW

Rewards and benefits are known to affect motivation levels, which affects performance and the effort that the employee puts in. As per research studies, the effect of incentive pay and total monetary compensation on motivation is to be studied (Fama 1980). A lot of attempts have been made to merge psychological theories (Locke and Henne 1986) of motivation such as Maslow, Herzberg etc. with theories that are economically inclined (Frey 1997); (Osterloh and Frey 2000); (Frey and Jegen 2001). A specific and detailed attempt leads to the bifurcation of the concept of motivation into extrinsic and intrinsic motivation (Calder and Staw 1975). Extrinsic motivation is motivation that is acquired by externally influenced need and is thus related to monetary rewards (Frey 1997). According to Thierry (1987), the effectiveness of the compensation system, especially rewards, benefits and performance evaluation can be measured based on three factors, transparency, fairness and controllability (Langedijk and Ykema Weinen 2000). Three most important benefits; promotion at work, higher pay or compensation and challenging and engaging role at work contribute to work motivation and job satisfaction levels. Young workers are more drawn towards the incentive aspect as promotion is not the only aspect in their mind (Ishida 1985). Victor H. Vroom (1964) defines motivation "as a process governing choices among alternative forms of voluntary activities, a process controlled by the individual. Motivation is a product of the individual's expectancy that a certain effort will lead to the intended performance, the instrumentality of this performance to achieving a certain result, and the desirability of this result for the individual, known as valence."

In the past a lot of theories have been used as motivation for employee job satisfaction. One of the theories being the Maslow's need theory that talks about human needs ranging from physiological to self-actualisation. On the basis of this theory many researchers like Kuhlen (1963) and Conrad et al (1985) got to know the level of employee satisfaction. Whereas on the other side were researchers like Herzberg and Mausner (1959), who wanted to base their research on traditional views like achievement, recognition, base pay, relations with the colleagues, healthy or unhealthy working conditions, responsibility, etc. Job training and motivation is also an important parameter to know the employee attitudes (Shields and Wheatley, 2002; Schmidt 2007a,b). Remuneration plays a very important and critical role in an organization (Heneman et al 2002). In compensation studies, process of social comparison with relevant others are a major determinant of job satisfaction and motivation. In the context of pay satisfaction, Adams' equity theory of motivation argues that one compares one's job input/pay ratio with certain referents. Heneman and Schwab (1985) conceptualized pay satisfaction as a multidimensional construct and defined a four facet structure of pay satisfaction - pay level, benefits, raises, structure and administration. Pay satisfaction is an important determinant of turnover and an employee's intent to leave the organization ((Hom and Griffeth, 1995).

Job satisfaction is a predictor of absenteeism, suggesting that increment in job satisfaction and organisational commitment, are good indicators to reduce turnover intentions and absenteeism. There is a correlation between motivation among the employees and pay that they receive, which directly leads to either satisfaction or dissatisfaction in their job. Transparent pay communication would help in increasing the performance of the organization, maintain trust among the employees, lead to organizational commitment and improve pay satisfaction (Cappelli and Sherer, 1988; Dyer and Theriault, 1976; Heneman and Judge, 2000; Judge, 1993; Lawler, 1981; Mulvey 2002).

For employees to be satisfied with their pay, they must be justly distributed and determined amongst everybody (Berkowitz 1987; Folger and Konovsky, 1989; Greenberg, 1993, 2006; Jones 1999; McFarlin and Sweeney, 1992; Scarpello and Jones, 1996; Sweeney and McFarlin, 1993). According to the condition of communication over-load or under-load could lead to discontentment and lower levels of job satisfaction and thereby attrition (Hom and Griffeth 1995). Another factor that has major influence on job satisfaction is the superior- subordinate communication. The research conducted by Lambert (2003) emphasized the impact of procedural justice on employee job satisfaction and found that that the impact was positive. Furthermore authors and researchers say that in case of absence of procedural justice, job dissatisfaction prevails and this forces the employee to attrite. Dailey and Kirk (1992) also emphasized the need for procedural justice in order to retain the employees and keep them happy. Folger and Konovsky (1989) analysed the impact of justice on employee job satisfaction in private organisations of USA. McFarlin and Sweeney (1992) studied the same in context of public sector organisations and banking sectors, respectively. Equity Theory posits that if the person perceives that there is inequality, where either their output/input ratio is less than or greater than what they perceive as the output/input ratio of the other person in the relationship, then the person is likely to be distressed. Social exchange theory was formulated by scholars like Emerson (1976, see also Ekeh 1974) in the 1970s. If there is reciprocity, a trusting and loyal relationship is evolved (Cropanzano and Mitchell 2005).

Compensation is an important aspect in the relationship between employees and employers (Gerhart and Milkovich 1992). It is a vital part of the contract between the employee and employer especially in the psychological context (Lucero and Allen 1994). Proper compensation practices used by the employers encourage the employees to work harder and put in lot of zeal and effort (Aggarwal and Bhargava 2009). Most of the researchers found a negative relation between organisational commitment and turnover intention (Addae et al 2006; Zhao et al 2007; Pare and Tremblay 2007).

According to researchers such as Ajzen and Fishbein (1980) and Igbaria and Greenhaus (1992), intentions to quit are very important to determine the actual behaviour of the employee. The reasons to leave a job can also be assessed from Sager's (1991) study of salespeople. A pay structure that is looked upon as not equal among the employees, leads to reduction in job satisfaction (Petrescu A and Simmons R, 2008). Study of pay structure and turnover intention creates a disparity between both the factors (Montowildo 1983). Vandenberghe and Tremblay (2008) and Tekleab, Bartol and Liu (2005) have explained two forms of organisational justice as important attributes of pay satisfaction that are negatively inclined towards turnover intention.

From the review of literature, it is thus seen compensation components in terms of rewards, benefits and organisational justice could impact motivation and job satisfaction levels which in turn impact turnover intentions. In addition, it is seen that factors such as supervisor's intervention, work environment, leave policies etc. could impact job satisfaction levels.

RESEARCH METHODOLOGY

The research is exploratory in nature and the approach towards the design includes getting questionnaires filled and possible secondary sources. The primary data was collected through a well structured questionnaire to ascertain the impact of compensation in terms of rewards, benefits and organisational justice- distributive and procedural justice, on motivation, job satisfaction and turnover intentions. The data was collected from a sample of 127 people, who were working as store managers and customer service representatives in retail outlets spread in Delhi and NCR regions. The employees were approached personally for their responses. The secondary data was collected through a lot of sources: reports, articles, cases, journals and internet data.

ANALYSIS AND INTERPRETATION

Reward

The Chronbach alpha is a coefficient of reliability. The reliability of questions for analyzing the Reward satisfaction level was 0.753 which is good. With regards to rewards, questions such as 'is the merit pay increment satisfactory', 'are incentives motivating and paid on time', 'are the benefits that are offered satisfactory' etc. were asked. On calculation of mean and standard deviation it was seen that employees felt incentives would motivate them and that target based incentives were a true judge of performance. However, they found that benefits offered and remuneration levels in the Retail industry and benefits were unsatisfactory. Overall mean for rewards was 3.488 which is moderate and thereby shows that on average employees are dissatisfied with the rewards.

Organizational Justice

The reliability of questions for analyzing the distributive justice's is .608 which is fair. Questions such as 'when compared to peers in other retail companies and in my company I am underpaid', 'I invest more than I receive in return' were asked. Based on mean and standard deviation employees felt that they were being treated unfairly in their job, the management did not score high in fairness and providing of equal treatment in terms of compensation, the employees felt that they were underpaid compared to peers both in other retail companies and in their own company and they felt that they were not adequately appreciated. The mean analysis shows that employees believe that they work too hard considering outcomes received and the rewards that they receive are not proportional to their investments. The employees ie Store Managers and Customer Service Representatives in the Front end in the Retail Industry in Delhi and NCR region are of the view that there is no distributive justice in the organisation. Overall mean for distributive justice is 3.293 which means that employees are not very happy with their salary payouts and reward. Thus we see that for employees both pay relative to referent others and pay relative to work performed are important and in both cases the management in the Retail industry needs to strategise.

The reliability of questions for analyzing the procedural justice is .768 which is good. The mean analysis shows that employees agree that there is procedural justice in their organisation. Supervisors are fair and helpful and the management is consistent in administration of pay policies.

On the whole, employees are not satisfied with their salary levels and in comparison to their peers in other retail companies and they feel that they are not wanted in their organization which leads to an increase in attrition rate. But they are hopeful that management will listen to their suggestion and consider their feedback.

MOTIVATION

The reliability of questions for analyzing the motivation level is .518 which is fair. Questions such as 'the company is sensitive to needs of the employees' were asked. From the mean analysis it is clear that incentives and recognition motivates the employees. The overall mean is 3.698 which shows that incentive payouts and recognition received motivate employees to perform better.

JOB SATISFACTION

The Chronbach alpha for reliability of questions for analyzing Job satisfaction test is .682 which is satisfactory. Employees are satisfied with their job as overall mean for job satisfaction is 3.396 or near to 4. The mean analysis shows that most of the employees are satisfied with their work content and they have enough opportunity to work their best. Whilst satisfaction level with the number of breaks that they get is low, the problem is with the benefits that they are receiving (like medical reimbursement, health insurance), merit pay increments and promotion and career development opportunties which most of the employees think is not satisfactory.

JOB TURNOVER RATIO

The Cronbach Alpha for reliability of questions for analyzing the Job turnover ratio is .665 which is good. The mean analysis exhibited the fact that employees intention to leave the company for higher incentives is high. Employees in this sector in the front end are clear that they are likely to look for higher paying jobs in the next year. This is a big concern for the companies in the retail sector for which they need to rework their strategy. The average mean of turnover intention is 3.319 which is high and is a cause of worry for companies it would lead to increased cost for hiring and training of newly acquired manpower and bring down the return on investment in case of employees.

HYPOTHESIS TEST

From the study of literature and the above analysis, the following hypothesis for this case study is derived:

H0: There is no significant relationship between reward and Organisational justice

H1: There is a positive relationship between reward and Organisational justice

Model Summary

Model	R	R Square	Adjusted R Square	Std. Error of the Estimate
1	0.601	0.361	0.307	0.835

The multiple correlation Coefficient (R) value of these variables is .601 which shows a moderate correlation between variables. The coefficient of multiple determinations is 0.361; therefore, about 36.1% of the variation in the financial and non financial rewards is explained by these five independent factors of organisational justice. The regression equation appears to be useful for making predictions.

ANOVA

Model		Sum of Squares	Df	Mean Square	F	Sig.
1	Regression	32.654	7	4.665	6.69	0
	Residual	57.873	83	0.697		
	Total	90.527	90			

The sig level is .000 so we can reject null hypothesis and accept H1 which shows that there is a positive relationship between Reward and organisational justice.

COEFFICIENTS

Model		Unstandardized Coefficients		Standard-ized Coefficients	t	Sig.
		B	Std. Error	Beta		
1	(Constant)	2.26	0.944		2.393	0.019
	I work too hard considering my outcomes	-0.156	0.109	-0.138	-1.43	0.156
	I invest more in my job than I receive in return	-0.19	0.097	-0.194	-1.97	0.052
	When compared to peers in other Retail companies, I am underpaid	0.154	0.115	0.133	1.335	0.186
	The management is available to discuss issues	0.218	0.148	0.162	1.479	0.143
	My supervisor is fair and just while doing my performance appraisal	-0.064	0.137	-0.045	-0.46	0.645
	Incentives are based on performance	0.361	0.101	0.389	3.562	0.001
	The management is fair and provides equal treatment in terms of compensation	0.013	0.091	0.014	0.14	0.889

Result

In the above table Constant means when all the other variables of organisational justice are zero average mean for reward level is 2.260. This means without organisational justice, rewards has low mean. The next variables explain the relation of dependent variables with independent variables. Employees are not happy with the remuneration they are getting.

Hypothesis Test 2

H0: There is no significant relationship between Reward and Motivation levels.

H1: There is a positive relationship between Reward and Motivation levels.

Model Summary

Model	R	R Square	Adjusted R Square	Std. Error of the Estimate
1	0.603	0.363	0.309	0.619

The multiple correlation Coefficient (R) value of these variables is .603 which shows a moderate correlation between variables. The coefficient of multiple determinations is .363; therefore, about 36.3% of the variation in the motivation level due to incentives is explained by these independent factors of reward. The regression equation appears to be useful for making predictions.

ANOVA

	Model	Sum of Marks	Df	Mean Square	F	Sig.
1	Regression	18.144	7	2.592	6.763	.000a
	Residual	31.812	83	0.383		
	Total	49.956	90			

The sig level is .000 so we can reject null hypothesis and accept the H1 which shows that there is a positive relationship between reward and motivation

COEFFICIENTS

	Model	Unstandardized Coefficients		Standardized Coefficients	t	Sig.
		Model B	Std. Error	Beta		
1	(Constant)	2.32	0.407		5.7	0
	Current remuneration is satisfactory	-0.059	0.085	-0.077	-0.688	0.49
	Benefits offered to me such as medical reimbursement, health insurance etc are satisfactory	-0.064	0.069	-0.098	-0.929	0.36
	Timely recognition is received	0.138	0.1	0.168	1.381	0.17
	The merit pay increment given is satisfactory	-0.171	0.094	-0.229	-1.812	0.07
	Target based incentives are a true judge of my performance	0.47	0.08	0.578	5.903	0
	The rewards I receive in terms of financial and non financial are in accordance with my needs	0.075	0.08	0.1	0.933	0.35
	Incentives are timely paid	0.027	0.079	0.033	0.337	0.74

Result

In the above table Constant means when all the other variables of rewards are zero average mean for incentive motivation is2.320. Incentives without help of other factors can motivate the employees. So it is clear that reward motivates employees but currently the incentives provided to employees in the retail industry especially retail store operations are not satisfactory. Employees are also not satisfied with benefits like medical reimbursement and health insurance schemes.

HYPOTHESIS TEST 3

From the study of literature the following hypothesis for this case study is derived:

H0: There is a no significant relationship between Reward and Job Satisfaction

H1: There is a positive relationship between Reward and Job Satisfaction

Model	R	R Square	Adjusted R Square	Std. Error of the Estimate
1	.731a	0.534	0.489	0.733

The multiple correlation Coefficient (R) value of these variables is .731 which shows a high correlation between variables. The coefficient of multiple determinations is 0.534; therefore, about 53.4% of the variation in the satisfaction level of work content is explained by these 8 independent factors of reward. The regression equation appears to be useful for making predictions.

ANOVA

Model		Sum of Squares	df	Mean Square	F	Sig.
1	Regression	50.611	8	6.326	11.759	.000a
	Residual	44.115	82	0.538		
	Total	94.725	90			

The sig level is .000 so we can reject null hypothesis and accept the H1 which shows that there is a positive relationship between reward and job satisfaction

Coefficients

Model		Unstandardized Coefficients		Standard-ized Coefficients	T	Sig.
		Model B	Std. Error	Beta		
1	(Constant)	0.08	0.569		0.147	0.883
	current remuneration is satisfactory	-0.049	0.101	-0.047	-0.49	0.627
	Benefits offered to me such as medical reimbursement, health insurance etc are satisfactory	0.06	0.083	0.071	0.776	0.44
	Timely recognition is received	0.58	0.12	0.507	4.794	0
	The merit pay increment given is satisfactory	0.16	0.114	0.158	1.423	0.159
	Target based incentives are a true judge of my performance	0.22	0.112	0.196	1.948	0.055
	Incentives motivate me to perform better	0.09	0.13	0.064	0.673	0.503
	The rewards I receive in terms of financial and non financial are in accordance with my needs	-0.1	0.095	-0.064	-0.69	0.491
	Incentives are timely paid	0.06	0.094	0.05	0.598	0.552

Result

In the above table Constant means when all the other variables of rewards are zero average mean for job satisfaction level is .084. This means without rewards there is very less interest in work content. The next variables explain the relation of dependent variables with independent variables. That is, for every 1% of timely recognition is received, the average mean for satisfaction in current work will increase by. 576 and for every 1% of current remuneration level, satisfaction decreases by .049. In this correlation matrix it is clear that remuneration and rewards are not satisfactory and these factors lower the overall satisfaction level of employees.

Hypothesis Test 4

From the study of literature the following hypothesis for this case study is derived:

H0: There is a no significant relationship between Job Satisfaction and Organisation justice

H1: There is a positive relationship between Job Satisfaction and Organisation justice

Model Summary

Model	R	R Square	Adjusted R Square	Std. Error of the Estimate
1	0.6	0.36	0.322	0.845

The multiple correlation Coefficient (R) value of these variables is .600 which shows a moderate correlation between variables. The coefficient of multiple determinations is 0.360; therefore, about 36.0% of the variation in the satisfaction level of work content is explained by these independent factors of organisational justice. The regression equation appears to be useful for making predictions.

ANOVA

	Model	Sum of Squares	Df	Mean Square	F	Sig.
1	Regression	34.066	5	6.813	9.547	.000ª
	Residual	60.659	85	0.714		
	Total	94.725	90			

The sig level is .000 so we can reject null hypothesis and accept the H1 which shows that there is a relationship between positive relation between job satisfaction and organisational justice

Coefficients

	Model	Unstandardized Coefficients		Standardized Coefficients	t	Sig.
		B	Std. Error	Beta		
1	(Constant)	0.436	0.894		0.488	0.627
	I work too hard considering my outcomes	-0.07	0.109	-0.056	-0.59	0.556
	I invest more in my job than I receive in return	-0.04	0.096	-0.041	-0.42	0.673
	When compared to peers in other Retail companies, I am underpaid	0.08	0.114	0.067	0.699	0.486
	The management is available to discuss issues	0.359	0.135	0.261	2.662	0.009
	My supervisor encourages and promotes my work	0.574	0.121	0.441	4.738	0

Result

In the above table Constant means when all the other variables of Organisational justice are zero average mean for job satisfaction level is .436. This means without rewards there is very less interest in work content. The next variables explain the relation of dependent variables with independent variables. That is, for every 1% of encouragement from the supervisor, the average mean for satisfaction in current work will increase by .574 and because employees are not happy with the organizational justice in the organisation, job satisfaction variable shows negative relation with most of organizational justice variables.

HYPOTHESIS TEST 5

From the study of literature the following hypothesis for this case study is derived:

H0: There is no significant relationship between Job Satisfaction and motivation

H1: There is a positive relationship between Job Satisfaction and motivation

Model Summary

Model	R	R Square	Adjusted R Square	Std. Error of the Estimate
1	.545[a]	0.297	0.246	0.709

The multiple correlation Coefficient (R) value of these variables is .545 which shows a moderate correlation between variables. The coefficient of multiple determinations is 0.297; therefore, about 29.7% of the variation in the companies' sensitivity towards employees is explained by these independent factors of job satisfaction. The regression equation appears to be useful for making predictions.

ANOVA

Model		Sum of Squares	Df	Mean Square	F	Sig.
1	Regression	17.826	6	2.971	5.902	.000a
	Residual	42.284	84	0.503		
	Total	60.11	90			

The sig level is .000 so we can reject null hypothesis and accept the H1 which shows that there is a relationship between positive relation between Motivation and Job satisfaction.

Coefficients

Model		Unstandardized Coefficients		Standardized Coefficients	T	Sig.
		B	Std. Error	Beta		
1	(Constant)	1.283	0.43		2.983	0.004
	I am satisfied with my work content	0.145	0.094	0.182	1.542	0.127
	I have enough opportunities to work my best	-0.08	0.103	-0.087	-0.776	0.44
	I get enough breaks while working	-0.031	0.081	-0.039	-0.375	0.708
	Benefits offered to me such as medical reimbursement, health insurance etc are satisfactory	0.188	0.076	0.261	2.473	0.015
	The merit pay increment given is satisfactory	0.167	0.086	0.204	1.93	0.057
	Promotion/Career Development Process in my organization is satisfactory	0.225	0.084	0.269	2.687	0.009

Result

In the above table Constant means when all the other variables of Job satisfaction are zero average mean for Motivation level is 1.283 which is quite low. This means without job satisfaction, employees have very low motivation. The next variables explain the relation of dependent variables with independent variables. It shows that higher merit pay increase, larger opportunities for promotion and better benefits can increase an employee's motivation level.

SUMMARY

Thus, from the analysis it has been seen that employees in Retail Store operations in Delhi and NCR area believe that remuneration levels are not satisfactory and providing incentives would be a source of motivation for them. Keeping in mind the effort and long hours that they put in and in comparison to referent others in other Retail Companies and the Industry, on an average the employee's feel that the salary that they get is insufficient. The above analysis show that employees believe that there is no distributive justice in the organisation and employees are not very happy with their salary and reward. On the other hand, employees agree that there is procedural justice in their organisation. Supervisors are fair and helpful. Management is also consistent with policies and employee's suggestions are considered by management. Incentives and recognition act as a motivating factor for employees in the Retail sector.

Job satisfaction levels are high and most of the employees are satisfied with their work content and they have enough opportunity to work their best. It is thus seen that in the Retail industry managers and supervisors are doing the best that can be done with regards to work content, however, with regards to rewards the management needs to re-strategise.

The problem is with the benefits that they are receiving (like medical reimbursement, health insurance) which most of the employees think is not satisfactory. The average mean of turnover intention is 3.319 which is high and is a cause of worry for companies. While distributive justice could be one reason for high attrition rates, it could also be higher incentives offered by other Retail Companies.

As analysed above, from the study it can be seen that most of the employees are motivated by higher incentives. Employees believe their supervisor's are good to them and management will listen to their suggestion and feedback while they also feel that the supervisors in times of appraisal are not fair and just. It should be noted that rewards and job satisfaction are directly proportional. Moreover, if the incentives are timely paid, job satisfaction would increase. Recognition of work on a timely basis and appreciation in front of other employees would result in motivation. Moreover, if the remuneration is not up to the mark and satisfaction level of the employee, the employee feels demotivated to work. Employees feel that they deserve more pay when compared to the amount of work they do. As one increases the other is also favourable. The employees feel that management is unfair and does not provide equal treatment in terms of compensation. Benefits are not updated and as per the requirements of the employees, due to which their intention to leave the company is very high. They feel they are not appreciated in the organisation. Job dissatisfaction leads to lower motivation. Better promotion and career development opportunities and benefits can improve employee's motivational level.

BIBLIOGRAPHY

Adams, J S (1963), "Towards an understanding of equity", Journal of Abnormal and Social Psychology, Vol 37 pp 422-36.

Bloom M.C. Milkovich, G.T. (1996), "Issues in managerial compensation research", in Cooper, C.L., Rousseau, D.M. (Eds), Trends in organizational behavior, Wiley, New York, NY, Vol-3 pp 23-47.

Carr, S.C., McLoughlin, D., Hodgson, M., MacLachlan, M. (1996), "Effects of unreasonable pay discrepancies for under- and over-payment on double demotivation", Genetic, Social, and General Psychology Monographs, Vol. 122 pp.475-94.

Deci, E.L., Ryan, R.M. (2008), "Facilitating optimal motivation and psychological well-being across life's domains", Canadian Psychology, Vol. 49 No.1 pp 14-23.

Emmanuel, C.R., Kominis, G., Slapincar, S. (2008), "The impact of target setting on managerial motivation and performance", paper presented at the American Accounting Association Annual Meeting, Anaheim, CA,.

Festinger, L.A. (1954), "A theory of social comparison processes", Human Relations, Vol. 7 No.2, pp.117-40.

Frey B.S, Jegen, R. (2001), "Motivation crowding theory", Journal of Economic Surveys, Vol .15 No.5, pp 589-611.

Frey B.S., (1997), "On the relationship between intrinsic and extrinsic work motivation", International Journal of Industrial Organization, Vol. 15 No.4, pp 427-39.

Gardner, D.G., Van Dyne, L., Pierce, J.L. (2004), "The effects of pay level on organization-based self-esteem and performance: a field study", Journal of Occupational & Organizational Psychology, Vol. 77 No.3, pp.307-22.

Greenberg, J., Ashton-James, C.E., Ashkanasy, N.M. (2007), "Social comparison processes in organisations", Organizational Behavior and Human Decision Processes, Vol. 102 No.1, pp.22-41.

Heneman, H.G. (1985), "Pay satisfaction" in Rowland, K.M., Ferris, G.R. (Eds), Research in personnel and Human Resource Management, JAI Press, Greenwich, CT, Vol 3 pp 115-39.

Heneman, H.G., Schwab, D.P.(1985), Pay satisfaction: its multidimensional nature and measurement", International Journal of Psychology, Vol. 20 No.2, pp 129-41.

Herzberg, F. (2003), "One more time: how do you motivate employees?", Harvard Business Review, reprint from 1968, Vol. 81, No.1, pp. 53-62.

Igalens, J., Roussel, P. (1999), "A study of the relationship between compensation package, work motivation and job satisfaction", Journal of Organisational Behaviour, Vol. 20 No.7, pp.1003-25.

Jenkins, G.D., Mitra, A., Gupta, N., Shaw, J.D. (1998), "Are financial incentives related to performance? A meta-analytic review of empirical research", Journal of Applied Psychology, Vol. 83 No.5, pp.777-87.

Jenkins, G.D., Mitra, A., Gupta, N., Shaw, J.D. (1998), "Are financial incentives related to performance? A meta-analytic review of empirical research", Journal of Applied Psychology, Vol. 83 No.5, pp.777-87.

Kohn. A.(1993)," Why incentive plans cannot work", Harvard Business Review, Vol. 71, No. 5, pp. 54-63.

Lawler, EE (2003), "Pay practices in Fortune 1000 corporations", Worldatwork Journal, Vol. 12 No.4, pp 45-64.

Leventhal G.S. (1980), "What should be done with equity theory? New approaches to the study of fairness on social relationships", in Gergen, K., Greenberg, M., Willis, R. (Eds), Social Exchange : Advances in theory and Research, Plenum, New York, NY, pp. 27-55.

Locke, E.A., Latham, G.P. (1990), A Theory of Goal Setting and Task Performance, Prentice-Hall, Englewood Cliffs, NJ.

Mc Farlin, D.B., Sweeney, P.D. (1992), "Distributive and procedural justice as predictors of satisfaction with personal and organizational outcomes", Academy of Management Journal, Vol. 35 No. 3, pp 626-37.

Osterloh, M., Frey, B.S. (2002), "Does pay for performance really motivate employees?", in Neely, A. (Eds),Business Performance Measurement: Theory and Practice, Cambridge University Press, Cambridge, pp.357-63.

Porter, L.W., Lawler, E.E. III (1968), Managerial Attitudes and Performance, R.D. Irwin, Homewood, IL, .

Ronen, J., Livingstone, J.T. (1975), "An expectancy theory approach to the motivational impacts of budgets", The Accounting Review, Vol. 50 No.4, pp.671-85.

Skinner, B.F. (1953), Science and Human Behavior, Macmillan, New York, NY, .

Thibaut , J., Walker, L.(1975), Procedural Justice: A Psychological Analysis, Erlbaum, Hillsdale, NJ.

Tremblay, M., Sire, B., Balkin, D.B. (2000), "The role of organizational justice in pay and employee benefit satisfaction, and its effects on work attitudes", Group and Organization, Vol. 25 No.3, pp 269-90.

Vroom, V.H. (1964), Work and Motivation, Wiley, New York, NY.

Weiss, D.J., Dawis, R.V., England, G.W., Lofquist, L.H. (1967), Manual for the Minnesota Satisfaction Questionnaire, Industrial Relations Center, University of Minnesota, Minneapolis, MN, .

Wright, B.E., Kim, S. (2004), "Participation's influence on job satisfaction: the importance of job characteristics", Review of Public Personnel Administration, Vol. 24 No.1, pp.18-40.

Competency Assessment of the Retail Staff and Preparing to Launch Retail HR Processes in Top Stores of ADIDAS India

Sakshi Puri* and Manosi Chaudhuri**

ABSTRACT

ADIDAS aimed to change the way its franchisee stores managed their human resources. It wanted to structure and benchmark the various HR activities at the store level. It used the competency assessment approach which has long demonstrated value to the HR departments in the areas of recruitment and selection, training and development, performance management and in total for the staff's self-development. An exploratory study was conducted for the purpose of analysis by using the techniques of in-depth interviewing and observation. After critically analysing the data in different ways, recommendations and suggestions were made to increase the performance of stores by making improvements in training programs and adding new dimensions to the already existing behaviours.

Keywords: Competency, competency assessment, competency gap, competency rating.

INTRODUCTION

ADIDAS is a name that stands for competence in all sectors of sports around the globe. The vision of the company founder, Adolf ("Adi") Dassler, has long become reality and his corporate philosophy, the guiding principle for successor generations. The idea was as simple as it was brilliant. Adi Dassler's aim was to provide every athlete with the best possible equipment. It all began in 1920, when Adi Dassler made his first shoes using the few materials available after the First World War. Today,

* Sakshi Puri is pursuing post graduate studies in management at Birla Institute of Management Technology, Greater Noida, India.

**Manosi Chaudhuri is Associate Professor,OB & HR at Birla Institute of Management Technology, Greater Noida, India.

E-mail: sakshi.puri13@bimtech.ac.in, manosi.chaudhuri@bimtech.ac.in the ADIDAS product range extends from footwear and apparel to accessories for all kinds of different sports. Currently based in Herzogenaurach, Germany it has well over 46,000 employees worldwide, with more than 3,000 working at the company's headquarters in Herzogenaurach. Today, the ADIDAS Group is Europe's biggest supplier of athletic footwear and sports apparel. It did a business of 13.34 billion Euros in the year 2011(http://www.adidas.com/). ADIDAS first entered India in 1989 through a licence agreement with Bata and later re-entered India for the second time in 1996 through a joint venture with Magnum International Trading Company Ltd., with an initial investment of $2.5 million to form ADIDAS (India) Trading Pvt. Ltd. ADIDAS holds a 100 percent stake in the company.

ADIDAS long felt a need to bring about a change in the way they operated through a franchise model in India (one of the most important channels through which ADIDAS products reached the consumers). Its presence is noted in about more than 250 cities in India. The retail strategy of ADIDAS is focused on 5 Ps: People, Product, Process, Premises and Profit. Competitive situations demand higher productivity with present resources. ADIDAS India has been able to structure and align its products and premises through various processes. One of the most important resources is people, where there is still scope of development. The training department planned their first step in the direction of the Competency Approach, as it offers direction in the areas such as recruitment and selection, performance management, employee development, succession planning, and organizational change. The competency study data set provides deep insights into the company culture and identifies the targeted developmental needs of the worker population. The competency study at ADIDAS uses a Behavioural Interviewing and Observation format, which is an extraordinary tool for setting standards and routinely measuring an organization's progress. Implementation of the recommended solutions of the competency research in the right direction would lead to strengthening of the already existing processes at the store level, bridging the competency gaps and ensuring productivity in the future. Also, one would come to a conclusion as to how to increase a store's performance in terms of increasing sales, better customer service and improved team performance.

Now it was time for Natasha, Management trainee at ADIDAS training department who joined six months back, to prove how well she could take up the responsibility assigned to her by Mr. Rawat (Manager, Retail training) of executing the competency assessment programme at all the top stores of Delhi and National Capital Region (NCR). She realised it was a huge opportunity for her to learn and also to get recognition in the organization if the research materialises in the right direction. She decided to start reading literature on Competency and Competency Assessment in organizations as well as various methods of mapping and assessing these competencies.

LITERATURE REVIEW

First discussed and assessed by McClelland in the early 1970s, competencies, or individual characteristics, were recognized as significant predictors of employee performance and success, equally as important as an individual's academic aptitude and knowledge content as indicated by tests scores or results (Lucia and Lepsinger, 1999; McClelland, 1973). A competency is the capability of applying or using knowledge, skills, abilities, behaviours, and personality characteristics to successfully perform critical work tasks, specific functions, or operate in a given role or position. Personal characteristics may be mental / intellectual / cognitive, social / emotional / attitudinal, and physical / psycho-motor attributes necessary to perform the job (Dubois, 1993; and Lucia and Lepsinger, 1999). Boyatzis (1982) and Fogg (1999) extended this definition to include both internal and external constraints, environments, and relationships related to the job or occupation. Motivations and perceptions of the work and one's self or talent also are viewed as influential in competently and successfully performing in a position (Boyatzis, 1982; Fulmer and Conger, 2004; Gangani, McLean and Braden, 2006; Sandberg, 2000). In summary, competencies are specific personal qualities that are "causally related to effective and/or superior performance" (Boyatzis, 1982); are common across many settings and situations, and endure for some time (Delamare Le Deist and Winterton, 2005).

The turning point for competency movement was when the article titled "Testing for Competence Rather than Intelligence" was published in American Psychologist in 1973 by McClelland wherein he presented data that traditional achievement and intelligence scores might not be able to predict job success and what was required was to profile the exact competencies required to perform a given job effectively and measure them using a variety of tests. McClelland argued that traditional intelligence tests, as well as proxies such as scholastic grades, failed to predict job performance. Instead, McClelland proposed testing for competency. This article, combined with the work done by Douglas Brey and his associates at AT&T in the US wherein they presented evidence that competencies could be assessed through assessment centres and on the job success could be predicted to some extent by the same, had laid foundation for the popularization of the competency movement. Competency-based approaches gained popularity and acceptance within the human resources community through the work of McClelland and his associates, particularly McBer and Company. They even developed a new and yet simple methodology called the Behaviour Event Interviewing (BEI) to map the competencies.

It is not easy to identify all the competencies that are required to fulfil the job requirements. However, a number of other methods like Critical Incident techniques, Psychometric tests, Questionnaires, etc. have also been developed and successfully tried out. These methods have helped managers to a large extent, to identify, reinforce and develop suitable competencies both for the growth of the individual and the organization.

OBJECTIVES

The main objectives of the study were to determine whether the existing workforce possesses the competencies critical for the organization's success and to identify the problem areas which need development.

APPROACH TO THE PROBLEM

After two days, Mr. Rawat followed up with Natasha to find out how far she had reached in understanding the history and concepts behind competency assessment. He brought with himself, the competency interview and rating guide for each of the positions in the stores, i.e. for Retail Professional (RP), Advanced Retail Professional (ARP), Stepping into Management Professional (SIM) and Store Manager(SM). The career of a store employee advanced from being an RP to becoming an SM.

When Mr. Rawat felt that Natasha had made a sincere effort, he started giving her tips on how to frame questions and assess the respondents on the various parameters without making them feel uncomfortable. He suggested her to be natural in her approach and not make use of the rating guide while interviewing. She was instructed to visit each store and have a 20-30 minute discussion individually with each staff member, observe them on the floor with customers, record their responses and then finally rate them in their absence on various parameters (competencies) like Sales and Business Acumen, Customer Service, Brand and Products, Operations and Processes, and Leadership and Teamwork. For the first few visits at the stores, Monica (Assistant Manager, Retail Training) guided her through the whole process.

Finally, when all the responses were generated, they were put to statistical testing.

RESEARCH METHODOLGY

The research relied mainly on the primary data collected from 100 respondents who were retail staff at the ADIDAS stores. Samples were selected from the top 15 stores in Delhi and NCR, in a non-probabilistic manner using convenience sampling. The primary reason for choosing convenience sampling was not to disturb any employee while he was at customer service and only that employee was chosen who was not addressing any customer issue at that time. This data was collected with the help of competency assessment rating interview guide and observation technique. The assessment used a five-point scale that had a number and a brief description associated with each of the categories which were: "Below expectations", "Met most expectations", "Fully met expectations", "Exceeded expectations" and "Outstanding performance", where 1 was the lowest and 5 was the highest on the scale. These helped Natasha to set clear performance expectations and conduct focused and fair interviews. The interview guide had questions which were based on the competencies required for various positions in the organization. Apart from establishing rapport and asking about the demographic details of the respondent, the total number of questions was 15. At the time of interview, a list of interview questions along with the competency rating sheet was used to extract information about specific and relevant behaviour. Natasha insisted on asking at least three to four job related behaviour examples of each competency and noted incidents of effective and ineffective behaviour. She kept detailed notes, which were later studied and used by her for evaluating respondents against the relevant competencies. Pretesting was done by giving the results of the initial samples to the HR manager for plotting competencies. The pre-test was found to be satisfactory and thus the interviews were continued as before.

DIAGNOSIS AND ANALYSIS

Natasha collated the data and analysed it in three different ways. In the first study, the staff members at the four positions in the stores were compared separately on all the five competencies on a rating scale of Low, Medium and High (Ref. Annexure 1). It was observed that the Retail Professionals were more or less in the low and medium category on each competency; hardly any RP staff was observed to be in the high category. Advanced Retail Professionals and Store Managers were generally found to be in the medium range on all the competencies. Stepping into Management Professionals scored very high when it came to knowing their customers and having brand knowledge.

CORRELATION AND REGRESSION ANALYSIS

The second analysis was done to find out if any relationship existed between the tenure i.e. time spent with the company and the competency rating of an individual. This study was restricted to 54 staff members. A scatter plot was used to show whether a linear regression existed between the two variables, i.e., tenure and the total of competency rating across five competencies for each level. A correlation coefficient for each of the four regression equations was also generated. Correlation analysis was used to measure strength of the association (linear relationship) between the two variables.

RPs showed a weak but positive correlation between competency rating and their tenure with the company. So, increasing the tenure contributed to improvement in competency rating of RPs, but not at a very effective level. In case of an ARP there existed a negative relationship which meant that even after increasing the duration (in months) with the company, the staff at the ARP level had not improved on its competencies. The trend line showed a negative relationship between the SIM competency rating and the tenure with a negative correlation coefficient. Lastly, SM competency rating showed a positive relationship with the tenure, but again it was a weak one as the correlation coefficient r = 0.1797, which was closer to zero.

TWO WAY ANOVA WITH INTERACTION

Finally, an Analysis of Variance (ANOVA) was done with the competency data since there were two independent and one dependent variable to analyze. The two independent variables, Position and Competency were considered in relation to the dependent variable, mean rating. Position had 4 levels and Competency had 5 levels (Ref. Annexure 2). This analysis helped in calculating the main effect for each independent variable and their interaction effect by considering null hypotheses as follows:

Main Effect, *Null hypothesis,* $H_{0\,(p)}$ = There was no difference between mean rating of staff at different positions.

Main Effect, *Null hypothesis,* $H_{0(c)}$ = There was no difference on mean rating across the five competencies.

Interaction Effect, *Null hypothesis,* $H_{0\,(pc)}$ = There was no difference on mean rating of staff for the 4*5 combinations of Position and Competency.

The results showed that position had an F-value of 17.96, and a significance level of .00 which was less than .05. So, the null hypothesis was rejected (Ref. Annexure 3). This meant there was a difference between positions i.e. RP, ARP, SIM and SMs when it came to competency rating. For competency again, the significance value was very close to zero and obviously less than 0.5. The null hypothesis was again rejected and it was concluded that there was a difference in mean rating between the five competency levels. The most important was the interaction effect between position and competency (Ref. Annexure 3). Here, the F-value was found to be 13.464 and significance level was much less than 0.05. The null hypothesis was rejected since an interaction effect did exist. The effect of competency depended upon the level of position one was at and vice-versa. One major noticeable fact from this analysis was that the interaction mean between the position SIM and the competency Teamwork and Leadership produced a very low value of 0.6389 as compared to the interaction means of RP, ARP and SM with Teamwork and leadership which were in the range 2 and 3 (Ref. Annexure 4).

Other findings were that SMs scored the highest on Sales and Business Acumen, followed very closely by SIMs. In Customer Service, and Brand and Product Knowledge, SIMs topped the list. A clear parallel movement was there from the RP level to the ARP level on each competency which showed very sharp results. But Annexure 4 also represented ARPs to be more aware of the Operations and Processes at the stores which came as a surprise because SIMs and SMs were expected to be more experienced in that domain. Natasha thought that after this research got over it would be a good idea to look into the competency rating questionnaire once again to find if certain specific things were lowering the rating of SIMs and SMs.

RECOMMENDATIONS

The recommendations Natasha gave were closely linked to the findings and outcomes of the study undertaken. She identified the competency gaps and suggested a specific and unique action plan for all the four levels in the store (RP, ARP, SIM and SM).

Retail Professional

Current Status and Observations: Training sessions for an RP are conducted for 3 days, 8 hours each, which covers his basic understanding of all the five competencies. Most of the RPs did not necessarily take training even after working for a month or two in the store either because of their own or franchisee's disinterest.

Problem Areas: RPs were rated in the low range on almost all the competencies. A weak positive relationship between tenure and competency rating was seen.

Recommendations: RP is the entry level position in the company and the company needs to build its values and culture in them at a very initial stage. It was recommended that the company and franchisees get into a training contract which facilitates RPs' training without fail and within the stipulated time. The training sessions need to build more on the important competencies for them like customer interaction, understanding their needs and serving them the right way. This would help the recently appointed staff to feel a level of connection with the brand and the high attrition which exists amongst them could also be controlled.

Advanced Retail Professional

Current Status and Observations: An ARP is trained for one day in the whole year. Their training module includes understanding Retail Key Performance Indicators (KPIs) and mathematics involved around it; giving and receiving feedback and training RPs. It was observed that they lack a separate identity in the stores and were often confused with either RPs or SIMs.

Problem Areas: The competency results revealed that almost all of them lay in the medium range on all the competencies. A negative relationship between tenure and competency rating was found.

Recommendations: Building on ARPs a little more would prove profitable for the business. The company can increase a few training modules in the category of Sales and Business acumen and Teamwork and Leadership because a few of them were still lagging behind on these competencies. More number of training sessions would also make them feel that some investment is done on them. The identity issue could be sorted by giving them a badge on their completion of ARP training, which they could wear at the store. The above two suggestions, if followed, would motivate them and also make them feel an important part of the store and the brand.

Stepping into Management Professional

Current Status and Observations: SIMs undergo a two day training program annually. Mostly two or more than two SIMs were found in a single store and only one of them is given the opportunity to train the other staff members.

Problem Areas: Due to their experience with the brand, they mostly score the highest on every competency across all the four positions except Teamwork and Leadership.

Recommendations: The concern for poor performance on one competency could be attributed to a specific reason that there was a lack of equal opportunities for all the SIMs at one store. It should be made mandatory for every SIM to take at least one training session in a month. This would boost their confidence and will enhance their leadership and teamwork skills. A tracking system of SIMs should also be maintained by the Store Manager so as to help in succession planning.

Store Manager

Current Status and Observations: Twelve training sessions on all the five competencies are scheduled for the Store Manager in a year's time. The SM is burdened with the task of generating the given target of sales on a daily, weekly, monthly and annual basis. Through his sales staff, he maintains trackers for each staff member and is also accountable to the franchisee owner and the Head Office of ADIDAS, India.

Problem Areas: The SM is unable to display his competencies on the floor to his staff as he gets too carried away with numbers the whole day.

Recommendations: The twelve training sessions should also include sessions on stress management other than focusing on the five core competencies. It is important for them to deal with stress first, which would eventually lead them to improve on their skills. A Floor Manager should be present in every store to assist the store manager. This would help the SM to delegate his work and give him more opportunity to display his competencies to his staff and also coach his people in the store.

CONCLUSION

When the findings were displayed by Natasha to Mr. Rawat and Ms. Monica, they agreed that the competency rating done was fair and also agreed that they should spend more time enhancing the competencies of ARPs and SIMs which showed negative relationship with the tenure in the company. In case of a significant low performance on teamwork and leadership by the SIMs, Mr. Rawat agreed that lack of equal and fair opportunities was the reason. Franchisee's disinterest in training and developing its staff was a major hindrance for a store's growth. They were impressed the way Natasha had correctly and accurately assessed individuals and analyzed the data with a clear understanding of the job roles in spite of many limiting factors like reluctance to share information by the Store Manager about his store staff and also misleading answers given by the staff. It could be seen that Natasha had built trust with her interviewees who led them to have a candid approach.

Mr. Rawat knew it was time to take action on the factors which were prohibiting the growth of the individuals and store. Considering Natasha's recommendations and his own understanding of the problems he decided to arrange for a meeting with the Director (Retail), Mr. Jai Prakash.

ACKNOWLEDGEMENT

The authors wish to place on record their sincere thanks to Devmalya Ghosh, Manager Retail Training, Adidas India Marketing Ltd for support in developing this case, permission to present the same at ICMC 2012 and publish in the conference proceedings.

REFERENCES

Boyatzis, R. E. (1982). *The competent manager: A model for effective performance.* New York: Wiley.

Delamare Le Deist, F. & Winterton, J. (2005). What is competence? *Human Resource Development International, 8(1)*, 27-46.

Dubois, D. D. (1993). *Competency-based performance improvement: A strategy for organizational change.* Amherst, MA: HRD Press, Inc.

Fogg, C. D. (1999). *Implementing your strategic plan: How to turn "intent" into effective action for sustainable change.* New York: American Management Association.

Fulmer, R. M., & Conger, J. A. (2004). Identifying talent. *Executive Excellence, 21(4)*, 11.

Gangani, N., McLean, G. N., & Braden, R. A. (2006). A competency-based human resources development strategy. *Performance Improvement Quarterly, 19(1)*, 127-139.

Lucia, A. D., & Lepsinger, R. (1999). *The art and science of competency models: Pinpointing critical success factors in organizations.* New York: Pfeiffer.

McClelland, D. C. (1998). Identifying competencies with behavioural event interviews. *Psychological Science, 9(5)*, 331-340.

McClelland, D.C., 1973. Testing for competence rather than intelligence. *American Psychologist, 28(1)*, 1-14.

Sandberg, J. (2000). Understanding human competence at work: An interpretative approach. *The Academy of Management Journal, 43(1)*, 9-25.

Sanghi, S. (2007). *The handbook of competency mapping: Understanding, designing and implementing competency models in organizations.* New Delhi: Response Books.

Shermon, G. (2004). *Competency based HRM.* New Delhi: Tata McGraw-Hill.

Latest News, Retrieved from http://www.adidas-group.com/en/home/Welcome.aspx

ANNEXURE 1

SCALE	RANGE (rating)		
	LOW	*MEDIUM*	*HIGH*
10	2-4	5-7	8-10
15	3-6	7-11	12-15
20	4-9	10-14	15-20

COMPETENCY RATING SCALE

Total rating under each competency per each individual across various positions i.e. RP, ARP, SIM and SM was calculated. It was further bifurcated on the basis of three different scales depending on the number of questions in each competency. A competency having two/three/four questions under it was rated on a scale of 10/15/20 respectively. Each scale was divided into three parts namely, Low, Medium and High.

ANNEXURE 2

		Value Label	N
Position	1	RP	125
	2	ARP	190
	3	SIM	90
	4	SM	95
Competency	1	Sales and business acumen	100
	2	Customer service	100
	3	Brand and products	100
	4	Operations and processes	100
	5	Teamwork and leadership	100

ANNEXURE 3

Source	Type III Sum of Squares	df	Mean Square	F	Sig.	Partial Eta Squared
Corrected Model	141.511[a]	19	7.448	14.756	.000	.369
Intercept	3629.987	1	3629.987	7.192E3	.000	.937
Position	27.208	3	9.069	17.968	.000	.101
Competency	47.654	4	11.913	23.603	.000	.164
Position * Competency	81.551	12	6.796	13.464	.000	.252
Error	242.272	480	.505			
Total	4369.389	500				
Corrected Total	383.783	499				
R Squared = .369 (Adjusted R Squared = .344) Tests of Between-Subjects Effects						

ANNEXURE 4

Estimated Marginal Means of mean_rating

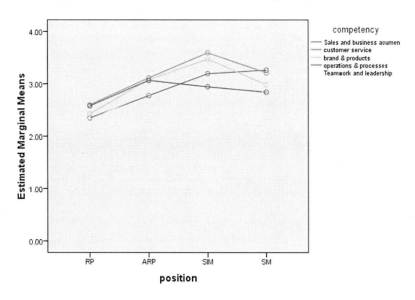

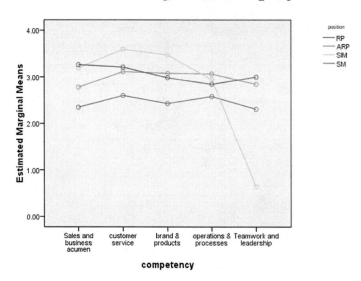

Estimated Marginal Means of mean_rating

Interaction effect between independent variables

If the interaction was not found to be significant then the lines in the above plots would be parallel.

PART IV: Cases in Leadership, Organization Development

Emerging imperatives of new business environment call for solutions to seek low cost of production and services, enhanced quality, higher flexibility, faster delivery and increased customer satisfaction. Businesses all around the world are seeking creative responses to new competitive realities. New organizational forms are evolving. The nature of work is being redefined. Leadership is being looked at from multiple angles such as quiet and invisible leadership (Thatchenkery & Sugiyama, 2011). Size and volume are not the top priority anymore.

The six chapters in this section discuss several cases from new perspectives on leadership and organization development. They are chosen from diverse fields to highlight application of these approaches to differing circumstances, cultural, political, and economic. The first chapter by Arnold Anderson and Cheryl Anderson explores leadership issues in administration of a large church facing a vocal minority group in blocking an effort to relocate and expand the church. The narrative showcases dependencies between followership and leadership and brings out the fine balance between faith and autonomy.Ronald Newton in the next chapter explores the theory and characteristics of charismatic leadership behavior with the goal of illuminating various perspectives of transformational leaders through their understanding of existing charismatic leadership behavior. Such a topic is of significance as corporations today try to balance the need for valuing multiple styles of leadership, not just charismatic.

Based on their long years of experience and research, DaphneDePorres and Monty Miller explore the inner working of international student programs. Their study provides ten steps that faculty engaged in overseas students visiting programs may use to build and reinforce the attitudes, behaviours, and commitments (ABCs) of students participating in such programs. Their advice is both pragmatic and supported by data. The next research case from Thailand-based Vilas Wongtrakuland and U.S-based Bruce Hanson discusses the impact of an Organizational Development Intervention (ODI) on the improvement of employee motivation, commitment, and customer satisfaction in a Thai subsidiary of a multinational hotel chain. The lessons learned are highly valuable for anyone looking for insights about managing staff in multinational corporations. The last case study is from Nathan Walla who examines the processes needed to guide professionalization of organizations in the cleaning industry from both environmental and social sustainability standards. All together these cases bring to surface the nuances and subtleties of organizational development and leadership.

How do Leadership Styles Affect Followership Styles in a Large Christian Church?

Arnold R.* and Cheryl R. Anderson*

ABSTRACT

A large Christian church experienced organizational behaviour issues over a period of approximately ten years. The church went from over 3,000 members to approximately 2,000 members. A vocal minority group attempted to block an effort to relocate and expand the church. Strife continued after the purchase of land and a small building and recruitment of a new congregation with no psychological or physical relationship to the initial campus. The financial burden placed on the membership because of the new facility further stretched the Christian faith of the members at the home campus. The interplay between formal and informal leaders and between leaders and followers of this church presents examples of the dependencies between followership and leadership.

Keywords: Leadership, followership, transformational stewardship, group efficacy, minority dissent, resistance to change.

INTRODUCTION

Organizational behaviour problems began about 2002. Due to significant membership and activity increases, a decision to sell the existing church and move to a new location with a new worship and music centre triggered negative reactions and subsequent organizational behaviour issues among a vocal minority of the membership.

A SHORT CHURCH HISTORY

On February 3, 1980 the first formal worship service of the church was held at a children's day care centre with about forty persons attending. The rapidly expanding

---

* Faculty membes and Doctoral students at Colorado Technical University, Colorado Springs, Colorado, USA.
E-mail: arnoldanderson@comcast.net

congregation soon outgrew this location and moved to a larger children's care centre in April 1980. Charter Sunday for the new congregation was celebrated in this facility on June 15, 1980, with 75 members joining (History of [name withheld for confidentiality reasons], 2012).

In November 1980, the 280-member congregation of a neighbouring church within the same denomination voted to merge with the new church. The neighbouring church's site had no room for expansion so the combined congregation decided to move to a newly developing residential area. By February 1981, the congregation, let by the pastor of the original forty-person congregation, moved to the third temporary site:a former restaurant and bar. The worship service that united the two congregations was on Easter Sunday, April 19, 1981(History of [name withheld for confidentiality reasons], 2012). This merger, the subsequent sale of the neighbouring church's property, and a bond drive became the keys to the financing of land and a new building where the church was currently located. These activities occurred over a period of years and under the tenure and guidance of two pastors, both ordained ministers, and well-liked by congregants.

The third senior pastor, a converted ordained minister from a different denomination, continued to attract and increase membership, requiring an expansion of the original building. That construction brought a large room that was used as both the Sanctuary and a multi-purpose room and several offices and classrooms. A second expansion, also during this pastor's tenure and completed in 1988, brought an 800-seat Sanctuary plus additional offices and classrooms, children's Sunday School area, and youth gathering areas. The Sanctuary built during the first building expansion became the multi-use Fellowship Hall. County building codes and the physical limitations of the site dictated the building could not be expanded a third time.

In the final decade of the 20th century and into the 21st century, membership grew 300% from 900 to over 3000, with weekly attendance at one of the seven services averaging over 1,800. A fourth minister led this explosion in membership through lay leaders, small groups' members, and charter members' support. Close affiliation between goals of these individuals and the pastoral staff worked well to propel attendance and collect members into the Faith, as demonstrated by the resulting membership numbers. The church became the largest of its denomination between Kansas City and San Francisco, much to the credit of a hard-working senior pastor and new associate pastors. Directors of Care Ministries, Children's Ministries, Youth Ministries, and Music became full time positions, and support staff,including both paid staff and volunteers,increased as well. The full-time staff positions were managed by the associate pastors, while the senior pastor concentrated on increasing attendance at worship services and in classrooms. Volunteer efforts focused on growing missionaries and candidates for seminary study. Ongoing Preschool and Mother's Morning Out continued to be important programs(History of [name withheld for confidentiality reasons], 2012).

EXPANSION ISSUE

By 2000, membership had grown to over 3,000 and the worship schedule was expanded to accommodate seven services. Two building expansions had enlarged the original church, but they were inadequate to house the growing need for more classrooms, children's and youth's programs, as well as adult ministries and the multiple worship services and social activities. The large attendance numbers more than exceeded the classroom capacity, which inhibited small group meetings and Sunday school class meetings. The building expansion possibilities had been maximized with the second expansion and now there was no way to grow on that property, either physically or in membership.The pastors preached from the pulpit how the capacity of both the sanctuary and the parking lot were exceeded on holidays, often resulting in visitors being turned away, but the obligation of members was to continue inviting people.

LEADERSHIP

In 2001 a small group of church members selected by the Senior Pastor became a Discernment Team (a common church method of trying to determine what is God's will by prayerful reflection, NYAC, 2012) to addressthe problems caused by the significant increase in church membership and activities. The Discernment Team suggested the church examine moving to a new location. Coupled with the recommendation to relocate the church was the suggestion to sell the original building as soon as a new Sanctuary could be built in the new location. These actions were by followers who assumed leadership roles (Baker, 2007). As followers of the Faith and the direction of the spiritual leaders, these individuals also exhibited characteristics of Kelley's Exemplary followership style (Flower, 1991).

The church council authorized a committee of volunteers to form a building committee to hire a consulting company to lead efforts in evaluating growth options and recommending a course of action. Most of these committee members were involved in other areas of church business or outreach, and were willingly advised by the Senior Pastor, exhibiting signs of Kelley's Conformist followership (Flower,1991). Several groups of volunteers were recruited by the Senior Pastor to analyse growth history and projections, donation records, and demographics for the geographic area from which the congregation drew members and visitors. The analysis revealed that the income level of the geographic area was above average for the metropolitan area, and that population growth for the city would see an increase in households in the specific geographic area of the church. All demographic indications were that the economy of the city could easily support the relocation of the church if membership continued to grow at its present rate. The recommendation from the consulting company, the building committee members, and the Senior Pastor was to locate another parcel of land for purchase and future building of a new Sanctuary and classrooms.

FOLLOWERSHIP

The church council accepted the recommendation and put the issue to a vote of the membership. This denomination uses an Episcopal system of polity (governance), which means bishops provide the top leadership (United Methodist Church, 2012). At a 'town hall' meeting presided over by the Bishop, the church membership voted to follow the recommendation (74% in favor of the expansion, 26% opposed to the expansion). The 26% were vocally and passionately opposed to any consideration of relocating the congregation to a new building, without any justification for their opposition. A second vote of the members upheld the majority opinion of the need to plan and search for a new property. Many members were disgruntled that so few people had participated in either vote, in addition to the minority that continued to complain and criticize. No effort was made by the pastors or the church leadership to determine why one-quarter of the vote was opposed to the relocation (De Dreu & West, 2001).

This final town hall meeting and the majority affirmation to continue with the relocation efforts led to the purchase of land and a warehouse about one mile from the existing church campus. A purchase agreement was worked out with the building committee chairperson (one of the original charter members of the church), the finance committee chairperson (a local realtor), and the Senior Pastor. The owner would finance the purchase with an option for the church to purchase an adjoining 8.8 acres. After significant renovations, the building no longer bore any resemblance to a warehouse. It was now renovated to include a chapel, classrooms, youth centre, thrift shop, and a worship centre that alsodoubled as a performing arts centre. This second campus was rededicated in August 2006.The Senior Pastor turned over administration of the second campus to the associate pastor, who handled worship services on Saturday evening and Sunday morning, as well as children's classes and nursery services with assistance from lay leaders. This effectively divided the congregation between two locations, resulting in both a psychological and physical division (informal conversation with second campus attendees). Additional negativity, as well as financial challenge, was laid on the membership because of the difference in congregations and perceived unequal contribution and benefits the two locations engendered.

Negative attitudes and comments continued to be obvious in small group study sessions, church dinners, choir meetings, and planning meetings for the new location and the subsequent purchase of the property. Several members complained to the staff of receiving negative and libellous anonymous emails. Many families left to join other congregations; one member complained at a monthly dinner that they were convinced the study that resulted in the effort to relocate the church was based on false information, and they felt the church's leadership had lied to the congregation. However, no evidence was offered to substantiate this accusation, nor any specifics identified as the basis for this perception. The escalating friction between the two campuses exacerbated an already precarious situation. Activities planned by staff and volunteers at the home campus received little support or participation from members of the second campus, and attendees at the second campus complained about not being included in home campus activities. Integration of the services or the people from the two campuses was not publically promoted by either pastor or lay leaders.

When the church council requested the membership to agree to put the existing building up for sale to help defray the mounting costs of maintaining two campuses, many of the older congregants were very vocal about losing "...their church." These researchers were approached by five different couples regarding this action. Planning teams continued with their efforts to gather space and functionality requirements for the new building, to interview the leaders of the different ministries, to identify an architectural firm for design proposals, and to ensure on-going communication of decisions and plans to the congregants (Bridges, 2003; Ogden and Hills, 2008; Avey, Hughes, Norman, and Luthens, 2007).

PERSONAL INVOLVEMENT

Both authors have been members of this church since the early 1980s. We met at the church in 1985, and were married there in 1988. We continue our membership and hope to work to heal some of the problems described in this case study.

One author was on the Finance Committee that hired the first round of consultants. We both were on the committee that gathered and examined demographics for the average income in the geographical area served by the church. We both have served in various capacities at the church, never considered ourselves leaders, but apparently many church members consider us to be informal leaders. This comment is based on the number of private opinions church members shared with us over the last several years. We were part of the communications team and participated in the purchase of the additional 8.8 acres adjoining the new classroom building. We also supported the recent bond issue that stabilized the mortgage payments to enable more planning for the new sanctuary (Kahn, 2004).

We were also the recipients of several anonymous 'spam' emails sent to the entire church membership, and were approached by at least 20 members (informal conversations with the authors) who expressed their dissatisfaction with the church leadership. It was unclear to whom these references were made, since this denomination had dual leadership: one group to see after the business side, and the ordained appointees to minister to the spiritual side. Others who received the emails and were approached individually by dissenters were persuaded to oppose relocation efforts; some of those people eventually moved to different churches to avoid the conflict. These negative actions were mainly after church membership voted to relocate (Pederit, 2000).

ORGANIZATIONAL CULTURE

This large church very rapidly lost about one-third of its membership over a several month period. Now, however, new members arrive almost every Sunday. The culture that attracted so many to the church still appears to exist, but is undergoing some shifts due to the departure of many members who were unhappy with the disruptions and changes. Several of those people were major financial contributors, as well as volunteers and informal leaders.

The economic structure of the demographic attracted to this church is at the higher end of the city's income-earning population. People living in the regional area typically have higher and more stable incomes than those living in other regions of the metropolitan area. This may partially be due to the large number of active duty and retired military who live in the area. Many of the church volunteer leaders and those active in committees have spent a career in the military, which means many have extensive experience in organizing and running large organizations.

There has always been a significant sense of cohesiveness and friendliness within the church. Many members feel the church members are warm, feel the church is home, and sense this is where they belong (Corley, 2004; Kirkman and Shapiro, 1997).A group of volunteers was continually engaged in community outreach, and congregation growth was perpetuated by personal invitation and word of mouth advertising. Informal leadership appeared to be consistently the same people. This sometimes discouraged new members from stepping forward to help.

The church has many elder members. There is a strong sense of resistance to change among some of these members (Diamond, 2008), as well as resentment that the existing building would have to be sold to fund the new one. Even the routine transferring of pastors into and out of the church can be quite unsettling for a while. Financially, many members do not donate in amounts commensurate with their incomes. They do not even approach tithing (giving 10% of net income). Members who attended church in the second location but now are brought into the main congregation at the original location have a history of low or no monetary donations. They also have a history of non-volunteerism.

ANALYSIS

Strategic management at the church consists of a senior pastor, an associate pastorand the volunteer chairpersons of several church committees. These are all key positions within the church and are critical to running an efficient operation. Church members attend services and activities in order to fulfil a spiritual need; the strategic managers are critical to helping members fulfil that need (Bommer, Rich and Rubin, 2005).

Formal leaders for this denomination are separated between management of business activities and management of spiritual activities. Leaders for both areas over the past 20 years have demonstrated a transformational stewardship style (Kee,

Newcomer, & Davis, 2006). Transformational stewardship reflects the leader's personal beliefs, approach to situations, involvement of followers, and commitment to change and innovation (2006, pg.7). According to Curry (2002), adult identity development is transferred from leaders to the followers in the organization, and the organization's identity influences the leadership style exhibited by the leaders. Transformational stewardship, then, depending on the success of its implementation, can propel people and organizations into very specific courses of action.

Kelley (Flower, 1991) tells us that the majority of followers fall into five types. The largest is a group called Pragmatic Survivors. These are individuals who don't commit to action until they see what is most popular with the rest of the organization. Exemplary Followers are critical thinkers, initiate change, and chance some risk in order to attain a goal; this group comprises 10 to 20% of the followers. This type of followers appeared in the early days of this church, with a few Pragmatic Survivors. A Passive Follower shows no initiative and is usually the result of aggressive leadership. This style was reflected when the various town hall meetings were called for the purpose of voting on actions that affected the entire congregation. Less than half of the registered members participated in any of the three voting opportunities. The Conformist Followers are those who go along with the majority in order to avoid conflict. This style is evident during the tenures of all five pastors. Alienated Followers are effective followers who have been disillusioned or let down and focus exclusively on the shortcoming of a situation, idea, or organization. This style is most evident toward the later part of this church's lifespan, although the quantity of followers exhibiting this style is minimal. These are the followers who mostly began as Exemplary Followers, but through a breakdown in execution of transformational stewardship, either intentional or unintentional, have adopted these characteristics.

In 2010, the Senior Pastor who was present during the relocation activities was reassigned to another district as a District Superintendent to expand church membership in a neighbouring multi-county area. By increasing membership 300% over a period of more than 14 years, this Pastor catapulted the church into the largest church of its denomination between Los Angeles and Kansas City. Although non-profit organizations have no standard for measuring effectiveness (Herman & Renz, 1999), it became evident through this promotion and transfer that numbers are at least one measure of success for religious non-profits of this denomination.

IMPLICATIONS

Communication was one of the main underlying problems. When the church membership voted 74% to 26% to relocate, no pastor or other church leader attempted to discover why 26% voted not to relocate. Leadership assumed majority ruled, and they could conveniently ignore the 26%. Church leaders also assumed the 26% would change their minds once they saw they were in the minority, although no attempt was made to discern what would change the minds of these people (Natemeyer &

Hersey, 2011; Seidman & McCauley, 2011).Some of that 26% formed immediately into the vocal negative group and began undermining the relocation effort. One person stated 'They will never get us out of this building.'

CONCLUSION

Previous formal and informal church leaders initiated a massive and risky change (i.e., the relocation effort) through a belief in the ability of the community of faith to pull together and support this undertaking. The relocation project, because it was under the auspices of a religious non-profit organization, was perceived to be above reproach so far as motives and ethical behaviour by all concerned (Pinnington, 2011).These leaders were able to influence the majority of the church membership in this belief of group efficacy (Pescosolido, 2001)because they had been influenced by formal leaders in whom they had implicit trust. Continued erosion by the vocal minority, and continued erosion of the members' faith in the leadership and its ability to accomplish the relocation and the supporting financial challenges was manifested by decreased volunteerism, declining attendance and membership, and severely diminished contributions. The resulting resistance to change, albeit by a minority, became divisive to the completion of the task (Armenakis, Harris, & Mossholder, 1993). The organization's apparent disregard for the opinions of one quarter of the membership in making decisions that culturally and financially affect the entire body quickly created a schism that has yet to be repaired (De Dreu & West, 2001).The lack of perceived fair process (Seidman & McCauley, 2011) continues to handicap changes that have been undertaken to repair the goodwill and trust of the congregation.

REFERENCES

Armenakis, A.A., Harris, S.G., and Mossholder, K.W. (1993). Creating readiness for organizational change. Human Relations, 46(6), pp. 681-703.

Avey, J. B., Hughes, L. W., Norman, S. M., & Luthans, K. W. (2007). Using positivity, transformational leadership and empowerment to combat employee negativity.

Bommer, W. H., Rich, G. A., & Rubin, R. S. (2005). Changing attitudes about change: longitudinal effects of transformational leader behavior on employee cynicism about organizational change. Journal of Organizational Behavior, 26(7), 733-753. doi: 10.1002/job.342

Bridges, William (2003). Managing Transitions, Second Edition. Cambridge, MA: Da Capo.

Baker, Susan D. (2007). Followership: The Theoretical Foundation of a Contemporary Construct. Journal of Leadership and Organizational Studies, 14:50.

Corley, Kevin G. (2004).Defined by our strategy or our culture? Hierarchical differences in perceptions of organizational identity and change. Human Relations, 57(9) 1145-1177.

Curry, Barbara K. (2002). The Influence of the Leader Persona on Organizational Identity. Journal of Leadership & Organizational Studies, 8:33.

De Dreu, C.K. and West, M.A. (2001). Minority dissent and team innovation: the importance of participation in decision making. Journal of Applied Psychology, 86(6), pp. 1191-1201.

Diamond, Michael A. (2008).Telling them what they know: organizational change, defensive resistance, and the unthought known. The Journal of Applied Behavioral Science, 44(3), 348-364.

Flower, Joe (1991). The Art and Craft of Followership. Healthcare Forum Journal, Jan/Feb 1991; 34,1.

Herman, Robert D., & Renz, David O. (1999). Theses on Nonprofit Organizational Effectiveness. Nonprofit and Voluntary Sector Quarterly, 1999 28:107.

Kirkman, B., & Shapiro, D. (1997). The impact of cultural values on employee resistance to teams: toward a model of globalized self-managing work team effectiveness. Academy of Management Review, 22(3), 730-757.

History of (name withheld for confidentiality reasons). (2012). About Us page. Retrieved March 16, 2012, from (name withheld for confidentiality reasons)Church Web site: http://www.(name withheld).com/about-us

Kee, James E., Newcomer, Kathryn, & Davis, Mike (2006). A New Vision for Public Leadership: The Case for Developing Transformational Stewards. The Center for Innovation in Public Service, Working Paper #4, The George Washington University School of Public Policy and Public Administration, and BearingPoint, Inc.

Natemeyer, W. E. & Hersey, P. (Ed.) (2011). Classics of Organizational Behavior (4th ed.). Long Grove, IL: Waveland Press, Inc.

New York Annual Conference, The United Methodist Church (2012). Home Page. Retrieved September 3, 2012 from http://www.nyac.com/site/search?controller=&keywords =discernment

Ogden, J. & Hills, L., (2008). Understanding sustained behavior change: the role of life crisis and the process of reinvention. Health: An Interdisciplinary Journal for the Social Study of Health, Illness and Medicine, 12(4), 419-447. Los Angeles, CA: Sage.

Pescosolido, A.T. (2001). Informal leaders and the development of group efficacy. Small Group Research, 32 (1), pp. 74-93.

Pederit, S.K.(2000). Rethinking resistance and recognizing ambivalence: a multidimensional view of attitudes toward an organizational change. Academy of Management Review, 25(4), 783-794.

Pinnington, Ashley H. (2011). Leadership Development: Applying the Same Leadership Theories and Development Practices to Different Contexts? Leadership 2011 7:335.

Seidman, W. and McCauley, M. (2011). Transformational leadership in a transactional world. OD Practitioner, 43(2), pp. 46-51.

United Methodist Church (2012). Home Page. Retrieved September 3, 2012 from http://www.umc.org/site/c.lwL4KnN1LtH/b.1720699/k.528D/Structure__Organization_ Governance.htm

Perspectives of Charismatic Leadership

*Ronald Newton**

ABSTRACT

This study explores the theory and characteristics of charismatic leadership behavior, with objectives of determining effects of charismatic leaders on different fields and backgrounds. The objective of this case study is to examine and provide perspectives of transformational leaders through their understanding of existing charismatic leadership behavior. Primary and secondary sources on charismatic leaders from diverse fields and backgrounds analyzed qualitatively and themes relevant to this study determined. This study reveals that charismatic leaders have different perspectives and characteristics that play a major role in enhancing the relationship between followers and the leader. Their ability to provide visionary leadership to gain the confidence of the followers is one of the most distinct leadership traits of the charismatic leader.

Keywords: Charismatic leadership, leadership theory, motivation.

INTRODUCTION

Volumes of empirical leadership cases in every discipline imaginable support leadership theory. Hunt (1996) provides "A new synthesis" or an expanded view of various leadership theory based on an open-minded aspect to both the knowledge content and knowledge approach toward leadership. Bass(2008, p.11) indicates "… there are almost as many different definitions of leadership as there are persons who have attempted to define the concept". Charismatic leaders are people distinguished by dominance, self-confidence, their need to influence, and by their strong conviction in their beliefs. Charismatic leaders appeal to the emotions of their followers by energizing their need for achievement, affiliation, and quest for power. By motivating task accomplishment, high expectations from followers can be displayed leading to results (Hunt, 1996).

* Colorado Technical University Colorado Springs, CO, USA.
E-mail: ronjnewton@hotmail.com

Charismatic leadership has been the subject of considerable research for the past two decades, a trend that informed by realization of the critical role that the leadership style plays in success or failure of organizations. Researchers have conducted numerous studies investigating the distinguishing characteristics and behaviors of charismatic leaders from other leadership styles. According to Bass (2008, p. 69), people follow charismatic leaders because they are "considered extraordinary, possessing exceptional powers and qualities that are uncharacteristic of the ordinary human being". Similarly, charismatic leadership is based on the reverence and unwavering commitment that the charismatic leader commands from the followers (Clark, & David, 2011; Murphy, & Ensher, 2008).

ISSUES

In spite of the voluminous studies on charismatic leadership, researchers have yet to come up with universally acceptable criteria outlining characteristics and behaviors of charismatic leaders. The case study reviewed here examines the perspectives of charismatic and non-charismatic leadership behavior. Interviews with leaders managing various operations, driven by strict schedule performance are analyzed to obtain information about their recognized use and the effects of charismatic leadership. This study explores the theory and perspectives of the charismatic leader, with the objectives of recognizing their influence on the attainment of targeted results.

CONTRIBUTIONS

Since Max Weber introduced the concept of charismatic leadership in the early twentieth century, it has been subjected to intense investigations by different scholars from diverse fields and applied in various circumstances as well. Initially, charismatic leadership theory focused on religious, political and military organizations but it has since expanded to encompass diverse segments in the contemporary management practices (Waldman, Javidan, & Varella, 2004). The major principle of charismatic theory is founded on the influence that the leader has on his or her followers in promoting positive results such as enhancing their motivation, productivity, dedication and job satisfaction (Annebel et al, 2005; Mumford, 2006). Thus, charismatic leadership is applied by diverse leaders in different fields to attain targeted strategic goals.

Various researchers on leadership agree that certain personal characteristics and behaviors are essential for developing charismatic leadership style (Sosik, John, & Chun, 2011: Mumford, 2006; Clark, & David, 2011). Bass (2008) identified self-image and self-presentation as the two major characteristic elements necessary for developing a charismatic image. According to Bass (2008, p.143), self-image is "the manner in which an individual perceives herself or himself in terms of appropriate identities, characteristics or features". From this perspective, charismatic leaders view themselves capable of inspiring others;while non-charismatic do not perceive this element as a component of their identity. A charismatic leader should be self presentable (Murphy & Ensher, 2008; Bass, 2008). This implies that he or she should control or regulate their identity so that they can be in a position to influence their followers and achieve the intended objectives. However, these characteristics are not limited to charismatic leaders alone. Mumford (2006) argued that charismatic leadership is a relationship between the leader and the followers established on the behavior of the leader and accompanied by favorable reactions from the followers. From this definition, Mumford (2006) indentified several major behaviors and traits the leader should possess to inspire followers. These include offering followers a clear sense of direction and coherent articulation of an inspiring future oriented vision. Moreover, charismatic leaders demonstrate remarkable persistence in pursuit of their goals and they anticipate high performance from their followers. On the other hand, followers should have confidence on the leader's ability and demonstrate unwavering respect and loyalty (Mumford, 2006; Annebel, et al, 2005; Waldman, Javidan, & Varella, 2004).

Certain behaviors distinguish charismatic leaders from their non-charismatic counterparts. Charismatic leaders demonstrate high levels of self-confidence, enthusiasm and creativity in addition to being focused on attaining their goals. Moreover, charismatic leaders demonstrate high social responsibility to people and they are also motivated by desire to gain social influence (Sosik, John, & Chun, 2011; Mumford, 2006; Campbell, et al, 2008). These behaviors are conspicuously absent in non-charismatic leaders. In addition, charismatic leaders are orderly during crisis and they focus on future oriented goals. Campbell et al (2008)summarized characteristics demonstrated by charismatic leaders into six behaviors, namely strategic vision accompanied by excellent expression, being sensitive to the environment, high propensity to take personal risks, and they are also sensitive to the needs of their followers. In addition, they demonstrate conspicuous deviation from the established or recognized order of doing things (Campbell et al 2008).

Charismatic leaders and their behaviors arouse followers. Over the last 20 years, a new genre of organizational leadership theories have surfaced as transformational, inspirational and charismatic (Howell, 2005).Charismatic leadership in organizational settings has undergone a significant evolution in terms of both theory development and empirical investigations. As a result, transformational leadership knowledge forms have expanded resulting ingoverning theories that are in use as leadership paradigms in the management field. At the same time as new theories develop, there are several unique transformational leadership perspectives evolving that we know little about. Theories of charismatic leadership have been promoting a heroic leadership influence by depicting leaders as results- minded heroes in many organizations and companies. Reviewing the theoretical convergence of empirical data from Hunt (1996) et al, this genre of leadership theory is considered "charismatic leadership" (Howell, 2005).

Because of their distinctive relationship with followers, charismatic leaders can be influential agents of organizational change and progress. Many theories discussed by Hunt (1996) of charismatic leadership have stressed the personality traits and behavior of charismatic leaders and their influence over followers. This interaction can be very powerful in transforming and managing change.

Hunt (1996) indicates that a large amount of the charismatic literature clearly argues that there must be a crisis situation for charismatic leadership to be established. Hunt (1996) cites Bass, et al with literature supporting a crisis as opportunities needed to foster charismatic leadership. The belief here is that for transformationally oriented leaders to perform there must be some relationship to a crisis versus a vision (Hunt, 1996). Hunt (1996) further provides that research provide two different types of charismatic leadership applications, induced by visionary and crisis situations. The *visionary* approach begins with an idea or vision and is furthered into action by the charismatic leader. In contrast, *crisis* induced charismatic leadership is developed as a solution to a situation. Creating or heightening correspondences between the leader and follower enhances the emotions and need for performance. While many leadership opportunities relate to a problem or something out of the ordinary, the application of charismatic leadership behavior in these situations is somewhat subjective and likely in need of further research.

Followers who share a charismatic bond with a leader are prepared to rise above their self-interests for the sake of the organization or purpose. By engaging in altruism for the concern of the corporate vision, and to accommodate the mission by the leader, a solid emotional connection to the leader's values and goals are produced by the follower (Howell, 2005). In a theoretical analysis of the follower's function in the charismatic leadership process, Jane Howell and Boas Shamir (2005) distinguish between two types of charismatic follower roles, *personalized* and *socialized*. In the *personalized* role, the followers are confused and uncertain of their responsibilities before entering the relationship with the charismatic leader. Here the charismatic leader provides a sense of purpose and greater self-confidence to the follower. This category of follower is most dependent on the leader and vulnerable to fulfill a need. This personalized follower relationship to the charismatic leader is based on a personal identification "with" the leader rather than an acceptance to the leader's vision. The *socialized* relationship between followers and a charismatic leader is based on a clear sense of the follower's identity and values. Here the socialized followers express their own important ideals within the structure of a collective, organizational, action. Followers in the socialized relationship participate in an active role in determining the values expressed by the leader, are less dependent on the leader, and are less open to manipulation by the charismatic leader (Howell, 2005).

Charismatic leaders motivate followers by exciting their abilities, shaping their aspirations and directing their energy toward the leader's view. Charismatic leadership theories focus on effective leaders who have exceptional effects on their followers and on social systems. Furthermore, they influence followers to become highly committed to the leader's mission by going above and beyond the normal call for duty. Theories of charismatic leadership highlight effects of emotional attachment to the leader on part of the followers through emotion, self-esteem and purpose (Shamir, 1993).

Charisma is a central concept used by leaders and followers either explicitly or implicitly. Unfortunately, charismatic leadership ability is often not seen as an existing character, ability or behavior pattern by presumably average leaders or followers. Many studies focus on known charismatic leaders but these studies fail to examine whether average leaders exhibit charismatic leadership behaviors on a routine basis or whether they believe themselves to be charismatic leaders. Clearly, more field research is needed to determine if charismatic leadership styles and behaviors exist and recognized by leaders with routine leadership roles. Once determined, a greater awareness may be placed on charismatic leadership principles as a recognized management tool for the leader.

NEED FOR STUDY

Numerous research studies have established that charismatic leaders influence their followers by inspiring and motivating them to become active participants. In addition, they instill a sense of purpose to previously disillusioned or dispirited followers, which spur them to take collective action (Bass, 2008). However, research on the effects of a charismatic leader on followers in diverse fields and backgrounds is scant. This case investigated the effects of charismatic leaders in various fields and their influence in achieving success in the respective operations.

RESEARCH METHODOLOGY

The objective of this case study was to examine the perspectives of transformational leaders through their understanding of existing charismatic leadership behavior. To collect the data, secondary sources on charismatic leaders from diverse fields and backgrounds were analyzed qualitatively and themes relevant to this study are determined. In addition, ten leaders took the opportunity to participate in this research. These leaders, chosen at random, have experience in leading operations where schedule performance is mandatory. This method was suitable for the case study because it combines the voluminous research studies available about charismatic leadership and its effects on followers and a society. The main secondary sources applied in the study were scholarly and peer reviewed journals about different charismatic leaders in the world.

Semi-structured interviews were conducted as a method for this study. Ten interviews were conducted and provided from leaders in operational management. These interviews supplied qualitative data to analyze and further report. An inductively based qualitative interview approach was used to recognize the use of transformational "charismatic leadership" by leaders. The option of a grounded study was not chosen here since the purpose was not to build theory but rather to evaluate the use of an existing leadership perspective.

A questionnaire consisting of six questions (Appendix A), designed for this case study, based on empirical charismatic leadership research and familiar leadership perspectives was used as part of an interview instrument for this study. The questionnaire reflects leadership principles of Hunt (1996), and research concerning charismatic leadership. The qualifications of participants were that each must have leadership experience in a schedule driven operation. The participants were invited exclusively for the conduct of this interview. The set of six interview questions were sent to the participants before the interview with an introduction and general explanation of charismatic leadership including references to House (1977), Hunt (1996), and Burns(1978).

RESULTS

DESCRIPTION OF HOW RESULTS WILL BE ORGANIZED

All participants responded to the same six questions. The information collected from each participant compiled and categorized by each question related to the subject as follows.

1. *Description of work the leader is involved in.* All the leaders interviewed in this study live in the United States and perform in a schedule driven manufacturing environment as follows:

- Production Operations Manager (5 interviewed)
- Operations President (4 interviewed)
- Supply chain Manager (1 interviewed)

2. *Describe a routine situation in which you demonstrate charismatic (transformational) leadership behavior.* When the participants described examples of their charismatic leadership behavior it led to an association of empowering their followers to meet their vision as a charismatic leader. The following behavior attributes revealed: humor, common goals, daily reviews, migrating to something new, enabling motions.

3. *The percentage of charismatic leadership traits you routinely apply.* All participants routinely apply charismatic leadership traits to lead others on a daily basis. Most recognized the need to "turn-off" this behavior during personal lulls and a need for quiet-time to re energize their charismatic leadership behavior.

4. *Do you believe charismatic leadership behavior can be learned? Explain.* All participants believe that everyone can learn charismatic leadership behavior. The answers here indicated that people in general are born with charismatic leadership traits as attributes or tools that can be developed and put to use based on the leader's desire to hone them.

5. *Do you consider yourself a charismatic visionary who leads ideas into action or a crisis-induced charismatic leader who develops solutions for crisis?*

All participants thought deeply about their response before answering. The majority indicated they considered themselves primarily to be a charismatic visionary who charismatically leads others to a planned goal or vision. One participant indicated over 90 percent of leadership behavior is spent on developing solutions to crisis or supported a crisis situation outside of normal.

6. *Do you ever use non-verbal charismatic leadership tactics such as body gestures or facial expressions to lead others? Identify examples.*

Most participants indicated they use non-verbal charismatic leadership tactics to lead others. One participant indicated never. The rationale to intentionally never use non-verbal was to avoid sending mixed messages to followers. Examples of those who use non-verbal charismatic leadership tactics include facial expressions such as smiles or frowns, handshakes, pats on the back, slight physical contact to reassure direction.

Summary of Survey Results

Leader (Participant)	Demonstrate Routine Charismatic Leadership	Daily use of Charismatic Leadership Behavior	Can char-Ismatic Leadership be Learned	Charismatic Leadership Usage: Vision / Crisis	Non-verbal Charismatic Leadership Tactics *
1	Yes	70%	Yes	Visionary	Yes
2	Yes	75%	Yes	Visionary	Yes
3	Yes	90%	Yes	Crisis	Yes
4	Yes	50%	Yes	Visionary	No
5	Yes	30%	Yes	51 / 49	Yes
6	Yes	45%	Yes	Crisis	Yes
7	Yes	50%	Yes	50 / 50	Yes
8	Yes	50%	Yes	Visionary	Yes
9	Yes	50%	Yes	Visionary	Yes
10	Yes	45%	Yes	Crisis	Yes
*Note: Virtual leadership roles limit the ability of non-verbal leadership tactics.					

Implications from this analysis provide further understanding of a leadership theory that engages personal and social emotion from the follower. Most respondents did not consider themselves a charismatic leader or having a charismatic behavior until they understood further the transactional leadership dimensions associated. This data is a new insight or deepens the leadership perspective concerning charismatic leadership theory. Hunt (1996) reminds us that regardless of the questions asked, there are likely implicit theories that appear in our responses. "Once again, we are reminded that it is wise not to treat questionnaires as if they reflect objective reality" (Hunt, 1996, p214).

DIAGNOSIS AND ANALYSIS

In a research study investigating charismatic leadership at strategic level, Waldman, Javidan, andVarella(2004) noted that charismatic leadership in corporate sector enhance teamwork and cohesion among members indentifying with the vision of the charismatic leader. By investigating charismatic leaders of several successful American firms such as Walt Disney, General Electric, and the Triumph Group, the researchers noted that their influence promoted team cohesion among senior level employees and junior workers. Annebel, et al (2005) investigated the effects of charismatic leader on performance of corporate organizations and noted that their innovation and propensity to take risks, especially during crisis enhanced survival and performance of the organization. In another study Clark and David (2011) observed that excellent oratorical skills, with visionary orientation as a major character of charismatic leader. The skill enhanced interaction between the leader and the audience. This promoted unity among followers and increased the influence of the leader to the masses, enhancing attainment of intended goals. Clark and David (2011) concluded that excellent oratory skills was one of the major influential charismatic attributes in careers such as politics and others related to public speaking and engagements.

RECOMMENDATIONS

Extensive research studies have examined behaviors and characteristics of charismatic leaders in different fields. Although they have come up with some diverse findings, the studies indicate that the character and personality of charismatic leaders enhance their interaction with the followers. However, more research studies will determine the implications of the enhanced leader-follower relationship on attainment of the intended organization's goals.

CONCLUSION

Charismatic leadership plays a major role in enhancing the relationship between followers and the leader, which is an important element in promoting teamwork and motivation in an organization. Although charismatic leaders have different perspectives and characters, their ability to provide visionary leadership to gain the confidence of the followers is one of the most distinct traits that distinguish them from others using different leadership styles.

The contribution from this study reveals a new insight or deepens the leadership perspective concerning charismatic leadership theory. Most leaders interviewed did not recognize their use of charismatic leadership principles until they understood more about their own leadership perspectives. This new insight could help future development of charismatic leadership theory by identifying behavior, observations, and insights from charismatic leaders. This information serves to address prominent issues about transformational leadership from actual leaders, which could provide as new direction for future studies and further empirical research. The findings presented here represent areas that transformational leaders should consider in their leadership behavior. In additional to practical knowledge, this information can be used for developing leadership-training material for charismatic leaders to successfully develop their leadership skills.

REFERENCES

Antonakis, J., (2011). Can charisma be taught? Tests of two interventions. *Academy of Management Learning & Education,* 10(3) 374-396.

Annebel, H., et al.(2005). Leader motives, charismatic leadership and subordinates work attitude in the profit and voluntary sector. *The Leadership Quarterly,* 16, 17-38.

Bass, M.(2008). *Handbook of leadership.* New York: Free Press.

Burns, J., (1978). *Leadership.* New York, NY: Harper & Row.

Clark, T., & David, G.(2011). Audience perception of charismatic and non-charismatic oratory: The case of management gurus. *The Leadership Quarterly,* 22, 22-32.

Heifetz, R., Grashow, A., & Linsky, M. (2009). *The practice of adaptive leadership: Tools and tactics for changing your organization and the world.* Boston, MA: Harvard Business Press.

House, R., (1977). *Theory of charismatic leadership.*Carbondale, IL: Southern Illinois University Press.

Howell, J., (2005). The role of followers in the charismatic leadership process: Relations and their consequences. *Academy of Management Review, 30*(1), 96-112.

Hunt, J.G. (1996). *Leadership: A new synthesis.* Newbury Park, CA: Sage Publications.

Livingston, R., (2011). MGMT_845_REL_Syllabus_OCT2011Final, Colorado Technical University, Doctor of Management (Online) Program, Colorado Springs, Co.

Mumford, M.(2006). *Pathways to outstanding leadership; A comparative analysis of charismatic, ideological and pragmatic leadership.* Mahwah, NJ: Erlbaum Press.

Murphy, S., & Ensher, E.(2008). A qualitative analysis of charismatic leadership in creative teams: The case of television directors. *The Leadership Quarterly,* 19, 335-352.

Shamir, B., (1993). The motivational effects of charismatic leadership: A self-concept based theory. *Organizational Science,* 4(4), 577-594.

Sosik, J., John, J., & Chun, J.(2011). Effects of moral reasoning and management level on ratings of charismatic leadership, in role and extra role performance of managers: A multi-source examination. *The Leadership Quarterly,* 22, 434-450.

Waldman, D., Javidan, M., & Varella, P.(2004). Charismatic leadership at the strategic level: Anew application of upper echelons theory. *The Leadership Quarterly,* 15: 355-380.

APPENDIX A: CHARISMATIC FIELD INTERVIEW QUESTIONS

"Transformational leadership is a theory where leaders and followers raise one another to higher levels of morality and motivation" (Burns, 1978, p.20). Charismatic leaders have their greatest effects on the follower's emotions. A charismatic leader seeks to satisfy the follower's needs by stimulating the follower's emotions and elevating the follower's relationship to the leader's level (Hunt, 1996). The following questions serve for interviewing leaders who include charismatic leadership behavior and theory as part of their leadership tactics.

1. Description of work the leader is involved in.
2. Describe a routine situation in which you demonstrate charismatic (transformational) leadership behavior.
3. The percentage of charismatic leadership traits you routinely apply.
4. Do you believe charismatic leadership behavior can be learned? Explain.
5. Do you consider yourself a charismatic visionary who leads ideas into action or a crisis-induced charismatic leader who develops solutions for crisis?
6. Do you ever use non-verbal charismatic leadership tactics such as body gestures or facial expressions to lead others? Identify examples.

Forging the ABCs in Graduate International Programs: Team Performance and Leadership Development

Daphne D. DePorres* and Monty G. Miller**

ABSTRACT

International student programs provide opportunities to learn about new cultures, see different paradigms in action, and find practical applications for the knowledge and skills through experiential learning as students prepare for global leadership and managerial roles. During international programs, learners often conduct projects in teams, often experiencing significant inter and intrapersonal conflict prompted by being in an unfamiliar environment and culture. This paper provides ten steps faculty may use to build and reinforce the attitudes, behaviours, and commitments (ABCs) that support both learning and successful projects while students participate in international programs. A survey is conducted and findings shared on the frequency a sample of experienced faculty historically use the ten steps.

Keywords: International programs, Interpersonal conflict, Intrapersonal conflict, "Use of self".

INTRODUCTION

As co-author, I experienced this first hand at 18 years of age, as a Rotary Exchange student in Brazil in 1974-75. For a very independent, only child from a farm in eastern Colorado, being accepted into my first Brazilian family was a life changing experience, truly a pivotal moment in my life. Speaking only one word of Portuguese and not even pronouncing "no" correctly, "nao" was challenging, and I was homesick for my culture. After two weeks, I had significant "cabin fever" and needed to regain some independence. My mother in my first Brazilian family arranged for me to meet my

---

* Colorado Technical University, Colorado Springs, Colorado.

**Colorado Technical University & International Performance Solutions.

E-mail: ddeporres@coloradotech.edu, monty@ipsltd.inf.

first Brazilian father at his office in downtown Belo Horizonte, a city of more than a million people. Mind you, my community in Colorado had a population of 2,500. I needed to take three different buses to get from home to my Brazilian father's office and I was game. As I headed out the door, Brazilian Mom pinned a note on my shirt in case I got lost, disoriented, or killed (lord knows why). Here I was, 18 years old and had driven tractors since the age of five, but if this was the price of freedom, so be it! What I learned in that year changed my life forever and has impacted all the people in my sphere of influence. As a result of this experience, I coined the phrase, "My Being Is Bigger Than Me."

How often do we think of ourselves as simply the physical bodies that our minds occupy? Our influence is so much larger than we realize, in terms of our ability to have a positive or negative impact on others. Moving our "being" beyond our human frame is advanced with conversations, presentations, phone calls, emails, publications and now social media. In a matter of minutes, thousands in cultures far beyond our own can perceive us positively or negatively.

Accompanying students to study in foreign environments, if properly executed, has significant ramifications of understanding self in a new and different context that may be otherwise never realized if one stays in the comforts of their primary culture. However, diligent and candid coaching is required for this understanding to emerge, which can be challenging. How introspective do people want to be, when experiencing a world into which they have been newly dropped? This is especially relevant when there are the rigors of time zone changes, food change, creature comfort changes and there is a project to do on top of it all. It is a challenge, but a must if the students are to maximize learning and the project is to be of value to the cooperators.

INTERNATIONAL PROGRAMS

International student programs provide short-term opportunities to learn about new cultures, see different paradigms in action, and find practical applications for knowledge and skills through experiential learning, as students prepare for global leadership and managerial roles. During international programs, learners often conduct projects in teams. These teams must stay on task and create value for clients, even when they are challenged by being in an unfamiliar environment and culture. Faculty who facilitate these programs often find they are called to reinforce the desired attitudes, behaviours and commitments (ABCs) needed for team compatibility, function and success. This paper addresses a method faculty can use to build and reinforce the ABCs that support both learning and successful projects, while students participate in international programs. For the conclusion to the paper, we surveyed seven faculty acquaintances, who have taken students on international study/action research projects to learn their utilization of the ABCs.

The authors have significant experience working with graduate students to not only improve their effectiveness in their current leadership and managerial roles, but to prepare them for future roles on a global stage. Through their work with two very different universities in North America, the authors have facilitated short-term international programs in which students engage in actual projects with real clients and undergo personal and professional development. This article focuses on the development of the student's ABCs within a project team while executing a project in-country.

THE CASE FOR THE ABCs

A common assumption is that global leaders must have knowledge about how other cultures function in order to operate competently within a culture. It is true that needed Leadership styles transcend national boundaries and encompass non-linear thinking (Mishra and Mohapatra, 2010).However, while cultural knowledge is an important dimension of the global leader's repertoire, the leader's own self-awareness is equally important (Goodman, 2009). Leaders who are able to function effectively with the demands of the global environment and the necessity for actionable self-awareness in response to the unfamiliar are valuable, yet not commonly found (Kok-Yee, Dyne, and Soon, 2009).

Although the term "leader" is understood in various styles across cultures (Steers, Sanchez-Runde, and Nardon, 2012), leadership effectiveness, as discussed by Elmuti, Minnis and Abede (2005), requires an "inner locus of control." Thus, it is incumbent upon the faculty to reinforce desired attitudes, behavioursand commitments (ABCs) and ensure that students take full advantage of the learning opportunities associated with performing as consultants to organizations outside their own culture. Faculty must also reinforce students' development, both personally and professionally, as leaders and managers through awareness and conscious choice, related to how they self-manage when in the global field.

Thus, graduate level management students will find themselves in an enviable position if they acquire the skills and competencies to lead in a global environment, especially as it concerns the critical ability to be self-aware and to act on their self-awareness. However, Pless, Maak, and Stahl (2011) point out the dearth of models that can be used to help leaders gain important competencies such as self-awareness. The authors propose a mechanism for graduate students to develop the skills and competencies needed to lead and manage within a global environment,while participating in international programs.

The fact that students are in a different environment than their day-to-day exacerbates the challenges of performing as a team, where the team must stay on task and create value for clients, fulfilling agreements established with their clients. The authors have found this is often a challenge for students, whose focus and ability to function as high performing individuals in a high performing team is challenged when virtually everything around them differs from their usual routines.

RELEVANT CONCEPTS

Three Theoretical constructs lend themselves to the ABC approach: Self Leadership, "Self as Instrument of Change" and Emotional Intelligence. With these constructs in mind, the authors integrate their experience in facilitating international programs and present a ten-step process we have both used during student international experiences.

Emotional Intelligence: A recent article in Forbes points out that only 15 percent of a person's success is due to technical skills born of a traditional understanding of intelligence, while 85 percent is due to other factors(Jensen, 2012). Given that traditional forms of intelligence may not be the most significant determinants of managerial and/or leadership success, it would be prudent to explore the other side of the coin. Emotional Intelligence (EI) is considered a type of intelligence through which a person who possesses it has the facility to recognize and interpret his own emotions and feelings, as well as the emotions and feelings of others, and to incorporate this knowledge as he chooses how to think and act (Law, Chi-Sum and Song, 2004). As leaders exercise their EI, they are able to better lead, foster teamwork and enhance job performance (Chopra and Kanji, 2010). Team members with high EI are able to foster positive interactions and trust amongst the team, which supports the successful execution of tasks (Chang, Sy, and Choi, 2011).

Self as Instrument: A construct in which one's entire being impacts effectiveness through the management of self. Highlights include self-awareness, giving and receiving feedback, and paying close attention to group dynamics (Jamieson, Auron, and Shectman, 2011).

Self-Leadership: An internally driven motivation to influence oneself to perform via awareness and navigation of beliefs and ways of thinking (Stewart, Courtright and Manz, 2010). Similarly, self-leadership is the process through which persons consciously execute their thinking and actions for the purpose of achieving greater effectiveness in their endeavors (D'Itino, Goldsby, Houghton, & Neck, 2007). Manz (1991) noted that everyone practices self-leadership to some extent, for example, but that not everyone is effective in this practice. Yet, he asserts that self-leadership can be developed.

INTERNATIONAL PROGRAMS

Gosling and Mintzberg (2004) advocate the position that managers not only realize self-development (and the attendant benefits) as a result of their participation in programs that feature it, but should embrace the responsibility to diffuse this learning into his or her environment. Gosling and Mintzberg (2004) argue that the opportunities and issues that managers face in business are not presented in tidy packages, with the educational equivalent being the course. They posit that management education should oscillate between theory and practice, linked by reflection. Mintzberg (2011) shares, "When you slow down, reflect, and take stock, and when you truly meet yourself, you can see past the pressures of managing and thus become able to function less frenetically and more effectively."

This article discusses how faculty has attempted to integrate this approach into our real-time experiences with students as we have worked in international settings. Learners may obtain feedback from either their own observations or from the environment. While this article discusses the interactions between the faculty and the learner, the learner is encouraged and expected to do his or her part.

Self-observation is thus an important feedback mechanism. Self-observation leads to self-awareness as the learner focuses on when, why and how they exhibit behaviours. The resulting self-awareness can be utilized to facilitate deconstructing or changing behaviours that are not effective (D'Itino, Goldsby, Houghton, & Neck, 2007). Building the capacities that enable both leadership, on a grand scale, and effectiveness in a team setting on a more localized scale, international programsare a significant development opportunity. Cameron and Quinn (1999) state, "Unfortunately, people are unaware of their culture until it is challenged, until they experience a new culture, or until it is made overt and explicit through, for example, a framework or model." International programs provide a unique framework of building greater facility with the ABCs.

THE ABCs

The authors have experienced situations when mature students, who are quite effective in their home culture, propagate heightened team and interpersonal conflict during an international program, disrupting the program and projects as well as souring the experience for all participants, faculty included. Tensions rise as negative comments or problematic interactions limit the ability of the team to perform successfully and achieve desired ends (Sinha, 2011).

The basic question is, how do the faculty and students effectively handle the conflicts and ensure that the project is completed, resulting in creation of a positive learning experience for all? We like to say, "Nip it in the bud!"but how do we accomplish this feat?When there are any indications of conflict, don't assume it will work itself out. Don't assume mature adults will find the common ground to inspire their work and overlook their differences. If it happens, great! If it doesn't happen, the conflict may have serious and disruptive consequences for everyone involved. In the Tuckman model of small group development, we should expect some degree of "storming," characterized by "lack of unity and polarization around interpersonal issues," before the group norms and begins to perform. Hence, our ability to perform effectively during an international program starts before the experience at beginning of the quarter. Below are steps we believe to be helpful when creating a positive environment for learning and a collaborative team to provide benefits to clients:

Step 1: Project: Establishing clarity about the proposed project. Students and faculty must clarify the who, what, when and where of the international program. What is the opportunity and scope of the project? What are the project deliverables? What is the culture we will experience? What do we know about the people with whom we will interact? What is it going to cost? What do individuals pay for and what does the institution pay for? What are the deliverables and expectations of the students? What are the timeframes for accomplishing the tasks? How will the students lead the effort and how will the facility support the effort? Many details need to be addressed and action plans created.

Step 2: Team: Build the Team before departure. Basic team building needs to be conducted where participants are given an opportunity to appreciate the experiences, talents, competencies, world views and nuances of each person involved in the project. By exposing as many aspects of the self as possible early in the process, in a relatively non-stressful environment (the home culture), the team builds a foundation that will allow it to withstand the rigors and challenges of foreign travel while being expected to perform. At a minimum, the team will develop mutual understandings that indicate, "We can agree to disagree."

One method of team building that has shown to be effective, and can be performed in a virtual environment, is for each person to create his or her life story, represented as a trail, pathway or journey. On paper, the team members capture their pathway's zigs and zags, high points, low points and learning. We couple this with an introspective assessment of sensory and cognitive preferences and have participants tie their preferences to life events. All participants will begin to realize that many of our life choices and events have an interesting connection to our sensory and cognitive preferences. Hence, our self, or being, is not a matter of happenstance or chance. It is, in many cases, a matter of how we are wired, or our neurodiversity. The instrument we use to assess sensory and cognitive preferences is called *Brain Pathways*™.

When we discuss diversity at a neurological level, it moves beyond ethnicity, gender, sexual orientation, etc. It reinforces how we are different neurologically. Recognizing our neurological differences is reaffirming and satisfying and helps team members appreciate idiosyncrasies.

Step 3: Norms: Create team norm and determine how challenges and issues will be dealt with. Again, what will be the role of the participants and what will be the role of the faculty?

Step 4: Journaling: Create a mandatory method of journaling and reflection. This is absolutely critical if participants are to enhance their understanding of self, gain a deeper understanding of their being and become aware of how they influence the many people around them. Additionally, emoting onto the page serves to counteract stressful situations (Horneffer and Chan, 2009).

Step 5: Dynamics: Work the plan and pay attention to group dynamics. As team members gather at the airport, in preparation for their flight to the project site, all should pay close attention to group and participant dynamics. As the team(s) work their action plans, faculty pays close attention to the participant dynamics.

Step 6: Meeting: Conduct daily team meetings focusing not only on task, but also on the emotional and physical health and maintenance of the team and its members, opening the space for the honest and respectful expression of thoughts and feelings. The storming will occur, and the earlier it occurs, the better. Daily meetings allow for the "lancing of the boil" to prevent festering and infection. Revisit team norms and remember to leverage knowledge of the team's neuro diversity from the pre-trip team building.

Faculty pays close attention to incipient conflict. It is never too soon to intervene. Our experience is that, with the implementation of the previous steps, a teamoften deals with its issues within a day or so. The team must be willing to speak honestly and frankly, hence, prepared to "nip it in the bud."

Step 7: Nip It! Bring the entire team together to address the issue. Bring those with conflicts and challenges together to understand what is occurring. What are causes and history of the issues? Most important, what harm is being done? Not only between individuals, but also to the team, project and client.

While at first this approach may appear to have a problem-solving orientation, in fact, it is a positive, solution-building stance. There is a strong emphasis on, "What are the assets of the people who are directly involved? How do diversity and neurodiversity play into this?" The community discusses how they will begin to repair the damage done and develops a plan for moving forward. Most importantly, the stakeholders address,"What are the consequences of not dealing constructively with these issues?"

Step 8: Consequences: The team continues to perform the contracted tasks and duties, while attending to the team maintenance plan. The faculty must model confidence and courage throughout, and be prepared to level appropriate consequences if corrective action must be taken, which may include sending a participant home.

Step 9: Learning: At or near the end of the program, explore the learning from a"self as instrument" perspective. What have participants realized about personalities, behaviours and their self-as-instrument, while practicing within a different culture, alongside others who are similarly stressed? How can they apply this learning in their professional lives, educational venues and family settings? What are the positive and negative attributes of their being bigger than their human frame? Encourage deep dialogue, continued journaling and repeated cycles of learning.

Step 10: Celebrate: Look for what worked well and celebrate it!Purposefully identify the successful elements of the project as the deliverables are completed.

DATA COLLECTED

We shared the Ten Steps with colleagues who had conducted international student study and action research projects to learn how they apply the steps. The information provided was,"We have developed 10 steps to prepare and execute a graduate student international program and want your <u>candid</u> evaluation on frequency of conducting the steps in your past programs. Below are the steps and their descriptions, following the description is a place to capture your answers."

The data collected from seven professors shows the least frequently used step is Building the Team before departure (Step 2), the second least frequent step, is creating team norms and determining how challenges and issues will be dealt with (Step 3), and third is Nip It! (Step 7). For faculty who have years of experience conducting organizational development and behavior programs,it is enlightening to find that our sample least frequently conducts the basics of what we know will enhance team performance.

Our opportunity is to conduct the basics of team building and coaching to create enhanced student collaboration and synergy resulting in a heightened learning experience for the students and likely a more positive impression with our cooperators.

International student programs provide a platform upon which students may develop many different competencies and knowledge-of-self as they prepare for global leadership and managerial roles. During international programs, learners find themselves challenged by being in an unfamiliar environment and culture. By reinforcing desired attitudes,behaviours and commitments (ABCs),particularly basic team building processes and coaching students, teams are better able to secure team compatibility, in order to function successfully and take full advantage of the international opportunity.Leaning about how one is perceived versus intentions is valuable and often is magnified when under pressure or in a different culture, hence realizing our "Being is Bigger than Me" will have positive personal development ramifications. Finally a smooth operating team has many benefits including giving faculty time to enjoy their surroundings and leave knowing all stakeholders have gained from the positive experience.

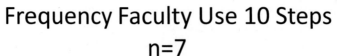

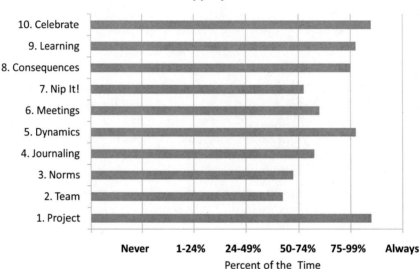

REFERENCES

Bonebright, D. A. (2010). 40 years of storming: a historical review of Tuckman's model of small group development. *Human Resource Development International*, *13*(1), 111-120.

Chang, J.W., Sy, T.& Choi, J.N. (2011). Team emotional intelligence and performance: interactive dynamics between leaders and members. Small Group Research. Issue 43, Vol. 75.

Chopra, P. K.& Kanji, G. K. (2010). Emotional intelligence: A catalyst for inspirational leadership and management excellence. *Total Quality Management & Business Excellence*, *21*(10), 971-1004.

Elmuti, D., Minnis, W., Abebe, M., (2005). Does education have a role in developing leadership skills? *Management Decision*, Vol. 43, Issue 7/8, pp.1018 - 1031.

D'Itino, R.S., Goldsby, M.G., Houghton, J.D.& Neck, C.P. (2007). Self-Leadership: A process for entrepreneurial success. *Journal of Leadership and Organizational Studies*. Vol 13, No. 4.

Goodman, N. (2012). "Training for cultural competence", Industrial and Commercial Training, Vol. 44, Issue 1, pp.47 - 50

Gosling, J. and Mintzberg, H. (2004). The education of practicing managers. *MIT Sloan Management Review*. Summer 2004 Vol. 45, No. 4.

Horneffer, K. J.& Chan, K. (2009). Alexithymia and relaxation: Considerations in optimising the emotional effectiveness of journaling about stressful experiences. *Cognition & Emotion*, Volume 23, Issue 3, 611-622.

Jamieson, D. W., Auron, M.& Shechtman, D. (2011). Managing 'use of self' for masterful facilitation. *T+D*, Vol.65, No.7, 58-61.

Jensen, K. (2012) Intelligence is Overrated: What you really need to succeed. *http://www. forbes.com/sites/keldjensen/2012/04/12*, retrieved May 22, 2012.

Kok-Yee, N., Dyne, L.& Soon, A. (2009). From Experience to Experiential Learning: Cultural Intelligence as a Learning Capability for Global Leader Development. *Academy Of Management Learning & Education*, 8(4), 511-526.

Law, K. S., Chi-Sum, W. & Song, L. J. (2004). The construct and criterion validity of emotional intelligence and its potential utility for management studies. *Journal Of Applied Psychology*, Volume 89, Issue 3, 483-496.

Manz, C.C. (1991). Helping yourself and others to master self leadership. Supervisory Management. Vol 36, No. 11.

Mintzberg, H. (2011). Looking forward to development. *Training and Development*. Feb 2011. Vol. 65, Issue 2.

Mishra, P.& Mohapatra, A. (2010). Relevance of Emotional Intelligence for Effective Job Performance: An Empirical Study. *Vikalpa: The Journal For Decision Makers*, 35(1), 53-61.

Pless, N. M., Maak, T.& Stahl, G. K. (2011). Developing Responsible Global Leaders Through International Service-Learning Programs: The Ulysses Experience. *Academy Of Management Learning & Education*, 10(2), 237-260.

Sinha, A. (2011). Conflict Management: Making Life Easier. *IUP Journal Of Soft Skills*, Volume 5(4), 31-42.

Steers, R. M., Sanchez-Runde, C. J.& Nardon, L. L. (2012). Culture, cognition, and managerial leadership. *Asia Pacific Business Review*, 18(3), 425-439.

Stewart, G.L., Courtright, S.H.& Manz, C.C. (2010). Self-leadership: A multilevel review. *Journal of Management*. Volume 37, Issue 185. DOI: 10.1177/0149206310383911

Harmonizing Western OD Methods and Thai Hospitality Culture: A Case Study of a Hotel

Vilas Wongtrakul* and Bruce Hanson**

ABSTRACT

This research specifically focuses on determining the impact of an Organizational Development Intervention (ODI) on the improvement of employee motivation and commitment, and customer satisfaction in a Thai subsidiary of a multinational hotel chain. The intervention used a corporate employee training exercise which had been found historically to be effective in many international contexts. It followed the intervention and examined the results. The study found that the training exercise (ODI) demonstrated no significant impact on the employees' sense of motivation and commitment nor the customers' sense of satisfaction. The researchers suspect that intervening variables associated with Thai Culture might have mitigated the effectiveness of the internationally recognized and sponsored training. It recommends that future studies adapt training to specifically address and incorporate a Thai culture of hospitality which will not only affect the employees' motivation and commitment, but will also become evident in enhanced customer satisfaction.

Keywords: Action research, Western values & organization development, employee commitment & motivation, customer satisfaction, Thai hospitality and culture.

INTRODUCTION

An organization chart is not a company, nor a new strategy an automatic answer to corporate problems. When trouble lurks we tend to call for a new strategy and then reorganize.The odds are that nothing much will change. The old culture will prevail and old habit patterns persist. If we want change, we fiddle with the strategy or we change the structure. At present, the ways to develop a company are by innovating products, improving the organization, and evaluating it against other competitors.

---
* Vilas Wongtrakul is with Assumption University Bangkok, Thailand
**Bruce Hanson is with Concordia University Irvine, California, USA
E-mail: wongtrakul.vilas@gmail.com, dochnson@mac.com

This action research study was designed to investigate the effects of employee commitment and employee motivation upon customer satisfaction.The Organization Development (OD) consultant seeks and maintains a collaborative relationship of relative equality with the organization members. Collaboration means, "to labor together". OD consultants conduct interventions – structured sets of activities and events designed to foster or enhance employee commitment and motivation in providing customer satisfaction. The nature of these interventions is that they are reflective, self-analytical, self-examining, proactive, diagnostically oriented, and action oriented. They focus on the organization's culture and its human processes. The organization's members must be able to diagnose situations accurately in order to arrive at successful solutions. Finally, this study attempts to assess the impact of OD interventions (ODIs) on employee commitment and employee motivation before, during and after the interventions.It also seeks to evaluate their impact on customer satisfaction in order to recommend ways for these organizations to become more competitive and to grow in the turbulent Bangkok tourism market.

STATEMENT OF THE PROBLEM

The main problem is the perennial issue of creating satisfaction in the hotel industry. This problem is particularly acute under current economic conditions since management's ability to increase employee commitment and customer satisfaction should result in increased revenues.

RESEARCH OBJECTIVES

1. To investigate the relationship between employee commitment and motivation, andcustomer satisfaction.
2. To investigate the applicability of western OD concepts inthe Thai cultural and social environment.

This case study on enhancing Employee Commitment, Motivation, and Readiness (ECMR) for Customer Satisfaction (CS) through harmonizing Thai & Western ODI processes aims to investigate the effects of employee commitment and employee motivation on customer satisfaction. It also attempts to identify the impact of ODIs on employee commitment and employee motivation.This case study on enhancing ECMR will help to strategically build relationships that may help the hotel industry to make effective connectionsamong staff. Upholding cultural integrity may be a key factor for ensuring customer satisfaction.

REVIEW OF LITERATURE

Although we cannot easily control or change government policies, political situations, markets, local and international competitors, and other external forces, there are some factors we can affect.We can try to gain higher employee commitment and stronger employee motivation. The organization's workforce is the key to better company performance. Employee commitment can lead to higher customer satisfaction. Therefore, to raise customer satisfaction a service industry such as a hotel needs to conduct action research to identify appropriate ODIs that can increase employee commitment and employee motivation.

In the hospitality industry, customer satisfaction is of paramount importance. Customer satisfaction is a measure of how services supplied by a hotel meet or surpass customer expectation. To measure satisfaction, hotels ask customers whether their product or service has met or exceeded expectations. Expectations are a key to satisfaction. When customers have high expectations,which are not met, they will be disappointed and will likely rate their experience as less than satisfying. For this reason a luxury hotel might receive a lower satisfaction rating than a budget motel— even though its facilities and service would be deemed superior in 'absolute' terms. Customer satisfaction ratings focus employees on the importance of fulfilling customers' expectations. When these ratings dip, they warn of problems that can affect sales and profitability.Furthermore, "Although sales or market share can indicate how well a firm is performing *currently*, satisfaction is perhaps the best indicator of how likely it is that the firm's customers will make further purchases *in the future*." (Farrisetal, 2010)

Employee Commitment is defined as the attachment of an individual to an organization as demonstrated by accepting the company goals, being willing to work hard for the organization and desiring to stay with the organization (Mowday et al, 1979). According to Meyer and Allen (1997), it includes affective commitment, continuance commitment and normative commitment. An employee might feel like staying, be rewarded to stay, or stay because of their values respectively. If employees have no emotional attachment to the organization, they will not desire to remain a part of the organization. If they could not obtain benefits or opportunities to grow, employees would have no continuance commitment. And without normative commitment, they would not be loyal to the company. Low employee commitment leads to low performance, which would consequently affect customer satisfaction with employees' service.

Employee Motivation is a process by which employees' behavior is mobilized, responsibly conditioned and sustained in the interest of achieving organizational goals (Cummings & Worley, 2005 and DuBrin, 2007). In this investigation, the assumptions of our organizational development intervention saw motivation as affected by the 4 factors of:

1. job design,
2. behavior modification,
3. recognition and pride and
4. financial incentives.

Without considering design,the job would likely not be meaningful. If there were no motivation through appropriate reward or punishment, employees' behavior might not be changed. Without recognition and pride as reinforcers,there would be no self-esteem and self-fulfillment. If pay was not linked to performance and gainsharing there would be no employee involvement. All these factors certainly affect employees' performance and consequently affect customers' satisfaction with employees' service performance.

The conceptual framework is summarized in Figure1 below.

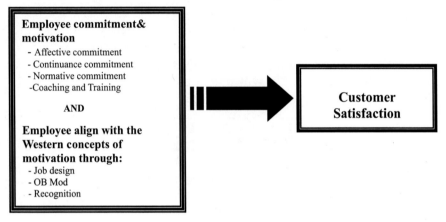

Fig. 1: Conceptual Framework

The employee survey respondents included a Training Manager, four other managers and twenty-five employees of the hotel. The researcher handed out the questionnaire of 70 items compiled from a variety of measures commitment and motivation along with job characteristics to everyone in this group for quantitative evaluation.

The qualitative data collection techniques for this action research were in – depth interview, focus group discussion, and observation. This action research was designed to use data cluster analysis and cause – and – effect diagram technique for qualitative analysis.

In addition, ten employees were interviewed by the primary researcher in face to face sessions. The interview form contained two parts. The first part was general information about the interviewee and the second part contained the core questions of the study. The six female and four male interviewees represented five departments in the Hotel. Most of the participants had bachelors' degrees. Four were less than 27 years old, four were between 27 and 49 years old, and two were above 50 years of age.

The data analysis presented and interpreted in this report is based on the collected qualitative data and quantitative data conducted to assess current employee commitment and motivation in the organization. However, it relied more on qualitative analysis in view of the small size of the organization.

To evaluate the effects on customer satisfaction this study relied upon customers of the Hotel who provided data through the Medallia Guest Feedback online system. While an imperfect measure due to self-selection, it was consistently applied over the time of the test. The researchers did not have direct control of this monitoring system, as it was a routine customer satisfaction survey.

RESEARCH RESULTS

The researcher distributed thirty questionnaires to employees working in different departments. And, thirty completed questionnaires were returned to the researcher, accounting for 100%. Table 1 shows that for the seventy questions in the questionnaire, cumulative Cronbach's alpha is .994 which implies that the questionnaire is reliable.

Table 1: Reliability Analysis of the Questionnaire

Cronbach's Alpha	Cronbach's Alpha Based on Standardized Items	N of Items
.994	.995	70

However, there were no significant employee results regarding commitment or motivational changes from pretest to post test. We will not spend time with further details of this quantitative test at this time.

In addition, overall customer satisfaction with the Hotel was unchanged from the previous year. (Medallia Satisfaction: 2010). The Medallia Guest Feedback system enables all staff to be aware of company objectives (e.g. Customer Satisfaction) & enables guests to transmit responses that are stored in the Medallia reporting system. Guest responses provide valuable feedback, as shown in the following Satisfaction Table 2 which covers the period before and after the ODI which occurred in May of 2009.

Table 2: Satisfaction 18535 (RAM) D'ma Bangkok – 04/01/09 to /08/30/09

	Apr	May	Jun	Jul	Aug	total
Sample size	144	88	71	82	93	478
GX Satisfaction Score	8.00	8.21	8.11	8.27	7.99	8.10
Experience	8.01	8.16	8.00	8.12	7.92	8.04
Service	7.86	8.23	7.99	8.29	7.80	8.01
Accommodations	8.01	8.25	8.19	8.23	7.87	8.09
Food & Beverage	7.69	7.87	7.97	8.01	7.72	7.82
Security	8.23	8.34	8.32	8.57	8.25	8.33

Thus, there was no support for our first research question. In assessing the quantitative measures of employee motivation and satisfaction, and attendant increase in customer satisfaction, no increase was observed. This study failed to find significant effect from the OD/Training intervention. This was indeed disappointing.

FURTHER EXPLORATION OF THE DATA

The qualitative data did however provide some interesting clues as to what was going on in the study, even though they were not conclusive answers.Providing an attractive career path and pleasant working conditions can motivate employees to attempt to increase customer satisfaction, according to their responses to question number six: "How can the company raise customer satisfaction?"

The most frequently mentioned recommendation for raising Hotel customer satisfaction was to improve communication within the organization and with the customer. Four respondents added that Customer Relation Management and product knowledge would help employees to be confident when dealing with customers.

Table 3: Employees' suggestionsfor the Organizational Development Intervention obtained from their open questionnaires compare Pre-ODI and Post-ODI.

Suggestion	Pre-ODI	Post-ODI
1. Improve communication between management and employees within the organization	4.15	4.75
2. Increase employee collaboration and participation	4.04	4.38
3. Foster a closer relationship among employees	4.43	4.00
4. Create a sense of pride in the employees towards their work	4.00	4.12
5. Maintain the Thai culture by having seniors teach the younger ones; depending on each other in the Thai way	3.65	3.69
6. Create a good balance between work life and personal/home life.	3.86	3.80
7. Offer training that develops employee talent	3.94	3.97

The employees felt closer together as a result of the training as evidenced by suggestion number three. This created a perceived need to further improve communication and further collaboration.Thus the result of the intervention from the employees' perspective was to heighten the desire to further improve their relationships through communication and collaboration.

INTERVIEW ASSESSMENT

All the interviewees mentioned that employee recognition made them feel that they wanted to do a better job, feel motivated and feel committed to giving good service. They felt that the employee was an important person in helping to initiate the improvement of work. Training and development were useful and created awareness in employees to give better service and help the organization to reach its goals. Three respondents felt that training was not useful because it was usually too basic for employees to help guests who needed better service.

According to the data provided by the interviewees, the two main problem areas affecting the Hotel employees' commitment and motivation were the lack of a communicated vision and mission to all levels of the staff, and an unclear career path. The Hotel was weak in communication as shown in the Pre-ODI Phase. Also, commitment and motivation were not optimal due to poor levels of employee collaboration and participation, as well as poor communication among the employees. The researcher observed that before the ODI, the working environment was tense and people complained because they didn't understand the Western concepts they were being asked to adopt. We will next consider the mitigation of these results given Thai and Western cultural assumptions.

REFLECTION ON RESEARCH QUESTION 2: WESTERN OD METHODS AND THAI CULTURE

This study adopts the Marvin Bower definition of culture as,"The way we do things around here". A limited degree of Thai culture was incorporated into the corporate training ODI. We looked at the rituals of how we greeted people. The staff members were taught to greet the guests using Thai greeting "SawasdeeKrubor Ka", which means "Hello" followed with "Good morning" and the name of the person receiving the call. When meeting the guests, they give the "Wai" gesture by putting the hands together under the nose as a sign of saying hello in Thai culture.

Below is a brief comparison of Thai vs. Western culture using Maslow's hierarchy of needs (Shepard, 2002). The primary difference may be the distinction between collectivist Thai values and individualistic Western values observed by Shepard.

Table 4: Maslow Hierarchy of Thai and Western Needs

Thai/Collectivistic ('We') Prioritization of needs	Western/Individualistic ('I')
1. Affiliation Needs	1. Self Actualization
2. Harmonious Relationships	2. Self Esteem
3. Face saving (Self Esteem)	3. Affiliation Needs
4. Safety/ Security Needs	4. Safety/ Security Needs
5. Physiological Needs	5. Physiological Needs
Team Group Achievement	Individual Achievement
"The Team That Eats Together	"The Team That Plays Together
Stays Together"	Stays Together"

What is particularly striking is the replacement of self-actualization with affiliation needs, closely followed by the need for harmonious relationships. This dramatically affects motivation in social settings, and the aims of achievement. Western assumptions of individual motivation are not nearly as operant, and the language from the head office's Western programs therefore does not make sense.

The work of Hofstede is perhaps the best or most broadly known in the area of corporate culture (Hofstede, 1980). The data used for the empirical part of Hofstede's research were extracted from an existing bank of questionnaire results collected within subsidiaries of one large multinational in 40 countries and covered among others, many questions about values.In spite of this limitation it might still lend some useful insights.

Hofstede identified 4 dimensions of national culture:

Power Distance: The term 'power distance' is taken from the work of Mulder (1977:90) who defined power distance as 'the degree of inequality in power between the less powerful individual (I) and a more powerful other (O) in which I and O belong to the same social system'. Thai culture is seen as having a relatively high degree of power distance, or granting the Other power.

Uncertainty Avoidance: The second dimension of national culture has been labeled Uncertainty Avoidance (UA) by Hofstede (1980). UA indicates ways in which a society copes with living on the blink of an uncertain future. That Thailand has a middle of the continuum score instead of a lower UA is surprising if one considers several socio-religious factors. This dimension is however perhaps not a significant factor of comparison.

Individualism: The third dimension of national culture is labeled Individualism by Hofstede (1980). It describes the relationship between the individual and his reference groups in a given society and is reflected in the way people make decisions. Thailand ranks well below the mean at 20 and the USA ranks highest with 91. While this is a qualitatively precarious dimension from a communal societies perspective, this may easily be a major source of difference between US based corporate training and Thai employee cultural expectations.

Musculinity: Hofstede (1980) has assembled the various correlates of the Masculinity Index (MAS) into a coherent picture of 'masculine' and 'feminine' types of national culture. Thailand ranks at 34, scoring in the middle compared with the US at 62. Masculine behavior is associated with autonomy, aggression, exhibition, and domination, whilst feminine behavior with nurturance, affiliation, helpfulness and humility. Thai culture is considered relatively more feminine and this would certainly affect it's style of hospitality and general acceptance of difference.

In summary, Thailand according to Hofstede (1980) is a country that exhibits: large power distance (as characterized in the tall organization structures in organizations, and by managers who make decisions autocratically and paternalistically); moderate uncertainty avoidance (as evident in the containment of conflict and confrontation, loose society and limited regimentation); low individualism (demonstrated in strong affiliative ties among employees, promotion from within, and policies and practices based on loyalty and a sense of duty); and femininity (emphasized by more women in qualified and well-paid jobs, as small-scale entrepreneurs, and weaker achievement motivation of the general population).

The effect this may have on Thai hospitality culture might be that all people are subordinate to the broader needs of cultural institutions and yet sympathetic to the situation of others. Thai hospitality culture is feminine in characteristic displaying an accepting and or tolerant nature. This approach can potentially be disrupted by forceful corporate influence from masculine/individualistic orientations, including survey and inquiry methods.

Organizational Development applications in Asia, must take cultural differences into account, since cultural differences could adversely affect work relationships. (Golden &Veiga, 2005; Karahanna, Evaristo&Srite, 2005) note that it is risky to impose a Western operating style in a social milieu that treats certain Western behaviors as alien and disrespectful.

Garg and Ma (2005) demonstrated that there was a difference in the organization culture and management style followed in local Chinese companies as compared to the American companies based in China. Cross – cultural researchers Lung – tan and Yuan – Ho (2005) examined the relationship between culture, management style, and performance amongst senior managers from Japan and Taiwan whose firms had joint ventures in China. Using Hofstede's dimensions of power distance and individualism, they tried to correlate differences in management style with the differences in cultural dimensions. However, they found that many of their hypotheses based on Hofstede's theory could not be supported. They concluded that cultural dimensions had little impact on management style and performance. Interestingly, one of their main suggestions for further research was to use qualitative methods such as in-depth interviews or case studies as these methods would generate deeper insight. One limitation of Hofstede's approach was using a purely quantitative approach to understand a complex phenomenon like culture. This encouraged contemporary researchers to explore mixed methodologies (combining quantitative with qualitative techniques) and purely qualitative approaches to cross – cultural research (Bartel-Radic, 2006; Burke-Johnson & Onwuegbuzie, 2004; Gummesson, 2006; Williamson, 2006). One advantage of using qualitative methods is an increase in the validity of the findings since the qualitative component using open-ended questions helped researchers cross check if respondents understood the issues being discussed in the same way as the researchers. (Hurmerinta-Petomaki & Nummela, 2006)

SUMMARY OF FINDINGS

Western OD Concepts do not easily fit with Thai Culture and Social Process

Explanation : Thai and Western cultures are very different. For example, in Thai culture we are taught to be disciplined, passive and often learn only by rote memorization whereas in Western culture we are encouraged to use critical thinking and to question, explore, experiment and analyze until we understand.

No change was seen in Employee Commitment or Motivation as a result of the ODI.

Explanation: Collectivist Social desirability mitigates attitudinal study.For example, in Thai society, individualism as practiced in the West is not generally accepted as a social value, because individuals seek identity not so much in terms of who they are as in terms of whom they are associated with.

No change was seen in Customer Satisfaction as a result of the ODI .

Explanation: The majority of the respondents thought that the motivational system in the organization was not good and could not motivate employees. Employees preferred group rewards over individual rewards.A motivational system needs to be created with uniquely Thai values.

The development of a Thai style of management and hospitality is open

As to what are the Thai social systems and behavior, it is impossible to give a simple answer. There are different theoretical frames, different units of analysis and different analytical tools available to dissect Thai social behaviors and Thai social systems. The resulting analyses and interpretations of Thai social behaviors are therefore varied, and some are even in conflict. Therefore, it is essential and beneficial to know the coverage of each theoretical and / or propositional view, with strength and limitations provided where appropriate. At present, there are three existing different interpretations of Thai social systems and behaviors which can be briefly presented as follows:

First, the "Loose structure" interpretation in Thai social system is in contrast tothe "Tight structure" interpretation from Western social systems. For example: When Thais in organizations have disagreements, the ideal approach is to continue superficially cordial relations without engaging in open debate or challenging the other's actions or ideas.In contrast, Western values tend to push for agreement, rationale dialogue and value winners, as in a zero sum game. There is a great tolerance of difference in Thai values. In the past few decades, there have been serious attempts to describe and analyze Thai behaviors and social systems, mostly conducted by foreign scholars in the fields of anthropology, sociology and political science. These studies have somehow highlighted a number of unresolved controversial issues, which are largely due to different levels of analyses as well as theoretical frameworks, and unproved speculations. It has been difficult to codify a core Thai way with Western methods, and they still appear to be illusive.

Second, it is commonly agreed among cultural anthropologists and sociological theorists like Robin Williams that "values always have a cultural dimension" (Williams, 1971; 1979), The present researcher holds that the selection of values itself is a perceptual evaluative process which could contain cultural bias. Thus, Rokeach's two sets of values, although they may be quite comprehensive for American people, may not be sufficiently comprehensive to be useful for non-Western cultures, particularly for Thai culture. We are still at a beginning stage of the construction of a Thai Value Scale.

Third, the interpretation of "Individualism" in Thai social behaviors differs from Western social behaviors. Since reciprocal rights and duties are not clearly marked, the Thai have relative freedom of choice in social action. As Phillips (1965) states, Thais have a "profound sense of self-concern and freedom of choice" as a major dimension of their loosely structured relationships (Phillips, 1965, p.206). And because of this individualism dimension, the Thais seldom show a sense of obligation, solidarity, ideological commitment, and possibly even loyalty to anything beyond personal values. A more specific definition of individualism was offered by Waterman who characterized it with four attributes: a) a sense of separate personal identity; b) striving for self actualization; c) internal locus of control; and d) principled moral reasoning, with emphasis on equity in interpersonal relations (Waterman, 1984). From this, one starts to see the difference between Thai individualism and American individualism. While the Americans are characterized by a high score on the four attributes, Thais can be seen as relatively lower on all four attributes.

CONCLUSIONS

The application of corporate training methods in this international hotel chain may have little demonstrable effect on employee motivation and commitment, and resulting customer satisfaction. The training however may have more effect on the interrelationships of the staff and indirectly aid the development of corporate solidarity. However the mitigating impact of Thai culture moderates the impact of this training and may be modified to achieve the intended effect without the observed intermediate behaviors and attitudes seen in the staff. In short, things don't work the way in a Thai hotel as they might in other cultural settings. The development of a unique theory of Thai hospitality may be a different mechanism or process which is more community based, and not individualistic. Gender roles are also different, as the overall culture can be seen as more receptive and accepting which has globally been seen as feminine characteristics. Other cultural traditions may be more imposing, and this accepting approach is more contextual and is disrupted and/or obscured by mechanistic individualized management systems.

REFERENCES

Anderson, E.W., Fornell, C. (2000), "Foundations of the American customer satisfaction index", Total Quality Management, Vol. 11 No.7, pp.S869-82.

Barnard, Janet. (1994). "Benchmarking in the Service Sector," Organizational Development Journal, 4: No. 4: 65 -71.

Bartel-Radic, A. (2006). Intercultural learning in global teams. Management International Review, 46, 647-677. Retrieved March 26, 2007, from Pro Quest database.

Bennett, Rebekah and Rundle-Thiele, Sharyn (2004). "Customer satisfaction should not be the only goal." Journal of Services Marketing, Volume 18 Number 7 2004 pp. 514-523

Bruhn, M., Grund, M.A. (2000), "Theory, development and implementation of national customer satisfaction indices: the Swiss index of customer satisfaction", Total Quality Management, Vol. 11 No.7, pp.S1017-28.

Burke Johnson, R., &Onwuegbuzie, A. J. (2004). Mixed methods research: A research paradigm whose time has come. Educational Researcher, 33, 14-26. Retrieved March 20, 2007, from Pro Quest database.

Chathoth,Prakash, Brenda Mak, Vinnie Jauhari and Kamal Manaktola (2007), "Employees' Perceptions of Organizational Trust and Service Climate: a structural Model Combining Their Effects on Employee Satisfaction." Journal Hospitality & Tourism Research, 31, pp 338 – 357

Coghklan, David and Brannick, Teresa. (2002). Doing Action Research in your Own Organization. London: SAGE Publications

Cummings, Thomas G., and Worley, Christopher G. (2005). Organization Development and Change. (8thed.) Mason, Ohio: Thomson South-Western

Denton, D.K. (1993), "Total customer satisfaction: the next step", Industrial Management, Vol. 35 No.6, pp.18-21.

DuBrin, Andrew J. (2007). Foundations of Organization Behavior. Mason, OH: Thomson South-Western

Farris, Paul W.; Neil T. Bendle; Phillip E. Pfeifer; David J. Reibstein (2010).Marketing Metrics: The Definitive Guide to Measuring Marketing Performance. Upper Saddle River, New Jersey: Pearson Education, Inc.

Ford, Robert, William Heisley and William McCreary (2008), "Leading Change with the 5-P Model."Complexing" the Swan and Dophin Hotel at Walt Disney World." Journal Cornell Hotel and Restaurant Administration Quarterly, 49; pp191 - 205

Gilbert, G. Ronald and Veloutsou, Cleopatra. (2006), "A cross-industry comparison of customer satisfaction," Journal of Services Marketing, Volume 20 Number 5 2006 pp. 298-308

Griffin A. Mark, Malcolm G. Patterson, Michael A. West. (2001). "Job Satisfaction and Team work: The Role of Supervisor Support," Journal of Organizational Behaviour, Vol. 22 No. 5 pp. 537 - 550

Gummesson, E. (2006).Qualitative research in management: addressing complexity, context and persona. Management Decision, 44, 167-179. Retrieved March 20, 2007, from Pro Quest database

Hansemark, Ove C. and Albinsson, Marie (2004). "Customer satisfaction and retention: the experiences of individual employees," Managing Service Quality, Volume 14 Number 1 2004 pp. 40-57

Hempel, Paul and Maris G. Martinsons (2009), "Developing International Organizational Change Theory using cases from China, Human Relations; 62, 459 – 498

Hinkin, Timothy and Chester A. Schriesheim, (2004) "If You Don't Hear from Me You Know You Are Doing Fine": The Effects of Management Non-response to Employee Performance. Journal Cornell Hotel and Restaurant Administration Quarterly, 45, pp. 362 – 371

Hofstede, G., &Hofstede, G. J. (2005). Cultures and organizations: Software of the mind (2nd ed.). New York: McGraw Hill.

Maragas S.V. Amandte (2008). "Knowledge and Practice of OD in East Asia. What are the gaps?", AODN , October 2008,

Meyer, J.P. and Allen, N.J. (1997). Commitment in the Workplace: theory, research and application. USA: Sage.

Mowday, R.T., Steers, R.M. and Porter, L.W. (1979). The Measurement of Organizational Commitment. Journal of Vocational Behaviour, 14:224-247

Naumann, E., Jackson, D.W. Jr, and Rosenbaum, M. (2001), "How to implement a customer satisfaction program", Business Horizons, Vol. 44 No.1, pp.37-48.

Phillips, Paul and PanosLouiveris (2005). Performance Measurement Systems in Tourism, Hospitality, and Leisure Small Medium-Sized Enterprises: A Balanced Scorecard Perspective. Journal of Travel Research; 44, 201 -211

Reis, D., Pena, L., Lopes, P.A. (2003), "Customer satisfaction: the historical perspective", Management Decision, Vol. 41 No.2, pp.195-8.

Roongrerngsuke, Siriyupa and Adith C. (2001), "Overview of HRM in Organizations in Thailand," Sasin Journal of Management, 1: 4 -5

Sachin Gupta, Edward Mc Laughlin and Miguel Gomez, "Guest Satisfaction and Restaurant Performance." Journal Cornell Hotel and Restaurant Administration Quarterly, 48; pp.284- 298

Seonghee Cho and Misty M. Johanson (2008), "Organizational Citizenship Behavior and Employee Performance: A Moderating Effect of Work Status in Restaurant Employees." Journal of Hospitality & Tourism Research, 32; 307 – 326

Shephard, Peter.- (2002). Leading Diverse and Multi-Cultural Teams: The Whole Brain Way. Brain Dominance Technologies SDN BHD, Malaysia

Walsh, Kate and Masaka, S. Taylor (2007), "Developing In-House Careers and Retaining Management Talent, Journal of Cornell Hotel and Restaurant Administration Quarterly, 48:pp. 163 - 180

Wong, A. (2000), "Integrating supplier satisfaction with customer satisfaction", Total Quality Management, Vol. 11 No.4-6, pp.S826-9

ELECTRONIC SOURCES

www.coachu.com

www.iftdo.org/tgr.htm

www.e-apic.com

www.nwlink.com/-donclark/hrd/glossary

www.thomsonedu.com/infotrac

http://www.spherion.com/press/ew;wases/2005/Emerging_Workforce.jsp

http://www.gainsharing.com

www.thomsonedu,com/infotrac

http://jam.sagepub.com

http://www.jstor.org/stable/364957

http://www.jstor.org/stable/2488033

http://miranda.emeraldinsignt.com/Insight/ViewContentServlet?Filename=Published/EmeraldFullTextArticle/Articles/0260241006.html#b7

http://www.spherion.com/press/releases/2005/Emerging_Woprkforce.jsp

Guided Professionalization in the Cleaning Industry with CIMS and CIMS GB: A Case Study

*Nathan Walla**

ABSTRACT

The purpose of this case study is to examine the processes neededto guide professionalization of organizations within the cleaning industry from both environmental and social sustainability standpoints. The ISSA is a trade association which has created the Cleaning Industry Management Standard Certification and the Cleaning Industry Management Standard Green Building Certification. These programs require that an operation meets or exceeds numerous criteria throughout six core objectives ranging from customer service to human resource, and environmentally friendly endeavors. Organizations seeking these certifications are required to pass a third party assessment which monitors whether or not these criteria are met. My hypothesis is that programs like CIMS and CIMS GB can easily be used by any cleaning operation to professionalize their operation and therefore increase their potential for success within the cleaning industry. In this study, a qualitative approach was taken as I shadowed a medium sized, Midwestern land grant university throughout their certification process. Field notes were taken for organization and reporting purposes. This organization was easily able to achieve their certifications, with honors. However, this ease of certification is not common among organizations seeking this type of credential. Most utilize the criteria for this certification in order to implement changes which align the organization with the standard in order to improve operations and move toward the overall achievement of obtaining certification.

Keywords: CIMS, CIMS GB, ISSA, cleaning industry management

INTRODUCTION

Today's cleaning industry is made up of different levels of professionalism when it comes to both the efficiency of services provided and the employee relations within their businesses. The ISSA is a trade association that has identified the need

---

* Colorado Technical University, Colorado Springs, Colorado COI, USA.
E-mail: nathan.walla@my.cs.coloradotech.edu

to streamline operations and lessen the differences of professionalism between the different levels of the cleaning industry. This professionalization is beneficial to cleaning organizations because in today's economy, it is quite difficult for less than standard operations to be cost effective and efficient. Creating an industry standard for operations is a key objective of the ISSA's Cleaning Industry Management Standard Certification and Cleaning Industry Management Standard Green Building Certification. These programs are designed to guide cleaning operations toward becoming an environmental steward as well as the most efficient operation they can be for both internal and external customer bases.

The ISSA was founded by Alfred Richter in 1923 as the National Sanitary Supply Association but changed its name to the International Sanitary Supply Association in 1966, due to growing international membership (ISSA, 2012). In 2005 the company changed its name again to better reflect the growing cleaning service provider membership population to ISSA – The Worldwide Cleaning Industry Association (ISSA, 2012). The ISSA recognizes the need to professionalize the cleaning industry and embraces or partners with other trade associations which value the same common principles of professionalism and introduces for the first time ethics as a dimension, and not just improved efficiency and effectivenessISSA, being an international organization, is a key stakeholder in cleaning industry interests and operational education and training worldwide.

The United States and the European Union are very much alike in their cleaning sectors. According to a European study by Mormont, in 2004, the European Federation of Cleaning Industries conducted a survey which showed that growth in the number of cleaning companies in Europe rose by a steady six point six percent throughout the previous 13 years and that the majority of companies within the cleaning sector are micro-companies that employ ten or fewer employees (Mormont, 2004). Much like in Europe, the cleaning sector continues to grow at a steady pace here in the United States as more emphasis is placed on healthy indoor air quality and the benefits of a sanitary environment. Another driving factor is the economic shift from manufacturing work to service work within the United States.

These micro-companies make it increasingly difficult to control ethical and efficiency aspects of a public sector operation due to smaller workforces that are not offered benefits, may be uneducated, or not able to legally work within the United States. This also puts monetary strain on professional operations by means of unfair bid submission by those that don't follow tax law, pay benefits or have the ability to provide satisfactory services governed by strict contract regulations.Substandard safety regulations and equipment used by employees cause dangerous work environments for both cleaning staff as well as customers who work in the cleaned spaces. Professionalization includes ensuring that proper safety procedures and training are in place alongside equipment that stays in optimal operating condition.

The solution to streamline professionalization is to create a standard for the larger or more proactive entities to follow in order to help educate the public on what type of operation to hire. This helps to educate the public on the difference between what type of service is provided by a professional organization and that of a substandard micro-company, thus shifting the consumer demand back toward utilizing the professional organizations. A professionalized organization will be able to offer better services at a lower cost as well as build trust with the general public. This study was needed to help prove my hypothesis that these guided standardization processes can be used in even the most complex cleaning organizations in order to promote professional operations.

I chose to complete this case study to see how the process of installing a guided program would work within a complex cleaning organization in order to standardize operations to a more professional and organized approach. This process took four months which was short in terms of time needed for most operations taking part in ISSA's certification programs according to the third party assessment consultant who recommended certification of this operation. For most organizations, this certification process and all of the preparation involved in achieving it can easily take six months to a year to accomplish depending upon what types of policies, procedures, and products they utilize currently which all coincide with the standards objectified through CIMS. ISSA's Cleaning Industry Management Standard certification is based upon an organization meeting a minimum number of criteria from the five core standards of a cleaning operation which are; quality systems, service delivery, human resources, health, safety, and environmental stewardship, management commitment, and in order to earn the Green Building designation the organization must meet the stringent requirements of the sixth green building core (ISSA, 2012).

OBJECTIVE

The overall objective of this case study was to shadow the ISSA Cleaning Industry Management Standard certification process of a complex, medium sized cleaning operation within a land grant university. The case study was used to determine the overall ease and effectiveness of the guided systematic program in assisting the organization in achieving the highly sought after industry certification. By taking a systems thinking approach, this study was designed to examine the effectiveness of a systematic approach to professionalizing the organization. The core criteria requirements to pass the certification are representative of the working parts of the cleaning operation system. In order to be considered a system, there must be three things present; elements, interconnections, and a function or purpose (Meadows, 2008). The six core standards are in relate to the elements of the system.

Quality systems are the element that refers to the physical equipment and training programs needed to do the work of the organization. Service delivery is the core standard that refers to the company's ability to provide world class service. The human resources standard is the element with reference to whether or not proper and ethical employee relations and performance management systems are in place. Health, safety, and environmental stewardship are all parts of the element which constitutes the company's ability to keep employees, customers, property, and the environment safe from harmful conditions and the green building standard ensures that all parts of the element of environmental stewardship are held at industry leading levels of care.

The other objective to this study was to determine if it was feasible for most of cleaning industry organization to follow the same systematic steps in earning this certification in order to professionalize their operations. It was a goal of this study to determine the effectiveness of this guided systematic approach to professionalization as operations could not halt work activity to revamp operational systems. Can most cleaning organizations meet the criteria by slowly introducing certain aspects of the standardized operations that they don't already meet?

RESEARCH METHODOLOGY

This case study was conducted based upon qualitative observation and analysis principles. In this study of a select case, my "sampling strategy" included the collection of data from only one cleaning organization that chose to pursue a certification as proof of industry professionalism (Loftland, 2006). A qualitative approach was taken as I shadowed a medium sized, Midwestern land grant university throughout their certification process. Field notes were taken for information organization and reporting purposes. The field notes did not contain any personal or private organizational information and were not shared with the organization or the ISSA. Based upon my observations with this organization, my hypothesis is that programs like the ones offered by ISSA such as CIMS and CIMS GB can easily be used by any cleaning operation to professionalize their operation and therefore future potential for success within the cleaning industry.

It was recorded in the field notes (Walla, 2012);that the process begins with very specific instructions being given to the cleaning organization in a step by step format. These instructions guide the organization's project manager or CIMS task force through the requirements needed to meet the expectations of each core standard. The cleaning organization is then contacted by a third party certification consultant who will be provided relevant proof of requirements met by the CIMS Champion. This step by step process gets the consultant familiar with the organization and its structure. The independent third party consultant ultimately visits their selected site to confirm that physical requirements of the organization are in order with the core standards. Once the consultant is provided proper evidence of meeting or exceeding ISSA requirements, the certification is awarded to the cleaning organization.

Since this test organization has had both the monetary and personnel resources available, they have been making great efforts in becoming an efficient and environmentally friendly operation for many years leading up to the desire to achieve a certification which proves this standard of operation. Therefore, the timeline of the certification process was shortened significantly. For this organization, the preparation process was the longest aspect of the process. According to my field notes, the preparation process was started in the first week of October, 2011and spanned into January of 2012 (Walla, 2012). The preparation process was delayed for two weeks in the month of December due to an annual university shutdown between the Christmas holiday and the beginning of the New Year.

In the first week of January, 2012 the preparation process shifted to open communication and exchange of documents between the third party certification consultant and the organization liaison based upon the checklist guidelines provided by ISSA (Walla, 2012). A sample of the certification checklist that outlines the core guidelines which is provided to the certifying organization can be found as an attached appendix to this case study. Based upon observation, this portion of the certifying process took the first two weeks of January, 2012 and ended with the third party certification consultant passing approval of the initial preparation phase and a visit was scheduled for February, 2012 (Walla, 2012).

The visit by the third party certification consultant was scheduled as a three day visit to the operation. This three day visit consisted of a viewing of physical documentation on the premises which show proof of the policies, procedures, and training mechanisms required by ISSA to be certified as well as physical evidence of a professional green cleaning operation (Walla, 2012). The visit ended with both internal and external customer interviews and interviews with the front line staff in order to gauge the true performance of the operation and the commitment of management in relation to the certification requirements. It was noted that the entire cost of the certification process for an organization of this size and demographic was typically between $6,000 and $10,000. Return on investment is also typically measured differently from certified organization to certified organization. This is solely dependent upon the reasoning behind the desire to achieve this certification.

DIAGNOSIS AND ANALYSIS

Based on the information in the field notes and the outcome of the certification process, my diagnosis is that hypothesis is correct for organizations of this size and nature. Further comparison of the certification process within different levels of organizations will need to be made in order to prove that programs like the ones offered by ISSA such as CIMS and CIMS GB can easily be used by any cleaning operation to professionalize their operation and therefore their potential for success within the cleaning industry, just as they did with the demographic studied.Even if the criteria are not met upon the initial phases of the certification process, there are structured ways of introducing different operational ideas and processes that have proven successful for other cleaning operations that can ensure a near future certification. My analysis of this type of guided structured program is that it can be implemented in any size organization and that it can also be implemented at any state of preparedness.

The entire certification process for the shadowed organization was four months. As stated in the field notes, "the third party consultant made it evident to his client that this was a faster certification in comparison to other equally complex organizations" (Walla, 2012). Given the state of preparedness of the certified to be company, the process can be long and structured or short. The process however, is step by step in nature and designed to guide the organization through meeting the core standard expectations. Organizations can choose to organize the certification process in any configuration which may suit their needs. Some organizations may split up the core standards or some may choose to assign a liaison, task force, or manager of such a project. The ease of the process is satisfactory in accordance with the objectives of this research case study.

RECOMMENDATIONS

Based upon my research, programs like ISSA's CIMS and CIMS GBcertifications are sufficient to serve as a structured method of company professionalization. I would recommend these types of guided programs to cleaning organizations similar in size and demographic from both private and public sector work environments. I would recommend to any organization that chooses to pursue such certifications in an effort to reach a higher level of professionalism or industry success, to form a task force if possible, or assign an individual who can help to organize the documentation needed and to serve as liaison for the consultant. This would drastically speed up the process and efficiency of the certification process and individuals from within the organization or independent contracted experts can play these key roles.

CONCLUSION

My conclusion is that there is a great need to begin a professionalization process for the cleaning industry as it will continue to grow at unprecedented rates into the foreseeable future. As stated earlier in this case study, the majority of the companies that make up the cleaning industry are micro-companies that employ less than ten people (Mormont, 2004). These smaller organizations operate on a vastly differentiated set of professionalism and operational standards. The more cleaning companies that can learn to meet or exceed professional and ethical industry-wide standards, the more profitable and trustworthy the industry as a whole will become.

Professional standardization of cleaning companies can offer many benefits to the industry from both environmental and social sustainability aspects. Using the core standards presented in ISSA's CIMS and CIMS GB certification programs, or similar certification programs offered by other trade associations, will play a key role in the process of the professionalization movement. Gaining industry respect for organizations that operate with employee and environmental wellbeing as part of their operational guidelines is essential to building cross industry partnerships and other successful ventures. For example, the CIMS GB certification offers the certified cleaning operation points toward LEED and LEED EBOM certifications for facilities who work with them or those in house operations at large organizations.

The future of the cleaning industry is likely to see smaller companies entering the market at an increasing rate. During the "Industrial Age Bubble", in most industries, we saw a major increase in the formation of very large corporations which became the norm in organizational structure (Senge, 2010). However, smaller and more robustly different operations will add to the diversity of the industry which will create new and healthy competition and a new "future of enterprise variety" (Senge, 2010).

REFERENCES

ISSA (2012) "CIMS Certification", from: *http://www.issa.com/?id=introduction&lg=*, retrieved on 7/12/12

Loftland, J., et. al. (2006) "Analyzing Social Settings A Guide to Qualitative Observation and Analysis Forth Edition", Wadsworth Cengage Learning, California

Meadows, D. H. (2008) "Thinking in Systems A Primer" Chelsea Green Publishing, White River Junction, Vermont 05001

Mormont, M. (2004) "Institutional Representativeness of Trade Unions and Employers' Organizations in the Industrial Cleaning Sector", UNIVERSITÉ CATHOLIQUE DE LOUVAIN Institute des Sciences du Travail, from: *http://tiny.cc/r73biw*, retrieved on 7/2/12

Senge, P. (2010) "The Necessary Revolution Working Together to Create a Sustainable World", Broadway Books, New York, NY

Walla, N. (2012) "CIMS GB Certification Field Notes", Guided Professionalization in the Cleaning Industry with CIMS and CIMS GB, unpublished research case study, Colorado Technical University, Doctor of Management Program

APPENDIX A

CERTIFICATION CHECKLIST - SHALL (MANDATORY) SHOULD (RECOMMENDED) MAY (HONORS)

1. Quality System: This section describes quality system requirements. It sets forth a general framework to ensure effective operations and continual improvement. Elements include:

1.1. Definition of Cleaning Service Requirements

1.1.1. There shall be a site-specific scope of work or performance outcome describing cleaning service requirements.

1.1.2 Changes to the service requirements shall be documented.

1.1.3. Cleaning service requirements should be consistent with the organization's stated mission and values.

1.2. Quality Plan

1.2.1 The organization shall have a written Quality Plan. The Plan is a written process for determining whether cleaning service requirements are met and for identifying improvement opportunities. It commits the organization to attaining the level of service as defined by the customer and the organization in the scope of work or performance outcomes.

1.2.2 The organization should communicate the plan to materially interested parties.

1.2.2.1 Each customer may receive a copy of the plan.

1.2.2.2 Each person in the organization may receive a copy of the plan.

1.2.2.3 The plan may define roles and responsibilities of operational personnel.

1.2.2.4 Each person in the organization should receive documented training related to the plan.

1.2.3 Service quality measurement/metrics

1.2.3.1 The organization shall measure and document its performance against the scope of work and performance outcome requirements.

1.2.3.2 The measurements should be taken at a frequency appropriate for scope of work and performance outcome requirements.

1.2.3.3 The factors being measured should be reasonable and suitable for scope of work and performance outcome requirements.

1.2.3.4 The organization shall use one or more of the following measurement tools:

1.2.3.4.1 Surveys

o Customers completing the surveys should submit them directly to appropriate representatives of the organization, rather than to the on-site supervisory personnel.

o Surveys should be reviewed with appropriate customer representatives.

1.2.3.4.2 Inspections

o Operational inspections by cleaning personnel should be performed as service is delivered.

o Site supervision should conduct site inspections.

o Management should conduct unannounced site inspections.

o Customers may participate in management-level inspections.

PART V: Cases in Global Culture and Organizational Change

Organizations today understandably face new realities in multiple domains, culture being one of the most intricate among them all. The organizations owe their existence to society and pay back to it in various forms as social responsibility and community development. There are new concepts such as conscious capitalism (Mackey & Sisodia, 2013[1]), corporate social responsibility (CSR), and social consciousness related to generation of capital. In the other extreme, as organizations move out to outsourcing or search for cheaper resources beyond the national frontiers they face cultural diversity among employees and customers. Cultural context has its own impact for the smooth functioning of systems, procedures, and human relations. This has been evident in several labor conflicts seen recently in several countries.This section examines some of these sensitive issues through case studies.

Beata Glinka and Tojo Thatchenkery present a case study to seek answers to the vexed question of how culture might influence management students from three radically different large world metropolises.This study covered management students in Warsaw (Poland), Delhi (India), and the Washington, D.C. (U.SA.). The authors collected data through a carefully designed questionnaire and carried out thematic analysis. Their findings reveal the role of bureaucracy in Poland and India and free markets in the U.S. They show how globalization has made the world more homogenous and yet how deep rooted cultural values persist. In the next chapter, Karla Peters-Van Havel focuses on a casestudy to develop an understanding of the psychological sense of community within a geographically dispersed organization. The objectives of her researchare to articulate a workable definition of community as applicable in a non-traditional environment and her analysis shows the ambiguities, challenges, and opportunities afforded by such an attempt.

Eiman Ibrahim, Siti Khalid, Dayana Jalaludin, andYousifAbdelbagi discuss a case about community engagement practice of JOC Petroleum (JOC), a petroleum company operating in the south of Sudan. The case examines corporate community engagement practice for a balanced and equitable development. In the next chapter Bhawna Anjaly and Arun Sahay illustrate a success story of a social entrepreneur who decided to improve the work-life of thousands of poor rickshaw pullers. The case study deals with demographic and socio-economic factors, health, and working conditionsin the city of Patna in India. The last case study in this section as well as the volume is from Ruchi Tyagi and Symphorien Ntibagirirwa. They study the economic success of South East Asia and compare it with failure of economic development in sub-Saharan Africa. The authors conclude that economic growth and development need to be a substantiation of a people's beliefs and values.

---

[1] Mackey, John.,& Sisodia, Raj. (2013). Conscious Capitalism: Liberating the Heroic Spirit of Business. Boston, MA: Harvard Business Review Press.

The Social Construction of Entrepreneurs, Success, and Wealth: A Case Study of Management Students' Perceptions from Three Different Cultural Contexts

Beata Glinka* and Tojo Thatchenkery**

ABSTRACT

Does culture influence how management students perceive success and wealth creation by entrepreneurs? Will students from a highly free-market oriented and internal locus of control oriented culture as the United States perceive wealth creation and success more positively than students from "post-socialist" or less "capitalism-friendly" and external locus of control oriented cultures? We put this question to test by having graduate management students in Poland, India, and the U.S fill out a carefully designed questionnaire. Using thematic analysis we explored the data to bring out underlying and deep rooted assumptions towards business, leadership, and wealth creation. The main purpose of the study is to compare beliefs and perceptions of entrepreneurs, success and wealth in three countries.

Keywords: Culture, wealth creation, success, beliefs, perceptions, external locus

INTRODUCTION: CULTURE AND ENTREPRENEURSHIP

As entrepreneurship is frequently perceived as the main source of economic and social development, the topic attracts considerable interest of researchers representing various disciplines (Acs&Audretsch, 2011). Researchers have explored various elements of the entrepreneurial process and bring to the field tools developed by their disciplines (Baron, 2004; Kirzner, 1973/2001; McClelland, 1961; Schumpeter, 1934/2004). Thanks to this inter-disciplinarity, it has been difficult to agree upon a

* Beata Glinka is with University of Warsaw, Poland.
**Tojo Thatchenkery is with George Mason University, USA.
E-mail: bglinba@gmail.com, thatchen@jamu.edu

definition of entrepreneur and entrepreneurship. Even then, most scholars agree that it is the opportunity that lies at the heart of the entrepreneurial process and offers a guideline to consider actions undertaken by individuals as entrepreneurs(Shane & Venkataraman, 2000; Timmons, 1999; Wickham, 2004).One of the most common manifestations of entrepreneurship is new venture creation or, as Timmons puts it, creating something of value from practically nothing(Timmons, 1999). Identification of opportunities can be perceived as a creative process and depends on the capabilities of potential entrepreneurs to interpret environmental changes. These individual capabilities are shaped in social interactions, and are strongly influenced by the cultural context (B. Berger, 1991; George & Zahra, 2002; Glinka, 2008; Hayton, George, & Zahra, 2002; LaVan & Murphy, 2007). It means that the scale and form of entrepreneurial activity depends on the specific context that forms beliefs, values and perception of potential entrepreneurs.Research supports the notion that culture not only supports but also constitutes an important obstacle to entrepreneurship (Baumol, 2004; Glinka, 2008).

Cultural context influences every stage of entrepreneurial process (Glinka & Gudkova, 2011) such as the decision to start a business (individual motives are influenced by perception of entrepreneurship and establishing own business as an attractive career path), nature of opportunity recognition/creation, types of businesses, ways of managing it, and development strategies.

CULTURAL DIFFERENCES – INDIA, POLAND, AND THE UNITED STATES

When researchers on entrepreneurship focus on culture, they tend to explore the concept of cultural diversity and cultural dimensions(e.g. LaVan & Murphy, 2007). Hofstede'sconcept of four (or later 5) dimensions of culture and national cultures of management is still among the most popular in the field(Hofstede & Hofstede, 2007/2005). Other concepts have recently gained momentum, such as GLOBE project(team of Robert House, 2004)or the "seven cultures of capitalism"(Hampden-Turner & Trompenaars, 1998/1993). All these modelsare often criticized as oversimplifying the phenomenon of culture, stereotyping them, and being too westernized[1]. It shows some differences, but seldom explains their causes. Most of the models are static, whilst culture tends to be a dynamic phenomenon, co-constructed and in a state of flux (Morgan, 1999) and continuously renegotiated through human interactions and dialogue.

Even if these cultural constructs are imperfect, they draw our attention to the topic of intercultural differences. In a highly globalized world these differences still exist

---

[1] According to critics, theories of cultural dimensions and differences created in Europe or US are biased by researchers' values and beliefs; some researchers decides to cooperate with Asian scholars, or on the basis of criticism decided to modify models, e.g. Hofstede decided to add 5th dimension (time) to his model.

and influence various kinds of economic action. In our research we decided to focus on three very different countries- India, Poland, and the United States.

The cultural uniqueness of India, Poland, and the United states have been prolifically described by Hofstede[2] and Trompenaars and Hampden –Turner (2002/1997). In Hofstede's research the three countries differ in various dimensions. Power distance[3] is highest in India (index 77), slightly lower in Poland (68), and lowest in the United States (40). The U.S. is understandably the most individualistic country (91). Though Poland is individualistic, it is much closer to collectivism (60) than the U.S., while India may be seen as a collectivistic country (48). According to Hofstede's data India is a long term oriented and pragmatic culture. Time for Indians is not linear, and not as important as to western societies which – like the U.S. (29) score low on this dimension. Poland is also short-term oriented, very close to the United States (32). In the masculinity – femininity dimension, all three countries are seen as masculine cultures (Poland 64, US – 62. and India – 56).

In one dimension - uncertainty avoidance – India (40) and the U.S. (46) are very close. Poland differs very significantly from India and the U.S.with an unusually high index of 93, making it a country with a very high preference for uncertainty avoidance. Countries exhibiting high uncertainty avoidance, according to Hofstede, maintain rigid codes of belief and are intolerant of unorthodox ideas.As we can see, these three countries differ in almost every dimension, with Poland being "in the middle," albeit close to the U.S., except for the significant difference in uncertainty avoidance. The cultural distance between India and the U.S. is quite high while Poland differs significantly from other countries in our analysis.

Trompenaars and Hampden –Turner (2002/1997) also compared several cultural dimensions. From the point of view of entrepreneurship research, the data about the locus of control is worth noting. For example, when asked if they believed that their fate is in their hands, 82% in the U.S. gave an affirmative answer, while only 66% in Poland and 63% in India felt so(Trompenaars & Hampden-Turner, 2002/1997, p. 173).

In entrepreneurship research some dimensions of culture are typically associated with the tendency for entrepreneurial behavior such as individualism rather than collectivism, low uncertainty avoidance and internal locus of control. Further, American culture is often perceived and described as the one that stimulates entrepreneurship (see Shane, 1992). The majority of influential concepts of entrepreneurship have originated from the United States (Thomas & Mueller, 2000). American success stories of rags to the riches are universally known.During economic crisis, the decline of American "culture of entrepreneurship" is often narrated by scholars and politicians as one of the causes. Many claim that in order to foster economic growth, the American

---

[2] http://geert-hofstede.com
[3] All the following data taken from: *http://geert-hofstede.com*. (Acces July 30th)

entrepreneurial spirit must be revived (Shapiro, 2011). Despite such occasional self-doubt, the U.S. is perceived as possessing one of the most favorable cultural climates for entrepreneurs.

Entrepreneurship in India has been studied since the mid-1960s. McClelland (1967) and McClelland and Winter (1978) conducted pioneering studies on entrepreneurship in India in 1964 and 1965. Believing that the need for achievement was a critical factor in entrepreneurship, McClelland sought to train young people in India to develop a desire for success. He conducted a five-year project known as the "Kakinada experiment" in one of the economically prosperous areas in Southern India. McClelland designed a three month long training program to train young people to set new goals and develop the need for achievement. To his surprise, he found that the traditional Indian values did not come in the way of achieving material success. Almost fifty years later, entrepreneurship continues to be a hot topic of research in India (Khanna, 2008; Prahalad, 2004; Pota, 2010; Nath, 2007).

Publications connecting Polish entrepreneurship and culture are scarce (Glinka, 2008). According to opinion polls (CBOS, 2009), social status of entrepreneurs is still quite low in Poland. The climate for entrepreneurship has been harsh for the last 200 years in Poland. First, in the end of 18th century the country lost its independence and had been divided among its neighbors for around 125 years. In the beginning of 20th century Poland experienced a short era of independence and economic freedom, and after the Second World War the socialist system was introduced. In official socialist propaganda, entrepreneurs were depicted as second class citizens, those who cheated and exploited honest working class. Only since the economic liberalization that began in 1989 could entrepreneurship develop without major obstacles. All these historic and other factors influence the Polish culture of entrepreneurship, which is still developing and cannot be perceived as fully supporting entrepreneurs.

CULTURE AND ENTREPRENEURSHIP IN THE CLASSROOM

There is a growing belief among scholars and public policy makers that sound legal environment and new ventures financing alone are not enough to foster entrepreneurship. As pointed out before, favorable social and cultural contexts are needed to encourage entrepreneurs and help them deal with their ventures. At the same time, values and beliefs cannot be created or changed by direct governmental or orchestrated initiatives, especially in the short term. Values change over time in a slow and complex process. Our reality is socially constructed (Berger & Luckman, 1983) through a process of human engagement in language. As a result, new values, beliefs, and the perception towards entrepreneurship may change only gradually.

Various factors play an important role in shaping values and beliefs. They include religion, history, globalization, mass media, and education. The last factor is particularly important in our project. In the process of education, one can build or fine-tune elements of entrepreneurial competences, defined by Bird (1995, p. 51) as "underlying characteristics such as generic and specific knowledge, motives, traits, self-images, social roles, and skills which result in venture birth, survival and/or growth."

Students' perceptions of entrepreneurs and entrepreneurship reflect their cultural context, but they may also indicate the quality and effectiveness of education as a way of promoting entrepreneurship and entrepreneurial behavior. Numerous studies have focused on entrepreneurial intentions of students (See Gassea & Tremblay, 2011 for a review). In addition, universities and business schools often try to measure entrepreneurial intentions in order to evaluate their performance in entrepreneurial education, and to define students' needs and preferences. As Gassea and Tremblay (2011)have stated, only a few studies have attempted to understand how the students' values, attitudes, and behavior can predispose them to create a new venture or have the intention to do so. The aim of this case study is to describe and explain students' perceptions and beliefs in three different cultural contexts. We do not examine (or measure) directly the influence of beliefs on entrepreneurial intent. Our focus is instead in understanding the socially constructed images of entrepreneurship.

The following research questions were raised in this project:

- How do students in different cultural settings perceive entrepreneurs? What are their beliefs about entrepreneurial processes and the roles of entrepreneurs?

- Does culture influence how management students perceive success and wealth creation by entrepreneurs?

- Will students from a highly free-market oriented and internal locus of control oriented culture such as the United States perceive wealth creation and success more positively than students from "socialist" or less "capitalism-friendly" and external locus of control oriented cultures?

It was assumed that cultural values in the three countries in threedifferent continents with different history, religion, and modes of development would differ significantly. The goal was to show the consequences of different cultural settings to the perception of entrepreneurship.We hope that our findings can be used not only to understand the cultural context of entrepreneurship, but also for designing better programs of entrepreneurship and innovation- oriented educationin universities.

RESEARCH METHODOLOGY

As the phenomenon under investigation is connected with values, motives and perceptions, we decided to use qualitative methods of data collection and analysis. Grant and Perren(2002) analyzed publications in the leading journals on entrepreneurship and concluded that 90% of them had been based on positivist assumptions. This means that most of the literature on entrepreneurship and its contextare based on the use of quantitative methods, often taking the form of surveys. After 10 years, the body of research is elaborate and exhaustive but positivistic assumptions still dominate the field. In contrast, this case study is based on interpretive assumptions and use qualitative methods as we believe that this approach leaves more space for open research and discovery and encourages the researcher to break new grounds and explore new phenomena. As many researchers have suggested, the utilization of methods other than quantitative can often lead to a better understanding of the phenomenon of entrepreneurship (Hjorth & Steyaert, 2004; Jennings, Perren, & Carter, 2005; Rae, 2002; Warren, 2004).

We decided to use narrative methods(Czarniawska-Joerges, 1998; Czarniawska, 2004)that proved to be highly useful in previous research projects of one of the authors. Students were given questionnaires with open questions and story lines. They were asked to interpret and comment upon stories about entrepreneurship, entrepreneurs, their success and wealth. We also asked them to write/finish a story prompted by us. We conducted our research in three universities in Poland, USA and India. They were

1. University of Warsaw, Poland, Faculty of Management (90 students, most of them 19-26 in age, about 60% male)[4]

2. School of Public Policy, George Mason University, Virginia, USA, (21 students, between 23 and 53 years in age, about 60% female), and

3. Birla Institute of Management Technology (BIMTECH), Greater NOIDA, India, MBA (52 students, most of them between 20 and 26 in age, about 60% male).

The Polish part of the research was conducted during 2005 and 2006. The Polish stories were translated into English. Appropriate corrections were made to adjust them to the U.S and Indian cultural setting (e.g. testing, changing names of entrepreneurs). Research in India and the United States were conducted in December 2011[5] and January 2012 respectively. We also decided to use 8 questionnaires that were collected from a group of American students in Poland in 2006. The data collected during the research was analyzed by two researchers separately (in order to triangulate results), compared, and discussed.

Our research has several limitations. (A) Qualitative methods do not allow for statistical generalizations. Yet, Bruyat and Julien(2001)point out that interpretative research fits the field of entrepreneurship better since it is a highly dynamic and not deterministic phenomenon that is deeply rooted in culture and social interactions. Qualitative methods are suited to the exploration of dynamic processes and they allow for a depiction of processes and generalization per analogy(Barbara Czarniawska-

---

[4] The first question, story of a wealthy business owner, was answered by almost 200 students, as it was included in 2 stages of the research in Poland.

[5] We would like to thank Professors Manosi Chaudhuri and doctoral student Nidhi Thakur of BIMTECH for their help in data collection.

Joerges, 1992). (B) Data were collected in different time, i.e. Polish data is 5-6 years older than the rest of the collected material. We are, however, convinced that this time gap didn't strongly influence the results. As Poland is a country that went through a systemic and major economic change relatively recently (1989), the cultural context of economic action is still quite turbulent. A modest amount of public opinion surveys and scientific research have shown that the social attitude towards entrepreneurs has become more positive in Poland(Glinka, 2008). This may mean that had the study were done in 2012, the results would have been even more positive about entrepreneurs than in 2005.

The research questionnaire consisted of three major parts. We discuss them below and present selected results of the study.

The Wealthy Entrepreneur

In the first part students were asked to finish the following story and propose its title "Mr (Name)[6] is the owner and CEO of a well-known company. For the last couple of years he has been listed among the richest people in (the country)".

Most of Indian students (over ¾) finished the story with a positive description of the entrepreneur and his business. Three types of interpretation were most common among them: (1) success through ethics and in connection with the society, (2) hardworking men can be successful and (3) success is rooted in mind; one's knowledge and ability to innovate will play crucial role.

1. The entrepreneur is successful, because of his strict moral rules and good relations with other people. His happiness is based on solving social problems; he helps others and serves the society. His business is built on ethics and social responsibility. He cares about other people: family, employees, friends, stakeholders.

Following sound ethical business practices has made his company achieve greater benefits. [M25]

> He wants to serve the society with this money and go for sustainable development. He wants to be a philanthropist. [M23]
>
> He has shown the example of simple living in spite of all the richness. He has many social initiatives developed for the welfare of children and women in the society [M23]
>
> He donates with free hand to many NGO's and has his own Cancer Kid's Foundation. People say he has a heart of gold [F21]

The entrepreneur not only thinks about his family, he also thinks about succession.

2. Success of an entrepreneur is a result of his hard work. He's gone a long way from "rags to riches".

---

6 Different names that were culturally familiar were used in each country.

He worked hard and raised an empire. [M28]

He attained this zenith by his hardworking [...] He is a self-made man as he has shown that if a person wants he has the ability to rise from rags to riches. [F20]

3. Success and wealth stem from good education, experience, and innovation.

His company works on innovation and finding solutions to problems faced by society. [M22]

The reason for Sharma's success is his innovative streak and his knack for grabbing new opportunities. [F22]

Indian students very often emphasized the meaning of balance in life – having family and friends, simple life within society, and helping others. They felt that success may come and go. Even if entrepreneurs work very hard, they may never know when the fortune may turn its back on them.

He was always considered to be in the control of things, had a first rate idea about the market. But things changed after he was diagnosed with a life-threatening cancer[M23].

Contrary to their Indian colleagues, the vast majority of Polish students (about 75%) interpreted the story in a very negative way. They felt that the entrepreneur was arrested since he earned the money in an illegal way as he was involved in a huge scandal. He was caught on money laundering or cooperation with mafia. Most of the stories were not only pessimistic but painted elements criminality and brutality. The entrepreneur is exploiting his employees, and cheating on various groups of stakeholders. Some students described this dishonest entrepreneur as a product of Polish economy.

Obviously, in Poland there is no place for decent business. Will it ever change? [M24].

Some students pointed out that even if the entrepreneur himself is a good man, there are people who will influence him and make him take part in "dirty business."

Despite honest work, he was dragged into shady business [K19].

A few stories focused on the moral side of entrepreneur's life, depicting him as a character in a sex scandal. Only few people (around 15%) suggested that hewas probably a successful entrepreneur and that they should learn from him, or he started another successful business.

Over 70% ofthe students from the U.S. presented a positive story of a business owner. Two students didn't give an answer and in two cases stories were ambiguous. Among the group of American students examined earlier in Poland,six out of the eight gave a positive interpretation. Most of the students wrote about the hard work of the successful entrepreneur who was seen as a good example of a self-made man.

> To be at the top of the Forbes list of billionaires has taken a considerable amount of hard work, ambition and dedication [F29].

One student presented a story of patience, persistence and tolerance to failure:

> His success was not handed to him easily. He failed in the past in several small companies he started – all went bankrupt. Mr. Smith didn't give up. He learnt the lessons from his failure and was able to create this successful enterprise he now enjoys [F52].

Some personal characteristics like ambition, creativity and ability to empower employees were also stressed. Good education was seen as important:

> During his childhood, Mr. Smith was supported entirely by family members who provided him with money to pay for the best education in the Nation [M34].

Some students stressed that now that the entrepreneur was wealthy, he could donate money to charity and that he could serve as an example for others who wanted to be successful. The role of entrepreneur's family was also crucial, and balancing business and family was one of the most difficult tasks of this entrepreneur. Here, we see a similarity between Indian and the U.S. students; both groups define the same problem, but for the Americans it is much harder to solve. Three stories, classified by us as ambiguous, were about the struggle for balance in life.

> This is what he has always dreamed about but with wealth didn't come happiness [M39].

> He is torn because he enjoys his job and the money is phenomenal. However, when is enough, enough in regards to money? Is it more important than his family? [M26].

A few students suggested that the next step of entrepreneur's career will be politics (and almost all of them were skeptical about it).Negative interpretations of the story were connected with exploiting workforce in countries with poor human rights protection and rampant with fraud.

In all countries the titles reflected the character of stories (see Table 1). Title of positive stories stressed success, while those proposed to negative stories – crime, scandal, or fraud.

Table 1: Selected titles of wealthy entrepreneur story proposed by students

	Examples of titles	
	Positive	*Negative*
India	▪ A Leaders Tale ▪ Story of a Pioneer ▪ The Rich and Successful ▪ Hard work Always Pays Off ▪ Inspiring Story of a Self-made Man ▪ Innovation creates great success stories ▪ From rags to riches ▪ The Rich and Successful Entrepreneur ▪ All that makes a difference is "Passion" ▪ A Philanthropist ▪ Good work needs no helping hand. It has the hand of God ▪ Mr. Sharma who made it big ▪ The man who owns – the heart of gold ▪ The Innovative and Ethical Business	▪ Two Sides of a Coin ▪ Illegal practices leading to fall in profit ▪ Power: a wicked temptation
Poland	▪ Success in a Polish style, ▪ Work, work…. success! ▪ Happy end!	▪ Another scandal in Polish business world ▪ Pol$ka?? ▪ Dirty money ▪ Another businessman in jail ▪ Dark side of impressing career ▪ Polish businessman ▪ The fortune built on harm and exploitation ▪ Iksiński-gate ▪ The truth about III RP
USA	▪ American, "Boot-straps" success Story ▪ How leaders are made? ▪ Jimmy's Innovation Challenge ▪ From rags to riches: The Story of how Mr. Smith rose to the top ▪ Mr. Smith saves the Day ▪ Go for it! ▪ Success: Through and Through ▪ The American Dream	Negative: ▪ The Enron story Ambivalent: ▪ Is it Possible to Have a Balanced Life: The Advantages and Disadvantages of Success ▪ The True Meaning of Life

Source: Own research.

STORIES ABOUT THE ECONOMY

The second part of the questionnaire consisted of 10 stories,[7] given in pairs. In every pair one story was more positive (gave a positive image of entrepreneur or economy), and the second was usually connected with a kind of illegal or unethical action. We asked students to choose in every pair one story which, in their opinion, was more probable. We also asked them to indicate 3 of 10 stories that, in their opinion, were

---

[7] In Polish part – 12 stories, but 2 of them were irrelevant to other countries, as they were based on EU regulations.

most typical for their county's economy and explain the choice. The short version of stories is presented in table 2.

Table 2: Stories about entrepreneurs/business

1. Anthony's company of just six people is really innovative and conquered the market with their new product.	2. Anthony's company of just six people is really "innovative" and thanks to illegal practices managed to hide real earnings for many years.
3. "Strawberry," a company from a small town, is a victim of a dishonest contractor, who vanished with their productand never paid for it.	4. "Strawberry", a company from a small town, is successful thanks to close relations with its business partners based on trust.
5. (Mr. Name) is awell-known entrepreneur, owner of some giant companies from Fortune 500. Recently he was arrested on charges of corruption, breaking labor laws, misappropriation of property and many other violations.	6. (Mr. Name) is a well-known entrepreneur, owner of some giant companies from Fortune 500. Born in a poor family he is a classic example of a self-made man.
7. Hard work is a main source of(Ms. Name) company. She had some hard times in her business – but now it's over, thanks to her business attitude.	8. Relations and connections are main sources of (Ms. Name) company. She works with people, who have "something to offer": an uncle in IRS, sister working for a member of congress etc. She knows she can go through hard times thanks to them.
9. (Mr. Name)'s company has vanished from the market because of a dishonestassociate and accountant, who had been pulling out money from the company.	10. (Mr. Name)'s company has vanished from the market because of his inability to listen to good advices of smart associates and accountants, who suggested that the company needed a new strategy. (Mr. Name) ignored them and they both left the company.

Source: Own research.

The results in three countries differ significantly (see Table 3). Polish students tended to give very balanced answers in 4 out of 5 pairs. Only in one case certain option was assessed as more plausible – Polish students did not believe in a "self-made man" story and thought that the option of an entrepreneur in jail was more likely. On the contrary, in the U.S. and India about 2/3 of students thought that self-made man was closer to reality than the entrepreneur being seen as a criminal. The positive story was assessed as more plausible than the negative one in both India and the U.S. Such beliefs are much stronger in the U.S. (pairs 1\2, 7\8 and – especially – 9\10).

Interestingly, in Poland students indicated as most characteristic to the business environment the stories that were among the rarest choices. Story number 5 (entrepreneur ending up in jail) was indicated by half of the respondents. Story number 8 (relying on people that has something to offer) was a second popular choice (41%). This story was also popular among Indian students. But it is important to note that connections have different social connotations in these two countries (generally in Poland this story sound much more negative than in India). Stories 2,3 and 9 came next (between 25 and 30% of choices). It's worth noting, that all this scenarios are in Polish context negative, giving pejorative image of entrepreneurs and economy.

Table 3: Students opinion of plausibility of stories about entrepreneurs/business

	Percent of students finding a certain story more likely									
Country:	1	2N	3N	4	5N	6	7	8N[8]	9(N)[9]	10
India[10]	80%	20%	37%	63%	34%	66%	52%	49%	50%	50%
Poland	51%	49%	52%	48%	72%	28%	53%	47%	53%	47%
USA	81%	19%	10%	90%	38%	62%	62%	38%	19%	81%

Source: own research.

We asked students to explain their choice. Most of Polish students offered explanations criticizing business practices in Poland. Almost one quarter of the students claimed that their choice was influenced by mass-media that showed examples of dishonest entrepreneurs and business scandals.

> In Poland people build their fortune by cheating [M20]
>
> Lots of business people steal. [M22]
>
> The central role In Polish economy is played by connections, corruption and exploitation. [M19]
>
> You can hear about all these spectacular situation in the media. [F28]
>
> These cases are most often described in different media. [M20]

Students felt helpless and frustrated. Some of them felt that there was no way to change situation while others hoped for governmental intervention:

> I hope that state will introduce proper regulations that will limit such situations. [F28]

Only few voices were more optimistic:

> [Good] entrepreneurs are in majority. There are companies that cheat, but it's a minority. Most entrepreneurs try to be honest. [M21]

On the contrary, in India and the US, student tended to indicate much more positive visions of business as characteristic to their countries. In India stories 1 and

---

[8.] The negative interpretations of that story are especially characteristic to Poland where even the Polish word for "network" has almost purely negative connotations (so it's used in English).

[9.] In his case both stories end with company's failure. In the first case (9) – the failure is connected with fraud, and in the second (10) – with ignoring good advices by entrepreneur.

[10.] In India almost 1/3 of students didn't follow instructions and didn't indicate themost likely story in every pair. All the students marked the stories that, in their opinion, were most characteristics to the business/ economy in India.

6 were chosen by over 40% of students. In the first we see innovation as a source of success, in the second – a successful self-made man. Description 8 came third, and we have discussed it earlier in this case study.

When commenting their choice most Indian students wouldn't give an in-depth analysis of Indian economy. However, they stressed some important aspects of it which were good and bad. They included the role of trust, business networks, hard work and innovation, numerous examples of self-made men, but also some shady practices.

> The business environment in India is very healthy and has a bright future. [M25]
>
> People in India are innovative in the sense they get output from minimum possible resources.[M21]
>
> Every business in India starts from a scratch and within no time they expand like anything. [M22]
>
> Trust is an essential aspect in Indian business. [F21]
>
> Also there is a lot of corruption in India. [M21]

In the U.S. descriptions 4 and 6 were chosen by almost half of the studrnts, i.e. self-made man, and relation based on trust as a source of success. Stories number 10 (failure of an entrepreneur who didn't listen to smart advice) and number 1 (innovation) were next. Positive remarks dominated among the explanations behind the choices which stressed the American entrepreneurial spirit.

> Most people in the United States operate through relationships, hard work, creativity and trust. There are some famous bad apples but the majority of people are good. [F41]
>
> Small business are the life-blood of the American economy.[F29]

Some students tried to present different sides of economy which were not always trouble free and filled with honesty. On the other hand, students felt that negative images promoted by media and politicians were exaggerated and did not reflect the state of businesses in the U.S.

> While the media and politicians like to publicize the negatives, I believe that the wide majority of business on the US are hardworking and strive to operate ethically. [M39]
>
> Both legally dubious and strategically clever paths to success seem possible. They often are present at the same time. [M39]

Some students compared corporations and small businesses.

> I think there are many small businesses that work hard and with integrity. However I also think that there are many corrupt corporations. [F24]
>
> Corruption from large companies seems fairly common in todays' world. [F52]

Sources of Success – Unfinished Sentences

In the third part of the questionnaire, we asked students to finish 5 sentences connected with success of entrepreneurs, or in business in general. The list of sentences is shown in Table 4.

Table 4: Unfinished sentences. Source: own research.

1	The owner of the Bemex company started his business in 1997. His company is doing very well, brings profits and gradually enters new markets. The success of Bemex is caused by…….
2	Owners of companies make big bucks because…….
3	The best recipe to create a good business is…….
4	(Name) works in the gardening industry. He is a hardworking, decent and scrupulous man. These characteristics mean that (name)…….
5	"The first million has to be stolen". Comment on that statement……..

After answering questions in the first two sections in very pessimistic ways, Polish students surprised us by proposing more balanced argumentation in the last section of the questionnaire. The most popular source of success and wealth (sentence 1 and 2) were: finding a market niche, good management, designing good strategy and using market analysis.

Hard work and commitment also help.

A minority of students pointed to exploitation of employees, cheating on taxes or other illegal/unethical practices.

Almost all American students named only positive reasons for success and wealth. They were vision, innovation, hard work, leadership and teamwork. They stressed that business was inherently a risky venture and that one could not succeed without taking some risk.

> 'A culture of innovation and hard work along with taking calculated risk.' [M34]

Only a few students mentioned negative sources of wealth. All were concerned about the differences in wages in top-down structures or extra bonuses.

Indian students pointed out mostly positive sources of company success, but were mixed when it came to sources of wealth. As far as success is concerned, factors such as innovation, ethics, creativity, hard work, honesty, and good HR practices were felt to be behind it. One student stated that the success was based on "pure luck." Those factors are also important when students are discussing sources of wealth, but this time also some negative elements may appear, like cheating, exploiting people or overcharging for products.

They beg, borrow and steal. They are cheaters. [M21]

According to Polish students, there was no clear recipe to create a good business. Some focused on idea, innovation and hard work, while a significant percentage of them suggested that contacts with politicians and evading the law as a more simple way.

... 'become a member of parliament' [M19]

American students saw this thing differently. All of them connected good business with entrepreneurial action: his/her motivation, willingness to learn, vision and creativity. They also felt that good location and resources also may help.

'Do what you love – and hopefully people will need it.' [F52]

Students in India too presented a clear recipe to create a good business and all of them were based on positive business attitude:

'Think+ initiate+ lead+ trust+ persevere' [M22]

'Hard work+ honesty+ care+ belief' [F21]

'Always be innovative and creative in doing business and never cheat your customer and be transparent.' [F20]

Being a hardworking man (sentence 4) for Polish students may mean both: success in life (but in a long term) or being poor and clumsy. People may like him, but probably his success will be very limited. Obviously it is not a best way to do a fast career. For American students having those characteristics means being prepared for success, trusted by clients and the community. For Indians this man is prepared for success and high earnings. In all the three countries students had difficulty in determining whether their fictional character was a worker or an entrepreneur, but the second possibility prevailed in most instances.

In the last question ("the first million has to be stolen"), almost 40% of Polish students avoided direct answer, 30% disagreed and 27% agreed. Almost all American students disagreed with that statement, and one person ironically stated:

'Sounds good to me, but where?' [M39]

Indian students mostly disagreed with that statement and felt that business requires honesty. But some of them noticed that in real life corruption does occur.

CONCLUSIONS AND DISCUSSION

Management students' images of entrepreneurs, success and economy in general were different in the three countries explored in this case study. The most negative images emerged from Poland.

Results in India were closer to the U.S than results in Poland. It was surprising since Asian cultures are generally perceived as more distant from the U.S. than

European. The reason for this may lie in high uncertainty avoidance of Poles and their risk aversion (Hensel & Glinka, 2012). This can explain low status of entrepreneurs (they have risky job), but not the fully negative stereotypes of them. This can be better explained by historically rooted beliefs.

These case studies reveal interesting aspects about entrepreneurship from three diverse cultures. Despite the rapid homogenization of cultures (Thatchenkery, 2006) arising mostly out of advanced state of globalization, the results of this study indicate that deep rooted cultural values still play a key role in how people think of entrepreneurship, material success, and wealth creation. While people in the three cultures seem to want to succeed and achieve, the ambivalence towards wealth creation is very clear among them. For the United States, entrepreneurship is the foundation of its economic engine and there is no ambiguity about the desirability of possessing wealth. The picture gets muddied for the Poles and Indians.

The findings of this study have significant implications for management education. MBA began as an American invention and has largely been exported to rest of the world. The popularization of MBA was done without much regard to cultural uniqueness of the local context in rest of the world. Influential researchers such as Mintzberg (2004) have called for the creation of "managers, not MBAs" in recognition of this important need for cultural appreciation in management education. This case study, while being a solid affirmation of such thinking, also highlights that the differences expected across national cultures are not what they used to be.

BIBLIOGRAPHY

Acs, Zoltan.,&Audretsch, David. (2011) (Eds).*Handbook of Entrepreneurship Research: An Interdisciplinary Survey and Introduction*. New York: Springer.

Baron, R.A. (2004). The Cognitive Perspective: A Valuable Tool For Answering Entrepreneurship's Basic "Why" Questions". *Journal of Business Venturing, 19*(2), 221-240.

Baumol, W.J. (2004). Entrepreneurial Cultures And Countercultures. *Academy of Management Learning and Education, 3*, 316-326.

Berger, B. (Ed.). (1991). *The Culture of Entrepreneurship*. San Francisco: ICS Press.

Berger, L., & Luckman, T. (1983). *Społeczne tworzenie rzeczywistości (Social construction of reality)*. Warszawa: PIW.

Bird, B. (1995). Toward a Theory of Entrepreneurial Competency. In J. A. Katz & B. R.H. (Eds.), *Advances in Entrepreneurship, Firm Emergence, And Growth* (Vol. 2): JAI Press.

Bruyat, C., & Julien, P.-A. (2001). Defining the Field of Research in Entrepreneurship. *Journal of Business Venturing 16*(2), 165-180.

CBOS. (2009). *Prestiż zawodów*. Warszawa: CBOS.

Czarniawska-Joerges, B. (1992). *Exploring Complex Organizations: A cultural perspective.*

Newbury Park-London-New Delhi: SAGE.

Czarniawska-Joerges, B. (1998). *Narrative Approach in Organization Studies*. Thousand Oaks, CA Sage Publications.

Czarniawska, B. (2004). *Narratives in Social Science Research*. London: Sage Publications.

Gassea, Y., & Tremblay, M. (2011). Entrepreneurial Beliefs and Intentions: A Cross-Cultural Study of University Students in Seven Countries. *International Journal of Business, 16*(4), 303-314.

George, G., & Zahra, S. A. (2002). Culture and its Consequences for Entrepreneurship. *Entrepreneurship: Theory and Practice, 26*, 27-29.

Glinka, B. (2008). *Kulturowe uwarunkowania przedsiębiorczości w Polsce (The cultural context of entrepreneurship in Poland)*. Warszawa: PWE.

Glinka, B., & Gudkova, S. (2011). *Przedsiębiorczość* Warszawa: Wolters Kluwer.

Grant, P., & Perren, L. (2002). Small Business and Entrepreneurial Research: Meta-theories, Paradigms and Prejudices. *International Small Business Journal, 20*(2), 185-209.

Hampden-Turner, C., & Trompenaars, A. (1998/1993). *Siedem kultur kapitalizmu (The seven cultures of capitalism)*. Warszawa: Dom Wydawniczy ABC.

Hayton, J. C., George, G., & Zahra, S. A. (2002). National Culture and Entrepreneurship: a Review of Behavioral Research. *Entrepreneurship: Theory and Practice, 26*, 33-52.

Hensel, P., & Glinka, B. (2012). *Urzędnicy i przedsiębiorcy (Bureaucrats and entrepreneurs)*. Warszawa: Poltext.

Hjorth, D., & Steyaert, C. (Eds.). (2004). *Narrative and Discursive Approaches in Entrepreneurship*. Cheltenham: Edward Elgar.

Hofstede, G., & Hofstede, G. J. (2007/2005). *Kultury i organizacje (Cultures and organizations. Software of the mind)*. Warszawa: PWE.

House, R. J. (Ed.). (2004). *Culture, leadership and organizations: GLOBE Study of 62 Societies*. Thousand Oaks: Sage Publications.

Jennings, P. L., Perren, L., & Carter, S. (2005). Alternative Perspectives on Entrepreneurship Research. *entrepreneurship Theory and Practice, 29*(2), 145-152.

Khanna, Tarun. (2008). Billions of Entrepreneurs: How China and India Are Reshaping Their Futures--and Yours Boston: MA: Harvard Business School Press.

Kirzner, I. M. (1973/2001). *Competition and Entrepreneurship*. Chicago, London: The University of Chicago Press.

LaVan, H., & Murphy, P. J. (2007). Southeast Asian Culture, Human Development, and Business CompetitivenessHelen. *Journal of Asia Business Studies*(Fall), 14-22.

McClelland, D. C. (1961). *The Achieving Society*. Princeton: Van Nostrand.

McClelland, D.C., & Winter, D. (1978). Motivating Economic Achievement. New York: Free Press.

Mintzberg, H (2004). Managers Not MBAs: A Hard Look at the Soft Practice of Managing and Management Development. San Francisco: Berrett-Koehler.

Nath, Kamal. (2007). India's Century: The Age of Entrepreneurship in the World's Biggest Democracy. New York: McGraw-Hill

Pota, Vikas. (2010). India Inc.: How India's Top Ten Entrepreneurs are Winning Globally. Boston, MA: Nicholas Brealey Publishing.

Prahalad, C.K. (2004). The Fortune at the Bottom of the Pyramid. Eradicating Poverty Through Profits Philadelphia, PA: Wharton School Publishing.

Rae, D. (2002). Understanding Entrepreneurial Learning: A Question of How? *International Journal of Entrepreneurial Behaviour and Research, 6*(3), 145-159.

Schumpeter, J. A. (1934/2004). *The theory of economic development*. New Brunswick, London: Transaction Publishers.

Shane, S. (1992). Why do some societies invent more than others? *Journal of Business Venturing*(7), 29-46.

Shane, S., & Venkataraman, S. (2000). The Promise of Entrepreneurship as a Field of Research. *Academy of Management Review, 25*(1), 217 – 226.

Shapiro, G. (2011). *The Comeback: How Innovation Will Restore the American Dream*: Beaufort Books.

Thatchenkery, T. (2006). Organization development in Asia: Globalization, homogenization, and the end of culture-specific practices. In B. Jones & M. Brazzel (Eds.). *The NTL handbook of organization development and change: Principles, practices, and perspectives* (pp. 387-403). San Francisco: Pfeiffer/Wiley.

Thomas, A. S., & Mueller, S. L. (2000). A Case for Comparative Entrepreneurship: Assessing the Relevance of Culture. *Journal of International Business Studies, 31*(2), 287-301.

Timmons, J. (1999). *New Venture Creation. Entrepreneurship for the 21st Century – 5th Edition*: Irwin/McGraw-Hill.

Trompenaars, A., & Hampden-Turner, C. (2002/1997). *Siedem wymiarów kultury (Riding the wawes of culture)*. Krakow: Oficyna Ekonomiczna.

Warren, L. (2004). A Systemic Approach to Entrepreneurial Learning: An Exploration Using Storytelling. *Systems Research and Behavioral Science, 21*(1), 3-16.

Wickham, P. A. (2004). *Strategic Entrepreneurship*: Prentice Hall – Financial Times.

The 'Sense of Community' in Geographically Dispersed Organizations: A Case Study of the Organization of Burners

Karla R. Peters-Van Havel*

ABSTRACT

The focus of this case study is to develop an understanding of the psychological sense of community within a geographically dispersed organization. This is embarked upon through a case study of Black Rock City, LLC (also known as Burning Man), which lacks traditional physical boundaries. The objectives of this research are to articulate a workable definition of community as applicable in a non-traditional environment, to explore the psychological sense of community, and to identify the communal aspect of Burning Man. The methodology used is a qualitative case study with a variety of data collection procedures including in-depth exploratory interviews of self-defined Burners, a history, direct observations, an ethnographic study, and primary research using The Sense of Community Index-2, commonly referred to as the SCI-2 (Chavis, Lee, & Acosta, 2008). Results from the case study are that a "shared emotional connection" is the most important factor to this geo-dispersed community and that acceptance, collaboration, and shared symbols and rituals can create a "sense of community" despite ambiguous boundaries.

Keywords: Community, geo-dispersed, burning man, gemeinschaft, gesellschaft, black rock city, burner, organization.

INTRODUCTION

What is a community and is a communal feeling measurable? Is Burning Man a community or a society consisting of a web of systemic communities? Why do some people feel connected to a group while others do not? Is a community intentional or fortuitous? Black Rock City is a limited liability corporation with offices in San Francisco, CA and Gerlach, NV. It is the organization that hosts the Burning Man

* Vice President of the Institute of Management Studies; Ph.D student Schoool of Human and Organizational Development Fielding Graduate University.
E-mail: karla@ims-online.com

festival, from which self-described "Burners" have evolved. The semantics are in a perpetual flux and "Black Rock City" is used interchangeably with "Black Rock Desert," yet "Black Rock City, LLC" is the designation of the current establishment. "Burning Man" refers to the art piece built in the likeness of a man burned in the Black Rock Desert during the festival, it also refers to the entirety of the festival itself, and finally, to the organization which extends beyond the playa and the Burners that define themselves as a part of the system of Burning Man. The organization is in the process of transforming into a not-for-profit organization (501c-3) branded "The Burning Man Project." There are presently 19 Year Round Staff, a Senior Staff of 16, an Executive Committee of 4 plus the Burning Man Board of 6 (Burning Man, 2012). Self-defined Burners illustrate their milieu as consisting of those that participate in the annual Burning Man retreat located in the Black Rock Desert of Nevada or any of the year-round regional Burning Man related activities. Further, being an active Burner is a psychological state reflected in behaviour, emotional intelligence, and culture. This group consists of well over 100,000 (Burning Man Census, 2011). Both the organization and the event are separate but inclusive of the culture (Heller & Minedew, 2012). The Black Rock City, LLC organization deals with many of the same issues other associations deal with, such as legal affairs, taxes, government regulations and politics, commercialism and marketing, communicating across cultural divides, market appropriate pricing, and competition in the form of other art events around the world. The organization has regional representatives who organize local events, fundraisers for projects, and market the culture and art of the Burners. While this populace is unconventional in many ways it is also familiar in the construct and systemic nature to unbounded organizations.

Defining the boundaries of Burning Man for the sake of clarifying who is a member of this assembly requires non-traditional thought due to the virtual and remote relationships amongst members. The uniqueness of a morphing culturally diverse city that is annually rebuilding and destructing its infrastructure, as Burning Man is, creates ambiguous borders. Additionally, the organization of Burners is continuously redefining its meaning and purpose supplementing the intellectual merit of this research. Finally, the migratory nature of Burners command an understanding of an internalized sense of community that does not depend on geographical boundaries for theoretical definition. Culminating in a portrait of community that can be extended to other groups not limited by physical space or the boundaries of time, such as online learning groups or virtual organizations, Burning Man is a hub for interdisciplinary studies. The topic of community became an interest of mine through discussions with colleagues on internalizing ones community. After my ethnographic study of Burning Man in 2011, I further questioned what it is that makes some feel that they are a part of this particular "community" while others function as observers, passive and without commitment. This was my fuel for deeper exploration. The realization of the diverse applications of the concepts associated with the development of a psychological sense of community occurred ex post facto. There are numerous researchers and interdisciplinary studies contributing to the study and definition of community, but there are a few that stand out as being particularly pertinent to the understanding of the Burning Man ecosystem. Ferdinand Tönnies' (1957) explanation of *gemeinschaft* and *gesellschaft*, and Emile Durkheim's (1964) studies of social density provide the baseline for understanding what Burning Man is as a totality, the organization and the Burners that consider themselves functioning as a single unit. A template for future applications based on the Burning Man experience, along with a deeper understanding of questions regarding the internalization of community, stems from the "sense of community" as defined by McMillan and Chavis (1986) and the revised theory of psychological sense of community by McMillan (1996).

In today's transient and global world, many organizations are looking for commitment, accountability and passion. These attributes can go from latency to fulfilment on an individual level through a sense of belonging, a difficult motivational tool to develop in a geo-dispersed organization. The sense of belonging evolves from a psychological sense of community and an internalization of commitment to a community. This case study contributes ideas on developing a sense of community and social capital (McMillan & Chavis, 1986; McMillan, 1996; Putnam, 2000; Fukuyama, 1999). As a strong sense of community increases group cohesion (Narayan & Cassidy, 2001), it is my intention to explain the interrelationships among citizens within this specific environment and to explore what it is that creates the sense of community.

Burning Man may be perceived as a festival similar to that of Kumbh Mela (a large religious gathering) India without the religious perspective and instead focusing on radical artistic expression. Others view it as an experiment of social construct or an event. Founder Larry Harvey uses the term "community" as an adjective and a noun to describe his image of what Burning Man has become and what it can be (personal communication, August 31, 2011).

COMMUNITY THROUGH THE AGES

Mankind's natural habitat was recognized as developing from, and taking the form of, family (Auguste Comte, 1875). As communal areas expanded differentiation and interdependence recrudesce and cities became a positive evolution of community. Fostering specialization and growth, economic structure was the societal bond to primitive communities (Engels, 1892; Marx & Engels, 1850; Bruhn, 2005).

However, some sociologists, such as Ferdinand Tönnies (1957), originally published in 1887, emphasized the negatives of a mature society, city or State, which he coined a *gesellschaft*. He contrasted what he saw as the negatives of interdependence and specializations with the benefits of a *gemeinschaft*, a unit focusing on familial relations and close-knit interconnections where all people have general knowledge and skills to provide communal self-sufficiency (Tönnies, 1957; Bell & Newby, 1974). The two terms, *gesellschaft* and *gemeinschaft,* encapsulate the dichotomy of analysis regarding territory and the people of that territory by dividing the social groups of people based on feelings, interpersonal connections, population size, and purpose.

These theories convey fundamental characters for defining Burning Man's context. Burning man in its totality has matured from a familial group in 1986 to a *gesellschaft* with specializations and interdependence of a systemic nature (Tönnies, 1957; Capra, 1996; Meadows, 2008). Black Rock City, whether a positive evolution or negative maturation, has continued to expand its presence on the playa and abroad.

Social density, the physical space an individual inhabits with others, effects individualism and interdependence (E. Durkheim, 1964). In a higher social density situation there is greater contact and thus greater connection with a group. The Burning Man event provides intense physical social density through its infrastructure with areas that are remote, demanding radical self-reliance for survival. The two extremes present on the playa offer attendees individualism and interdependence. This diverges from the virtual connections amongst Burners that continue year round. Randall Collins (1994) describes Durkheim's conscious and unconscious societal structure stating, "we think ourselves rational, masters of our own destinies; in fact our rationality itself is given to us by the social structure we inhabit, a structure that forms us to think in one particular way rather than another" (p. 192). The variable social density present in many of today's geo-dispersed organizations, such as Burning Man, can be detrimental to the sense of community if such a social structure is unavailable.

Georg Simmel (1950) proposed in his original work in 1903 that with increased population density humanity would face an increase in psychological disturbances. Community would be disrupted by urbanization to the point of self-destruction of spirit and creativity. Detachment was the answer to maintain individuality (Simmel, 1950; Bruhn, 2005). A shared belief among many Burners who perceive going "home" to Burning Man is that it is a chance to rediscover themselves without the constraints and expectations of attachments to modern traditional society while at the same time offering social connectedness to those that desire it (S. Edison, personal communication, May 19, 2011).

There is a paradox and a conflict in the need for relationships and the need for individual freedom (Hesselbein, Goldsmith, Beckhard & Schubert, 1998; Wheatley & Kellner-Rogers, 1998). This yin-yang of complementary opposites can bring upheaval in any environment and achieving personal balance is a subconscious effort. Organizations are finding this topic of work/life balance to be one of current significance and in looking at building community structures within organizations that are for-profit it is a significant factor of design.

The depth of understanding of communities and societies, including "citizenship from within," and cultural pluralism in society, matured to a definition of social interaction in 1971 (T. Parsons, 1954; 1964; 1971). "Societal community," a term coined by Parsons, is explained as "a patterned conception of membership which distinguishes between those individuals who do and do not belong" (as cited in Sciortino, 2010, p. 243). Taking this social interaction further, the sense of community is a group of people who perceive similarities between themselves and others. This group knowingly participates and nurtures an interdependent relationship to contribute to a stable structure. Seymor B. Sarason (1974) described the sense of community as a group having a unique connection. This search for similarities brings attendees to the playa and the ability to contribute diversely to the structure and creativity of Burning Man creates Burners who make the pilgrimage annually.

The theory of a sense of community was developed by David W. McMillan (1976) as a working paper describing the sense of community as a feeling of belonging, emotional interdependence, and a shared confidence that individual needs will be met. In 1986, McMillan and Chavis presented an updated theory of the sense of community along with a tool for measurement, The Sense of Community Questionnaire (Chavis, Hogge, McMillan, & Wandersman, 1986). McMillan (1996) later revised the theory and created the SCI-II (Sense of Community Index second edition) allowing researchers to observe variation in communities (Long & Perkins, 2003). However, it is a qualitative tool and not a definitive instrument. It is the predominant tool used by researchers to compare and measure the sense of community and it is apropos to the study of Burners.

A community cannot be purposefully created according to research published in *The Sociological Category of Communion* (Schmalenbach, 1977). Community is something that happens without awareness. Biologists, Humberto Maturana and Francisco Varela from Chile advised in congruence that "we can never direct a living system; we can only hope to get its attention" (Hesselbein, Goldsmith, Beckhard & Schubert, 1998, p. 11). However, community is no longer limited to a geographical region, and with virtual worlds and alternative personas, along with new technology widely available for communications, we are seeing a paradigm shift.

The previous research describes the differences between a community and a society, the sense of community, and the measurables of a community. If Bowlby's (1969) attachment theory, which describes attachment as a "lasting psychological connectedness between human beings" (p. 194), were integrated in to the theories on community there could be potential for a more definitive explanation of why or how an individual leaps to become an active member of a community. Additionally, the life course theory (G. H. Elder, 1998) may offer another perspective on the connection between the patterns and dynamics of an individuals' historical context and their willingness to commit.

INSIDE THE BURNER

Five methodologies were used to develop this single case study. They include primary research using the Sense of Community Survey Index-II, or SCI-II (McMillan, 1996), six in-depth exploratory interviews of self-defined Burners, a history, direct observations, and an ethnographic study completed in 2011. These methodologies were chosen to give a complete picture of the Burners and the organization that has developed, to remove researcher bias, and to get a broader and more geographically diverse response. Research continued approximately 2 years.

The SCI-II was given to 222 geographically dispersed self-defined Burners. The survey has 1 question to be answered on a 6-point Likert scale and 24 questions answered on a 4-point Likert scale. The range of answers for the 4-point scale varied from "not at all" to "completely." The link and a request for participation in the SCI-II were sent out through the Burning Man global blogs, FaceBook site and through email. All respondents were volunteers and confidential responses were limited to one per person. The responses were coded and included in the form of thematic analysis. Since respondents to the SCI-II were given complete anonymity, the six involved in the in-depth exploratory interviews may also have participated in this survey.

The in-depth informal exploratory interviews were done individually and in person. The interviews were done in Reno, Nevada by a single interviewer, K. Peters-Van Havel, between May and August of 2011. All participants were volunteers and had attended Burning Man multiple times (averaging 10-15 years of attendance), the subjects made up a diverse population, with an age range from 35 to 60. To protect the anonymity of the research subjects, names have been altered for this paper and pseudonyms are used.

A history was developed using the Burning Man census, the official Burning Man website, historical books on Burning Man, the TV Free Burning Man archives, documentaries, interviews with members of the Board, published essays and speeches, and conferences at Playaskool in the Black Rock Desert. Karla Peters-Van Havel did ethnographic research from May through September of 2011. Direct observations were done in Reno during preparation for the Burning Man festival at the building of The Temple, Compression, the Nevada Museum of Art, the Burning Man Fashion Show, art project fundraisers, and on the Playa itself throughout Burning Man. The method of direct observation continued with Decompression, local art fundraisers, the Burning Nerds, and participation in a film project about Burning Man and Reno titled Event Horizon (Heller & Minedew, 2012).

The case study method using thematic analysis was chosen to answer the "how" and "why" questions of community as seen in Burning Man. Furthermore, it was selected for the distinct advantages of being able to look at a contemporary event which, as a researcher, I had little to no control (Yin, 2009).

THE KINDLING THAT LED TO BURNING MAN

The communal atmosphere at Burning Man was an unintended and unplanned phenomenon. It started simply. The annual city of over 50,000 commenced with Larry Harvey and a small group of friends going to Baker Beach in San Francisco, California in 1986 to burn a wooden frame of a man (Doherty, 2004). Strangers were drawn to the installation and burn of this 'man.' Newcomers to the group brought music and performance art. Interaction, as well as alcohol, flowed freely creating a commonality of shared space (Doherty, 2004; R. Johnson, personal communication, May 24, 2011). Friendships sparked and a sense of temporary community developed through a shared participatory experience. Larry has not acknowledged his reason for burning the first man except to say it was not a religious event, "It was a spontaneous act of radical self expression" (personal communication, September 1, 2011). The participation and the effigy grew in a transitory partnership with the Cacophony Society (Doherty, 2004).

In 1991 Burning Man moved to the Black Rock Desert to avoid potential legal and safety issues in San Francisco. In what was to be termed Black Rock City, participants found freedom and detachment from modern civilization that appealed to them. Growth was exponential and by 1996 had reached 8,000 participants (Burning Man Timeline, n.d.). Rod Garrett was brought in as the City Planner of Black Rock City in 1997. He created the clock shape by which the city is now known (Garrett, 2010). "When (Mr. Garrett) sketched a circle, with the Man in the middle and the system of radial roads, things started falling into place. The area closest to the Man would be reserved for art installations, creating a park-like zone that complemented the 'residential neighbourhoods' in the same way Central Park makes Manhattan liveable" (Bernstein, 2011). This development in city planning provided structure and a formalized neighbourhood.

Burners follow local, state and federal laws while at Burning Man. To formally recognize community norms and expectations the Ten Principles were developed. They are "core guiding concepts" with no governing body or form of enforcement. These principles are: gifting, inclusion, decommodification, radical self-reliance, radical self-expression, communal effort, civic responsibility, leave no trace, participation and immediacy (Burning Man, 2012). Gifting is most often apparent in volunteer work and Black Rock City is built and run almost exclusively by volunteers.

While the Ten Principles do offer the connection between knowledge and behaviour lending to cohesion and personal mastery (McMillan, 1996), they are open to interpretation that can lead to discontent. For example, for some radical self-expression means anything goes. However, others may find this attitude offensive or intrusive and tolerance is tested.

As attendees return to the "default world" (the world outside of Burning Man) they return with social norms and the hope for cohesion through shared expectations.

The regional events, web-based communications, gatherings to celebrate shared experience and to work toward common goals for future events, are all still done under the muse of the Ten Principles. The intention of Burning Man founder Larry Harvey is to see these guidelines implemented in the global world at-large (personal communication, August 31, 2011).

UNEARTHING THE FINDINGS

The initial question on the SCI-II, 'How important is it to you to feel a sense of community with other community members?' is a validating question to assist with result interpretation. "We have found that total sense of community is correlated with this question – but keep in mind this may not be true in every community" (Chavis, Lee, et al., 2008). In the SCI-II 4-point Likert Scale survey of self-defined Burners, the majority of the 222 responders claimed that the feeling of a sense of community between themselves and other community members was 'very important' or 'important'. Interestingly, the subscale for scoring the SCI-II shows that Burners rate 'shared emotional connection' as the greatest gain from their involvement with the Burner populace. Stepping down fairly equally in scale were the other explanations for a desire to sustain a sense of community in Burning Man: 'reinforcement of needs,' 'membership,' and 'influence.'

Within the group of respondents there was significant variation in several of the responses and a slight variation in others. One of the questions, "community members and I value the same things," led a majority of respondents to answer 'mostly' with a high secondary response of 'somewhat.' Trust rated fairly low on the SCI-II with only 18.9% of respondents stating that they completely trust people in this community. A strong argument that Burning Man is created of multiple communities comes in a question about whether or not community members actually "know" the respondent. Surprisingly 37.8% of those surveyed said 'not at all,' '39.6% 'somewhat,' and 20.3% answered 'mostly.'

McMillan and Chavis (1986) offer mutual influence as a contributing factor to the sense of community as measured in this index, yet the vast majority of those questioned answered that they only somewhat feel they have influence over Burning Man. Respondents did recognize that there are symbols and expressions completely unique to the members of this group, which leads to a strengthening of community. Shared language, symbols, tradition, and ritual further develop the cohesiveness of a group and all of these are present, and recognizable by Burners (McMillan & Chavis, 1986; Pieterse, 2009; Sarason, 1974).

In an attempt to discover the borders of the Burning Man community, society, and culture, those same 222 responders were asked two exploratory questions separate from the SCI-II. If the entire group of active Burners (estimated in the hundreds of thousands by Burning Man, LLC., 2012) were one community then we would expect solidarity in the answers. The distribution, however, suggests a society made up of smaller communities, which is a strong proponent for structuring an intentional community into smaller groups so that fortuitous internalization and development can occur.

The first of these two questions was 'Where is the Burning Man Community? The graph below shows that the majority of respondents selected multiple answers rather then all choosing one clearly defined conclusive response. This suggests either that there is no clear answer or that one has not been communicated to Burners.

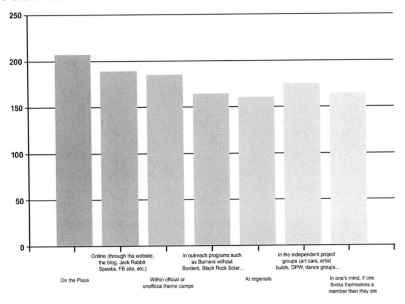

Fig. 1: Where is the Burning Man Community? (n = 221)

The second question allowed for each respondent to choose one answer to define the 'borders of the community' as seen in the following graph. These answers were again varied suggesting that Burners are not of a single psychic unity although interdependent and placing a high value on feeling a sense of belonging. However, the question did allow for 'other' responses where respondents could elaborate on their definition. Some of the responses pertaining to this discussion reiterate the ambiguity of the boundaries of the community. For example, a few of the responses were, "this is an existential question. The borders are fluid and transient - sometimes very well defined, the other times ambiguous," "In my opinion, the borders of the burner community are permeable," and, "…it is so ambiguous and open to each participant's experience, whatever that is defined as. I certainly think it is a global border, or non-border, on a fundamental level."

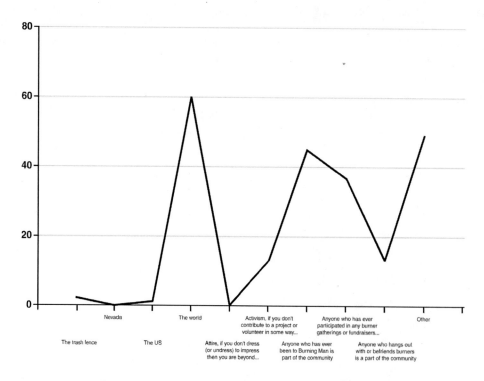

Fig. 2: Where are the borders of the community ? (n = 220)

The exploratory interviews showed similar results. Friendship, connection, and collaboration, as reflected in the Ten Principles, were common themes among those interviewed even though the boundaries and definition of the Burning Man community were hazy and scattered. There was a clear feeling of acceptance within the Burner society that subjects felt they lacked in the 'default world.' This acceptance creates not only a feeling of membership and shared experience, but also a reinforcement of needs, the need in this case being the need for acceptance without limitations or judgment. In general, most of those interviewed, felt they live a more authentic life because of their experiences as a part of Burning Man.

Through observation and ethnographic study, I saw that there were many groups that functioned as small communities. Some friendships and connections extended beyond Burning Man, but a fair share of these communities were limited to the time on the Playa and did not extend beyond the border of the desert.

Gifting is a big part of the Burner experience and it is done with no expectation for return. A Burner can gift time and services, finances or objects. Theme camps consist of volunteers working together on and off the Playa to make the experience a positive one for all involved. Often those that join a theme camp do so to share in a unique experience different then what they might share with colleagues or co-workers in the default world. This further suggests Burning Man is a society created of small communities, each distinct in their belief and level of interdependence.

DISCUSSING THE DUST

Tradition and goals are not things that in and of themselves define a community. There is little agreement on the definition of community besides that it involves people, and even that could now be questioned if we cross disciplines into anthropology or ecology. So the goal is to examine the Burning Man populace and to identify the communal aspect of Burning Man, and how this could potentially be replicated or not, using theoretical definitions.

With 64,000 people officially in attendance of the Burning Man event in 2012, and well over 100,000 who consider themselves in some way to be a part of the active Burning Man "community" (Burning Man Census, 2011), the size alone dictates the gesellschaft label (Tönnies, 1957). Additionally, the SCI-II reflected the majority response as 'somewhat' to the question of being able to recognize others in the community. However, this group cannot be defined by size alone. Anthony P. Cohen (1982, 1985) states that it is commonalities that bind a group and function as a boundary to outsiders. He also explains, in conjunction with Tönnies, that not all boundaries are physical, "They may be thought of, rather, as existing in the minds of the beholders" (Cohen 1985, p. 12).

Burning Man is a unique milieu rarely, if ever, considered in terms of theoretical community and, although the group remains active throughout the year, the gathering in the Black Rock Desert appears and disappears annually. Although these groups are not homogeneous and do not have the loyalty expectations that Tönnies (1957) described in a gemeinschaft, they instead offer "radical inclusion" without expectation or demands. Perhaps even these sub-groups are a pseudo disjointed urban sub-society. On these points I agree with Emile Durkheim (1964) in that these two groups, gesellschaft and gemeinschaft are not mutually exclusive, and they also may not be fully descriptive of all the options.

Looking at this group through a different lens and placing it in a different context, Burning Man might be better examined as a global society with an annual tradition that takes place on the Playa, instead of as an annual gathering that reaches outward to communities. In this way, Burning Man can be examined in relation to distance education programs with a global reach or geo-dispersed corporations. Often these contain systems of communities and culminate periodically with an event such as seminars, planning meetings, keynote speakers, or ceremony. They share a similar format of global connection coming together occasionally for a face-to-face gathering.

The social density at Black Rock City is high in most areas. The infrastructure has the theme camp areas designated in a clock-like layout, keeping campers together and artwork in the rural sands, creating a shared journey to reach the art. The positioning of the first stake that initiates the infrastructure build, the burn of the Man, the burn of the temple, and the burn of the regional effigies, are all symbols of Burning Man that culminate in a ritualistic endeavour. For those who do not attend these events they are streamed live via the internet until the conclusion of Burning Man.

The sense of community is defined through four dimensions: (1) the sense of membership, which is construed as a feeling of connectedness, investment, and emotional safety; (2) mutual influence; (3) integration and fulfilment of needs; and (4) a shared emotional connection, this could be shared history or shared experiences (McMillan & Chavis, 1986). According to McMillan, "it is not necessary that group members have participated in the history in order to share it, but they must identify with it" (McMillan and Chavis, 1986, p. 13).

The Sense of Community Index-II was later developed to measure the 1986 definition of the sense of community. The four dimensions previously used to define community were also updated. The new dimensions were articulated by McMillan as: (1) spirit, similar to membership but newly emphasizing friendship, boundaries, and a sense of belonging; (2) trust, heavily reliant on an authority structure and a knowledge of expectations or rules; (3) trade, highlighting continuous bargaining and mutual benefit; and (4) art, which takes the previously sited category of "shared emotional connection" and states that these connections in time and space are symbolized in art (McMillan, 1996).

Based on the SCI-II and the ideas laid out by McMillan (1996), Burning Man features many of the qualities outlined in the theories of the Psychological Sense of Community and the SCI-II reflects this. According to the SCI-II, "shared emotional connection" is the most important factor to Burners. Defined as shared history, shared experiences, places, or time, it is a need that 37.3%, answered was 'completely' met and 34.5% stating this need was being 'mostly' met. Nevertheless, the SCI-II is not a definitive measurement that can actually determine or define a specific community.

AFTER THE ASH

The term community has been defined in a multitude of ways. For the purposes of this research Burning Man was illustrated as a year-round event culminating in the annual eight-day ritual and tradition in the Black Rock Desert. Burners are best described as a society or a gesellschaft (Tönnies, 1957) consisting of multiple communities, called villages, theme camps, teams and/or networks. Since there is no geographical boundary to delineate what makes one an insider or outsider of Burning Man it is generally recognized as a cultural issue. The Burner culture is the mentality of belonging to something greater than the individual, lasting year round, and weaved in to one's life like a thread in a tapestry. It is an internalization of the Ten Principles reflected in all parts of an individuals' life. It can affect one's activities, relationships, employment, spirituality, and viewpoints.

Further research topics in this area of community and Burning Man could include: spontaneous versus planned communities, differences in growth to a community or society, and the affects on attendance due to the sense of community members do, or do not, feel. Burning Man is a unique area for research as it is born and buried every year, extends beyond traditional boundaries, and includes a diverse global population. Black Rock City, LLC. provides infrastructure, economic design, administrative necessities, and an autonomous zone for members of its cultural community to gather and participate. Safety, a shared emotional connection that comes through shared experiences and goals, communication, and inclusion with acceptance are primary necessities in establishing a sense of community in geo-dispersed organizations. While portions of this mix of community development can be intentionally created, other ingredients are serendipitous and must be allowed to happen without force. Internalizing a culture is a choice, one that can be encouraged like stoking a fire. Like a fire, a foundation and a spark can be given, yet if it takes or how well it illuminates is something then uncontrollable.

REFERENCES

Bell, C. & Newby, H. (1974). *The sociology of community: a selection of readings.* New York, NY: Frank Cass and Company Limited.

Bernstein, F. A. (2011) A vision of how people should live, from desert revelers to urbanites. *The New York Times.* Retrieved 10/20/11 from http://www.nytimes.com/2011/08/29/arts/rod-garrett-the-urban-planner-behind-burning-man.html.

Bowlby, J. (1969). *Attachment: Attachment and Loss: Vol. 1. Loss.* New York, NY: Basic

Bruhn, J. G. (2005). *The sociology of community connections.* New York, NY: Kluwer Academic/Plenum Publishers.

Burning Man. (2012). Retrieved on 6/10/12 from http://www.burningman.com

Burning Man census. (2011). San Francisco, CA: Black Rock City, LLC. Retrieved 5/15/12 from http://afterburn.burningman.com/11/census/

Burning Man timeline. (n.d.) San Francisco, CA: Black Rock City, LLC. Retrieved 7/6/2011 from

http://www.burningman.com/whatisburningman/about_burningman/bm_timeline.html

Capra, F. (1996). *The web of life: A new scientific understanding of living systems.* New York, NY: Anchor Books.

Chavis, D. M., Hogge, J. H., McMillan, D. W., & Wandersman, A. (1986). Sense of community through Brunswick's lens: A first look. *Journal of Community Psychology, 14*(1), 24-40.

Chavis, D. M., Lee, K. S., & Acosta J. D. (2008). *The Sense of Community (SCI) Revised: The Reliability and Validity of the SCI-2.* Paper presented at the 2nd International Community Psychology Conference. Lisboa, Portugal.

Cohen, A.P. (1985). *The symbolic construction of community.* London, UK: Tavistock (now Routledge).

Collins, R. (1994). *Four sociological traditions.* New York, NY: Oxford University Press, Inc.

Comte, A. (1875). *System of positive polity, Vol. 2.* (F. Harrison, Trans.). London, UK: Longmans, Green & Co. (Original work published 1852).

Doherty, B. (2004). *This is Burning Man.* Dallas, TX: BenBella Books, Inc.

Durkheim, E. (1964). The division of labor in society. (G. Simpson, Trans.). New York, NY: Free Press (original work published in 1893).

Elder, G. H. (1998), The Life Course as Developmental Theory. Child Development, 69: 1–12. doi: 10.1111/j.1467-8624.1998.tb06128.x

Engels, F. (1892). *The condition of the working-class in England in 1844.* (F. K. Wischnewptzky, Ed. and Trans.). London, UK: George Allen & Unwin LTD. (Original work published 1845).

Fukuyama, F. (1999, October). *Social capital and civil society.* Conference on second generation reforms, Washington, DC. Retrieved from http://www.imf.org/external/pubs/ft/seminar/1999/reforms/fukuyama.htm

Garrett, R. (2010). *Designing Black Rock City.* Retrieved 11/15/11 from http://blog.burningman.com/2010/04/metropol/designing-black-rock-city/.

Heller, N. A. & Minedew, S. (Co-Producers). (2012). *Event Horizon – Burning Man Burning Reno.* Reno, NV: Sun Productions.

Hesselbein, F., Goldsmith, M., Beckhard, R. & Schubert, R. F. (1998). *The Drucker Foundation: The community of the future.* San Francisco, CA: Jossey-Bass.

Long, D. A. & Perkins, D. D. (2003). Confirmatory factor analysis of the sense of community index and development of a brief SCI. *Journal of Community Psychology, 31* (3): 279-296.

Marx, K. & Engels, F. (1850, November 9). Manifesto of the Communist Party. (H. Macfarlane, Trans.). *The red republican.*

McMillan, D. W. (1976). *Sense of community: An attempt at definition.* Unpublished manuscript, George Peabody College for Teachers, Nashville, TN.

McMillan, D. W. (1996). Sense of community. *Journal of Community Psychology, 24* (4): 315-325.

McMillan, D. W. & Chavis, D. M. (1986). Sense of community: A definition and theory. *Journal of Community Psychology, 14* (1), 6-23.

Meadows, D. H. (2008). *Thinking in Systems: A Primer.* White River Junction, VT: Chelsea Green.

Narayan, D., & Cassidy, M. F. (2001). A dimensional approach to measuring social capital: Development and validation of a social capital inventory. *Current Sociology, 49*(2), 59-102. Retrieved from http://www.google.com/url?sa=t&rct=j&q=&esrc=s&source=web &cd=1&ved=0CCcQFjAA&url=http://info.worldbank.org/etools/docs/library/9748/12064_ a020037.pdf&ei=jGU_UOzkLcX5igKz2oCYDg&usg=AFQjCNE2yLWZjhdZ4PcOhXk DA_FGiDyxTw.

Parsons, T. (1954). *Essays in sociological theory.* New York, NY: The Free Press.

Parsons, T. (1964). *Social structure and personality.* New York, NY: The Free Press.

Parsons, T. (1971). *The systems of modern societies.* Englewood Cliffs, NJ: Prentice-Hall.

Pieterse, J. N. (2009). *Globalization and Culture: Global Mélange.* Lanham, MD: Rowman & Littlefield Publishing Group.

Putnam, R. (2000). *Bowling alone: The collapse and revival of American community.* New York, NY: Simon & Schuster.

Sarason, S. B. (1974). *The psychological sense of community: Perspectives for community psychology.* San Francisco, CA: Jossey-Bass.

Sarason, S. B. (1986). Commentary: The emergence of a conceptual center. *Journal of Community Psychology, 14:* 405-407.

Schmalenbach, H., Lüschen, G., & Stone, G. P. (1977). *Herman Schmalenbach on society and experience: Selected papers.* Chicago, IL: University of Chicago Press.

Sciortino, G. (2010, August). 'A single societal community with full citizenship for all': Talcott Parsons, citizenship and modern society. *Journal of Classical Sociology,* vol. 10 no. 3 239-258.

Simmel, G. (1950). *The sociology of Georg Simmel.* (K. H. Wolff, Ed. and Trans.). Glencoe, IL: Free Press. (Original work published 1903).

Tönnies, F. (1957). *Community and society.* (C. P. Loomis, Ed. and Trans.). New York, NY: Harper Torchbook. (Original work published 1887).

Wheatley, M. J. & Kellner-Rogers, M. (1998). *A simpler way.* San Francisco, CA: Berrett-Koehler Publishers.

Yin, R. K. (2009). *Case study research design and methods, fourth edition.* Thousand Oaks, CA: SAGE Publications, Inc.

Community Engagement Practice of a Joint Venture Petroleum Company Operating in Sudan

Eiman H. Ibrahim*, Siti Nabiha Abdul Khalid**, Dayana Jalaludin*** and Yousif Abdelbagi****

ABSTRACT

The case is about community engagement practice of JOC Petroleum (JOC), a petroleum company operating in the south of Sudan. JOC is a joint operating company between Sudapet, a local petroleum company and Petrosedan, an Asian multinational oil company. As a company that gives immense concern to community needs, JOC has established Community Development Department (CDD), a department specifically responsible in the development of projects for local communities living in its oil extraction areas in the southern part of Sudan. The CDD, together with the state government, operates community development projects with a broad focus, concentrating on service provision, infrastructure development and community empowerment. In year 2011, the newly formed Republic of South Sudan has declared 'Development and Equitable Sharing of Wealth Guiding Principles' for all its oil and gas investors, under the Transitional Constitution of the Republic of South Sudan 2011. As a result, community development projects are now no longer merely voluntary company initiatives but have evolved into regulatory requirements, with demand for better transparency and accountability. This case examines corporate community engagement practice of a petroleum company to promote a balanced and equitable development that creates a lasting benefit to the beneficiaries.

Keywords: Community development, community engagement, sustainability, stakeholder dialogue, corporate social responsibility.

*   Eiman H. Ibrahim is with Graduate School of Business.
**   Siti Nabiha Abdul Khalid is associated with Graduate School of Business,Universiti Sains Malaysia.
***   Dayana Jalaludin is with School of Management, Universiti Sains Malaysia.
****   Yousif Abdelbagi is with School of Management Studies, University of Khartoum.
E-mail: ihi.mohamed@gmail.com, nabiha@usm.my, dayana@usm.my, yousif3a@hotmail.com

INTRODUCTION

Nasser Ali (name is changed) is the Community Development Manager of JOC Petroleum (JOC), a petroleum company operating in the south of Sudan since April 2006. JOC is a joint operating company between Sudapet, a local petroleum company and Petrosedan, an Asian multinational oil company. The secession of south Sudan from Sudan in 2011 and the formation of the new government known as Republic of South Sudan have brought various changes to the regulatory landscape for the oil and gas companies operating in South of Sudan. In year 2011, the 'Development and Equitable Sharing of Wealth Guiding Principles' under the Transitional Constitution of the Republic of South Sudan 2011 was declared. As a result, community development projects are now no longer voluntary company initiatives. It is now mandatory for all oil and gas companies operating in the south of Sudan to conduct corporate community engagement with a high level of transparency and accountability.

Corporate social responsibility is not a new agenda for JOC. Its company's mission "to become an effective petroleum operator with innovative technology and a proficient workforce, while contributing to the development of the nation" clearly spells out JOC's strong interest towards improving the life quality of society at large including the local community. There is a dedicated department in JOC known as Community Development Department (CDD) specifically entrusted with the task to develop projects for communities living in JOC's oil extraction areas. Accordingly, CDD operates with specific strategic goals as per below;

- To contribute to the improvement of quality of life and socio economic status of host communities
- To respond appropriately in event of crisis
- To support people with special needs
- To advocate the culture of peace
- To mainstream gender in community development activities with emphasis on women empowerment programs
- To create partnership with government bodies NGO's in development activities.
- To promote community awareness towards different development aspects and develop their capacities and skills.

All CDD projects, as mentioned by one of the CDD executives, "are not carried out merely as philanthropy or charity but are done in the context of being responsible towards the community". At present, CDD works closely with the state government and runs project under three designated sectors i.e. service provision; infrastructure development; and community empowerment. The CDD, throughout its years of operation, has drawn several recognitions for JOC including the prestigious Petrosedan Group Health, Safety, Environment and Sustainable Development Award and Best Major Project Award in Management Development Project.

JOC COMMUNITY DEVELOPMENT AREAS

Service Provision	Infrastructure Development	Community Empowerment
• Water supply • Health • Education	• Hospitals • Schools • Roads • Bridges • Docks	• Trainings • Capacity building

Nasser Ali noticed that JOC's current community development activities are centred on providing better infrastructure facilities for the local community. Although CDD does host community empowerment projects, the scope is limited to areas of training that has been suggested by the government. Majority of the CDD projects focuses on assisting the government in developing the oil extraction areas, and are one-off in nature. Recognizing the above mentioned newly announced regulation, Nasser Ali speculated that there will be some impact towards JOC's present corporate community engagement practices. He called for a meeting with his community development team to discuss on the future of JOC's community engagement practices, particularly in response to the regulatory changes. The team members were assigned to evaluate JOC's present community engagement practices. The meeting discussed several questions that needed to be addressed by Nasser Ali and his team. Should JOC conduct its community engagement practices like before or there need to be some changes? Aren't the current practices able to fulfil the needs of its beneficiaries? Does the involvement of the local community justifiably considered during the engagement? What is the next step that could be done by Nasser Ali and his team?

JOC COMMUNITY ENGAGEMENT IN A NUT SHELL

JOC operates in the state of Unity, South of Sudan. Population of Unity is close to 600,000, comprising different ingenious tribes of nine clans from the Nilotic ethnic groups. Traditionally, the people of Unity depend on agricultural production, cattle keeping (goats/sheep), fishing, hunting and local trading (RSSDDRC, 2012). Similar to many post conflict areas, formerly there was very little access to formal education, healthcare and infrastructure in Unity. Nowadays, the people of Unity are hired by the various oil companies operating in Unity including JOC. In JOC, the local people are mostly employed as unskilled labor while a few are hired as professional, servicing in diverse aspect such as medicine, engineering and management.

At present, JOC is engaged in the exploration, development and production of hydrocarbon resources in three areas known as Block 5A, Block 5B and Block

8. Accordingly, the beneficiaries of JOC's community engagement projects are the community of Block 5A, Block 5B and Block 8. Given its limited resources, it is a challenge for JOC to manage the expectation of this heterogeneous community who expects drastic transformation for development, as voiced out by one of CDD team member "the high expectation unrealistic to our budget and unrealistic to our role as an operating company".

COMMUNITY VS STAKEHOLDER

Generally, the discourse of engagement for community development projects in JOC varies with the nature of each project. As a rule of thumb, the community is engaged in at least one phase of each project life cycle. Here, parallel to the perspective of JOC, the word *community* mainly refers to its *stakeholders*, particularly the authorities of the country, state and community. JOC believes that these authorities are parties that would have the best view on the issues and needs of the local community. Thus, all JOC's community projects are initiated and approved by the above mentioned authorities. A project will only go forward if it is needed by the community as per suggested by the authorities. The local community will be then informed about what has been decided from the consensus between the authorities and JOC. Likewise, the involvement of the local community representatives is minimal in terms of negotiation and consultation, except for a few tribal chiefs who are occasionally engaged during the stakeholder dialogue. It is the state government via county commissioner who would play domineering roles in determining JOC's community projects.

STAKEHOLDER DIALOGUE

The embracement of community engagement compels sincere consciousness and genuine commitment. Ideally, community engagement is about "need for those within a community to plan to think clearly about the communities they are working with, to understand their history, culture and nature of their current existing organization and networks, in addition to their scope of local needs and the issues that arise and how the community encounters them, strengths of the community that may be built on, and the nature of existing dialogue and participation in the community" (Hashagen, 2002).

In JOC, community engagement requires the involvement of the stakeholders in the planning, implementation and evaluation phases of community project and activity. The stakeholders are engaged in at least one phase of the project cycle, mostly at the planning and implementation stage. Community project development in JOC starts with annual budget allocation for each designated projects. Budgets are diverted to the preferred need according to the request of the abovementioned authorities. These authorized elite are used as a focal point in determining the type of community project that JOC will be embarking for residence of Block 5A, Block 5B and Block 8. Their influence and final say are an important aspect in relation to JOC's community engagement strategy.

The issues that are brought up by the authorities tend to be limited and few, confined to infrastructure provisions and social responsibility of the government. As a consequence, JOC's community projects are usually about fulfilling the governmental role in providing development for Block 5A, Block 5B and Block 8 residence. The voices of the NGOs or development experts representing the local community are unlikely visible during the stakeholder dialogue sessions. The stakeholder dialogue sessions do not exist as bridges for JOC to get a deeper insight as to what the local community has to say regarding its community projects. Obviously, the restricted participation of representatives from the local community refrain the presence of new voices that would raise new issues on behalf of the community. In adjacent with the highly bureaucratic political environment of Sudan, JOC primarily listens only to the calling of the authorities who may have the ability to pose significant threat toward their operation.

During the planning stage of each community projects, JOC will coordinate with the country, state and local authorities through a process of multiparty dialogue in order to select the projects that will be implemented. Each project will then need to be approved by the authorities. In the implementation phase, the involvement of the local community is highly visible, usually as construction workers. Additionally, JOC does have some participatory contracts with a few national NGOs for some of its projects. These NGOs are normally hired in a short term as subcontractors that provide trainings, for example basic healthcare training for the local community. The local community is also noticeably involved in JOC's compensation process. Negotiations on compensation for any developments by JOC will be done via the compensation committee which comprises of both representatives from JOC and the local community. The compensation committee is responsible for the decisions regarding the amount and disbursement of compensation to local community for any property damage caused by JOC's operations.

EVALUATION OF OUTCOMES

Evaluations for all JOC's community projects are done through baseline survey where assessments on before and after are carried out to see whether there are changes over time due to the projects. For instance, a clinic project aims to alleviate the health status of the community. Therefore health status for the targeted community is measured before and after the clinic operates. Among examples of the measurements used for evaluation are in terms of service delivery such as number of patients treated and number of immunization given.

Apart from the baseline surveys which are internally evaluated in nature, JOC does not conduct any voluntary reporting or external auditing method with regards to its community engagement projects. There is no public access for any information regarding the outcome from stakeholder dialogue. The degree of transparency is modest with no imprecise evidence of accountability, especially on the contribution of JOC and its specific community engagement benefits for the local residence. At present, there is no systematic learning or generation of ideas being made based on existing or prior community projects.

TOOLS FOR ANALYSIS

Nasser Ali suggested for his team to evaluate the relevancy of JOC's current corporate community engagement practices. In order to arrive at a conclusion, they need to investigate several aspects of JOC's practices. First, he mooted for a debate regarding JOC's present conceptualization of *community* as *stakeholders*. Next, he requested for the team to evaluate JOC's level of engagement during the process of its stakeholder dialogue based on the five dimensions of stakeholder dialogue as suggested by Torfing (2004) and Young et. al. (2003). The relevance and significance for each dimension is explained as under.

Table 1: Stakeholder Dialogue: Level of Engagement

Dimension	Level of Engagement	
	Low	*High*
Inclusion	Only few privileged stakeholders are included in dialogue	All relevant stakeholders are included in the dialogue
Openness	Dialogue is structured around a fixed set of questions/problems/ issues	Dialogue is structured around open questions/problems/issues
Tolerance	One position has priority over all others	New alternative and critical voices are respected
Empowerment	One stakeholder dominates the dialogue decisions	Freedom and equality in dialogue as well as in decisions
Transparency	No access to information about the process and outcomes of the stakeholder dialogue	Full access to information about the process and outcomes of the stakeholder dialogue

- Inclusion refers to the recognition of the whole range group of interest, formal and informal representatives (Hashagen, 2002).
- Openness refers to absence of eradication of potentially controversial issues before or during stakeholder dialogue (Lukes, 2005).

- Tolerance refers to nil prioritization of rationales hence the dialogue is tolerant to all views. All issues, be it profit related or not, are viewed as equally important (Young et. al. 2003).

- Empowerment refers to balance in power where there is freedom and equality in dialogue (Pedersen, 2006).

- Transparency refers to access of information hence demonstrating accountability (Young et. al. 2003).

Furthermore, Nasser Ali asked for his team to identify JOC's form of community engagement based on the scale of public participation ranging from the passive recipients of information (i.e. inform) to self self-empowered communities that initiate actions independent of external agents (Thompson et. al. 2009). Based on this analysis, the corresponding level of engagement and longevity (ranging from passive and non-ongoing to proactive and on-going) can be identified. Table 2 indicates the engagement continuum that may be used as guidance for Mr. Nasser Ali and his team.

Another important aspect that Mr. Nasser Ali suggested his team to look at is on the participatory elements of JOC's community engagement practices. Sustainable community engagement practices may be achieved when the participatory process is comprehensive. The details of Flora's (2004) nine generic elements of participatory process are as per below.

- Context specificity- The dissimilarities each place posses and how it is addressed.

- Collective vision- The acknowledgement of the community capital to be made explicit as well as allowing the building up of a communal vision between the company and community.

- Diversity of perspectives- The involvement of all the relevant parties in order to reach well rounded comprehensive decisions.

- Use of facilitator- Having someone whom the community trusts as aids for the company during decision making.

- Involving government official and representatives

- Participatory Contracts- Clear terms of agreement between the company and other parties.

- Monitoring and feedback of outputs and outcomes in relation to objectives.

- Sustained Systematic Learning in terms of monitoring and reporting.

- Evaluation in the context of the relevant community.

Table 2: The Engagement Continuum

Type of Engagement	Description	Examples	Level of Engagement & Longevity		
Inform One way communication			Passive		Non-Ongoing
Listen : One or two way communication with decision making not resting with community					Increasingly
Involve : Creating shared understanding and solutions pursued by one partner only			Increasingly Level of Engagement	Of Engagement	Self Ongoing
Partners: Developing shared action plans through collaboration					Sustaining Nature of Energy
Mobilise and Empower : People take independent initiatives and develop contacts with external institutions for resources and advice			Proactive		

Source: Adapted from Hashagen (2002); Tamarack (2003); Neilson (2005); Dare & Schirmer (2008)

THE NEXT STEP AHEAD- PROSPECT AND OBSTACLES

Nasser Ali felt that his department needed plan on the changes or refinement that could be done for JOC's community engagement practices. Among the aspects that need to be addressed are community conceptualization, stakeholder dialogue, community engagement typology and participatory element. He believed a critical evaluation based on the given tools for analyses would initiate useful assessment and generation of ideas from his team. Besides that, he also requested suggestions for other method of evaluation from his team. Two central issues emerge from this case. First, does the present community engagement practice of JOC would fulfill the agenda for 'a balance and equitable development with lasting benefit to the beneficiaries'? Second, what are the improvements that need to be done? This case constitutes some specific questions that need to be resolved as per below;

1. What are your views of JOC's community engagement practice of JOC. Determine the suitability of;

   a. Conceptualizing community as stakeholders (i.e. commissioners, state authority, authorities within the community).

   b. Level of engagement during the stakeholder dialogue.

   c. Type of engagement and tools applied.

   d. Participatory elements in the engagement process.

2. What is the nature of change required in JOC's community engagement practice?

3. What other course of approach and action that could be taken by Mr. Nasser Ali and his team?

REFERENCES

Dare, M., & Schirmer, J. (2008). A Brief Guide to Effective Community Engagement in the Australian Plantation Sector Tasmanian Institute of Agricultural Research, University of Tasmania ,Cooperative Research Centre for Forestry Retrieved 10 February 2012 from *www.crcforestery.com.au*

Flora, C. (2004). Social Aspects of Small Water Systems. Journal of Contemporary Water Research and Education, 128, 6-12.

Hashagen, S. (2002, May). Models of community engagement. Scottish Community Development Centre. Retrieved 12 February 2012 from *www.dundeecity.gov.uk*

Lukes, S. (2005). *Power: A Radical View*. Hampshire: Palgrave MacMillan.

Neilson,L. (2005). Effective Engagement: Building relationships with community and other stakeholders. The Community Engagement Network Resource and Regional Services Division, Victorian Government Department of Sustainability and Environment Retrieved 11 February 2012 from *www.dse.vic.gov.au*

Pedersen, E. (2006). Making Corporate Social Responsibility (CSR) Operable: How Companies Translate Stakeholder Dialogue into Practice. Business and Society Review, *111*(2), 137–163.

RSSDDRC, R. O. S. S. D. (2012, January). Demobilisation and Reintegration Commission.. States:Unity, from *http://www.ssddrc.org/states/unity.html*

Tamarack Institute (2003). Our Growing Understanding of Community Engagement. Ontario, CA. Retrieved 15 February 2012 from *www.tamarackcommunity.ca*

Thompson, L., Stenekes, N., Kruger, H., & Carr, A. (2009). *Engaging in Biosecurity:Literature review of Community Engagement Approaches* Australia: BRS Publication.

Torfing, J. (2004). Diskursive forhandlingsnevaerk i akterveringspolitikken. Poloticia, 36(2), 143-163.

Young, I., Bendell, J., Andriof, J., Waddock, S., Husted, S., & Rahman, S. (2003). *Inclusion and Democracy:Talking for change? Reflections on effective stakeholder dialogue*. Sheffield: Greenleaf Publishing.

Growth Concerns of a Social Enterprise: The Case of 'SammaaN Foundation'

Bhawna Anjaly* and Arun Sahay**

ABSTRACT

The case illustrates a success story of a social entrepreneur who decided to improve the work-life of thousands of poor rickshaw pullers who had no access to any bank even to borrow small amounts to pay daily rental for the rickshaws they pulled for their livelihood. The study deals with demographic and socio-economic factors , health and working condition of rickshaw pullers in a major town of Patna. These factors have been identified with the help of literature review and an exploratory study. The case explores how these factors are improved by SammaaN Foundation. The objectives of the case is to make readers aware of the scaling up issues of the start-up working in socio- development sector. The case could be used in sustainability, Innovation and entrepreneurship subjects in graduate and post-graduate management programme and management development programmes.

Keywords: Social entrepreneurship, innovation, sustainability, technical factors, health, working conditions, ownership

INTRODUCTION

Irfan Alam, the founder & chairman of SammaaN Foundation, was returning after addressing the students of India's prestigious Faculty of Management Studies (FMS), New Delhi on January 5, 2012. He was out of his office for only two days but the calls from office kept pouring in. Next day he had to return to his office in Patna.[1] His mind was occupied with the strategic and operational issues his start-up social enterprise was facing. Though occupied with issues of his enterprise, his thoughts kept on returning

---

[1] Patna is the state capital of Bihar one the fastest growing states in India.

---

* Research Scholar,Birla Institute of Management Technology, Greater Noida, India.
**Dean Research, Birla Institute of Management Technology, Greater Noida, India.
E-mail: bhawna.anjaly09@bimtech.ac.in, arun.sahay@bimtech.ac.in

to the question asked by a student. It was no extra ordinary question. Almost everyone could ask what he asked very casually, "What is next?" He was struggling to answer this question though he was confident to find answer to the questions coming in as calls from his enterprise at Patna.

His organization, SammaaN, was working since March 5, 2007 (under section 25 of the Indian Companies act 1956) on its mission to organize rickshaw[2] pullers on a business platform and free them from the vicious cycle of poverty and exploitation. They had achieved some success in their mission. Today, it was working directly with 15,000 rickshaw pullers and registered base of more than 500,000 potential beneficiaries. He had achieved this position on his own terms and without donations from anywhere. He was now standing at the cross roads where donors, lenders, angel and government funding were standing. He was wondering which direction to take!

BUT WHAT'S NEXT?

It was very clear to him that if his organization were to reach to a wider audience then he needed to grow and replicate his success at other places. He was so much involved in the operational issues that it was difficult for him to pull himself out of this and think afresh about the growth. He also did not have funds required to take it to the next level. This was not an easy situation to be in. He had to plan for a future course of action based on the options he had. He started with a recollection of his journey so far.

THE BEGINNING

It started in a hot afternoon of one of the hottest Indian summer, when Irfan was travelling on a rickshaw. He was thirsty and wanted some water. All that the rickshaw puller could offer him was a little bottle he was carrying for himself. This unavailability of water instigated a business idea in Irfan's mind. He started thinking that if a rickshaw puller starts selling bottled water to his passengers, won't he earn more and his passengers would be benefited? To do a quick check of his business idea Irfan questioned the rickshaw puller if he would like to sell water bottles to his passengers to earn a few extra bucks. The question started-off the rickshaw puller's stories of the miseries of in life.

"Sahib (sir), my rickshaw itself is so heavy that it's difficult to pull. Why would I want to increase the weight further by putting bottles of water? And even if I decide to sell, I don't have money to invest in buying those mineral water bottles. Moreover, people will not buy water from me because rickshaws are taken for small distance."

This gave set back to what Irfan was thinking but he kept on identifying a way to

---

[2] Rickshaw is a man pulled, non-motorized tri-cycle prevalent in the south Asian countries for small distance travel. See Annexure – for the picture.

realize his dream. Finally, it downed on him as to how he could make a business sense out of rickshaw. His idea was to use rickshaws as 'mobile billboard'. The more he thought about it, the more he got convinced about its feasibility.

IDEA DEVELOPMENT

Based on this thought, Irfan developed a business plan and started looking for a platform to test it. At the same time, one of the national TV channel was launching a reality show called 'Business Baazigar'.[3] They were looking for ideas & people who had the potential to make it big. Irfan sent his business plan to that competition. Competing with some of the best brains of the country, he won the competition. This proved to be a milestone in Irfan's life. The promoters of the show offered him money to sell his idea and/or work with them as an employee on this venture. He knew his business idea had a potential. He wanted to start it in his own way. He refused the big money and other offers and decided to be his own boss. Thus, began the journey to fulfill his dream.

TESTING THE WATERS

Initially, his dream met with harsh and difficult real world. No sooner had he started the execution of his idea, he came face to face with the operational hurdles. It was difficult to convince companies to put their ads on the rickshaw. It was even more difficult to persuade the rickshaw pullers to try out this idea because they did not own the rickshaw. Moreover, the traditional rickshaws did not have proper space for advertisement. Thus, the challenges were multiple, ranging from design of rickshaw itself to the hardships of rickshaw pullers' life. The issues related to rickshaw pullers' lives were far more depressing than expected. The issue was not only of their miserable economic condition but was a combination of the effect of the tyranny of police and municipal authorities over them. This convinced Irfan to pursue this business idea not only for generating profit for his business but for bringing a social change in the current status of marginalized rickshaw pullers. He decided to explore both the financial and social aspects of the proposed business further.

RICKSHAW AND RICKSHAW PULLERS

The concept of a tricycle rickshaw was not new or novel. In India as well as many South East Asian countries this was a prevalent mode of last-mile travel. This noise-less, environmentally friendly and cost-effective vehicle was also providing employment to millions of people. This vehicle had potential in terms of providing sustainable transport for small distance local travel. Still this medium of transportation had been ignored by and large. There were hardly any attempts made to improve or promote

---

[3] A popular business reality show on India's TV network.

it. On the other hand, deliberate policies in most of the urban towns of developing countries had been made by the concerned authorities to phase out rickshaws (Rajvansi, 2002).

Not only policy makers but academics, too, did not consider this for their research. The existing studies on rickshaw pullers are very few and the studies related to their contribution in providing sustainable transport are almost non existent in India (Kurosaki, et. al. 2007). These indicated the fact that though there were problems related to the sustainability of rickshaw and rickshaw pullers, no segment of the society was bothered about them. The existing literature yielded a few factors which were creating hindrance in the growth of rickshaw transport. The in-depth interviews with rickshaw pullers[4] added a few more factors to that list. This gave a list of factors which needed to be looked at to improve the condition of rickshaw and rickshaw pullers. The literature and interviews provided the following that could improve their lives: Technical (Rajvanshi, 2002; Exploratory study); Economical (Begum, and Sen, 2004; Kucukemiroglu, 1999) ;Social (Kucukemiroglu, 1999; Exploratory study);Demographic (Kucukemiroglu, 1999); Working Condition(Exploratory study);Health (Exploratory study).

Technical

The existing cycle rickshaw as mentioned earlier had hardly changed since it was introduced in India in the early 1920's from the Far East. The word 'rickshaw' is derived from the Japanese word jinriksha, which means hand drawn cart (Rajvanshi, 2002). Thus, most of the rickshaws were primitive with least consideration to the use of technology or removal of drudgery of rickshaw pullers. The average weight of a traditional cycle rickshaw is 115 kg (Alam, 2012). It requires massive energy to move the vehicle with passengers sitting in it. The high weight slowed down the speed considerably. Thus, the design was not user friendly. The rickshaw pullers had no room to keep his essentials. The seating arrangement was very uncomfortable and the bulky frame made the aerodynamic drag very high (Rajvanshi, 2002). Further, the frequent breakages in rickshaw at some common points were regular. The reason for this was that the rickshaw manufacturing was an unorganized industry with no quality control. These rickshaws were so poor in quality that they had to be replaced completely in about two years (Rajvanshi, 2002).

Economical

Buying a rickshaw was not perceived to be a sensible investment by the rickshaw pullers (Begum, and Sen, 2004). The migrant status, demands for upfront payment, registration cost, maintenance cost and lack of any identification proof were some of

---

[4] In depth interviews were conducted with 10 rickshaw pullers, in Patna to understand the ground realities.

the reasons behind it. Thus, majority of rickshaw pullers did not own a cycle rickshaw; they rented it from an owner-contractor. The contractor, as he was taking high risk by renting rickshaw to the people without any identification proof, charged very high rent. The rent was usually charged on daily basis. Thus, the amount was small so that the rickshaw puller could earn and pay on daily basis without realizing the enormity of the amount paid. Further, the lack of identification proof debarred them from access to any banking support. Neither, the bank recognized them nor any person was ready to be their guarantor. As a result, they deposited their savings with the only person trusting them: the contractor.

Interview with rickshaw pullers revealed that many times they got cheated by the contractors and they did not have anyone to complain to. As per Brijlal, one of the rickshaw puller in Patna, "The contractor never returns us our total money. He keeps back some amount saying that he does not have it at that moment. Later on he will deny having any remaining money". Many of the rickshaw pullers have similar experience.

Social

A very large number of people in this sector are poor rural-to-urban migrants. Most of the rickshaw pullers are migrant workers, of which nearly 60 percent are from Bihar, followed by 30 percent from UP, and the remaining 10 percent are from Bengal, Orissa, Rajasthan and other states (Muralidharan, 2009). These migrants have very little education and skills, so, rickshaw pulling provides an easy job opportunity and an escape from the rural poverty. Because of their migrant status, they have almost non-existent social security. In case of any exigency they do not have any one to rely-on. Even the other rickshaw pullers did not provide them any help or relief, though they wanted, because of their own livelihood being in danger.

Health

The food intake of rickshaw pullers is inadequate to sustain their health[5]. Their meal lacks nutrition required for physical labor. Many of them take alcohol or take drugs to get the instant high to put in massive amount of slog required. These habits develop because their poverty makes them vulnerable to systematic health risks (Begum and Sen, 2004). They have no health checks even when needed. Being away from family also made them prone to sexually transmitted diseases (Population Council, Dhaka, 2007).

Demographical

---

[5] During the in depth interview 7 out of 10 rickshaw pullers mentioned that they have only tea & biscuits for breakfast.

Majority of the rickshaw pullers belonged to the 20 to 40 years of age group.[6] The reason for this may be the physical stamina required for the job. The age and physical strength affects their income as well. As the rickshaw puller got old, his income reduced drastically.

Working Conditions

The high maintenance cost and complex registration process of rickshaw kept rickshaw pullers from owning the rickshaw. Its cost, too, for the initial purchase, was too high; out of their reach. The working hours were not defined; rickshaw pullers could decide it as per their convenience, which in turn depended on the time for which they had hired the rickshaw from the contractor. Most of them were illiterate or semi-literate. They were unaware of the traffic rules. This gave the police a chance to harass and exploit them. Many of them were migrants so they did not have place to stay. Some of them rented rickshaw for 24 hours and slept in it, while other migrant rickshaw pullers slept on railway platform, footpath or under the bridge.

These issues stated above indicated towards a structural problem which needed to be solved. As per the definition of social entrepreneur by Bill Drayton[7], (Bornstein, 2006) this sector needed a social entrepreneur. Clearly, this was an area where a social intervention was needed, wherein these rickshaw pullers could get maximum benefits from their hard work.

SammaaN Foundation

His rickshaw ride on that hot summer day, the success of business plan on the national TV and further the reflections on the plight of rickshaw pullers inspired Mr. Irfan Alam to convert his idea into a business; a social enterprise. He founded an organization named 'SammaaN Foundation' on the 25th January 2007 in Patna, India. This foundation undertook to organize and improve the whole set-up of rickshaw pulling sector.

THE BUSINESS MODEL

SammaaN Foundation believed in the potential of the bottom of the pyramid customer. This belief was based on the assumption that if their earnings will improve their spending and thereby their living standard. "This way the vicious cycle of poverty and exploitation could be broken and the down trodden could be included in to the main stream", thought he.

The changing of the whole set up in which rickshaw pullers operated needed innovative thinking. This required not only the structural change but also the behavioural change that needed continuous efforts and novel methods (Rangan, K. et.al 2009). However, to work with the rickshaw pullers, Irfan created an innovative business model that provided for sharing the advertising revenue with the rickshaw pullers. In this model, different places of rickshaw (redesigned) had been identified as advertising board. SammaaN approached many corporate and negotiated the deal with willing corporates. The revenue sharing model (from the advertisement) is depicted in Figure 1.

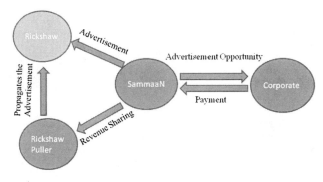

Fig. 1: Revenue Sharing

Soon he found that he could further contribute in uplifting the lives of the rickshaw pullers. This time his thought went from marginal gain to capital gain. He was wondering how the rickshaw pullers could be out of the clutches of the contractor. How could they own the rickshaw? How could they be relieved from the unreasonable rent that they were paying? Soon he found that he could solve this problem. He created a second business model which he called 'Ownership Model'. In this model, SammaaN tie-ups with nationalized banks for providing loan to the rickshaw pullers registered with them. SammaaN acted as the guarantor and/or facilitator for them. It also insured that the rickshaw pullers kept repaying installments of their loan. His ownership model is given in Figure 2 below.

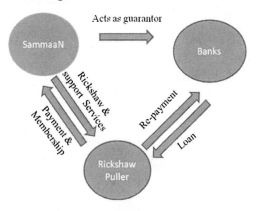

Fig. 2: Ownership Model

TECHNICAL CHANGES

SummaaN Foundation worked on the design and reduced its weight from 115 Kg to 70 -75 kg. In the process, he not only changed the design but used lighter material. The design change also provided space to rickshaw pullers to keep their essential things. Further, it had provision of first aid box, newspaper and mineral water bottle. Later, he also introduced a small radio transistor in the vehicle. Progressively, the foundation set-up a rickshaw manufacturing unit. This unit is producing the newly designed rickshaw (Figure 3) with the quality assurance. The foundation continues to work to remove the problem of frequent breakages that the rickshaws were having. To solve the perennial problem, they have hired engineers and technicians with whom they are presently working with.

Fig. 3: The New Rickshaw

Economical Changes

The rickshaw pullers working with SammaaN were given a SammaaN identity card. The identity card was issued to them after thorough background check. In case of migrants, the background check was done with the other native rickshaw puller already registered with SammaaN. This identity card and support from the organization helped rickshaw pullers in opening bank account and access to other financial resources. SammaaN also encouraged the rickshaw pullers to buy the rickshaw so that they could earn more by moving greater distance and paying lower daily installment. To help them in buying rickshaw, SammaaN worked on ownership model discussed earlier. SammuN also insured the rickshaw bought by them. Depending on the revenue sharing model, the foundation bears the maintenance cost which is provided by them to the rickshaw pullers. In case of any emergency the rickshaw pullers can get the insurance claim for damages.

Social Changes

SammaaN's identity card provided the rickshaw pullers a social status. The foundation organizes a weekly meeting of the rickshaw pullers. In this informal gathering they talk about their problems and their experiences. In this forum, they also discuss the possible solution to problems, with collective wisdom. Further, fortnightly meeting called 'SammaaN Sabhas' are also organized. In these meetings different topics like traffic rules, education, gender equity or anti-intoxicant campaign are taken up.

Working Condition

"SammaaN had given a social recognition to the rickshaw pullers. They had got a chance to a dignified life. No policeman could unnecessarily harass them now. "They have somebody to back them up" says 'Chandu', one of the rickshaw puller working with SammaaN. Chandu had also Provided a rickshaw tour to former US president Mr. Bill Clinton on his visit to the office of SammaaN. Foundation had 24 hour help line where rickshaw pullers could report in case of any exigencies. The nearest patrolling employee of SammaaN reaches to help them. Many ticklish issues that rickshaw puller face were solved by SammaN this way.

Health

One frequent problem SammaaN faced was of medical facility available to rickshaw pullers. The rickshaw pullers faced lot of health problems due to unhygienic living condition, malnutrition and poverty. When rickshaw pullers fell ill, they had to face lot of difficulty in getting admitted to the government hospital. The private hospitals were very costly. This inspired SammaaN to start a mobile medical unit. After seeing their efficient operation, Government gave them responsibility for running the government scheme of mobile medical unit called 'Dhanvantari' for the city of Patna.

Irfan's business was contributing to the removal of some of the problems that rickshaw pullers were facing. SammaaN's efforts had touched the lives of many rickshaw pullers. It had improved not only their income; it also created awareness towards a better life. A comparative chart of SammaaN and other rickshaw pullers spending pattern is given in Figure 4.

But all this was not giving any satisfaction to Irfan. He wanted to take his idea to million others. For this, it was important to have second round of funding. He was not in favor of taking grants and this was making his task of scaling up significantly difficult. The options he had were also spread out. Among various options his thought was going on the following:

He could wait for the Government projects like the 'Dhanwantari' project. But the problem was that decisions related to the projects were time consuming. Even after the award of the project, the disbursement of money took a lot time.

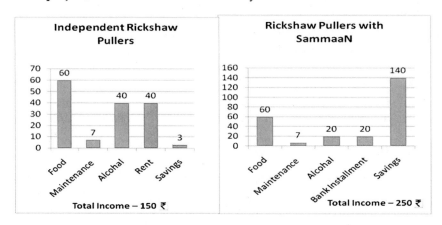

Fig. 4: Average Expenditure Pattern/day

The other option could be to talk to corporates for releasing more advertisements generating more funds. But the response from them till date had not been very encouraging and it was expected to remain so unless the number of rickshaw pullers increased dramatically that required more funds.

The rickshaw manufacturing unit of SammaaN was also struggling to keep itself afloat. It needed economies of scale to flourish which was not possible right away. It also needed funding for its ambitious research on solar panel rickshaws that would need a storage battery for which research departments of government were ready.

The last option could be to impress a genuine investor who could bring in the requisite money. SammaN could give him some stakes in the company but Irfan was not sure of the present value of the company and thus, how much share to give to the investor.

Can social entrepreneurship survive in this age of intense competition? What could be the *mantras* for success?

ACKNOWLEDGEMENT

The authors express their sincere thanks to Mr. Irfan Alam, Chairman and Managing Director of SammaaN Foundation for full support to develop this case and permission to present the same at ICMC2012 and publish the same in the conference proceedings.

REFERENCES

Alam, Irfan (2012). Interview conducted by the authors of this paper on February 6th, 2:30pm at SammaaN Foundation's office in SBI colony, Patna.

Begum, S. and Sen,B. (2004). "Unsustainable Livelihoods, Health Shocks and Urban Chronic Poverty: Rickshaw Pullers as a Case Study" CPRC Working Paper 46

Bornstein, David. (2004). *How to change the world: social entrepreneurs and the power of new ideas.* Oxford; New York: Oxford University Press

Population Council (2007). *Increasing Dual Protection among Rickshaw Pullers in Bangladesh,* Dhaka: Bhuiya, I. et. al.

Kurosaki, T. Sawada, Y. Banerji, A. and Mishra, S.N. (2007). "Rural-Urban Migration and Urban Poverty: Socio-Economic Profiles of Rickshaw Pullers and Owner-Contractors in North-East Delhi", retrieved from *http://www.ier.hit-u.ac.jp/~kurosaki/rick0702.pdf on 1st February 2012*

Kucukemiroglu, Orsay (1999)."Market segmentation by using consumer lifestyle dimensions and ethnocentrism: An empirical study", *European Journal of Marketing,* Vol. 33 (5) pp. 470 – 487

Muralidharan, Aswathi (2009). "Micro Financing Cycle Rickshaws," Retrieved on 26th July'12 from *http://www.dare.co.in/opportunities/idea/micro-financing-cycle-rickshaws.htm*

Rajvanshi, A. K. (2002). "Electric and improved cycle rickshaw as a sustainable transport system for India," *CURRENT SCIENCE,* Vol. 83, NO. 6

Rangan, V. K. Karim, S. Sandberg, S. K. (1996). "Do Better at Doing Good," *Harvard Buisness Review.* vol. 7, no. 3, p. 42-54.

ANNEXURE – 1

Traditional Rickshaw

Source: http://oldbike.wordpress.com/1980s-kw-engineering-works-heavy-duty-cycle-rickshaw-india/ Retrieved on January 12th, 2012.

SammaaN design (Irfan sitting)

Source: Sent by Mr. Irfan Alam

The Impact of Cultural Values in Shaping Economic Growth and Development: A Case of Ubuntu Economy

Ruchi K. Tyagi* and Symphorien Ntibagirirwa**

ABSTRACT

Neo-liberal economics is built upon the claim that the freedom to pursue one's self-interest and rational choice leads to economic growth and development. Against this background neo-liberal economists and policymakers endeavoured to universal this claim, and instantly argue that appropriate economic policies produce the same results regardless of cultural values. Accordingly, developing countries are often advised to embrace the neo-liberal economic credo for them to escape from the trap of underdevelopment. However, the economic success of South East Asia on the one hand and the failure of economic development in sub-Saharan Africa on the other, are increasingly proving that the 'economic' argument cannot be taken dogmatically: self-interest and rationality do not seem to be the sufficient explanations for economic development. One other avenue to be taken seriously is the link between cultural values and economic development. After viewing the principle of self-interest against its historic-cultural background, we consider this link in the African context, and argue that, although they cannot be taken as the sole factor, people's cultural beliefs and values are crucial for economic development. Economic growth and development need to be a substantiation of a people's beliefs and values. In African value system, this substantiation could lead to what one would call 'ubuntu economy' in which the state, the markets and the people are all agents in the process of economic growth and development.

Keywords: Ubuntu economy, cultural values, economic growth, development, rationality, people's beliefs

---

* Associate Professor and Dean Academics & Research, DIMS Meerut.

**Revue Ethique et Société,Fraternité Saint Dominique,Bujumbura (Burundi), Kigali (Rwanda).
E-mail: csractivist@yahoo.co.uk

INTRODUCTION

Cultural values in Africa have been mostly perceived negatively in economic matters both by African economists, policymakers and planners themselves as well as the consultants of the international institutions and foreign donors. As a consequence, there is a tendency to shift away from them, even from those values such as trust, solidarity and cooperation which, nowadays, are important in today's economic business. Much attention is concentrated on the claim that appropriate economic policies (mostly neo-liberal policies) necessarily achieve economic growth and development.

OBJECTIVES OR THE ISSUES AT STAKE

Few key issues are at stake in this reflection.

(a) Impact of people's cultural beliefs and values on economic development.

(b) The identity of people determines the way they produce, consume and exchange economic goods and services.

(c) The way people view themselves and live in the world can be enhanced or hampered by others with whom they do not share the ontological status.

LITERATURE REVIEW: QUESTIONING THE LINK BETWEEN SELF-INTEREST AND ECONOMIC GROWTH

The claim that 'the freedom to pursue one's self-interest leads to economic growth' comes from Adam Smith's reflection on how the wealth of a nation could be created and increased (Smith, 1965). The economic discourse of neo-liberalism lays much emphasis on self-interest rather than on the interest of the others; the centre of focus in neo-liberal economic ordering is self-interest (Sen, 1987: 21). Even if economic success were to be achieved, to what extent can one really say that it is only the principle of self-interest that led to such a success? Do people really behave in an exclusively self-interested way in economic matters? Are there no other aspects that may serve as catalysts of economic success such that self-interest is but one of them or not even necessary? Amartya Sen has this crucial question, to which we concur: 'the real issue is whether there is plurality of motivations, or whether self-interest alone drives human beings' in economic matters (Sen, 1987:13). This series of questions led Mark Lutz and Kenneth Lux to explore the possibility of a Humanistic Economics as can be seen in their conclusive observation:

> Where it has been acknowledged that human behaviour might have another dimension than self-interest, it has been decided that this part of the person is irrelevant to economics and therefore is outside the scope of science. […] Such an exclusion is theoretically wanting, empirically questionable, a serious social mistake with unfortunate consequences (Lutz & Lux, 1988:102).

According to Sen (1987), in the case of the economic success of Japan, there is empirical evidence showing that there were systematic departures from the self-interested behaviour in the direction of cultural values such as duty, loyalty and good will that played an important role in the Japanese economic success (cf. Lutz & Lux, 1988: 84). Sen himself was drawing on the reflection of Morishima (1982), a Japanese scholar who argued that what had played an important role in the Japanese economy was much more the Japanese spirit which was rooted in Shintoist and Confucian values (Dore, 1983, 1987; Aoki, 1989; Ikegami, 1995). Nowadays, it is being argued that the economic success in other South East Asian countries is also being achieved thanks to the same Confucian values (Franke et al., 1991; Granato et al., 1996; Hofstede and Bond, 1988). The group solidarity provides a ground for cooperation within the same East Asian society, while the hierarchical authority of the government provides incentives, political framework, the infrastructure and other means necessary for the enterprises of its country to compete on the international scene.

The argument that in the case of Africa, the state has been an obstacle to self-interest and, thus, a hindrance to economic growth and development is built on the debate between the libertarians defending the priority of the individual over the community, and the communitarians who defend the priority of the community over the individual. Hence, those who believe that in Africa the state is an obstacle to the principle of self-interest and its economic achievements are the libertarians who argue that in the African culture, the community is hampering individual freedoms and responsibilities, and hence an obstacle to the individual flourishing (Kenyan, 2006). It is true that the community can effectively be a limit or an obstacle to individual freedom and responsibility; however, it is equally true that the community can be a context in which the individual flourishes more than if one were left alone, particularly when the values which the community cherishes are harmonised with those which the individual cherishes for mutual advantage (Gyekye, 1997; MacIntyre, 1981; Mbiti, 1970; Sandel, 1982, 1996; Taylor, 1989; Tshamalenga, 1985).In the case of the Asian economic miracle, it has been observed that the state, far from being a handicap for the market economy that is thought to result from the principle of self-interest, played an important role in the economic development (Cypher & Deitz, 2004; Biel, 2000: 202; Dasgupta, 1998).

THE UBUNTU ECONOMY

The Bantu are a group of Africans who occupy almost all the Southern part of the Equator and its surroundings. They cover more than 60% of the African population in sub-Saharan Africa, and occupy geographically one-third of the whole African continent (Kagame, 1976). This may justify why most African and non-African thinkers tend to refer to Bantu philosophical principles to make the point of what unifies Africans (Eboussi-Boulaga 1981; Jahn, 1961; Tempels, 1959). According to

Alexis Kagame, the lowest common denominator of the Bantu people is the fact that their value system is structured according to the way they conceive of the categories of being in their ontology (Kagame, 1976; cf. Kagame, 1956). There are four of these categories (Figure 1), namely:

- The category of mu-ntu (plural: ba-ntu): intelligent (or rational) being(s). It is the category of human beings.

- The categories of ki-ntu (plural: bi-ntu): non- intelligent beings. It is the category of things including animals, plants and inanimate beings such as stones.

- The category of ha-ntu: spatio-temporal being. It is the category of time and space.

- Finally, the category of ku-ntu: modal being. It refers to the way different beings are shaped, their position, their relation, their colour, etc.

All these four categories (mu, ki, ha, ku) are built on the same root, *ntu* (being) and are arranged in a hierarchical order with the human being standing at the top of the hierarchy. Contrary to what Mkhize (2008: 41) holds, it is obvious from the above figure that *ntu* is not only reserved to human beings. Mkhize (2008: 38) rightly talks of the cosmic unity but fails to discover that *ntu* underlies it, maybe because the four categories seem to be unknown to him.

There has been a question of why 'bu' of *(u)buntu*,[1] for instance, does not constitute a fifth category. According to Kagame (1976), with the concept of u-bu-ntu, one is already in

the formal logic as a condition for (African) philosophising. In effect, the Bantu distinguish between the concrete and the abstract. They separate the abstract of accidentality expressing entities which do not exist independently in nature such as u-bu-gabo (courage, force and virility*); u-bu-shingantahe* (integrity, equity) and the abstract of substantiality. Both of them are connoted by - bu. Ubuntu (humanity or humanness) enters in the latter category. Of course, ubuntu as a metaphysical concept has moral implications. In effect, *ubuntu* is a moral character and even a value of people when they live, act and behave in the way that fosters harmony in the

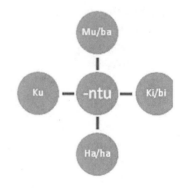

Fig. 1: The Structure of the Bantu Universe

society and the universe around them. The use of *ubuntu* of southern Africa refers to this moral character or value. In fact, when one says that people are living according to the value of *ubuntu*, one means that these people live in a way that fulfils their nature as intelligent beings.

What these Bantu categories of beings underlie is the notion of community and inclusiveness. The human being, the *mu-ntu*, is first of all part of the universal community (the community of *ntu*) which includes beings other than the human being. In other words, the different realities of the universe belong together. As Mkhize (2008: 38) rightly puts it, different realities of the universe form the cosmic unity. Secondly, the human being belongs to the human community (family, clan, village, etc.) from which one is born. One is *mu-ntu* among the *ba-ntu*. The *muntu* is conceived of as part of the social web which incorporates other Bantu. These Bantu include human beings actually living (the present generation), human beings who are dead (the past generation) and human beings who are not yet born (the future generation). It is not within the limits of the paper to treat the underlying conception of time. Suffice it to simply mention that the Bantu people have a communitarian conception of time. For instance, the proverb: "The best time to plant a tree is two years ago, the second-best is now" means that what our past parents might not have achieved for us to enjoy it today we have to do it now for our future generation to enjoy it. This sense of community which is not limited to the present generation is peculiar to African way of life. For Dickson Kwesi, it is a characteristic mark that defines African-ness (Kwesi,1977).

In southern Africa, this sense of the (human) community is expressed in the following popular Zulu and Xhosa saying: *'umuntu ngumuntu ngabantu'* [3] (a person depends on other people to be a person; or better, you are a person in that you carry within yourself your humanity and the humanity of others).

Thus, in the African value system, the first value is the value of the community. The ontological primacy of the community in the African value system may lead one to wonder what happens to individual agency. In effect, one may be made to believe that the individual is swallowed up by the community to the extent that one cannot have a freedom and responsibility of one's own. Gyekye (1997) felt uncomfortable with the seeming radicality of the African sense of community and asked himself whether a moderate perspective of the African community could be envisaged. In fact, his whole book, Tradition and Modernity is an effort to substantiate such a moderate perspective. However, the African value system naturally accommodates both the individual as well as the community as ontologically interdependent without reducing the ontological density and the primacy of the community. We have developed this point elsewhere by making a distinction between the human being as a being-with/in-self *(umuntu-w'-ubuntu)* and human being as being-with/in-others *(umuntu-mu-bantu)* (Ntibagirirwa, 1999, 2003: 75–77). Maybe what we could add here is the fact that the value of *ubuntu* is both an ontological and moral value of people individually as they live according to their nature as well as collectively when their interdependence is geared to achieving social harmony.

There is a host of moral values that go with the value of the community. We will not dwell much on them but will only refer the reader to the reflections of thinkers: Julius Nyerere who tried to build a political and economic system based on the values of the family (ujaama), cooperation, sharing, care and compassion (Nyerere, 1968); Kaunda (1968) whose humanism is built on such values as mutual aid, cooperation, responsibility and concern for others and Senghor (1964) who emphasised communion, participation and sympathy. All these thinkers who also happen to be the fathers of Africa's independence aimed at building a socialist type of economy on the community and the values that flow from it.

However, our observation is that their socialist response to the Africa's quest for economic development was rather a question in search of an answer: which economic system is most likely to harmonise with the African value system and its ontological structure?

Today's economic development involves three major actors which tend to compete in the economic order: the state, the markets and the people. What the Bantu conception of reality leads us to is the fact that the three forces have to constitute a triangle and interact in synergy for a meaningful development to be achieved. In other words, in the Bantu conception of reality, economic development should be inclusive rather than exclusive. Obviously, this goes in the opposite sense of the neo-liberal belief that self-interest and rational choice require that the market run the economic show alone, thus excluding the state and the people to the point of making them passive. The implication is that the market alone becomes the agent of economic growth and development, while the role of the state and the people is reduced to being the patients. On the contrary, the African value system, as can be seen from the Bantu conception of reality, would not divide the actors of economic development into agents and patients, producers whose responsibility, on the one hand, is to produce and accumulate, and on the other hand, the consumers. The African value system gives us a framework in which all could be agents whose solidarity and cooperation would lead to economic growth and development. In such a framework, one achieves one's humanity as a producer and a consumer, or a buyer and a seller, who responds not only to the forces of the market but also to both the material and spiritual needs of the being human. This is the very meaning of *ubuntu* i.e the *ubuntu* economy.

CONCLUSIONS

In this case we have demonstrated that cultural values are an important factor that needs to be taken seriously to achieve economic growth and development. The self-interest and rational choice themselves are part of a cultural value system. Thus the Bantu conception structures a whole system of values that could enhance rather than undermine economic growth and development in Africa. The major advantage of the African value system, we underlined, is the fact that it guards us against exclusion and the separation of people into categories of agents and patients in the process of economic development. Seen against this background, economic growth and development is a product of the synergy of all actors: the state, the market and the people forming the triangle in the process of economic development.

Thus, if the argument of the necessary link between cultural values and economic development is convincing enough, it is misleading to try to universalise the values of self-interest and rationality as the only ground of economic growth and development. Accordingly, our reflection has two major implications. The first implication is that our argument should be understood as a reflective invitation to political leaders, economists, policymakers, etc. To concentrate much effort on creating a political and socio-economic environment in which cultural values can catalyse economic growth and development. From this point of view, authors are in agreement to the World Bank which, in October 1999, declared that culture is an essential component of economic development, which should play an important role in economic processes.

The second implication is rather a warning based on the history of economic development. The experience of the last few decades of the twentieth century as well as the 2008 financial crisis have shown us that neither the state alone, nor the market alone, can lead societies to a meaningful economic growth and development. The last years have also witnessed to some kind of collective mobilisation of marginalised groups against the disempowerment tendency of the state and the market thanks to the development of civil society movements (Mohan and Stokke, 2000), particularly in developing countries. What one can learn from African values centred on the community is that what would work to achieve economic development is not exclusion but inclusion of all the actors. Accordingly, we are suggesting that, in the African context, what could achieve economic growth and development is the synergy of the state, the market and the people. Authors call this the *ubuntu* economy.

REFERENCES

Aoki, M. 1989. *Information, Incentives, and Bargaining in the Japanese Economy.* Cambridge: Cambridge University Press.

Biel, R. 2000, The *New Imperialism: The Crisis and Contradictions in North/South Relations.* London: Zed Books.

Cypher, M. C & Dietz, J L 2004. *The Process of Economic Development.* London/New York: Routledge.

Dasgupta, B. 1998, *Structural Adjustment, Global Trade and the New Political Economy of Development.* New York/London: Zed books.

Dore, R. 1983. Goodwill and the Spirit of Market Capitalism. *British Journal of Sociology. 36*

Dore, R 1987. *Taking Japan Seriously: A Confucian Perspective on Leading Economic issues.* Standford: Standford University Press.

Eboussi-Boulaga, F. 1981. *La crise du Muntu: Authenticité africaine et Philosophie* Paris: Présence Africaine.

Franke, R. H., G. Hofstede & Bond, M.H.1991. Cultural Roots of Economic Performance: A Research Note. *Strategic Management Journal*, 12, 165–173.

Granato, J., Inglehart, R & Leblang, D.1996. The Effect of Cultural Values on Economic Development: Theory, Hypotheses and Some Empirical Tests. *American Journal of Political Science*, 40(3), 607–631.

Gyekye, K.1997. *Tradition and Modernity*. Cambridge: Cambridge University Press.

Hofstede, G. & M. H. Bond, M.H. 1988. The Confucius Connection: From Cultural Roots to Economic Growth. *Organizational Dynamics*, 16, 4–21.

Ikegami, E 1995. *The Taming of the Samurai: Horific Individualism and the Making of Modern Japan*. Cambridge, Mass: Harvard University Press.

Jahn, J. 1961. *Muntu: An Outline of the New African Culture*. New York: Grove Press.

Kagame, A. 1956. *La Philosophie Bantu-Rwandaise de l'Etre*. Brussels : Académie Royales des Sciences Coloniales.

Kagame, A. 1976. *La Philosophie Bantu Compar*ée. Paris : Présence Africaine.

Kaunda, K. 1968. *A Humanism in Africa*. London: Longmans.

Kenyan. 2006. On a Communitarian Ethos, Equality and Human Rights in Africa. *http://iheu.org*. Accessed 11 Apr 2009.

Kwesi, A. D. 1977. *Aspects of Religious Life in Africa.* Accra: Ghana Academy of Arts and Sciences.

Lutz, M. A. & Lux, K. 1988. *Humanistic Economics: The New Challenge*. New York: The Bootstrap Press, New York.

MacIntyre, A. 1981. *After Virtue*. Notre Dame, Indiana: University of Notre Dame Press.

Mbiti, J. 1970. *African Religions and Philosophy*. New York: Doubleday.

Mkhize, N. 2008. Ubuntu and Harmony: An African Approach to Morality. In R. Nicolson (ed.), *Persons in Community: African Ethics and Culture*, pp. 31–45. Pietermaritzburg: University of Kwa-Zulu Natal Press.

Morishima, M.1982. *Why Has Japan 'Succeeded'? Western Technology and Japanese Ethos* Cambridge: Cambridge University Press.

Ntibagirirwa, S. 1999. *A Retrieval of Aristotelian Virtue Ethics in African Social and Political Humanism. A Communitarian Perspective*, University of Natal. Unpublished Masters Dissertation. University of Natal, Pietermaritzburg.

Ntibagirirwa, S. 2003. A Wrong Way: From Being to Having in the African Value System. *http://www.crvp.org/book/Series02/II-7/chapter_v.htm*. Accessed 22 Apr 2009.

Nyerere, K. J. 1968. *Ujaama: Essays on Socialism*. Dar-es-Salaam: Oxford University Press Onis, Z. 1995. The Limits of Neoliberalism: Towards a Reformation of Development Theory. *Journal of Economic Issues*, 29(1): 97–119.

Sandel, M. 1982. *Liberalism and the Limits of Justice.* Cambridge: Cambridge University Press.

Sandel, M. 1996. *Democracy's Discontent: America in Search of Public Philosophy.* Cambridge: The Belknap Press of Harvard University Press.

Sen, A. K. 1987. *On Ethics and Economics.* New York: Blackwell.

Senghor, L. S. 1964. *Liberté* I: Négritude et Humanism. Paris : Seuil.

Smith, A. 1965. *An Inquiry into the Nature and Causes of the Wealth of Nations.* Edited by E. Cannan, introduced by Max Lerner. New York: Modern Library.

Taylor, C. 1989. *Sources of the Self. The Making of Moral Identity.* Cambridge: Cambridge University Press.

Tempels, P. 1959. *Bantu Philosophy.* Paris: Présence Africaine.

Tshamalenga, N. 1985. Langage et socialité. Primat de la Bisoité sur l'Intersubjectivité. In Facultés Catholiques de Kinshasa (ed.), *Actes de la 9eme Semaine Philosophique de Kinshasa, du 1er au 7 décembre, 1985,* pp. 59–81. Kinshasa : Facultés Catholiques de Kinshasa.

Author Index

Abdelbagi, Yousif	412	Johns, Joan Marie	65
Agarwal, Shuchi	263		
Anderson, Arnold R. Anderson	325	Khalid, Siti Nabiha Abdul	412
Anderson, Cheryl R.	325	Khan, Mohammed Arshad	181
Anjaly, Bhawna	421		
		Lemons, R. Mikel	3
Beverley, E. Powell III	54	Long, Ken	126
Boje, David M.	52		
Brands, Kristine	21	Miller, Monty G.	344
		Miller, Monty	163
Carter, Barbara	65	Misra, Pooja	293
Chaudhuri, Manosi	263, 311	Montonen, Tero	242
Colvin, T. James Jr.	103		
Coppedge, Krisha M.	52	Nayak, Parameswar	278
		Newton, Ronald	334
DePorres, Daphne D.	344	Ntibagirirwa, Symphorien	433
Dighe, Parag	126, 163		
		Paul, Lapoule	251
Elam, Debora	21	Puri, Sakshi	311
Eriksson, Päivi	242		
Erwan, Lamy	251	Qureshi, Asma	115
Glinka, Beata	379	Rana, Geeta	210
Goel, Alok	210	Robertson, Alfonso	90
Gupta, Jaya	192	Roy, Santanu	181
Hagedorn, Rod	34	Sahay, Arun	421
Hanson, Bruce	354	Sood, Abhay	293
Havel, Karla R. Peters-Van	397	Srinivasan, Divya	141
Hay, George W.	224	Stevens, Jeff	115
Ibrahim, Eiman H.	412	Tenkasi, Ramkrishnan (Ram) V.	224
		Thatchenkery, Tojo	3, 54, 141, 379
Jain, Shreya	293	Thorpe, James M.	103
Jalaludin, Dayana	412	Tomar, Megha Singh	192

Tyagi, Ruchi K   433   Walla, Nathan   368
Tyagi, Sanjana   278   Washington, Anne L.   141
                                                 Wongtrakul, Vilas   354
Wakefield, Tonya Henderson   90
Wall, Kenneth   65, 90, 163   Yaw, M.   163

The Editors

DR. G.D. SARDANA, a chartered Mechanical Engineer, Ph.D. (IIT Delhi) and is presently Professor of Operations Management and Chairperson, Center for Development of Management Cases at the Birla Institute of Management Technology, Greater Noida (India).

He has corporate experience of over 40 years having worked in organizations of repute such as BHEL, ABB and Singer at senior positions. In academics, he has earlier worked with Institute of Management Technology, Ghaziabad for four years as Professor Operations Management, Dean-Academics, Editor Paradigm, and later for two years with the Institute of Management Education, Ghaziabad as its Professor Emeritus and Director.

He has to his credit over 80 papers. Three of his papers have won Best Paper awards from the Indian Institution of Industrial Engineering. He has published two books: Productivity Management (Narosa, 1998) and Measurement for Business Excellence (Narosa, 2009). The first book bagged Best Book awards from the Delhi Management Association, and Indian Society for Training and Development. He has co-edited six books on management cases.

DR. TOJO THATCHENKERY (Ph.D. Weatherhead School of Management, Case Western Reserve University) is Professor and Director of the Organization Development and Knowledge Management program at the School of Public Policy, George Mason University, Arlington, Virginia, USA. He is also a member of the NTL Institute of Applied Behavioral Science and the Taos Institute. Thatchenkery's recent books include Making the Invisible Visible: Understanding the Leadership Contributions of Asian Minorities in the Workplace (2011), Positive Design and Appreciative Construction: From Sustainable Development to Sustainable Value (2010), Appreciative Inquiry and Knowledge Management, and Appreciative Intelligence: Seeing the Mighty Oak in the Acorn. Thatchenkery has extensive consulting experience in organization development and knowledge management. Past and current clients include the United Nations, IBM, Fannie Mae, Booz Allen, PNC Bank, Lucent Technologies, General Mills, 3M, British Petroleum, the International Monetary Fund, the World Bank, United States Department of Agriculture, Pension Benefit Guaranty Corporation, United States Environmental Protection Agency, and Akbank (Turkey).